T O W E R Y   P U B L I S H I N G ,   I N C.

CHICAGO
SECOND TO NONE

▲ MARK SEGAL / PANORAMIC IMAGES, CHICAGO

BY TOM McNAMEE
AND
SARAH WALTON

ART DIRECTOR
BRIAN GROPPE

CORPORATE
PROFILES BY
PATRICIA SULLIVAN ZEFF

PRODUCED IN
COOPERATION WITH
THE CHICAGOLAND
CHAMBER OF COMMERCE

CHICAGO

◀ CHURCHILL & KLEHR

Library of Congress Cataloging-in-Publication Data

McNamee, Tom.
     Chicago : second to none / by Tom McNamee and Sarah Walton ; corporate profiles by Patricia Sullivan Zeff ; art director, Brian Groppe.
          p.   cm. — (Urban tapestry series)
     "Produced in cooperation with the Chicagoland Chamber of Commerce."
     ISBN 1-881096-00-9 : $39.50
     1. Chicago (Ill.)—Pictorial works.   2. Business enterprises—Illinois—Chicago— History.   3. Chicago (Ill.)—Industries.
I. Walton, Sarah, 1949-   .   II. Zeff, Patricia Sullivan, 1959-   .
III. Title.   IV. Series.
F548.37.M36   1993
977.3'11—dc20   92-62590
                                                                              CIP

TOWERY PUBLISHING, INC.
1835 UNION AVENUE, SUITE 142
MEMPHIS, TENNESSEE 38104

Publisher:	J. ROBERT TOWERY
Editorial Director:	PATRICIA M. TOWERY
Senior Editor:	MICHAEL C. JAMES
Articles Editor:	ALLISON JONES SIMONTON
Assistant Art Director:	ANNE CASTRODALE
Technical Director:	WILLIAM H. TOWERY
Copy Editor:	KAREN L. BEDSOLE
Editorial Contributors:	JIM MONTAGUE
	ANDREA GORDON ROSEN
	RENIE E. SCHREIBER
Production Assistants:	L.D. BEGHTOL
	TERRI J. JONES

ON CHICAGO'S SOUTHWEST SIDE IN THE MIDDLE 1960S, THE children played a game of hide-and-seek called ring-a-levio.

They chose up sides and, as one team counted to 100, the other team vanished into the summer night, shadows flitting across backyards and alleys.

Some children hid behind bushes; others huddled in basement stairwells or crouched in "gangways"—a Chicago term for that narrow walkway between two houses. One boy, without fail, climbed high in an elm tree in his own backyard.

He would sit in that tree for the balance of the game, until the moon had shifted in the sky, until his baby brother had gone to bed, until his friends had finally called, "alley, alley ocean free, free, free!"

And as the boy hid patiently in the elm, he would look out from that great height at the fabulous city.

To the north, swallowed in darkness, he could hear the train yards—the grinding of steel wheels and the crashing of coupling cars. To the south he could see the pitched roofs of a hundred homes crowding into the suburbs. And to the northeast, on the very edge of his visual universe, he could see a faint light—the beacon atop the Prudential Building, then the tallest building in Chicago. It blinked red in the black night, beckoning across 15 miles of bungalows and treetops and steeples like a night-light from the Land of Oz.

All of this filled the horizon of a child at play: One city—one Chicago—whole and together. ▶

By day the skyscraper looms in the smoke and sun and has a soul.

Prairie and valley, streets of the city, pour people into it and they mingle among its twenty floors and are poured out again back to the streets, prairies and valleys.

It is the men and women, boys and girls so poured in and out all day that give the building a soul of dreams and thoughts and memories.

—from *Skyscraper* (1916)
by Carl Sandburg

N THE '90S, SOME THREE DECADES LATER, THE VIEW OF THE CITY IS FAR
more obstructed. Greater Chicago is now the third largest metropolitan area in the United
States, and its neighborhoods and suburbs are such distinct entities that the city's essential
sense of community can be easy to miss, seemingly lost in a thicket of separateness.

But Chicago's underlying civic unity remains real, undeniable, and resilient. The city's
downtown—the Loop—serves the neighborhoods, and the neighborhoods serve the Loop. The
city needs the suburbs, and the suburbs need the city. Each and every ethnic and racial group
contributes richly to the polyglot whole.

Even North Siders and South Siders, forever divided by the backward-flowing Chicago
River and a famous Cubs-vs.-White Sox baseball rivalry, can't seem to go it alone. As far back
as 1834, when the first stationary wooden drawbridge over the river was built at Dearborn Street,
South Siders, fearing that North Siders would siphon off business, tore it down. But in time, a new
bridge went up, the first of 20 now spanning the river in the downtown area, each one a reminder
of those social ties that bind.

THE LOOP

HICAGO IS, TO BE SURE, THE GREAT AMERICAN CITY. NOT AS
cosmopolitan as New York. Nor as trendy as Los Angeles. Nor as exotic as New
Orleans. But more completely American than any other city, blending the myriad
social, spiritual, and aesthetic stirrings that define our national identity. Chicago
is a town of Eastern sophistication and Western straight talk, of intellectualism and common
sense, of refinement and simplicity. It is in Chicago, for example, in the revolutionary works of
Louis Sullivan, Frank Lloyd Wright, and Ludwig Mies van der Rohe that American architecture
has found its most celebrated homegrown expression. Sullivan, who liked to say "form follows
function," bridged the classical decorative traditions of Europe with the utilitarian designs yet
to come from Mies van der Rohe. Wright founded the world-famous Prairie School
of architecture, in which low-slung houses conformed to the topography of the Midwest, hugging
the prairie ground. And Mies, who liked to say "less is more," virtually invented the International
School of sleek and box-like glass and steel high-rises.

Chicago's American Blend is found elsewhere as well: in the vernacular speech of its best
and earliest writers, such as Theodore Dreiser and Nelson Algren; in the pioneering social welfare
movements of Jane Addams and Saul Alinsky; in the electrified Southern blues of Muddy Waters;
in the rock-and-roll stagecraft—high art and street tough—of the Steppenwolf Theatre Company.

The city's very name—Chicago—was made in America.

8

Chicago whirls at the foot of Lake Michigan in the middle of this country and sucks everything American into its vortex. American culture. American industry. American swagger. Indeed, the city owes its very existence to that most American of concepts, Manifest Destiny. Chicago was methodically platted on the Midwestern prairie in 1830 by a federal surveyor, James Thompson, for the express purpose of creating a great urban gateway to western expansion.

Which is precisely what happened.

Thompson drew up the street grid for what is today Chicago's heart—its fabulous Loop— and as this marked-off land was sold by the parcel to finance the construction of a major new canal, the big city rose out of the swamp. Thompson himself, by the way, was offered a chunk of land in payment, but seeing no future in it, accepted a nice horse instead.

Chicago, even now, begins and ends with the Loop—a little more than one square mile of Oz-like architectural grandeur where the Prudential Building is now dwarfed by greater giants, such as the 110-story Sears Tower, the world's tallest building. The Loop is, in a sense, Chicago's Home Office, headquarters for dozens of major banks, corporations, retailers, law firms, newspapers, TV and radio stations, and government agencies. It is home, as well, to the Board of Trade and the Art Institute, The MacArthur Foundation, and City Hall. It is where big decisions are made.

And everything else that is Chicago—the neighborhoods, the suburbs, the fishing holes— rolls out from there.

The Loop, of course, is not really Oz. It is a land far more magical. Oz, to be sure, has some good stuff. It has Dorothy and the Wizard and a horse of a different color.

But the Loop! It has the brass of the Chicago Symphony Orchestra…the cry of a sax from a street-corner jazzman . . . cops sipping coffee in the glow of neon at 3 AM…lovers who kiss in the spray of Buckingham Fountain . . . no-nonsense waiters at the famed Berghoff restaurant… screeching elevated trains and rumbling subway trains…bridges that draw up for bobbing sailboats …spooky subterranean green lights on Lower Wacker Drive…fastball cabbies who dust back tourists…a skyline that glistens like candlelight on crystal…a man who dances with his wife…and a sculpture by Picasso that looks like a woman or maybe an Afghan hound or maybe a dodo bird.

The Loop's overwhelming importance is obvious from the briefest glance at any city map. Every major train line and electric car line runs directly out of the Loop. All four major expressways touch the central city as well, linking it forever with the bungalow-belt neighborhoods, the freshly mowed suburbs, and the red-barn countryside.

Mayor Richard J. Daley, the mayor of Chicago from 1955 to 1976, planned it that way. Just as all roads led to Rome, he reasoned, all roads should lead to the Loop. And he willed it into being. The man they called "Boss" could do such things. ▮▷

T WAS HERE IN WHAT IS NOW DOWNTOWN, WHERE THE GRAYISH-GREEN of the Chicago River meets the blue of Lake Michigan, that the Midwest's first people—Native American Indians—traversed for a thousand years. They bartered and camped overnight here because they understood something golden about this spot.

Traveling by canoe, Indian tribesmen could hug the coastline of the Great Lakes for a hundred miles. When they came to the Checagou—a Potawatomi word meaning wild onion or skunk grass—they could turn up the flat slow river and paddle southwest with ease. Where the river finally went dry, at what today is Harlem Avenue just north of the Stevenson Expressway, they could lift their canoes onto their shoulders, portage eight miles through swampland to the Des Plaines River, and then float downstream to the Illinois River, the Mississippi River, and, eventually, the Gulf of Mexico.

Not a bad trip.

Better still for our travelers, when the rains were heavy and the swamps flooded, they could navigate the same route in lightly loaded canoes and never set foot on land.

The Indians understood all this, and they explained it to the early French explorers. That knowledge led Louis Joliet and Jacques Marquette to a profound realization: a short, man-made canal between the Chicago and Des Plaines rivers could link, by a route of water, the American East and West.

"Here someday," Marquette predicted in 1673, "will be found one of the world's great cities."

The man-made water link would be the Illinois and Michigan Canal, opened in 1848. The city would be Chicago.

In time, Native Americans were forced out of Chicago, pushed into increasingly smaller territorial corners by one bad-news treaty after another. Finally, in 1835, they gathered in the city one last time to collect treaty-arranged payoffs and moved west of the Mississippi.

But their legacy remains. Dozens of Chicago streets today carry Indian names. Northwest Side residents still unearth flint arrowheads in their gardens. The tradition of Checagou as a trading post continues at the Chicago Board of Trade, the world's largest futures and options exchange. And the legacy of this juncture as a crossroads continues as well. O'Hare International is the world's busiest airport, and Fords and Toyotas now roll where Indians once walked.

To be sure, a great many Chicago streets that run on an angle to the city grid were once high-ground Indian trails. Milwaukee Avenue. Clark Street. Vincennes Avenue. Archer Avenue. Blue Island Avenue. Grand Avenue. Longwood Drive. Travel them today and you follow in the paths of Chicago's first people. Travel them and they lead you out of the center city, away from the Loop into the neighborhoods, and beyond. ▶

In a big and sometimes crowded city, canoeing is a surprisingly popular pastime. On the Fox and Des Plaines rivers, in particular, the canoeing gets heavy as soon as the weather turns warm. The sport's major local event is the Mid-American Canoe Race on the Fox, from South Elgin to Aurora, held in June. Some 2,000 canoeists compete annually in the 22-mile race, the best of them crossing the finish line in a mere two-and-a-half hours.

THE NEIGHBORHOODS

WHAT ARE YOU?

Nobody lives in Chicago for long without being asked that question. Nobody lives here forever without asking the question himself.

Chicago is a town full of people who came from someplace else, their ethnic or national origins no more than a few generations removed. Those roots continue to matter profoundly. Ethnic festivals are big in Chicago. So are ethnic parades. Newspaper dispatches from Warsaw and Palermo and Mexico City are received like letters from home, and bilingual education in the public schools comes in 24 different languages. Everybody is *something* or so Chicagoans presume, and so everybody asks, "What are you?"

The question is usually innocent enough—another turn in a conversation. First you might ask, "Cubs fan or Sox fan?" And then you might ask, "What are you?"

But it can also be a search for a password:

"What are you?"

"Irish."

"Me too! County Mayo!"

The bonding is heavy and quick. In truth, *what* you are may say something about who you are in Chicago, but more predictably, it says volumes about *where* you are, as in where you live. Chicago is, after all, the City of Neighborhoods.

If, for example, you are a Chicagoan of Chinese descent, there is a fair

chance you live in Bridgeport or in Chinatown on Cermak Road. Unless, of course, you are of Chinese descent but come from Vietnam, in which case you probably live on or near Argyle Street.

From Chicago's very first days, racial and ethnic groups have organized according to neighborhoods, laying claim to one patch of flat prairie or another, often leaving acres of empty land between them. The Irish settled in Bridgeport on the Southwest Side. African-Americans moved up from the American South and settled on Chicago's Near South Side. Italians staked out Taylor Street, immediately west and south of the Loop.

Each group claimed its pavilion at a sort of permanent world's fair.

New arrivals continue the pattern today, supplanting earlier immigrant groups that have melded into the mainstream and moved out to the suburbs. Koreans on Lawrence Avenue. Russian Jews on Devon Avenue. Puerto Ricans in Humboldt Park. Chicago is their home now. They work and play here, and, day by day, contribute to a fabulous whole.

"We all live together in one giant, interlocked relationship, across 100 neighborhoods," Harold Washington, Chicago's first black mayor, once marveled. "How do we do it?"

As the mayor knew, it is not easy. But what you learn on a journey through the city's ethnic neighborhoods is that Chicago was built on the muscle and brilliance of untold thousands, men and women of every race and surname. No one crowd can claim an edge.

Perhaps the best way to explore Chicago's neighborhoods is to ride a bike along the city's "emerald necklace," a 28-mile ring of wide boulevards linking a half dozen major parks.

Created 130 years ago for pleasant Sunday carriage rides, the emerald necklace today is a string of all the sights, smells and voices of Sweethome Chicago—the Chicago most tourists never see.

The necklace begins on Garfield Boulevard in Hyde Park on the campus of the University of Chicago, a center of unsurpassed intellectual firepower that churns out Nobel laureates the way a nearby Nabisco plant churns out Oreos—in world-record numbers. ▶

As of 1992, the university could claim ties to 64 Nobel prize winners, a tally so absurdly high that one campus cafe posted this sign: "Free sandwich and soda to Nobel laureates. Limit one per customer."

Saul Bellow, the intellectually heady novelist who recently accepted a position at Boston University, is one of those Nobel wonders. He is also a homegrown Chicago boy, by way of Humboldt Park on the West Side, and a good example of a familiar side-of-the-mouth, street-wise Chicago persona. In Bellow's best books, such as *Humboldt's Gift*, his characters seem more amused than offended by Chicago's wise guys and hustlers. They exhibit a big-city skepticism that assumes virtually nothing is "on the legit," including, perhaps, a professed love for your hometown.

"Why do you still live in Chicago?" someone asked Bellow. "Because you have roots here?"

"Roots?" Bellow replied. "More like a lot of old wires."

From the brilliance of Hyde Park, Garfield Boulevard rolls west, zipping past streets that recall great songs and parks that recall great books. Touchstones of Chicago culture and history rush by, becoming almost a blur.

To the left is Washington Park, where the great defense attorney, Clarence Darrow, loved to stroll, and where Studs Lonigan, James T. Farrell's most famous character, sat in a tree and courted Lucy.

To the right is the mansion of Big Jim O'Leary, a flamboyant stockyard-district gambler and son of *the* Mrs. O'Leary—Catherine—whose cow is blamed for the Great Chicago Fire of 1871. (Truth is, the cow got a bum rap. The fire started in the O'Leary barn, but there is no evidence Mrs. O'Leary was milking her cow at the time.)

To the north lived Lorraine Hansberry, who died young but left behind one of America's most powerful plays, *A Raisin in the Sun.* Richard Wright, who resided nearby, worked as a postal clerk by day and wrote an American classic, *Native Son*, by night.

In this South Side world straddling Garfield Boulevard, Muddy Waters forged his electric blues, playing all night in smoky clubs; Louis Armstrong and Bix Beiderbecke pushed the limits of jazz; Mahalia Jackson raised her rich contralto to heaven; the Marx Brothers grew up; and Thomas A. Dorsey, the "Godfather of Gospel Music," wrote a timeless song, "Take My Hand, Precious Lord."

At Provident Hospital four blocks north, Dr. Daniel Hale Williams, the first black member of the American College of Surgeons, became the first surgeon to successfully operate on the heart.

And at a South Side firehouse in 1878, an all-black company invented the fire pole. The captain of Engine Company 21 came up with the idea after noticing that his men were responding remarkably fast to fire alarms by sliding down a hay-binding pole from the firehouse's third-floor hayloft.

Two miles west of Hyde Park, Garfield Boulevard crosses Halsted Street, one of the most history-soaked roads in all Chicago. Social reformer Jane Addams founded Hull House, the most famous settlement house, on Halsted. Benny Goodman, the "King of Swing," grew up on Halsted. And it was on this street that Chicago earned its nickname, "Hog Butcher to the World." The Union Stockyards, a square mile of stench and livestock, closed in 1971 after feeding the nation for 105 years.

At Western Avenue, the emerald necklace turns north, weaving through various ethnic European, African-American, and Puerto Rican neighborhoods, and some neighborhoods too topsy-turvy to be labeled. One block is spiffed up. The next is walking around in its bathrobe.

Pedaling past Humboldt Park, you recall that Sister Carrie, Theodore Dreiser's literary heroine, lived near here. Rolling across Division Street, you remember that Nelson Algren and his *Man With the Golden Arm*, Frankie Machine, haunted the dark corners a mile or two due east.

At Diversey Avenue on the North Side the boulevard ring turns east, toward the lake, slicing through the heart of that part of town best known to the outside world—the Chicago of Wrigley Field, Steppenwolf Theatre, Lincoln Park Zoo, and The Second City. This is cosmopolitan Chicago, where performance artists dressed in black date anthropologists dressed in tweeds.

The restaurants here in Lincoln Park and Old Town and on the Near North Side turn up in the gossip columns, usually when **Oprah** or **Michael Jordan** drops by. The sidewalks fill up with the stylishly young. The comedy clubs and sports bars card at the door all night. The dance clubs thump into the early morning.

The City of Neighborhoods, in such places and at such times, is transformed into That Toddlin' Town.

At this end of town, the names that are the measure of cultural and artistic achievement, the sights and sounds that recall the contributions of so many—from David Mamet to John Malkovich to Mike Nichols—are too many to tip a hat to. But as we

reach the end of our ride, arriving once again at the lakefront, we must brake to a stop and single out just one more: L. Frank Baum.

Baum was a traveling salesman who lived on Flournoy Street on the West Side some 95 years ago. He liked to make up stories and tell them to the neighborhood children.

One night, he was telling a humdinger about a Scarecrow, a Tin Woodsman, and a girl named Dorothy when one of the children, Tweety Robbins, said, "Oh please, Mr. Baum, where did the Scarecrow and the Tin Woodsman live?"

Baum looked around the room, spotted the label "O–Z" on the bottom drawer of a file cabinet, and informed little Tweety that his characters lived "in the marvelous Land of Oz."

THE SUBURBS

ALAN SHORTALL

THAT IS SOOOOO 708.

In Chicago's hippest dance clubs, when the chitchat turns to what is stodgy and safe and uncool, that is what they say: "That is sooooo 708." Which is to say, that is so suburban.

Chicago has one telephone area code—312. The suburbs have another—708. The differences do not end there.

Chicagoans play softball barehanded with a 16-inch ball. Suburbanites play with a glove and a 12-inch ball.

Chicagoans say "Chi-*caw*-go." Suburbanites, "Chi-*cah*-go."

Chicagoans think of the suburbs, when they think of the suburbs at all, as a decaffeinated land of Weber Grills, Twinkies, and McDonald's restaurants. (Which, come to think of it, might be the suburbs' own fault: They invented the Weber, the Twinkie, and the first McDonald's.)

Suburbanites think of Chicago as a double-strength espresso land of excitement and enticement . . . but no place you'd want to get lost in.

What we have here, of course, are stereotypes and terribly wrong-headed ones at that. In truth, Chicago's 250-plus suburbs conform to no easy descriptions of Levittown blandness. If they were in a coloring book, you'd need the whole 64-pack of Crayolas to do them justice. They are as different from each other as they are from the big city.

The suburbs owe their existence to Chicago. The oldest suburbs grew up along the train lines—beginning with the Chicago and Galena Railroad in 1848—that shot out from the city like spokes from the hub of a wheel. Pioneer settlements far from the new railroads, such as Bachelor's Grove, died off. Towns by the tracks, such as Elmhurst, Naperville, Tinley Park, and Evanston, prospered and grew. ▶

The city, in turn, leaned on the country towns. When the first frame house was built in Chicago in 1832, for example, the lumber was hauled in from suburban Plainfield, then called Walker's Grove.

Today, the suburbs are home to two-thirds of the 7.5 million people who live in the Chicago area. Dozens of these towns are expanding and radically remaking themselves each year. More subdivisions. More cul-de-sacs. More office parks.

In Lombard, a well-tended, half-acre cemetery sits amid a shopping center parking lot. The cemetery dates back to 1880. The parking lot does not.

Outside Naperville, the last dairy farm in DuPage County is such a curiosity that Clarence "Junie" Landorf finds it a challenge to get the afternoon milking done, what with all the kids piling out of the yellow school buses just to watch. And if he needed any further proof that he's looking awfully quaint, there was that artist who hopped the fence one Sunday and set to work sketching "Cows on Farm."

In 1991, DuPage County even lost its last one-room schoolhouse, the 77-year-old McAuley School in West Chicago. All six of its students graduated or moved away.

Farmland is giving way to new housing, the sort with a master bedroom suite, attached two-car garage, and backyard deck. And the fancier the deck the better—a flower box, a gazebo, maybe even a hot tub. The more Californian the better. Decks in the suburbs of Chicago are becoming so *de rigueur*, it may one day be possible to leap from deck to deck across the entire metropolitan area and never once touch actual ground.

And on every deck . . . a Weber Grill. Seventy-seven percent of all American households now own a grill, and that is probably an underestimate in suburban Chicago. Call it hometown pride, if you will. The Weber kettle—king of the barbecue—was invented by Chicago suburbanite George Stephens in 1951. He didn't like anybody else's grill, so he made one of his own enduring design at the Weber Brothers Metal Works (now the Weber-Stephens Products Co.) in Palatine, where he worked.

These are Chicago's—and America's—new suburban neighborhoods: winding streets, split-level houses, and storm-water retention ponds pretending to be lakes.

Big-city Chicagoans, like big-city folks everywhere, tend to scoff: You call that a *neighborhood?* Where's the corner drug store? Where's the neighborhood church? Where's the

grandpa on the front steps who yells at the kids to stay out of the street?

But they are neighborhoods all the same, if being a neighborhood means sharing a dream.

Whereas Chicago's most durable city neighborhoods formed along religious, ethnic, or racial lines, these new suburban communities have profound common denominators of their own—shared values, aspirations, and experiences. Nothing brings people together, any suburban parent will say, like the challenge of raising children.

Moreover, for every fast-growing Baby Huey of a suburb, the Chicago area includes 10 or 20 more established towns, many as old as the city itself. Their stories are long, and their pride is palpable.

Due west of Chicago's Loop, some 24 miles away, is Wheaton, dating to 1839. In the years before the Civil War, Wheaton was a major stop on the Underground Railroad. Billy Graham graduated from Wheaton College, a religious school famous for dispatching missionaries around the globe. And John and Jim Belushi—of The Second City and "Saturday Night Live" fame—grew up there.

Ten miles north of the Loop, on Chicago's border, is Evanston, dating to 1863. The Women's Christian Temperance Union—the ladies who gave us Prohibition—was founded in Evanston in 1874. The ice cream sundae was also invented there—not so coincidentally.

In the staid and proper Evanston of WCTU days, mere seltzer water—let alone alcohol— was considered a wicked indulgence. So Deacon Garwood, the owner of an ice cream parlor in town, complied with a local ordinance forbidding ice cream sodas on Sunday by serving ice cream and syrup without the soda. He called his concoction a sundae, rather than a Sunday, to avoid being sacrilegious.

Then there is Chicago Heights, due south of the Loop some 25 miles, a little town that in some respects looks more like the big city than parts of Chicago itself. In Chicago Heights, the entire history of Chicago—the blue-collar beginnings, the Babel of immigrant tongues, the classic downtown, and the patchwork of ethnic neighborhoods—is retold in miniature. This is a town rich in history and heritage.

Consider a single Chicago Heights neighborhood called The Hill. Four generations of Italian-Americans grew up there learning American ways, working unbelievably hard to give their children a softer life. The first generation settled the neighborhood, organizing according to Old Country hometowns—Neopolitans on one block, Sicilians on another. They built a church on the highest ground—St. Rocco's Roman Catholic—pouring the foundation and laying the bricks with their own hands. They labored as steelworkers and autoworkers on Monday through Saturday, and on Sunday they knelt in St. Rocco's and prayed for their children's future.

Today, their children's children are doctors and lawyers and teachers who live in pretty houses in pretty neighborhoods far from Chicago Heights. But on Sundays, what do they do? They pack up their kids and drive to *nonna's*—grandma's—for a spaghetti dinner on The Hill.

And this is a suburb?

Absolutely. A typical Chicago suburb. ►

The traffic reporters on the radio call it the "Circle Interchange." Others call it the "Spaghetti Bowl." It is where three major Chicago expressways converge. This brings to mind the oldest and silliest joke in Chicago:

"Does dis bus go to da Loop?"

"No, it goes beep beep."

At Great America, a 300-acre amusement park in suburban Gurnee, there's a ride somewhere that's got your number. Do you have the stomach of a fighter pilot? Then try the American Eagle, one of the world's largest wooden roller coasters. If, on the other hand, just sitting in a swing can make you queasy, then stick to something slow and earth-bound, like the Great America Scenic Railway.

CHICAGO:

FOR ALL THEIR DIFFERENCES, IF ANY ONE WORD DESCRIBES CHICAGO'S suburbs or, for that matter, the city proper, it is "change." Metropolitan Chicago is forever evolving, always becoming something new.

The suburbs, once predominantly commuter bedroom towns, are growing increasingly independent of the big city. High-technology industries are crowding into new office parks strung out along the East-West Tollway and the Northwest Tollway. Twenty-two Fortune 500 companies are based in the suburbs—two more than in the city.

It is possible today to live in the suburbs, work in the suburbs, dine in grand style in the suburbs, take in a good play in the suburbs, and never step into the city.

Indeed, tens of thousands of suburbanites do just that.

And yet, 160 years after Chicago built that first frame house with lumber from Plainfield, the entire metropolitan area remains wrapped in a common history, a common fate. The Great Swap continues. Chicago gives a lakefront festival, the suburbs give back a forest preserve. Chicago builds a convention center, suburban businesses dispatch the conventioneers.

The expressways of metropolitan Chicago are jammed each day with workers and goods moving to and fro, all part of the Great Swap.

And what everybody gets is this: One city—one Chicago—second to none. ▶

ALMOST 30 YEARS HAVE PASSED SINCE THAT NEIGHBORHOOD BOY played ring-a-levio on Chicago's Southwest Side. The tree he climbed on summer nights is gone, and the boy has long since moved to the suburbs, where he is "sooooo 708." He grills on a Weber and eats at McDonald's and thinks he might build a deck. He even plays softball with a glove, which makes him feel like a guy from Cleveland.

He married a woman from the suburbs who says "Chi-*cah*-go" instead of "Chi-*caw*-go"— and he can live with that, but now their children say "Chi-*cah*-go" too, which troubles him.

But he works in the Loop, which he still likens to Oz, and he doubts he will ever take such good fortune for granted. Indeed, as he walks across the Irv Kupcinet Bridge each morning and scans the horizon, he still marvels at Chicago's spirit and beauty and boundless energy.

Some things will never change. ●

GIVEN THE CITY'S REPUTATION AS A national transportation hub, Chicago's original downtown is often still called "the Loop," a name inspired by the elevated train tracks encircling the core business district.

And who, by the way, was this person Dan Ryan (BOTTOM), who ranks right up there with ex-presidents when it comes to being immortalized in an expressway name? He was president of the Cook County Board of Commissioners. In Chicago, where local politics are followed like sports, Ryan was an important man.

pages 24–25

OUR CITY IS STREETWISE AND ALLEY-hip of the casually familiar. Thus the Standard Oil Building and the John Hancock are, with tavern gaminess, referred to as Big Stan and Big John. Sears is simply that; never mind Roebuck. Ours is a one-syllable town. Its character has been molded by the muscle rather than the word.
                    —from *Chicago* (1985)
                        by Studs Terkel

PHOTO: WALTER DEPTULA

CHARLES FISHELMAN

THE VERY FIRST ELEVATED TRAIN LINE, erected in 1895, is the one pictured here—the Lake Street Line. The builder was Charles Tyson Yerkes (1837–1905), who also helped construct the first subways in London. Yerkes, famous in his day for his shady business practices, was the real-life inspiration for the villain in several of Theodore Dreiser's novels, including *The Titan* (1914).

▼ RICHARD YOUNKER

IT IS TRUE, AS THE NOTICE ON THE CAB
door says, that Chicago cabbies
sometimes carry no more than $5
in change, but they've got loads of
personality. The best ones have
been known to mist the interiors of
their cabs with perfume or incense,
provide a fresh daily newspaper,
or maybe even carry a portable TV.

CABS ARE CONVENIENT, BUT BUSES ARE inexpensive, which might explain why the Chicago Transit Authority chalks up 393 million riders per year.

CHARLES ESHELMAN ▼

JOHN WELZENBACH ▲

CHURCHILL & KLEHR ▼

MANY OF CHICAGO'S BEST-KNOWN landmarks, including the Chicago Board of Trade Building (**BOTTOM LEFT**) and the Wrigley Building (**TOP OPPOSITE**), display the time. Indeed, clocks are so ubiquitous in the Loop that pedestrians need not wear watches. They can look up, take half a dozen readings, and figure the average. The 24-story Merchandise Mart (**TOP**), owned by the Kennedy family of Boston,

occupies an entire city block and was the world's largest building at the time of its completion, 1929. The Mart, with more than 4 million square feet of floor space, is a center of wholesale merchandising, with showrooms for clothing, furniture, household appliances and accessories, and much more. In 1991, the Mart finally went retail, adding two floors of shops for the general public.

COMMODITY TRADING WAS INVENTED in Chicago. Farmers from across the Midwest came to Chicago by wagon and barge and sold their grain as best they could. What they failed to sell they dumped in the lake.

TODAY, CHICAGO'S FOUR INTERNATIONAL exchanges— the Chicago Board of Trade, the Chicago Mercantile Exchange, the Midwest Stock Exchange, and the Chicago Board Options Exchange— set world prices for everything from corn, wheat, soybeans, and pork bellies to U.S. Treasury bonds, foreign currencies, and stock options.

At the Chicago Board of Trade alone, some 130 million to 155 million contracts are traded each year, worth an estimated $12 billion to $14 billion.

When a Chicagoan walks into the fanciful James R. Thompson Center (**BOTTOM OPPOSITE**), he is likely to freeze in his tracks as quickly as any tourist from Iowa, stunned by the drama of this building. Designed by Helmut Jahn (**TOP**), one of Chicago's most innovative architects, the structure is a celebration of complex geometry, natural light, and festive colors. Not everybody, however, likes the place. At a ceremony in May 1993, in which the building was renamed for the former governor of Illinois, one elderly gent jokingly consoled Thompson, saying, "It could have been worse. They could have named a prison after you." Thompson himself said, "Chicagoans love it or hate it, but they talk about it. That's Chicago style."

THE TALLEST BUILDING IN THE WORLD
is the 110-story Sears Tower
(OPPOSITE), designed by the Chicago
architectural firm of Skidmore,
Owings & Merrill in the sleek,
glass-and-steel modernist style
associated worldwide with another
renowned Chicagoan, Ludwig Mies
van der Rohe. The tower, which
opened in 1973, stands 1,454 feet
high and, on a windy day, sways
6 to 10 inches from the verticle.

The Museum of Contemporary
Art (BOTTOM), which was founded
in 1967, is scheduled to move to a
larger space in the spring of 1995.
The MCA organized the first major
museum exhibitions for artists Jeff
Koons and Christo.

SOME FOLKS CALL IT "THE WINDY City." Others call it "Sweethome Chicago," "City of Big Shoulders," or "That Toddlin' Town." But perhaps the truest motto for Chicago is also the most prosaic—"The City That Works."

▲ CHUCK BERMAN

At the University of Chicago Law School (**bottom**), nobody has time to do anything but study. Supreme Court Justice Anthony Scalia taught here, and Edward Levi, the U.S. attorney general from 1975 to 1977, was dean.

▶ JIM WRIGHT

Page 40

All good Midwesterners, even those big-city ones who don't know a heifer from a combine, like their corn on the cob. Marina City Towers, dubbed the "Corncob Towers" by locals, embodies the brashness and energy of Chicago's modernist architecture.

PHOTO: KAREN I. HIRSCH

Page 41

In one of the more successful movies filmed in Chicago—*Hunter* (1980), starring Steve McQueen— an automobile roars right off the lip of an upper level of Marina City's parking garage.

PHOTO: CHARLES ESHELMAN

CHICAGO
PLACE

SAKS FIFTH AVENUE

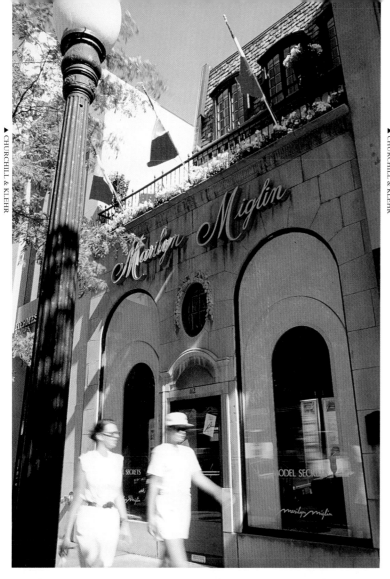

IF "GOD IS IN THE DETAILS," AS IT is sometimes said, then there can be few true atheists among the architecture buffs of Chicago. Exquisite ornamentation is the hallmark of dozens of the city's finest older buildings, from the decorative terra cotta of the Fisher Building (1895), at 343 S. Dearborn Street (**BOTTOM RIGHT**), to the almost obsessively intricate metal flourishes of the Carson, Pirie, Scott and Company Building (1889), at 1 S. State Street (**TOP RIGHT**). It was the designer of the Carson's building, Louis Sullivan, who coined that familiar aphorism of efficiency, "Form follows function."

NIKE TOWN (TOP LEFT), OPENED IN 1992, is first a spectacle and second a store, intended above all to be fun. It features a four-story atrium with life-size sculptures of sports stars, Lucite pneumatic tubes that shoot shoes from the fourth-floor stockroom to a first-floor sales pod, and fish swimming behind a display of aqua shoes.

NORTH MICHIGAN AVENUE, SOME- times called the "Magnificent Mile," is Chicago's poshest shopping district. Tourists and conventioneers from all over the world crowd the side-walks. Buses roar alongside horse-drawn pleasure carriages, and store windows compete to display the finest merchandise. Annual sales on the street frequently top $1 billion, and elaborate stores and elegant boutiques seem to open each year.

NEW YORK IS AMERICA'S FASHION capital, gloves down. But Chicago is home to an exceptional community of clothing designers. Among the very best are Hino & Malee (**TOP LEFT**), who operate their own boutique on Oak Street. Kazuyoshi Hino and Malee Chompoo, a husband-and-wife duo known for asymmetrical design, market their fashions to 400 stores across the country.

THE ART INSTITUTE OF CHICAGO, founded in 1879, houses one of the finest art collections in the world. In recent years more than 1.3 million people annually have visited the institute to view some of its 300,000 pieces. A hallmark of the museum is the Bertha Honore Palmer Impressionists collection.

Associated with the museum is the illustrious School of the Art Institute of Chicago, whose 1,700 students often study in the Ryerson and Burnham Library (TOP LEFT). Among the school's alumni are Ivan Albright, Thomas Hart Benton, Walt Disney, the cartoonist Herblock, the film-maker Vincente Minnelli, Leroy Neiman, Georgia O'Keeffe, Claes Oldenburg, Ed Paschke, and Grant Wood.

The Art Institute's two famous bronze lions (OPPOSITE) are almost as much Chicago landmarks as the Picasso sculpture and the historic Water Tower.

ONE OF THE MOST ENDURING
monuments of the Chicago School
of Architecture is the 10-story
Auditorium Building (1889), a masterpiece designed by Louis Sullivan
and Dankmar Adler. Now home to
Roosevelt University, it originally
included office and retail space, as
well as the acoustically perfect auditorium. The auditorium has been
called Chicago's Sistine Chapel.

SOMETIMES A BUILDING IS SO LOVELY
it belongs in an art museum. Such
is the case, quite literally, with the
Old Stock Exchange (OPPOSITE),
another masterpiece by Adler and
Sullivan. When the building, originally at 30 N. LaSalle Street, was
demolished in 1972—much to the
dismay of historic preservationists—
its Trading Room was salvaged
and restored in the Art Institute
of Chicago. The battle to save the
Old Stock Exchange marked the
beginning of a citizens' preservation
movement in the city, now spearheaded by the Landmarks Preservation Council of Illinois.

On North Michigan Avenue, one of the oldest buildings in Chicago and one of the newest grace the skyline together. The Water Tower, built between 1867 and 1869, survived the Chicago Fire of 1871 and has become a symbol of the city's resilience. Bloomingdale's, in the 900 N. Michigan building, opened for business in 1988 and brought a slice of New York to town.

One of the city's most respected architecture critics, M.W. Newman of the *Chicago Sun-Times*, once described the vintage Rookery at 209 S. LaSalle Street (OPPOSITE) as having "the ruddy air of a Victorian clubman living the blue-chip life." Completed in 1886, it was designed by two early masters of Chicago architecture, John Wellborn Root and Daniel Burnham. They built it with red brick and granite and gave it a bright skylit lobby. Then in 1905, the most celebrated Chicago architect of them all, Frank Lloyd Wright, completely remodeled the lobby in his inimitable Prairie style, using cream-colored marble and black wrought iron.

HOLY NAME CATHEDRAL (TOP), A
Victorian Gothic church dedicated
in 1875 and substantially renovated
several times since, is the principal
church of the Archdiocese of
Chicago. During Pope John Paul
II's visit to Chicago in 1979, the
cathedral was the setting for a
performance by Luciano Pavarotti,
as well as a concert by the Chicago
Symphony Orchestra—both events
in the pontiff's honor.

IN 1988, THE EXOTIC HOTEL INTERCON-
tinental (BOTTOM, TOP OPPOSITE)
held a huge rummage sale, hawking
just about everything that wasn't
nailed down, including 900 TV sets
and the quarterdeck from the ship
used in the movie *Around the
World in 80 Days*. In the following
months, every inch of the place
was rehabbed and restored to its
original glory. Particularly striking
are its intricately painted ceilings,
balustraded curved staircases, and
marble inlays. The hotel's most
distinctive exterior feature is a
Moorish-style minaret. You just
don't see a lot of those in Chicago.

A WALK THROUGH THE FIELD MUSEUM (BOTTOM) is a walk through exotic lands. Modeled after a Greek temple, the museum was built in 1919 with an $8 million grant from the will of Marshall Field, the department store king. Popular both with locals and tourists, the institution remains a center of scholarly research, devoted to the study of anthropology, geology, botany, and zoology.

page 54

THE HOTEL INTERCONTINENTAL WAS built by the Shriners and dedicated in 1929. Originally the Medinah Athletic Club, the hotel still features an Olympic-size swimming pool. And just how extravagant is this building? Consider this quote from a tour guide: "Now we're making the transition from the Celtic and Mesopotamian lobby to the Byzantine Empire with Assyrian influence in the Hall of Lions."

PHOTO: ALAN SHORTALL

page 55

A DETAIL FROM A SUBURBAN COUNTRY club built by the Shriners in the 1920s also reflects the organization's devotion to exotic architecture.

PHOTO: SAMUEL FEIN

THE **C**HURCH IN THE **S**KY (THIS PAGE), as it is called, stands 400 feet above street level in the lacy gothic spire of the Chicago Temple, First United Methodist Church, 77 W. Washington Street.

THE **S**ECOND **P**RESBYTERIAN **C**HURCH (OPPOSITE), at 1936 S. Michigan Avenue, was once among the most elite congregations in Chicago, favored by such business titans as meat-packer Ogden Armour and sleeping car-builder George Pullman. They spared no expense. The church, designed by architect James Renwick in an English Gothic style and built between 1872 and 1874, contains 22 stained glass windows, including 14 by designer Louis Comfort Tiffany.

CHICAGO IS A CITY OF IMMIGRANTS who erected many monuments to their faith. The architecture of the oldest cathedrals reflects a tradition rooted in faraway lands. There is an abrupt curve in the Kennedy Expressway just north of Division Street that would not be there, had there not been a beloved Roman Catholic Church in the way. The curve is called "the Catholic bend in the road."

pages 58–59

IN *The Wonderful Wizard of Oz*, the place of promise and mystery is called the Emerald City. In Chicago, it's more like the Golden City, especially as the setting sun bathes the western facades of the Loop.

PHOTOS: KEVIN O. MOONEY

THE ELKS NATIONAL MEMORIAL, unknown to many Chicagoans, is resplendent inside and out. The magnificent building houses the national headquarters for the Benevolent and Protective Order of Elks, a fraternal and charitable organization founded in 1868. The Elks have almost 1.5 million members across the United States and raise millions of dollars for programs that aid the sick, the needy, and the deserving.

GIVE ALL THANKS, AGAIN, TO ARCHITECT Louis Sullivan, who designed Holy Trinity Cathedral in an understated Russian Provincial style. Commissioned by a group of Russian immigrants, the lovely little church was dedicated in 1903.

FATHER JACQUES MARQUETTE (1637-1675) was a French Jesuit missionary priest who brought Catholicism to the Midwest. He is credited with saying the first Christmas mass in Chicago in 1674 to a small gathering of Native American Indians. Marquette and the Quebec-born explorer Louis Jolliet were the first Europeans to visit the site of present-day Chicago.

AS THE GOTHIC WINDOW SUGGESTS, the University of Chicago is steeped in tradition and history—or at least as much history as one will find in the fresh-faced Midwest. But as the martial arts disciples on the lawn demonstrate, this is one thoroughly alive and modern place of learning.

CHICAGO'S BRIDGES STITCH TOGETHER a patchwork city, and skilled iron-workers stitch together the bridges themselves, creating crisscrossing beds of steel cable to support the asphalt above.

THE EL ABOVE RUNS ALL NIGHT, WHILE Lower Wacker Drive lies in darkness all day. Lower Wacker, sometimes called the "Emerald City" because of its eerie green lights, is the bottom level of a two-tier boulevard that hugs the Chicago River around the outer rim of the old Loop. It is a wonderful street to get to know— an underground bypass to rush hour congestion—but no place for amateurs. The narrow, labyrinthine street was designed as a service road for downtown trucks making deliveries to basements.

IT IS ONE OF THE CHARMING, IF inefficient, anachronisms of Chicago that when a boat or barge is coming through, bridges must go up— even if that means a good bit of inconvenience for motorists and pedestrians. The policy dates to an early time in the city's history when river traffic was far more crucial to the economy. All the same, Chicagoans don't seem to mind. They stop their work, look out windows, and watch.

DRAWBRIDGES ARE A SYMBOL OF
Chicago. The first, the now inactive
Cortland Street Bridge, was built in
1902. The city still has 43 moveable
bridges, all of them operated by
trained city workers. Bridge-tenders
used to hole up in the little towers,
often with nothing much to do,
whiling away the hours between
boats by watching TV. But now, in
the interest of efficiency, they rove
the city in teams, going to this
bridge or that as they are needed.

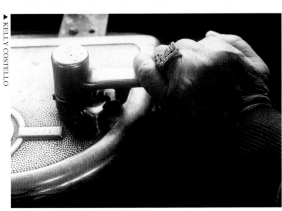

CHICAGO HAS TEAMS OF WORKERS WHO do nothing but paint bridges. Given the extremes of the weather, the toll of winter salt, and the constant automobile traffic, it is no wonder it's a full-time job.

WHILE MUCH OF THE PUBLIC ART ON view in Chicago is sponsored by the government or large corporations, some of the most moving pieces are works of folk art that show up on outdoor walls. The theme of these murals and chalk drawings frequently is one of ethnic or nationalist pride.

In the 1960s and early 1970s, a determined group fought to preserve this city's great architectural heritage from the threat of "urban renewal" efforts. Led by Richard Nickel, a Chicago photographer who devoted his days and nights to photographing neglected buildings, preservationists made progress. Today, it is not uncommon to see workmen touching up Chicago's brick-and-mortar works of arts.

RALPH FRESE IS A FOURTH-GENERA-tion, German-American blacksmith and master canoe builder. His company, Chicagoland Canoe Base, at 4019 N. Narragansett, opened more than 50 years ago as a blacksmith shop. Frese, an avid outdoorsman, built his first boat when he was 14.

HARPO MARX PLAYED A LYON & Healy Model 30. And, today, the company can make one for you, too. Lyon & Healy Harps, at 168 N. Ogden Avenue, is the nation's oldest maker of standing string harps. The business was founded in 1863 and survived the Great Chicago Fire and two other fires. The company now produces nearly 1,000 harps a year. Inside the frame of every concert grand harp are 2,000 moving pieces activated by the foot pedals.

MICHELE GIFFUNE

CHURCHILL & KLEHR

WHAT YOU SEE IN THE DETAILS SAYS
as much about you as it does about
the city.

"Man Against Crocodile"? It is
a sign (BOTTOM LEFT) that could only
have come from Riverview, that
glorious, seedy amusement park
that once lit up the night sky on the
Northwest Side. At Riverview, some
folks cheered for the crocodile.

AMONG CHICAGO'S QUAINTEST
buildings are the old firehouses, as
pretty as the day they were built.
But the very first firehouses (BOTTOM
RIGHT) looked altogether different—
three-story affairs with a hayloft
on the third floor, living quarters
on the second, and horses and
wagons on the first.

▶ CHUCK BERMAN

PARTS OF CHICAGO ARE A WALKER'S delight, full of warm buildings, quiet side streets, and whimsy, even in the rain. Gene Kelly, one suspects, might have liked to dance here.

STREET MUSICIANS, ONCE BANNED from the city's boulevards, now are a common sight and sound. Many are awful; many more are worth the dime or dollar you might drop their way. The best acoustics, the musicians say, are in the subways.

▼ JIM WRIGHT

ROCKEFELLER **C**HAPEL (1928) ON the campus of the University of Chicago is praised for its excellent acoustics and the fine quality of its pipe organ. It was named in honor of oil magnate John D. Rockefeller, who donated $2 million towards the chapel's construction.

SO, OKAY, THE HORN IS A LITTLE BIG for the child. At the moment. But remember—little Benny Goodman, back on Maxwell Street, probably looked just as ambitious at that age.

IN SUMMER, PARADES ARE AN ALMOST weekly occurrence— especially in the Loop—with seemingly each and every racial, ethnic, and social group taking a turn. The two biggest events are the St. Patrick's Day Parade and the Bud Billiken Day Parade, celebrating African-American Chicago and held on the South Side.

DID YOU DOUBLE BOGEY AND WRITE down par? Careful. These guys at the Medinah Country Club are watching you. *Golf Digest* magazine has rated this club as the 12TH best in the United States.

BUCKINGHAM **F**OUNTAIN **IN** **G**RANT Park—downtown's front yard— was patterned after a fountain on the grounds of Louis XIV's palace at Versailles. Interestingly enough, its jets are controlled by a computer 708 miles away in Atlanta.

ONE **OF THE MORE REMARKABLE** features of Chicago is the proximity of the lakefront to the central business district. But they're not this close. The fish pictured was a sign outside a seafood restaurant. Michael Jordan of the Chicago Bulls bought the place, and now, instead of a fish, there is a basketball outside the restaurant. In the background is the John Hancock Building (1969), the third tallest in Chicago after the Sears Tower and the Amoco Oil Building (1979).

THIS **C**HICAGO **WORKER IS ASSIGNED** to a water intake crib two miles out into Lake Michigan, which provides tap water for the city and its suburbs. Water is taken in through the cribs and chemically treated at a shoreline purification plant before it heads for the pumping stations.

CHICAGO IS JUSTIFIABLY PROUD OF its public art collection, especially its numerous outdoor installations, including the authentic Native American totem pole in Lincoln Park, the Indian warrior in Grant Park, and the fiberglass monument by French artist Jean Dubuffet in front of the James R. Thompson Center. The city and park district maintain about 150 pieces of sculpture.

CLAES OLDENBURG'S *Batcolumn* has got to be the most lighthearted public sculpture in Chicago, especially in light of the abysmal performances over the years of both Chicago baseball teams. Standing outside the Social Security Administration Building, at 600 W. Madison, the *Batcolumn* is 100 feet tall and weighs 20 tons.

CHICAGO PARKS ARE DOTTED WITH sculptures, statues, and other works of art. Among the skyscrapers looming over Grant Park in the background, by the way, is the Prudential Building, once the tallest building in the city.

THE ART INSTITUTE'S FAMOUS BRONZE lions, which actually root for every Chicago sports team, were sculpted by Edward Kemys and have stood on Michigan Avenue since 1894.

ALEXANDER CALDER'S STEEL *Flamingo* stands outside the Federal Center, where it was dedicated in 1974. Adults like it. Children find it hard to climb.

CHARLES ESHELMAN

It is Chicago's best known sculpture even if nobody quite knows what it's supposed to be. Pablo Picasso's untitled sculpture, made of Cor-Ten steel, was unveiled in 1967 in what is now called Daley Center Plaza. Some folks thought it might be an Afghan hound, others said a woman, others said a dodo bird, a baboon, a vulture, a giant cheese slicer, and an insult to Chicago's greatness. In time, Chicago came to accept it. Now, many even claim to like it.

THE CHARM OF PUBLIC ART IS ITS physical proximity. You can touch it, sit on it, or meet a friend under it.

THE NAME OF THE SHOW WAS "AM Chicago," and it wasn't very good. So in 1984, WLS-TV brought in a 30-year-old unknown, Oprah Winfrey, to be the new host. One year later, it was the top show in its time slot. The rest is talk-show history. In 1986 the program went into national syndication, and today it continues to be a daytime hit.

SAUL **B**ELLOW IS GENERALLY CONSID-ered to be Chicago's greatest living writer. Both intellectual and earthy, he embraces all the extremes that make up this city of his boyhood. He was awarded the Nobel Prize for Literature in 1976.

BACK IN 1952, WHEN LUSTY **H**UGH Hefner started his daring magazine for men, *Playboy*, who would have thought that his Phi Beta Kappa daughter, Christie Hefner, would take over one day? So it goes. While Hugh lives the life of leisure in California today, Christie is chairperson and chief executive officer of the corporate empire in Chicago.

PULITZER **P**RIZE-WINNING AUTHOR Studs Terkel, perhaps America's best oral historian, is the author of seven books of carefully crafted interviews. He is also a sometime-actor, host of a daily radio show, and an untiring champion of liberal causes, even now in his 80s. Studs' exuberant philosophy of life is "Take it easy, but take it."

Eppie Lederer (a.k.a. **Ann Landers**) is the queen of America's advice columnists, sharing the crown only with her twin sister, Popo Friedman Phillips (a.k.a. Abigail Van Buren). Her first bit of advice was published on October 16, 1955 in the *Chicago Sun-Times*, and, as everybody knows, she's been dishing it out ever since.

CALL HIM KUP. EVERYBODY DOES. AND he'll call you pal. He always does. Irv Kupcinet grew up in Chicago, played football alongside future president Gerald Ford on the 1934 College All-Star Team, and played professional football with the Philadelphia Eagles. He has written a daily newspaper column since January 18, 1943—first for the *Chicago Times*, and now for its successor, the *Chicago Sun-Times*. He's still a good read, and he's still got the best phone book of any reporter in town. When new reporters come to the paper, they usually meet Kup the first time they have to go begging for a phone number. "Kup, got a number for Sinatra?" Kup always does.

IN CHICAGO, THERE IS NO END TO the fine dining and no end to the nightlife. Among the cutting-edge restaurants drawing impossible crowds are Galleria Marchetti (where the owner also sells sports cars), Bice, and Cafe Ba Ba Reeba. On a more traditional note, there are evenings with the Chicago Symphony Orchestra (BOTTOM OPPOSITE), which always draws a crowd at orchestra hall.

THE FIRST LADY OF DANCE IN CHICAGO is Maria Tallchief Paschen (OPPOSITE), whose career as a prima ballerina began on an Osage Indian reservation in Oklahoma. Once married to choreographer George Balanchine, she was principal dancer with the New York City Ballet from 1947 to 1960. Paschen is currently director of ballet for the Lyric Opera.

▶ KAREN I. HIRSCH

CHICAGO WAS NOT ALWAYS MUCH OF A classical music town. Indeed, when Theodore Thomas, a respected New York musician, agreed in 1891 to be the first conductor of the new Chicago Symphony Orchestra, he explained, "I would go to hell if they gave me a permanent Orchestra" Fortunately, the times have changed. The Chicago Symphony, now considered to be among the finest orchestras in the world, was led to greatness by Georg Solti (TOP LEFT OPPOSITE), musical director from 1969 to 1991. The current musical director is Daniel Barenboim (TOP RIGHT OPPOSITE).

THE CHICAGO THEATRE, WHICH HAS had its ups and downs, is decidedly in the midst of an up. The Chicago opened in 1921, booked all the biggest stage stars in the United States for 30 years, and then fell on hard times. Blame it on the advent of TV, which kept audiences at home. But in 1986, the theatre was completely refurbished, and it reopened in style with entertainer Frank Sinatra. On the night pictured here (RIGHT), pianist Victor Borge performed.

THE MUSIC BOX THEATER IS CHICAGO'S leading revival house, where the films of Chaplin and Fellini, rather than Spielberg, are screened.

IT WAS ONCE OWNED BY "MACHINEGUN" Jack McGurn, and Al Capone was a regular patron. Now the Green Mill bar is one of Chicago's hottest and most respected nightspots, where excellent jazz can be heard every night but Monday. Why not Monday? That's Poetry Slam night, when local writers take to the stage and recite their best stuff for some tough customers. The worst poets get booed right off the stage.

BEFORE THERE WAS "SATURDAY NIGHT Live," there was "The Second City," the first crucible of the improvisational comedy skit. Among the dozens of comedic stars who apprenticed at The Second City in Chicago or at its branch clubs are Alan Alda, Ed Asner, Alan Arkin, Dan Aykroyd, Jim and John Belushi, Shelley Berman, John Candy, Robert Klein, Shelley Long, Elaine May, Paul Mazursky, Bill Murray, Michael Myers, Mike Nichols, Gilda Radner, Harold Ramis, Joan Rivers, David Steinberg, and George Wendt.

SOMETIMES A NIGHT OUT MEANS GETTING together with a couple of friends and making your own entertainment.

THE CHICAGO BLUES FESTIVAL, HELD for three days each June in Grant Park, showcases the loud, electric urban blues for which the city is famous. The sound is a jumped-up, electrically amplified reworking of the old 12-bar country blues of the Mississippi Delta. Muddy Waters, winner of six Grammy awards, was the king of Chicago bluesmen. It was Muddy who sang, "Got My Mojo Workin'."

MUDDY **W**ATERS DIED IN **1983,** BUT Chicago remains home to dozens of blues greats. They perform in clubs all over town, some so small there is no stage. Among the most famous performers are Koko Taylor (**TOP RIGHT**) and Junior Wells (**BOTTOM RIGHT**).

IN CHICAGO, AS IN ALL OF THE UNITED States, race does matter, although it should not. People are people. Santa is Santa. And the Lone Ranger symbolizes the good in us all. The actor who played the Lone Ranger on radio and TV for years, by the way, was Chicagoan Clayton Moore.

ROSA'S IS ONE OF CHICAGO'S MOST popular music joints. But the sign is a bit misleading. Rosa's is as well known for rhythm and blues as for the straight blues, especially when the great Otis Clay is on the bill.

IF YOU CAN'T FIND IT AT THE JAZZ Record Mart, you can't get it period.

FOR THE BEST BLUES IN TOWN, THE
South Side is the place to go,
especially the New Checkerboard
Lounge. But if you can't make it
that far, there's always Buddy Guy's
Legends, just south of the Loop.
Eric Clapton has called Buddy Guy
the "finest guitar player alive."

WALKING AROUND CHICAGO IS LIKE traveling around the world. From neighborhood to neighborhood the language, foods, and dress all change. Russian Jews and East Indians share Devon Avenue. Taylor Street near Racine Avenue is predominately Italian. For more than 100 years, North Lincoln Avenue has been a solidly German street. Chicago's old Greek Town still thrives on Halsted Street. Immigrant Poles get their income taxes figured out on Milwaukee Avenue. And Palestinians have found a new home on the Southwest Side.

▶ KAREN L. HIRSCH

MICHELE GIFFUNE

THE JEWISH POPULATION OF THE
Chicago area is growing once again,
as immigrants from the countries of
the former Union of Soviet Socialist
Republics flock to America. But
for all of Chicago's immigrants, the
yearning to become American is
offset by a wish to preserve beloved
ethnic traditions. At the Bernard
Horwich Jewish Community Center
(TOP), children learn traditional
dances. The shofar, or ram's horn
(BOTTOM), is sounded during
worship on Rosh Hashanah and
each of the following 10 days
of penitence.

At the Alliance of Polish Clubs
Building, 5835 W. Diversey
Avenue, young Polish Americans
in traditional Highlander dress
learn the music and the dance of
their forefathers.

AT PICKARD INCORPORATED, A
106-year-old china factory in
Antioch, the secret to success is
quality. Pickard china is used on
the president's jet, Air Force One,
and in United States embassies
around the world.

ANDERSONVILLE, ON NORTH CLARK
Street, once was the geographic
heart of the largest Swedish
population in the world outside
Stockholm. Although Chicago's
Swedish population has long since
dispersed and other ethnic groups
have moved in, the old street
retains much of its Nordic heritage.
Visitors today can still take part in
various Swedish festivals, including
the Santa Lucia procession of lights
in December and Midsummerfest,
a celebration of the longest day
of the year.

CHURCHILL & KLEHR

ELABORATE EGG-PAINTING IS A centuries-old folk art still practiced at Easter time in Chicago's Ukrainian-American community.

FOR A LITTLE TASTE OF SEOUL, TRY Lawrence Avenue on the Northwest Side.

ONE OF THE CITY'S MOST VITAL NEW immigrant populations is the Vietnamese community of Argyle Street in Uptown. Chicagoans wander over to Argyle for the food, which is excellent, and then marvel at how these new Americans have transformed one of the shabbiest old streets on the North Side. Trung Viet Grocery (**TOP**) was started by a family that came to Chicago from Saigon in 1979. Many of the proprietors of shops on Argyle actually are of ethnic Chinese descent and were among the first to flee to America after the Vietnam War.

FIRST SETTLED BY CHINESE IMMIGRANTS in about 1912, Chinatown on the Near South Side is one of Chicago's oldest and most exotic ethnic neighborhoods. Indeed, the neighborhood continues to grow, receiving hundreds of new arrivals each year from mainland China and Taiwan. Recently, an association of Chinese-American businesspeople managed to buy up a large tract of adjacent land, giving the overcrowded community room to grow.

FOR DECADES THE ON LEONG BUILDING was the unofficial City Hall of Chinatown. In the 1980s, federal agents raided the building and uncovered a multi-million-dollar gambling operation, but more recently it has become a legitimate social center.

ONCE A YEAR IN **G**RANT **P**ARK ALL
the ethnic neighborhoods of
Chicago—or at least their restaura-
teurs—gather together almost
within spraying distance of

Buckingham Fountain and chuck
their diets. Taste of Chicago, as
this annual rite is called, is a sort
of gustatory Woodstock.

MAYBE IT'S A FORM OF OVERCOMPEN-sation—like the guy who piles up scholarly degrees to convince himself of his own intelligence— but an authentic Chicago hot dog is loaded with extras. You got your mustard, your ketchup, your chopped onions, your hot peppers, your tomatoes, and your celery salt. So it ain't one of them famous New York dogs. It weighs more.

▲ JOHN BOOZ

▲ JOHN BOOZ

▲ JOHN BOOZ

IN MEXICO, RODEO IS THE SPORT OF THE gentry. It only stands to reason that in Chicago, where Mexican–Amer-icans are a sizable ethnic group, Mexican rodeo has found a second home. The "charreada" is a popular late summer diversion in parts of the city and in certain southern suburbs, attracting 5,000 to 10,000

pectators. The flamboyant charros
wear fitted rhinestone-studded suits,
and mariachi music fills the air.

IF THE NAMES ON THE GOVERNMENT buildings, expressways, and forest preserves don't give away the secret—Kennedy, Ryan, Dunne, Daley— then the green river should. The Irish are big in this town. On St. Patrick's Day each year, city workers in motorboats dump hundreds of gallons of green dye into the Chicago River, giving it a peculiar appearance that lingers for days. According to the 1990 United States Census, however, the number of Chicago area residents who actually identify their primary ancestry as Irish is less than 10 percent.

▶ CHARLES ESHELMAN

HE WAS BORN THE ELDEST SON OF the most powerful mayor in the city's history, Richard J. Daley (1902–1976). But Mayor Richard M. Daley (воттом), whose nickname in high school was "mayor," shies away from comparisons with his famous dad, fully aware that he and the times are very different. Daley was elected in 1989 and reelected in 1991. Like his father, the 51-year-old mayor loves his city. And like his father, he is extremely private in his personal life, always putting his family first.

IT WAS HER SMILE, HER INTELLIGENCE, and her flat-out refusal to play racial politics that brought her victory. On November 3, 1992, Carol Moseley-Braun became the first black woman to be elected to the United States Senate. She drew 53 percent of the vote in her race against a suburban Republican lawyer who had worked in Ronald Reagan's White House. Moseley-Braun's previous job? Cook County recorder of deeds.

CHICAGO'S PARADE HONORING THE soldiers who fought in Operation Desert Storm (**TOP, TOP OPPOSITE**) was one of the nation's largest.

SINCE 1988, CHICAGO'S ANNUAL FALL marathon has included a division for wheelchair athletes. The winners clock in at about one hour and 45 minutes, meaning they finish before those who go on foot. The route is typically lined with entertainment, from the Mariachi Azteca Band to the Chinatown Lion Dancers to the Shannon Rovers.

THE ANNUAL BUD BILLIKEN DAY
Parade (BOTTOM), the largest parade
in the city, celebrates a fictional
character created by the *Chicago
Daily Defender*, the city's leading
African-American newspaper.
Bud Billiken is said to be the patron
saint of the *Defender*'s news carriers
and all black children.

CHURCHILL & KLEHR

RICHARD YOUNKER

AS THIS HISTORIC PHOTO OF PARADING meat industry workers suggests, the stockyards were once the backbone of Chicago's economy.

THE FANCY OLD GATEWAY (TOP) IS about all that remains of the once internationally famous Union Stockyard. The last cattle pens were razed in 1976. In its peak year, 1924, the square-mile meat processing plant received 18,653,539 head of livestock. Forty thousand men and women killed, cut, cured, cooked, and canned the beasts. Workers also tanned hides, ground bones to fertilizer, and reduced knuckles to gelatin.

THE MEAT INDUSTRY THAT REMAINS IN Chicago today is involved largely in processing livestock that has been butchered elsewhere and shipped here by rail.

IN THE DAYS BEFORE EXPRESSWAYS and the inexpensive Model T Ford, industrial workers lived as close as possible to their places of employment. The ultimate experience in such living may have been the planned utopian town of Pullman. George Pullman, who built railroad cars, designed the town to meet his employees' every need. There were comfortable row houses (**RIGHT**), a library, a church, and a hotel named after his daughter Florence (**OPPOSITE LEFT**). But, in 1884, the residents had tired of Pullman's control over their lives and voted to annex themselves to Chicago. Pullman resisted, and blood was shed in a workers' strike. But in 1898, by order of the Illinois Supreme Court, the Pullman Company was divested of ownership of the town.

KEVIN O. MOONEY

A FAVORITE STYLE OF HOUSING IN Chicago is the sturdy, fireproof brick bungalow, whose design originated in India. On some blocks in some neighborhoods, every single house is a bungalow.

CHICAGO'S SOUTHEAST SIDE IS A LAND OF steel mills, factories, working rivers, and working people. On the North Side, the lake is a pretty diversion. On the Southeast Side, it is an integral part of an industrial economy.

CHICAGO IS STILL A SMOKESTACK TOWN, turning out Weber Grills, steel wire, Twinkies, farm machinery, Cracker Jacks, textbooks, and a whole lot more.

CHICAGO IS STILL A UNION TOWN.
The Chicago Federation of Labor
(CFL) claims some 500,000
workers. The International
Brotherhood of Teamsters, with
around 65,000 members, claims the
largest membership in the Cook
County area. Interestingly enough,
the head of the CFL today, Robert
Healy, is a former public school
teacher. For years, the union
movement in Chicago was dominated by blue-collar trade unions
and, appropriately, the CFL
president was a blue-collar worker.
Today, public employee unions
have grown in influence.

CHICAGO IS A TOWN OF PRIDE. **P**EOPLE here take care in their work, whether their job is in education, construction, watch repairing, or cigar making.

CHICAGO IS INCREASINGLY A HIGH-technology town. Firms specializing in research and technology have sprung up by the dozens, especially along Interstate 88 in the west suburbs and throughout the suburbs northwest of O'Hare International Airport. Each year, at least 35 Chicago-area companies are listed among *Fortune* magazine's Fortune 500.

MAGIC INCORPORATED, AT 5082 N. Lincoln Avenue, is one of about a half dozen top-ranked magic supply shops in the Chicago area. Jay Marshall (BOTTOM), a retired magician who works in the shop, performed 14 times on "The Ed Sullivan Show."

IN A TOWN OF CLOWNS—NORTH SIDE, South Side, Chinatown, and, some would suggest, City Hall—Bozo is number one. "The Bozo Show" has aired on WGN-TV in Chicago since 1961. Since the ticket backlog for the show is five or six years, some people send away for them before their children are even born.

CHICAGO NEVER QUITE GOES TO SLEEP, whether that means working the overnight shift at a steel mill or taking in another lakefront festival.

ON JULY 3 EACH SUMMER, TENS OF thousands of people flock to Grant Park for a night of music and celebration. The Grant Park Symphony plays a full program of classical music, culminating with Tchaikovsky's rousing "1812 Overture." Then, as the cannon in the final movement begins to blast, the night sky over the lake lights up with fireworks.

The Petrillo Band Shell in Grant Park is the place to be on summer weekend nights in Chicago. The Grant Park Symphony plays there. The jazz, blues, and gospel fests schedule their biggest talent there. And the Chicago Bulls—whenever they win a championship, which is often enough—take their bows there. And it's all free.

The alfresco music scene in the suburbs, typified by this pop music concert in west suburban Lisle, must inevitably lag behind the big lakefront productions, but it gets better by the year.

RAVINIA, IN HIGHLAND PARK ON THE North Shore, is best known as the summer home of the Chicago Symphony Orchestra. The music fans get there early, picnic on the lawn in style, and then settle back for a great open-air production.

IN MANY SUBURBS, SUCH AS DEERFIELD, the small-town feel is palpable, especially when everybody turns out for an old-fashioned summer celebration of patriotism.

DAY OR NIGHT, **C**HICAGO IS A GREAT family town. In summer, it's festival time on the lakefront, first with the Blues Festival, followed by the Gospel Festival, A Taste of Chicago, the Country Music Festival, Venetian Night, "Viva Chicago," and the Jazz Festival. Venetian Night (TOP), is like a "Rose Bowl parade on water," as one city official said, with 40 to 50 beautifully lighted boats gliding along the shoreline.

page 152

CHICAGO'S MOST PRESTIGIOUS cemetery is Graceland, on the North Side, and not just because it leads all others in ivy. It's just that such an interesting crowd is buried there: architects Ludwig Mies van der Rohe and Louis Sullivan, boxing champion Jack Johnson, meat packer Phillip D. Armour, and Cyrus McCormick, inventor of the reaper.

PHOTO: CHUCK BERMAN

page 153

THE UNIVERSITY OF CHICAGO, THIS city's most prestigious place of learning, prides itself on scholarship. Its favorite football cheer: "Themistocles, Thucydides, the Peloponnesian War, X Squared, Y Squared, H-2-S-O-4. Who for, what for, who are we gonna yell for? Maroons!"

The University is part of a century-old tradition of college-level education in Chicago, which includes DePaul University (1898), Loyola University (1870), Northwestern University (1851), Columbia College (1890), Illinois Institute of Technology (1892), and Chicago State University (1869).

PHOTO: JIM WRIGHT

THE BIGGEST UNIVERSITY IN THE Chicago area, measured by enrollment, is the University of Illinois at Chicago (TOP), with some 25,000 students. The school, which opened a four-year campus southwest of the Loop in 1965, was designed for urban commuters.

NORTHWESTERN UNIVERSITY IN Evanston (ABOVE) is nestled on 251 acres along the lakefront. The third-largest private university in the Chicago area (after DePaul University and Loyola University), it rivals the University of Chicago for academic prestige.

THE ART INSTITUTE OF CHICAGO, located on busy Michigan Avenue downtown, draws students from across the Midwest.

GRANT PARK WAS A CAREFULLY PLANNED park, built on hundreds of tons of landfill that pushed back Lake Michigan's waters. Some sections of the park almost suggest formal gardens, British-style, with rows of trees creating shady walkways.

BOB FIRTH

FAMILIES AND NATURE LOVERS ARE always welcomed at the Morton Arboretum near west suburban Lisle. The 1,500-acre arboretum was established in 1922 by Joy Morton, founder of the Morton Salt Company. Scientists there are working to develop strains of trees and shrubbery that withstand the harshest urban smog and slush.

CHICAGO'S FUTURE IS ITS CHILDREN— all of them, of every background. Increasingly, the city is international in complexion, home to growing numbers of not only European immigrants, but also people from around the world. Cook County's Asian-American population has jumped 69 percent in the last 10 years, while the Hispanic-American population has increased 39 percent.

MIKE TAPPIN

CHUCK BERMAN

IN SUMMER, THE LAKEFRONT, THE ART fairs, and the many parks of Chicago are favored by the elderly. But let us be truthful now. When the weather hits, oh, 10 below zero, a lot of older Chicagoans who can afford to do so fly like snowbirds to Florida and Arizona.

IT'S NOT EXACTLY KASPAROV VS.
Karpov, but, weather permitting,
chess skirmishes are waged every
day around the Chess Pavilion near
North Avenue on the lakefront. Some
contestants play almost every weekend. Strollers, bikers, and joggers
stop to watch. The only request?
No unsolicited advice, please.

THE WOODLAWN TAP ON THE SOUTH Side is tweedy Hyde Park's favorite neighborhood tavern. Or is it a coffee shop? At Jimmy's—as the place is better known—it is sometimes hard to tell.

OVER THE PAST FEW YEARS AS THE CITY
has become evermore a tourist
town, cruise boats have proliferated
on the Chicago River and Lake
Michigan. The Wendella, which
docks on the Chicago River at
Michigan Avenue, remains the most
popular cruise boat, with river and
lake excursions running a half hour
to two hours. Since 1962, the
Borgstrom family's Wendella line
has also offered commuter rides
between Michigan Avenue and the
Chicago & Northwestern Station
west of the Loop.

THIS IS WHAT THOSE PEOPLE IN
motorboats do: ride up the Chicago
River from the lake, putter to a stop
just short of one of the big downtown bridges, pop the top on a cold
beer or soda, and wave heartily in
the direction of all those hot, sticky
office workers trudging by overhead. Nice folks.

THE PADDLEBOATS FOR RENT IN
Lincoln Park are a Chicago favorite.
Good for first dates. For marriage
proposals. For delighting the children.

THE IDEA BEHIND GRANT PARK,
shown here with Buckingham
Fountain in the background, is to
make every regular Joe feel like a
rich man for a while. One of the
most startling features of Chicago,
visitors often say, is the pastoral
beauty of the park right outside
the noisy business district.

THE LINCOLN PARK CONSERVATORY
is part of Chicago's greatest civic
pride—its carefully preserved lakefront. The conservatory consists
of three acres of greenhouses in
which plants and flowers from
around the world are carefully
tended. Seasonal flower shows,
held four times a year, draw the
biggest crowds.

THIS FLIGHT OF FANCY IS THE UNITED
Airlines terminal (1987) at O'Hare
International Airport. Its daring
designer, architect Helmut Jahn,
explained his vision this way:
"Normally people get pushed
through some basement-like
concourse—totally dehumanized.
We have tried to make a building
that treats people in a way that is
exciting and pleasing." It is exciting.
And many would say pleasing.
But not everybody. Then again,
buildings that take chances seldom
please everybody. Or, as Michael
Hayden, who designed a light
sculpture for the terminal, said,
"Something that no one finds
complaint with means you are
serving pabulum."

Gates B9-B22 →

Gates B9-B22

▲ MARK SEGAL / PANORAMIC IMAGES, CHICAGO

CHICAGO HAS TWO MAJOR AIRPORTS: Midway on the Southwest Side and O'Hare International on the city's northwest edge. O'Hare, the busiest airport in the world, has handled the arrivals and departures of more than 69 million passengers per year in recent years, and the tally continues to grow. That "ORD" on every O'Hare baggage claim ticket, by the way, is short for Orchard Place, which was the airport's first name.

CHICAGO REMAINS THE RAILROADING
hub of the Midwest. The first
Chicago train was the Pioneer, which
made its maiden run on November
20, 1848, going 10 miles between
the Chicago River and the Des
Plaines River.

THE RAILROADS RUN OUT OF **C**HICAGO like spokes on a wheel and stretch across America. Here, a trainman stands on the tracks near Goodenow, immediately south of the Chicago metropolitan area.

THE **M**ILWAUKEE **R**OAD SWITCHING yards in northwest suburban Bensenville, where this trainman works, are some of the largest in the country.

FARMLAND SURROUNDS THE **C**HICAGO area, much of it devoted to corn and soybean crops. Pumpkin fields, however, are not uncommon. These farmers were selling pumpkins from a corner stand at Clark and Halsted streets a few days before Halloween.

ONE OF THE MOST POPULAR PAINTINGS in the Art Institute of Chicago is Edward Hopper's nighttime scene in a diner, *Nighthawks.* That's more than appropriate in a no-nonsense town like Chicago, where cheeseburgers and laminated menus are big. Some places, like Ed Debevic's on Wells (BOTTOM OPPOSITE), are friendly retro-Fifties joints, opened long after Elvis sang his last song. Others, like the Hard Rock Cafe (BOTTOM), offer ear-splitting music with the burgers. The Rock'n'Roll McDonald's across the street from the Hard Rock Cafe is a neon palace packed with 1950s memorabilia. At The Choo Choo Restaurant in Des Plaines (TOP), the food is shipped by rail to your plate. One of the real McCoys in Chicago diners, sitting on the same corner for decades, is White Palace Grills, 1159 S. Canal Street (TOP OPPOSITE).

▼ KAREN I. HIRSCH

ALTHOUGH **C**HICAGO WAS A CENTER of early filmmaking, with silent movie stars such as Charlie Chaplin, Douglas Fairbanks, and Gloria Swanson getting their start here, it was not until the middle 1970s that the movie industry really discovered the town. Now films are big time, and the sight of studio trailers along some back street is far from rare. *The Untouchables* (TOP, OPPOSITE TOP) was filmed in Chicago in 1986 using authentic locations well known to Elliot Ness and Al Capone. *The Babe* (BOTTOM, OPPOSITE BOTTOM), which starred John Goodman as the baseball legend, was filmed here in 1991.

GENE SISKEL IS THE TALL ONE. ROGER Ebert is the stout one. Together they are America's best known film critics, with a syndicated weekly television show, "Siskel & Ebert," that can be seen across 92 percent of the country. Siskel is a movie columnist for the *Chicago Tribune.* Ebert is film critic for the *Chicago Sun-Times.*

POOL HALLS ARE MAKING A COME-
back in Chicago, most of them
emphasizing a family atmosphere
and an upscale, wholesome
camaraderie. One has a dress code.
Another promotes coed leagues.
A third has a cappuccino machine.
Minnesota Fats wouldn't know
what to make of it.

CHRIS'S BILLIARDS, AT 4637
N. Milwaukee, was one of four
Chicago pool halls chosen for
filming *The Color of Money,*
starring Paul Newman and Tom
Cruise. It was picked because its
relaxed appearance captures the
classic flavor of a pool hall.

At the Woodlawn Boxing Club, the dream is still of knockouts, championship belts, and a ticket out of hard times. Chicago's two all-time greatest fighters were Barney Ross (1909–1967), who was the first boxer ever to hold both the lightweight and welterweight crowns, and Tony Zale, the so-called "Man of Steel." Zale fought 89 professional bouts, won 72, and was twice crowned middleweight champion.

MIKE TAPPIN

CHARLES ESHELMAN

MAXWELL STREET IS A LIVELY, GIANT flea market. You can buy almost anything on Maxwell, it is said. Hubcaps, shoes, oranges, chairs, cassette tapes, trousers, watches— you name it. Just don't expect a money-back guarantee. Maxwell Street is located directly south of the University of Illinois at Chicago, and, sadly, there has been serious talk in recent years of closing the market down to make way for an expanded campus. The best time to visit is early on a summer Sunday morning when the place comes alive with the sounds of raw street blues.

A CITY OF NEIGHBORHOODS MUST,
almost by definition, have a good
share of old-fashioned neighborhood barbershops—the kind with
the classic barber pole out front.
And Chicago certainly does.

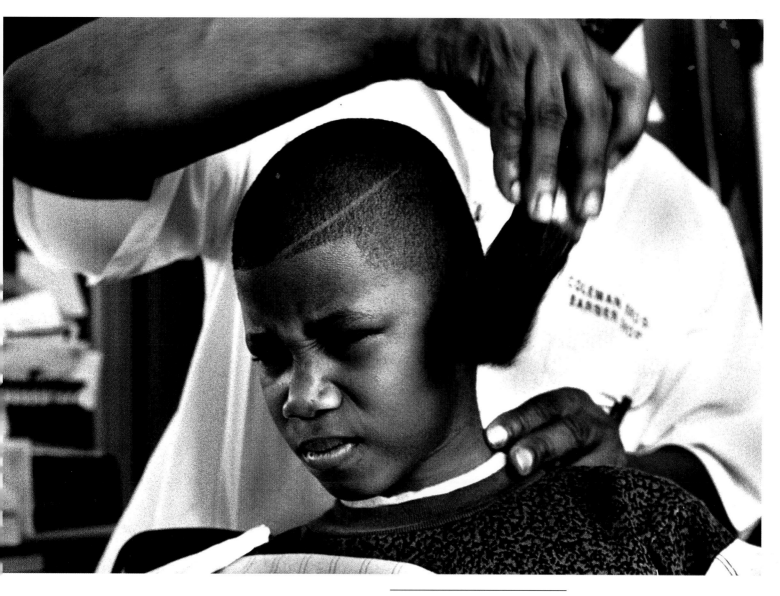

A GOOD HAIRCUT AT COLEMAN
Brothers Barber Shop, 6802 S.
Stony Island Avenue, ends with a
quick brushing up.

ALTHOUGH THE AVERAGE SUMMER temperature in Chicago is quite moderate, there are days when it's blistering hot and the mercury shoots into the three-digit range. In 1934, on the hottest day on record in Chicago, the temperature hit 105 degrees.

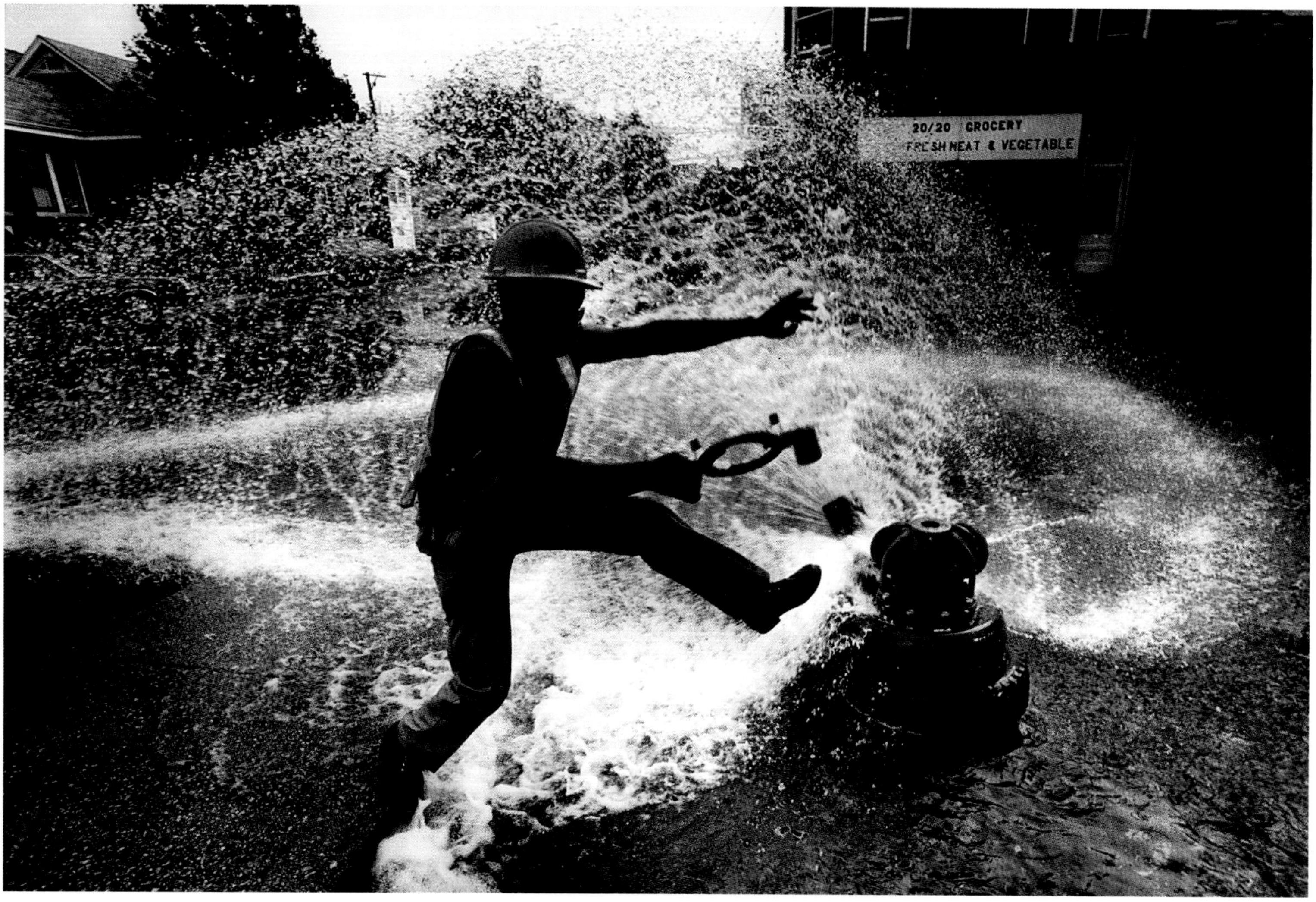
20/20 GROCERY
FRESH MEAT & VEGETABLE

THE AVERAGE BICYCLE RIDER IN
Chicago is daringly acrobatic only
in his dreams. The suburban forest
preserves and the lakefront area are
crisscrossed by many excellent bike
paths. The most ambitious cyclists
have been known to peddle the
entire length of a series of linked
trails that run from Chicago to
Milwaukee, Wisconsin.

ONE OF THE MORE POSITIVE TRENDS in urban education, exemplified at this North Side public school, has been the greater emphasis placed on celebrating children's ethnic heritage in song, story, food, and costume.

OPTIMISM IS A WAY OF LIFE AT THE El Hogar Del Nino Day Care Center, 2325 S. California Avenue, which offers after-school programs and other social services.

BECAUSE CHICAGO IS INCREASINGLY an international city, especially in its financial markets, a number of foreign schools have been established for the children of expatriates. The Futabakai Japanese School in suburban Niles is a private school subsidized by the government of Japan and by Japanese-related industries in the Chicago area.

AS PRINCIPAL OF A PUBLIC ELEMENTARY school on Chicago's South Side, Sylvia Peters has her work cut out for her. As in many cities across the nation, Chicago's public schools are struggling—nobody denies this. And nobody disagrees that improving the schools must be a crucial goal. With more than 500 elementary schools and 64 high schools, Chicago has the nation's third-largest public school system.

THE LINCOLN PARK ZOO, OWNED BY the Chicago Park District, draws 4 million visitors annually—more than any other zoo in the United States. It boasts 1,900 animals on 35 acres of land and features America's largest polar bear pool, with 266,000 gallons of water.

THE **J**OHN **G**. **S**HEDD **A**QUARIUM (OPPOSITE), which opened on May 30, 1930, has 6,000 specimens of fish, invertebrates, reptiles, amphibians, and mammals exhibited in 203 tanks.

THE **$45**-MILLION **O**CEANARIUM (ABOVE), a 170,000-square-foot addition to the Shedd Aquarium, holds 3 million gallons of saltwater. The Oceanarium is one of the most popular tourist attractions in the city.

CURIOUS TO KNOW WHAT THE HEAVENS looked liked in the year 30 AD? Try the Adler Planetarium, located on Northerly Island on the lakefront. The popular Sky Show, an audio-visual production that gives you a sense of flying through space, changes with the seasons. And once you've seen the Sky Show, check out the museum, especially the authentic moon rock. It looks exactly like an Earth rock.

THE FIELD MUSEUM OF NATURAL History is best known for its dinosaur skeletons and its impressive collection of Egyptian mummies, mummy masks, and other ancient relics. It is regarded as one of the best museums in the world for its research in the natural sciences.

LOCATED AT 800 S. HALSTED STREET, Hull House opened as a settlement house in 1889 to assist impoverished immigrant groups. In her classic autobiography, *Twenty Years at Hull House,* social worker Jane Addams described her mission as an attempt to "relieve" one level of society of its "over-accumulation" and another level of society of its "destitution." The building is now a museum.

THE **D**U**S**ABLE **M**USEUM OF **A**FRICAN-American History, at 740 E. 56TH Place, has a permanent exhibit, "Up From Slavery," which describes the slave experience and includes written accounts and artifacts. The museum has done much to preserve the story of African-Americans in Chicago and promote awareness of those who advanced black pride and the causes of freedom and civil rights.

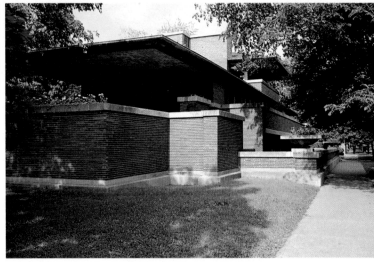

CHURCHILL & KLEHR

IN A TOWN OF ARCHITECTURAL GENIUSES, Frank Lloyd Wright (1867-1959) towers above the rest. His low-slung Prairie School of architecture was so far ahead of its time that Wright buildings erected some 70 years ago look modern still.

On the downside, it must be said, even Wright's best buildings have been faulted for cramped interiors and uncomfortable furniture, much of which he designed himself.

Wright's Unity Temple in Oak Park (TOP), completed in 1909, was constructed of poured concrete, in part to save the church money.

Wright's masterfully precise Robie House (BOTTOM RIGHT) in Hyde Park was designed in 1909 and is now something of an architectural shrine. The main entrance is in back, the rooms flow serenely from one to the next, and the beautifully leaded casement windows run in banners along the walls. The house is now used as offices by the University of Chicago.

Also pictured (BOTTOM LEFT) is the architect's home in Oak Park.

▲ JIM WRIGHT

ON ARMITAGE AVENUE ON THE North Side, the buildings are close together and recall the heritage of the street's original German immigrants. Hyde Park (BOTTOM RIGHT), on the other hand, is more leafy and sedate, befitting a neighborhood that was developed as a suburb and only later annexed into the city.

THE MUSEUM OF SCIENCE AND Industry, perhaps Chicago's most beloved museum, is housed in a building left over from the World's Columbian Exposition of 1893, the city's first world's fair. More than 2 million adults and children visit the museum each year. They tinker with the computers, try out the space suit, walk through a gigantic plastic reproduction of the human heart (it beats), venture through a coal mine reproduction, explore an actual World War II German submarine, and catch a movie at the five-story Omnimax Theater.

UNIVERSITY OF CHICAGO GEOPHYSICIST Tetsuya T. Fujita is called the "tornado man" by newspaper reporters. He is regularly called upon in emergencies to explain phenomena such as "microbursts," "micro-vortices," and "suction vortices."

ON A WINDY DAY, LAKE MICHIGAN crashes with fury against the city's beach walls, almost swamping Lake Shore Drive.

IN THE MIDWEST IT IS NOT SO MUCH
any one season that people love, but
the changing of the seasons. And so
an early snowfall is embraced as
beautiful, even if it does foretell of
hard weather to come.

"If you don't like Chicago's weather, stick around," goes the old saying. But in the dead of winter, snow and ice abound, no getting around it. It clogs streets, freezes rivers, buries cars, and wins elections. It was the famous snowstorm of 1979, dropping more than 20 inches of fresh snow on an existing eight inches, that probably got Jane Byrne elected mayor. In an inspired TV commercial days before the election, Byrne stood in the snow and asked why it was taking City Hall so darn long to plow the streets.

DURING THE CHRISTMAS SEASON, the city strings white lights on all the trees lining North Michigan Avenue. The stores fill their windows with ornaments, lights, and Christmas scenes, and an enormous tree is erected next to the Picasso in Daley Plaza. Chicago's castle-like Water Tower is always decked out for the season, somewhat like grandpa stepping out for the evening.

LIKE A SCENE FROM HANS CHRISTIAN
Andersen, children play through
the day and into the night on the
Midway Plaisance in Hyde Park.
When the weather is cold, a quarter-
mile stretch of the mile-long Midway
is turned into a skating rink.

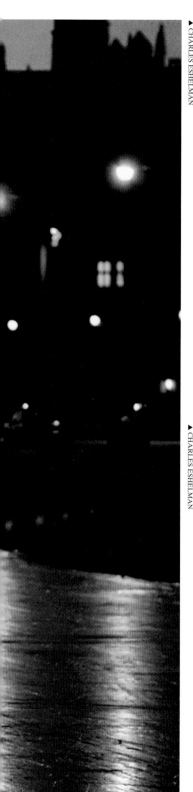

IN SOME CIRCLES IN CHICAGO, THE silvery little smelt, properly battered and fried, is considered a delicacy. The smelt season on Lake Michigan begins in late March or early April. Hordes of fishermen flock to the lakeshore with nets and warming refreshment, usually in the evening. In spring the smelt migrate into shallow water to feed and spawn.

THE CHICAGO BLACKHAWKS, LED over the years by Hall of Famers such as Bobby Hull, Stan Mikita, Pit Martin, and Denis Savard, are three-time winners of the Stanley Cup. The Blackhawks play their home games at Chicago Stadium, sharing the facility with the Chicago Bulls.

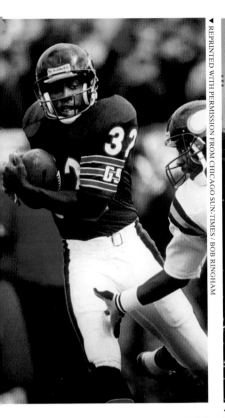

◀ REPRINTED WITH PERMISSION FROM CHICAGO SUN-TIMES / BOB RINGHAM

▲ MARK SEGAL / PANORAMIC IMAGES, CHICAGO

WHEN THE BEARS ARE PLAYING AT Soldier Field (TOP RIGHT), and the sun is up, it is always—always— a sold-out event. Football has a long tradition in Chicago. George Halas, who organized the Bears in 1920, virtually invented the National Football League. Among the greatest "Monsters of the Midway" were Walter Payton, Red Grange, Dick Butkus, Gale Sayers, Mike Ditka, and Bronko Nagurski.

BEARS FOOTBALL IS GRIND-EM-OUT, down-in-the-mud, hit-em-hard football. Number 72 in the middle (RIGHT), by the way, is defensive tackle William "The Refrigerator" Perry, locally famous for his amazing girth.

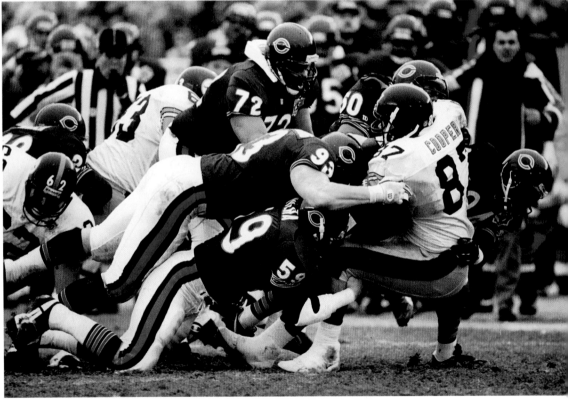

DA PICASSO LOVES DA BEARS.

SOLDIER FIELD, THE PARK DISTRICT
lakefront stadium in which the
Bears have played for about two
decades, is a combination of Greek
and Roman style architecture. A
memorable date in the stadium's
history is September 22, 1927, when
World Heavyweight Champion
Gene Tunney defeated Jack
Dempsey there.

A **BULLS TICKET IS THE HOTTEST IN** town. They play at the West Side Chicago Stadium on a removable court installed over the hockey rink used by the Chicago Blackhawks. For years the Bulls were terrible, and the Stadium was half empty at most games. Now, in the "Age of Air Jordan," you have to beg your boss for the corporate ducats. Beginning with the 1994 season, the Bulls will play in a new West Side stadium.

◀ CHARLES ESHELMAN

◀ KEVIN O. MOONEY

WHADDAYA THINK? DOES THIS LOOK like one happy town or what? Chicago is not used to excellence in professional sports. It's just been so long. So when the Chicago Bulls won their first NBA championship in 1991, the town was delighted. This souvenir edition of the *Chicago Sun-Times* (**RIGHT**) sold out in no time at all. Kids all over town still have that front page taped to their bedroom wall.

▲ ART SHAY

"SIR MICHAEL." "MICHAEL, THE Miracle." "Air Jordan." On the basketball court, he has no peers. He is, simply, the best. Michael Jordan is also a classy guy and an excellent role model for children. As the advertisement says, "Be like Mike." You could do worse.

He was the Bulls' first-round draft pick in 1984, rookie of the year for the 1984–85 season, and most valuable player in the NBA for three seasons . . . and counting. Jordan is swamped by reporters and fans wherever he goes.

NIGHT BASEBALL CAME TO WRIGLEY
Field—the last hold-out in
professional baseball—on August
8, 1988, after a long struggle with
local residents. They feared the
traffic, the noise, and the loss of a
fine tradition—baseball under the
sun. On the flip side, a lot of
baseball fans theorized that the
Cubs were so awful each year
because their strength was being
sapped by all that sun. As it
happens, night baseball has worked
out well, but the Cubs still can't
seem to win.

IT'S THE CHEAPEST TICKET IN TOWN—
a rooftop seat across the street from
the ballpark (BOTTOM LEFT). And
the view is not bad. Ivy-covered
Wrigley Field, built in 1914, is as
pretty as a picnic grove. The Cubs
have played at Wrigley since 1916.

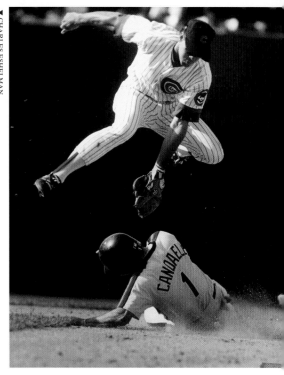

CHARLES ESHELMAN

CHUCK BERMAN

WRIGLEY FIELD HAS THE ONLY manually operated scoreboard (**MIDDLE RIGHT**) in professional baseball. A couple of guys sit up inside the board during the game and change every name and number by hand.

The voice of the Chicago Cubs is Harry Caray (**BOTTOM LEFT**), the veteran baseball play-by-play man on WGN television and radio. When a Cub hits a home run, Harry's signature exclamation is, "Holy Cow!"

THE OLD COMISKEY PARK, WHICH IS the smaller stadium on the left side of the street (**TOP RIGHT**), was beloved by generations of White Sox fans. But the truth? It was an old barn with bad sight lines. Really. Just don't say it too loudly. On the other hand, the new Comiskey Park (**LEFT, BOTTOM RIGHT**), which opened in 1991, is a gem. In the new park, as in the old, the scoreboard explodes with fireworks whenever a Sox player hits a home run.

REPRINTED WITH PERMISSION FROM CHICAGO SUN-TIMES / TOM CRUZE

THE CRITICS SAID BO JACKSON (RIGHT) was all washed up. Nobody with an artificial hip could possibly play baseball again. But Jackson, who sustained his injury playing professional football, started in the outfield with the White Sox when the 1993 season began. Better yet, he hit and fielded well.

A favorite of White Sox fans is veteran catcher Carlton Fisk (TOP), the team's all-time home run leader, with 213 at the end of the 1992 season.

White Sox outfielder Dan Pasqua (BOTTOM), slid safely into home this time. Now if only the Sox could pick up another American League Pennant. The Sox have won the pennant four times—the last time back in 1959—and the World Series twice, in 1906 and 1917.

▼ KAREN I. HIRSCH

IF BASEBALL IS AMERICA'S GAME, then softball is Chicago's game. As much as Chicagoans like to follow the Cubs and White Sox, the real summer ritual is playing softball on a corner lot. And for the most part, Chicagoans play barehanded with a 16-inch-circumference ball. In the suburbs, a 12-inch ball with a glove is more the rule. Softball evolved in the 1880s in Chicago from an indoor version of hardball. You pitch the ball with a high arc and hope it comes down almost verticle over the plate.

▲ CHUCK BERMAN

WHEN THE BLUE DEMONS PLAY basketball at DePaul University, it's an event. Thousands crowd into the stadium. When the DePaul women's softball team plays a game (TOP LEFT), the fans who show up at the little field below the El tracks are family and friends. Softball is a game, not an event.

CHICAGO'S ANNUAL FALL MARATHON winds through the streets of the city, messing up automobile traffic all morning. Covered live on both radio and television, the race attracts top runners from around the world, and thousands of residents turn out to cheer.

IN 1991, THE CHICAGO AREA BECAME home to its first minor league baseball team, the Kane County Cougars. The Cougars' presence on the edge of the metropolitan region symbolized a coming of age for the far western suburbs, where until recently, the population would have been considered too small to support a professional sports team.

RIVERBOAT CASINOS ONLY RECENTLY arrived in the Chicago region, beginning with a couple of boats in both Joliet and Aurora. But more are on the way. Land-based gambling casinos, adamantly opposed by Gov. Jim Edgar, remain illegal in Illinois. On the heels of the casinos has come another form of Las Vegas entertainment—concerts by big-name stars such as Frank Sinatra and Dolly Parton. Concert halls in the suburbs have always booked a few big acts, but never so many as now.

IN THE SUBURBS, ONE OF THE MOST striking examples of how to capitalize on a great natural resource is the picture-perfect Naperville Riverwalk. With a bike path, a pretty wooden bridge, a gazebo, and several thoughtfully placed scenic overlooks, it has added new luster to Naperville's original downtown district.

THIS LITTLE WATERWAY, NOW A scenic backdrop for bicycle riders in downstate Morris, is part of the historic 96-mile, man-made canal that put Chicago on the map. The digging of the Illinois and Michigan Canal, running from Chicago to LaSalle-Peru, began in the 1830s, creating a water link between Lake Michigan and the Mississippi River via the Illinois River. Much of the original canal in Chicago is now covered over by the Stevenson Expressway.

WHEN HOFMANN TOWER (OPPOSITE) was built on the south bank of the Des Plaines River in suburban Lyons in 1908, it was the tallest building west of Chicago. At that time, Lyons was a town of picnic groves. Chicagoans came out by train on weekends and hiked to the top of the tower for a spectacular view of the surrounding area. The Tower's original owner, George Hofmann, was president of Hofmann Brothers Brewery in Chicago. In 1985, the State of Illinois took ownership of the building and now is in the process of restoring it.

GRAUE MILL NEAR SUBURBAN Hinsdale was a center of lumber milling in the 1850s. It is best remembered today as a major and well-authenticated stop on the old Underground Railroad. Runaway Southern slaves, headed for Chicago where they could stow away on a steamship to Canada, were sheltered for a night or a day or a week, as need be, at the old mill.

THE GROSS POINT LIGHT STATION
in Evanston was built in the 19TH
century when commercial shipping
on Lake Michigan was a major
industry in Chicago. The 113-foot
lighthouse sits a mile or so down
the lakeshore from the Baha'i
temple (**OPPOSITE**).

THIS IS WHAT PEOPLE SAY WHEN THEY enter the lacy white Baha'i House of Worship: "What a great place to get married." The 191-foot, nine-sided temple in north suburban Wilmette was designed by architect Louis Bourgeois and completed in 1953. The Baha'i religion stresses the importance of a simple life dedicated to serving others, and it opens its beautiful houses of worship to people of all faiths.

page 234

AT THE MEDINAH COUNTRY CLUB, one of the biggest country clubs in the world, the emphasis is on golf. In the 1920s the Shriners built the club 25 miles west of the city as a rural retreat for themselves and their families. Not only did they create three separate 18-hole golf courses on the grounds, but at one time Medinah also had a clubhouse with a grand ballroom and a bowling alley, gun and equestrian clubs, a marina on a private lake, and facilities for cross-country skiing, ski jumping, and tobogganing. Most of those facilities today are gone, but the golf lives on. Medinah has been the site of the U.S. Open three times.

page 235

ST. PETER'S UNITED CHURCH OF Christ is the oldest and one of the most distinguished churches in suburban Skokie. The congregation itself celebrated its 125TH anniversary in 1992.

page 236

THE SCULPTURED WHITE WALLS OF the North Shore Unitarian Church in Deerfield are punctuated by 23 multicolored glass panels. The artist was Bob White, who specializes in the medium of fused glass which resembles stained glass, but entails the use of intense heat to make color flow into color.

ZENITH ELECTRONICS CORP. (ABOVE), with international headquarters in suburban Glenview, has been on the forefront of developing high definition television (HDTV), a technology that makes possible super sharp pictures and digital sound reproduction in television. HDTV will probably be available in the U.S. market by the mid-1990s.

THE FERMI NATIONAL ACCELERATOR Laboratory (TOP LEFT) is the site of the highest energy accelerator in the world. Fermilab, as it is usually called, is a direct outgrowth of the research done in Chicago during World War II to build the first atomic bomb. Working in a secret lab beneath an athletic stadium at the University of Chicago, a team headed by Italian-born physicist Enrico Fermi created the first controlled nuclear chain reaction in 1942. Fermi had immigrated with his family to the United States directly from Stockholm after accepting the Nobel Prize for Physics in 1938.

ONE OF THE TALLEST BUILDINGS in the suburbs is the 31-story Oak Brook Terrace Tower (TOP RIGHT), designed by Helmut Jahn.

RAY KROC BOUGHT THE NOTION OF producing assembly-line hamburgers from two brothers named McDonald in California. His first McDonald's restaurant—now a museum— opened on April 15, 1955, in north-west suburban Des Plaines. Kroc parlayed his hamburger stands into a national franchise that became the standard for—and envy of— the fast-food industry.

▼ JON CUNNINGHAM

▲ CHUCK BERMAN

IN THE PARKING LOT OF THE HOTEL Sofitel, a French hotel in suburban Rosemont, stands an iron structure, the Eiffel Tower (TOP LEFT). In Paris, folks say, there is another one.

MOST OF BERWYN DOESN'T LIKE IT, but the guy who owns the shopping center does, so it stays. In 1990, voters of the Chicago township, in an advisory referendum, voted 69 to 31 percent against *Spindle* (TOP RIGHT), a pileup of eight cars on a stainless-steel spike. But the owner of the Cermak Plaza, where the sculpture sits, said he would not budge. Actually, David Bermant said he was encouraged to see that 31 percent of the voters shared his taste in art. "I think," he told Zay Smith of the *Sun-Times,* "Berwyn is actually telling me it has great potential as a future home for modern art."

GURNEE MILLS, WHICH OPENED IN 1991 on the northern edge of the Chicago metropolitan area, is one of the largest discount shopping malls around. People drive in from all over the Midwest, check into a local hotel for the weekend, and shop till they drop.

IN METROPOLITAN CHICAGO, WHERE the county forest preserves are considered untouchable and where farmlands are giving way to housing developments, people are finding new ways to use landfills. Settler's Hill (BOTTOM OPPOSITE), an 18-hole course which sits in part on a landfill, was a big hit soon after opening in 1988. Golfers play about 32,000 rounds per year on the fairways in Geneva.

TWO HUNDRED YEARS AGO, LIGHTNING regularly set fire to the prairies, enriching the soil and stimulating new growth. Now the job of setting fires belongs to prairie preservationists, who start controlled burns in spring to destroy settler-introduced European grasses. The deep-rooted native plants grow right back. This fire was in the Nelson Lake Marsh State Nature Preserve in Kane County.

THREE OF THESE MEN ARE FIXING THINGS up. The fourth is probably wrecking something. The gardener in Chicago's Sheffield neighborhood (TOP), the Skokie homeowner looking to get a couple of windows repaired (BOTTOM), and the fence builder in Wilmette (BOTTOM OPPOSITE) are probably trying to make the old home place a little nicer.

The man from Underwriters Laboratories (TOP OPPOSITE), however, often tears things apart just to see how much abuse they can take. Underwriters Laboratories is the nation's largest, best-known, and most influential testing ground for consumer products. Underwriters works with 40,000 manufacturers each year, and the "UL approved" seal is marked on 6 billion products worldwide.

AT THE OAKLEY MILLWORKS IN Frankfort, a family-run business founded in 1956, shop foreman David Mead sands a pair of carefully tooled doors. Oakley Millworks supplies residential home contractors in the Chicago area with windows, doors, trim, and hardware.

CURTISS HALL IN THE FINE ARTS Building (TOP OPPOSITE), at 410 S. Michigan Avenue, is used for chamber music recitals, rehearsals, and auditions. The Fine Arts Building just might be the Loop's most curious office building, rented out by music studios, drama schools, architects, and the like. Among its former tenants were sculptor Lorado Taft, cartoonist John T. McCutcheon, architect Frank Lloyd Wright, and writer L. Frank Baum, best known for *The Wonderful Wizard of Oz*.

ARTIST AND POET TONY FITZPATRICK is co-owner of the World Tattoo Gallery (BOTTOM OPPOSITE), 1255 S. Wabash Avenue, where he recently organized a show devoted to Elvis art.

▶ ANDY GOODWIN

IN SUBURBAN CHICAGO, THE MID-
west's rural roots are sometimes
right around the corner—maybe
just behind an old barn, perhaps
recalled in an old-fashioned bake
sale in Deerfield, or at a vintage
farm equipment show in Harvard.
And sometimes farm life just rolls
right into town, like the tractor
crossing a street in Barrington.

▲ ROBERT C.V. LIEBERMAN

KLINE CREEK FARM (TOP) IS A 200-acre "living history" farm located about 40 miles due west of Chicago's Loop. Operated by the DuPage County Forest Preserve District, it is both a tourist attraction and a working farm, 19TH-century style. In the fall, city folk like to come out, pick corn by hand, and toss it into a wagon pulled by husky Belgian draft horses. They consider this rustic fun, not work—a bit like Tom Sawyer's pals whitewashing Aunt Polly's fence.

▲ JON CUNNINGHAM

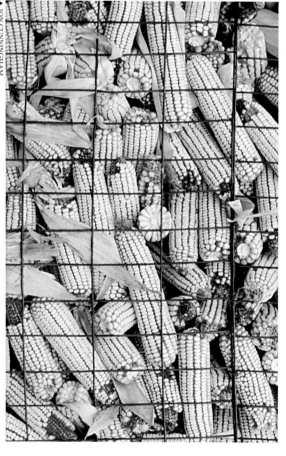

HEAD ON OUT TO NORTH AND NORTH-western suburbs, such as Barrington, Inverness, and Mundelein, and what you will find are the most graceful of thorough-bred horses, quite a few of them racers. Many of the farms have extensive stables and private training tracks.

ARLINGTON **I**NTERNATIONAL **R**ACE-course may well be the Taj Mahal of race tracks. After a devastating fire, it was rebuilt in 1989 at a cost of $200 million and is elegant at every turn. Arlington is flush with fountains and marble foyers, and, best of all, the view from every seat is unobstructed.

CRUISE SHIPS ON LAKE MICHIGAN,
such as the *Chicago Princess*, have
gained a large following in recent
years. Some ships give historic
tours; others offer twilight dinners
or play host to company parties.

WHO'S THE BEST SAILOR ON THE Great Lakes? The winner of the big Mac, that's who. The annual Chicago-to-Mackinac Island Yacht Race, a 333-mile run, is the oldest regularly scheduled, long-distance yacht race in the world. It began with five ships in 1898. Today, more than 300 boats compete. The most successful skipper in Chicago-Mac history was former Mayor William Hale Thompson, who piloted his boat, *Valmore*, to three straight victories from 1908 to 1910.

WHEN THE WEATHER IS WARM, Chicagoans take to the lake like children racing for the pool. They sail, windsurf, sunbathe, swim, fish, and anything else they can think of that's wet and fun. The lake is 307 miles long, 118 miles wide, and an average of 279 feet deep, so there's room for everybody.

A SURE SIGN OF WARM WEATHER TO come is Chicago Park District workers dropping buoys along the lakefront to mark swimming areas.

OAK STREET BEACH, LYING AT THE head of the North Michigan Avenue shopping strip, is generally agreed to be Chicago's "Beautiful People" beach. Office workers—both men and women—frequently stroll down on their lunch hour to catch a few rays of sun and ogle the beauties and hunks.

WARM WEATHER AT NORTH AVENUE Beach brings a touch of California to Chicago, with volleyball nets all over the place and lots of tanned and athletic bodies going for the spike.

THE MOST SCENIC EXCURSION IN Chicago has got to be a bike ride along the city's beautifully main-tained lakefront path, stretching from Hollywood Avenue on the far North Side to Hyde Park on the South Side.

page 258

LOVERS AND GENTLE PEOPLE WANDER down to Lake Michigan's endless shoreline at dawn and sunset. It has a tide, like the ocean, and a capricious mood.

IF THE KIDS HAD GOOD ENOUGH
throwing arms, those chunks of
rock and ice would land in the state
of Michigan, 118 miles away on
the other side of the lake.

LAKE MICHIGAN IS 10,300 YEARS OLD.
It was heaving and rocking and
spraying for ages before the first
people stopped to marvel. But you
just know that the very first ones—
the Native Americans who
discovered it—did just that.

THERE ARE PEOPLE WHO HAVE A penchant for cities—more than that . . . a gift of sensing them, of feeling their rhythm. And Chicago was a huge polyglot orchestra . . . leaderless, terrifyingly discordant, yet with an occasional strain, exquisite and poignant, to be heard throughout the clamor and din.
—From *Fanny Herself* (1917) by Edna Ferber

pages 264–265

WHEN 2.1 MILLION PEOPLE FLOCKED to the lakefront to watch the last Air and Water Show, a two-day affair sponsored each July by the Chicago Park District, city officials were a bit disappointed. In a really good year, attendance tops 2.5 million—plus another 2,000 or so spectators on boats. But, who's counting?

THE LEADERSHIP THAT MADE **C**HICAGO great was not the dictate of any individual leader at any time in our history. It was not the operations of a cabal in a smoke-filled room.

The leadership that made Chicago great, from its earliest origins, was the partnership of every sector of our city's society, working together. That partnership is the leadership that our times require.

> —From Mayor Harold
> Washington's second
> inaugural address,
> May 4, 1987

PHOTO: CHURCHILL & KLEHR

CHICAGO
SECOND TO NONE

A LOOK AT THE

CORPORATIONS,

BUSINESSES,

PROFESSIONAL GROUPS, AND

COMMUNITY SERVICE ORGANIZATIONS

THAT HAVE MADE

THIS BOOK POSSIBLE.

~

OUT ON THE MIDWESTERN PRAIRIE, a bolt of lightning now and again would spark a roaring fire. It was a natural phenomenon both deadly and life-giving, leaving the land scorched and barren, but replenishing the tired soil. So it was with the Great Chicago Fire of 1871, which proved to be the city's greatest disaster and greatest opportunity. The flames leveled four square miles, killed at least 250 people, and left 100,000 more homeless. But out of the ruins rose a sturdy, carefully planned, and thoroughly modern American city.

CHICAGO:

1837

RUSH-PRESBYTERIAN-
ST. LUKE'S MEDICAL
CENTER

1847

CHICAGO TITLE AND
TRUST COMPANY

1848

CHICAGO BOARD
OF TRADE

1852

MERCY HOSPITAL AND
MEDICAL CENTER

1857

THE CHICAGO DOCK &
CANAL TRUST

1872

MONTGOMERY WARD
AND CO., INC.

1881

ILLINOIS BELL

1881

MICHAEL REESE HOSPITAL
AND MEDICAL CENTER

1882

MIDWEST STOCK EXCHANGE,
INCORPORATED

1887

SEARS, ROEBUCK
AND CO.

1889

THE NORTHERN
TRUST COMPANY

1890

SEARLE

RUSH-PRESBYTERIAN-ST. LUKE'S MEDICAL CENTER

WITH A CHICAGO HISTORY SPANNING MORE THAN 150 YEARS, RUSH-PRESBYTERIAN-ST. LUKE'S MEDICAL CENTER IS WIDELY ACKNOWLEDGED AS ONE OF THE NATION'S LEADING ACADEMIC HEALTH CENTERS. RUSH MEDICAL COLLEGE, THE EARLIEST COMPONENT OF

Rush-Presbyterian-St. Luke's Medical Center employs almost 9,000 people and has a medical staff of more than 1,300 at its 22-building campus on Chicago's Near West Side (right).

The Medical Center is committed to using the most up-to-date equipment and techniques in diagnosis and care (below right).

Leo M. Henikoff, M.D., president and CEO.

today's medical center, was chartered by the State of Illinois in 1837, just two days before the City of Chicago was incorporated. Its founder, Dr. Daniel Brainard, named the school in honor of Dr. Benjamin Rush, the only physician with medical school training to sign the Declaration of Independence. Rush Medical College was the first institution of higher learning chartered in Illinois, and one of the first medical schools opened west of the Alleghenies.

The early Rush faculty, well known across the American frontier for its expertise, engaged in patient care, research, and teaching, and was associated with a number of scientific developments and new clinical procedures. As the city grew, so did Rush's involvement with other developing institutions such as St. Luke's Hospital (established in 1864) and Presbyterian Hospital (founded in 1883), the two of which later merged in 1956.

In the early 1940s, Rush discontinued undergraduate education, but its library was maintained and its faculty continued to teach at the University of Illinois school of medicine. The college reactivated its charter in 1969 and joined forces with Presbyterian-St. Luke's Hospital. Rush University, which now includes colleges of medicine, nursing, health sciences, and research training, was established in 1972 and has grown to an enrollment of 1,300 students.

Today, Rush-Presbyterian-St. Luke's Medical Center includes the largest private hospital in Illinois, as well as the Johnston R. Bowman Health Center for the Elderly, established in 1976 as a national prototype for geriatric care. The Medical Center employs almost 9,000 people and has a medical staff of more than 1,300 at its 22-building campus on Chicago's Near West Side. In 1992, the Medical Center logged more

than 29,000 admissions, nearly 20,000 surgical procedures, more than 37,000 emergency room visits, and more than 185,000 outpatient visits. Rush also maintains an extensive organ transplant program, a highly productive in vitro fertilization program, one of the nation's largest Alzheimer's disease programs, and a poison control center serving northern Illinois.

In addition to its resources at the main campus, the Rush regional system includes four affiliated hospitals as core components: Copley Memorial Hospital in Aurora, Holy Family Hospital in Des Plaines, Illinois Masonic Medical Center on the North Side, and Rush North Shore Medical Center in Skokie. Rush plans to add three more hospitals to its system by the year 2000, enabling it to serve 11 to 12 percent of the metropolitan population base.

THE RUSH INSTITUTES
One of the cornerstones of Rush's future is the Rush Institutes. The Institutes bring together in a central location the key clinical resources needed for diagnosis and care, thereby eliminating the need to move patients from area to area for different services. Building in areas where Rush is already a leader in patient care and research, they

include the Rush Heart Institute, the Rush Cancer Institute, the Rush Institute on Aging, the Rush Institute for Mental Well-Being, the Rush Neuroscience Institute, and the Rush Arthritis and Orthopedic Institute.

Five of the six institutes are housed in a new 11-story, 229,000-square-foot addition to the Medical Center's professional building. The Bowman Center serves the Rush Institute on Aging.

A FOCUS ON RESEARCH
The Medical Center is also one of the largest research facilities in the area. In fiscal 1992, Rush received more than $26 million in research grants—an 18.1 percent increase over the previous year. An impressive 1,488 research projects were under way in 1992 in the areas of

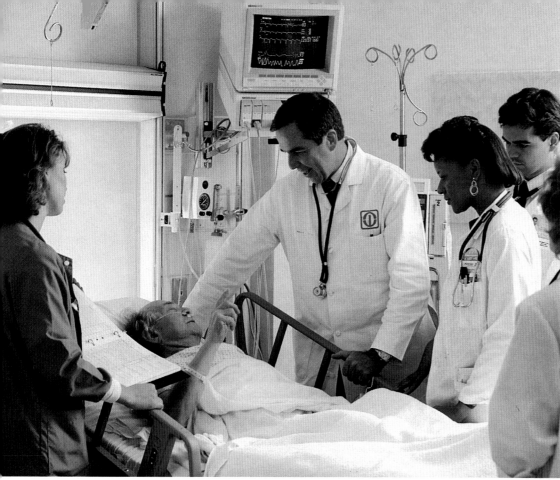

ancer (226 studies), neurological ciences (213 studies), cardiovascur disease (207 studies), and immuology (125 studies), among others. n addition, researchers from differnt departments collaborated on 175 ultidisciplinary projects.

VARIETY OF HEALTH LANS

he Medical Center's RUSH Health lans[SM] is a family of health benefit rograms designed to meet a variety f patient and employer needs. Comined, the RUSH Anchor HMO, USH Access HMO, and RUSH ontract Care PPO programs serve ore than 1,200 businesses throughut the metropolitan area.

RUSH Anchor HMO is the secnd largest staff model HMO in reater Chicago, with more than 10,000 members. It operates 17 edical offices and employs more an 130 physicians.

RUSH Access HMO is a network odel HMO with nearly 40,000 embers. The organization conacts with private-practice physiians to provide care to members at eir own medical offices.

RUSH Contract Care PPO is the ledical Center's preferred provider rganization, offering coverage to ore than 80,000 people in the hicago metropolitan area.

A GOOD NEIGHBOR IN CHICAGO

Rush has been at its present location since 1875, greatly expanding its resources in the past two decades. Over the years, it has had a strong influence on the surrounding neighborhood and has been a positive force for redevelopment on the Near West Side.

Through its Community Affairs office, Rush engages in a broad range of services to the community, including free health screenings, health fairs, immunizations, and school visits by health teams. A recent initiative pioneered by Rush and involving local businesses and nearby elementary and secondary schools is the development of the Westside Science and Math Excellence Network. The program is designed to interest young people in the health professions.

Beyond its influence on the Near West Side neighborhood, Rush-Presbyterian-St. Luke's Medical Center has been a major component in Chicago's health care system for more than 150 years. Its longtime commitment to education, medical research, and quality patient care will remain an important part of its future.

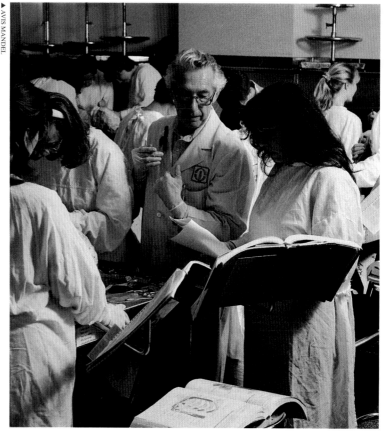

AVIS MANDEL

Basic sciences are the foundation of health education at Rush.

CHICAGO TITLE AND TRUST COMPANY

THEY SAY "YOU CAN'T GO HOME AGAIN," BUT CHICAGO TITLE AND TRUST COMPANY DID JUST THAT WHEN IT CONSTRUCTED A NEW HEADQUARTERS FACILITY ON THE VERY SITE WHERE IT WAS FOUNDED ALMOST 150 YEARS AGO. ◆ IN 1992, THE COMPANY MOVED INTO THE NEW 1 MILLION-SQUARE-

Richard P. Toft, president of Chicago Title and Trust Company (left), and Richard L. Pollay, president of Chicago Title Insurance Company, Ticor Title Insurance Company, and Security Union Title Insurance Company.

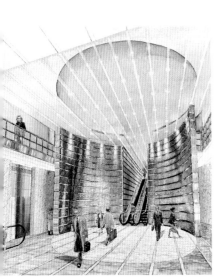

Even the walls of the 171 N. Clark Street lobby (above) reflect a world of craftsmanship. Their Quetzal green marble was mined in Guatemala, cut in Italy, and finished completely by hand.

foot Chicago Title and Trust Center, where it occupies the first 10 floors of the 50-story tower on the northeast corner of Clark and Randolph streets and the adjacent 13-story mid-rise at 171 N. Clark Street. Prior to the move, the company had been headquartered at 111 W. Washington Street since the mid-1940s.

"The creation of the Chicago Title and Trust Center, almost a century and a half after the company's founding on the same historic site, reaffirms our commitment to the city of Chicago. We're proud to return to the very site where Chicago Title and Trust Company originated," says Richard P. Toft, president of Chicago Title and Trust Company.

The company's ancestral firm, Reese and Rucker, opened in 1847 after law clerk Edwin A. Rucker developed a system of conducting a faster, more accurate title search. His innovative methods made it easier to conduct an examination of public records to uncover potential problems before a property is turned over to its new owner.

Today Chicago Title and Trust has two principal businesses: title insurance and related real estate services, and investment management and trust services. The Chicago Title and Trust Family of Title Insurers includes Chicago Title Insurance Co., the major subsidiary of Chicago Title and Trust, and two recent acquisitions, Security Union Title Insurance Company (1987) and the Ticor Title Insurance Companies (1991). This group of subsidiaries provides owners' and mortgage title insurance policies on property anywhere in the United States, Puerto Rico, the Virgin Islands, and Canada through a network of more than 4,000 branch offices and agents. The Chicago Title and Trust Family of Title Insurers is the nation's largest title insurance organi-

zation, with annual revenues in excess of $1 billion.

The Financial Services Group of Chicago Title and Trust offers a nationwide service in tax-deferred real estate exchanges and manages the investment of $4 billion in assets for corporations, not-for-profit organizations, and families.

INNOVATION AND GROWTH

The company, in its early days of growth and continued innovation, had a far-reaching impact on the real estate industry, as well as the Chicago economy.

About 40 years after Rucker's invention, a successor of Reese and Rucker, Title Guarantee and Trust, issued the first title guarantee policy in Illinois. The policy was designed to protect a new property owner against a potentially devastating loss if a title proved to be invalid. This new kind of protection for property

owners, which represented the birth of real estate title insurance in Illinois, encouraged financial institutions to make loans more widely available to property buyers and home builders.

Consequently, Chicago boomed and the company, which adopted its current name in 1891, followed suit. Chicago Title and Trust Company began expanding beyond Cook County in the 1920s, to the state capital of Springfield in 1930, and outside of Illinois in the 1950s.

TITLE INSURANCE TODAY

Throughout the years, the fundamental principles of title insurance have remained unchanged, but the process has been expanded.

In addition to conducting the initial title search, which is one of the first steps in obtaining title insurance, the title insurance companies of Chicago Title and Trust provide consumer information about all aspects of home buying and selling, including explanations of such important considerations as escrow and closing costs.

Title insurance protects a policyholder against challenges to rightful ownership of his or her property that typically arise from circumstances of past ownership. Each successive owner adds new risks of title challenges to the property. As a result, title insurance policies are designed to protect the property owner and/or lender against events that have already occurred but are unknown to the buyer at the time a title is transferred. For the cost of a one-time premium payment, a title policy also protects the holder for the entire time he or she owns the land.

"Title insurance protects the policyholder against events that may not be obvious from checking public records, such as forgery and real estate fraud," explains Richard L. Pollay, president of Chicago Title Insurance Co., Ticor Title Insurance Co., and Security Union Title Insurance Co. "If the title search misses a judgment against the seller because of confusion regarding his or her identity, that's covered too."

Chicago Title and Trust Company, which employs 1,800 people in the Chicago metropolitan area and 8,200 nationwide, is owned by Alleghany Corporation, a New York-based company engaged primarily through subsidiaries in industrial minerals, retail banking, title insurance, and investment management.

Through a family of insurers and a network of thousands of branch offices and agents, Chicago Title and Trust Company continues to provide comprehensive title insurance and related real estate services, and investment and trust services to customers throughout the United States and beyond.

Above street level, Chicago Title and Trust Center (right) soars an impressive 50 stories. Below, its use of existing moorings and tunnels neatly blends the new structure into the downtown pedway system.

CHICAGO BOARD OF TRADE

THE CHICAGO BOARD OF TRADE WAS FOUNDED IN 1848 BY 82 MERCHANTS TO STABILIZE CHICAGO'S CHAOTIC GRAIN MARKETS THROUGH A CENTRAL-IZED MARKETPLACE. FROM THAT BEGINNING NEARLY 150 YEARS AGO, THE 750-EMPLOYEE ORGANIZATION IS NOW THE OLDEST AND LARGEST FUTURES

The Chicago Board of Trade (right) has been an anchor of the city's financial district since it moved to 141 W. Jackson Boulevard in 1930.

Soybeans, corn, wheat, and other commodities are traded on the CBOT's agricultural trading floor (above).

and options exchange in the world.

Today, the Chicago Board of Trade provides a safe haven for investors seeking to minimize risk. Buyers and sellers meet on the bustling trading floors, and through an open outcry auction system "discover" a price for agricultural and financial futures and options contracts. The Board of Trade is also a laboratory for new ideas and new technologies designed to keep its members and the U.S. futures industry number one in the world.

With more than 3,600 members trading everything from soybeans to Treasury bonds, the Chicago Board of Trade reached an annual trading volume record of 150 million contracts in 1992. It is the largest trader of soybeans, and its 30-year Treasury bond futures contract is the most successful futures contract in the world.

Recently, affirmation of the Board of Trade's importance in the global commodities and financial markets came, as is often the case, in the midst of a crisis. In April 1992 during Chicago's underground flood, the Board of Trade was forced to close. As a result, grain elevators were paralyzed because prices could not be determined without the Board of Trade. Likewise, the government of Taiwan postponed a purchase of 54,000 metric tons of soybeans because the trading floor was not operating. World financial markets were similarly affected, as trading activity in New York slowed to a crawl.

LEADERSHIP THROUGH INNOVATION

Officials at the Board of Trade realize that innovation is the key to continued leadership in the futures industry. In 1992, the exchange announced the development of catastrophe insurance futures and options

designed to allow insurance companies to minimize their risk associated with major disasters caused by wind, hail, earthquakes, riots, floods, etc. This contract is the first in what will be a new line of risk-management tools targeting the insurance industry.

Another recent Board of Trade innovation is the creation of clean air futures in response to the 1990 Clean Air Act, which calls for free market incentives to help lower

pollution levels nationwide. Through clean air futures, a utility that is successful in reducing sulfur dioxide emissions before the deadline can sell its unused emissions allowances to other utility companies through the Board of Trade's markets.

While the Board of Trade has become renowned as the world's most innovative financial exchange, it remains firmly rooted in the agricultural markets that fueled its

arly growth. To complement those markets, the exchange has introduced the world's first futures contracts on diammonium phosphate and anhydrous ammonia, fertilizers so important to the agricultural community.

In addition to the many products it has created, the Chicago Board of Trade is developing some of the financial industry's most automated systems. Traders soon will move away from using pens and cards to record trades, in favor of the Board of Trade's AUDIT (Automated Data Input Terminal) electronic trading card. The device, which will be no bigger than a television remote control, will make traders and their markets more efficient and provide the Board of Trade with an instantaneous, tamper-proof audit trail of each trade.

A second electronic trading system now being used by the Board of Trade is called Project A. The system allows members and member firms to trade nonconventional products, such as scrap steel futures, during regular trading hours. Project A will serve as a cost-effective launch pad for potentially high-volume futures contracts which can eventually be moved onto the main

trading floor.

Recognizing a global need to manage financial risk around the clock, the Board of Trade and the Chicago Mercantile Exchange developed the GLOBEX® trading system in conjunction with Reuters, an international communications organization. Launched on June 25, 1992, GLOBEX is an around-the-world automated electronic trading system that allows conventional products to be traded while markets in other countries are active.

AN ARCHITECTURAL SYMBOL
Since 1930, the Board of Trade has been headquartered at 141 W. Jackson Boulevard in Chicago's financial district. Designed by Holabird and Root, the 45-story Chicago Board of Trade Building is an Art Deco beacon in a city renowned for its fine architecture. The structure is appropriately topped by a 30-foot cast aluminum statue of Ceres, the Roman goddess of grain, reflecting the organization's roots in commodities trading.

According to officials, the Chicago Board of Trade will continue its longtime mission to innovate,

unify, and lead the futures and options industry. Creating a better marketplace for its members, a stronger competitive position, and, most importantly, more efficient, effective, and liquid markets for farmers and investors the world over are the Board of Trade's primary goals for the 1990s and beyond.

World leaders such as Mikhail Gorbachev (above) have seen the CBOT's markets in action.

MERCY HOSPITAL AND MEDICAL CENTER

MERCY WAS CHICAGO'S FIRST HOSPITAL, AND IT IS STILL LEADING THE WAY IN CARING FOR THE AREA'S HEALTH NEEDS. THOSE NEEDS HAVE CHANGED DRAMATICALLY SINCE 1846, WHEN FIVE SISTERS OF MERCY TRAVELED FROM PITTSBURGH TO WHAT WAS THEN A FRONTIER

town plagued by yearly outbreaks of cholera, typhoid, and smallpox to carry on the healing ministry begun by Mother Mary Catherine McAuley. Today's health care is as much about keeping people well as it is about healing the sick. Mercy has evolved from humble beginnings to become a leading community-based health care system and a center of academic excellence.

Through cost-controlling partnerships with Chicago-area employers, MercyWorks documents ongoing health care expenses and outcomes for each employee, using the revolutionary Accutrak system.

PIONEERING SPIRIT

When the Sisters of Mercy arrived in Chicago, the city was only nine years old. In their first makeshift convent at Madison and Michigan, it was not uncommon for the sisters to awake on winter mornings under bedclothes dusted with snow. Nonetheless, they began immediately to visit the sick, and within a year they were nursing at a temporary hospital set up at the Tippecanoe Inn. This pioneering spirit led to an official charter for Mercy Hospital in 1852

and established a tradition of innovation and excellence that continues to this day.

When Dr. Nathan Davis, founder of the American Medical Association, sought in 1859 to reform the training of doctors by organizing what later became Northwestern University Medical School, Mercy affiliated immediately. Mercy's chief surgeon, Dr. Edmund Andrews, introduced antiseptic surgery techniques to Chicago in 1869. The hospital survived the Great Chicago Fire of 1871 and continued to make medical history.

President Theodore Roosevelt was Mercy's most prominent patient in 1912. Shot while campaigning in Milwaukee for the Bull Moose Party, Roosevelt took a train to Chicago to consult with Mercy's chief of surgery about the bullet lodged in his chest. (The decision was to not remove it: "It takes more than that to kill a Bull Moose," said Roosevelt.)

Mercy was the first American hospital to use the arthroscope (1924) and the first private hospital in Chicago to offer treatment with radioactive medicines. More recently, the medical center dedicated Chicago's first oncology unit and today is pioneering the use of stereotactic radiosurgery to treat previously inoperable conditions.

STILL LEADING THE WAY

After nearly a century and a half of service to Chicago, Mercy remains at the forefront of quality health care. A 477-bed teaching hospital anchors a growing network of health care facilities serving diverse communities and ethnic groups in Chicago and surrounding suburbs. More than 335 physicians representing 35 medical specialties provide compre-

hensive clinical, diagnostic, therapeutic, and rehabilitative services. Patients from throughout the Midwest—and across the country—come to Mercy for expert care in cardiology, oncology, orthopedics, diabetes, rehabilitation, and other medical specialties.

Mercy has played a leading role in medical education from the day it opened its doors. The medical center has a major teaching affiliation with the University of Illinois at Chicago Medical School and is also affiliated with the University of Chicago Medical School, Loyola University Stritch School of Medicine, Chicago Medical School, Northwestern University Medical School and Rehabilitation Institute of Chicago, and Saint Xavier College School of Nursing. Through numerous additional programs, Mercy educates allied health professionals in 32 disciplines.

With more than 2,400 employees, Mercy is a major contributor to the Chicago-area economy—and not just through its payroll. Its neighborhood facilities make a full range of preventive and therapeutic services convenient and affordable for patients and employers. Many procedures that once required expensive hospitalization can now be performed on an outpatient basis: Mercy logs some 160,000 outpatient visits annually and plays a key role in controlling Chicago's health care costs. The hospital's leadership works constantly with business and government to develop a more compassionate, equitable, and affordable health care system.

FOCUS ON WELLNESS

Mercy's community service and wellness programs promote physical, emotional, social, and spiritual well-being for Chicagoans of all

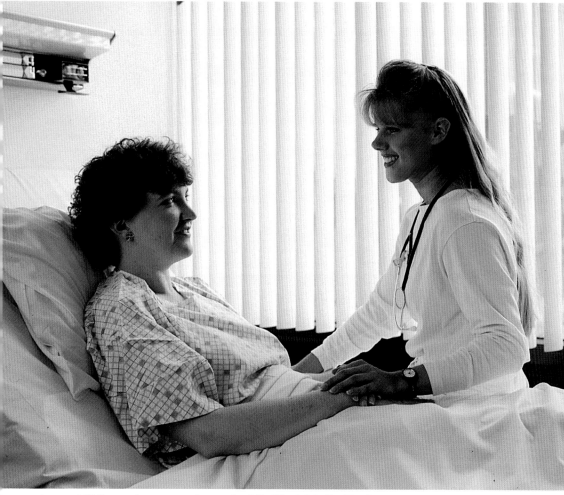

ages and races. OB Outreach ensures quality care for low-income women; Give Kids a Chance provides the medical and social services high-risk parents need to deliver and raise healthy, happy youngsters; the School Nurse program teaches Healthy Lifestyle wellness education through local schools; and Health Professionals for the Future gives high school students firsthand exposure to career opportunities in health care. House Calls provides in-home physician care for the homebound elderly, while people recuperating from surgery or extended illness are assisted through Home Health Services.

The Diabetes Treatment Center at Mercy was the first program in Chicago to meet national standards for patient education, providing multidisciplinary tools for effective self-management. Through Mercy's innovative Mind/Body Medical Institute, patients with high blood pressure, cholesterol imbalances, or diabetes can learn to combine medication with non-drug therapies to control cardiac risk factors and improve their quality of life.

CUTTING EDGE RESEARCH AND TECHNOLOGY

Mercy supports a number of research and development projects ranging from children's health issues to alcohol and chemical dependence. Ongoing research in neurosurgery has won the medical center national recognition, and Mercy is among the leading investigators of heart disease and cancer of the lung and breast.

Mercy's expert stereotactic radiosurgical team uses a state-of-the-art Linac system to treat patients with brain tumors, vascular malformations, and other conditions that can't be helped by conventional surgery. With the patient under local anesthesia, the equipment targets a beam of ionizing radiation precisely where it is needed, thus removing diseased tissue without hair loss, scarring, or damage to healthy surrounding tissue.

THE SPIRIT OF MERCY

Health care has changed radically since Chicago's first hospital was founded, but the Spirit of Mercy remains the same: to minister to all with dignity and respect; to provide quality care for the whole person; to meet the ever-changing needs of Chicago's diverse ethnic communities; and to provide the leadership needed to ensure progressive, compassionate patient care.

THE CHICAGO DOCK & CANAL TRUST

THE HISTORY AND SUCCESS OF THE CHICAGO DOCK & CANAL TRUST CLOSELY PARALLELS THE GROWTH AND DEVELOPMENT OF THE CITY IT CALLS HOME. FROM WAREHOUSES TO RETAIL SHOPS, FROM FACTORIES TO APARTMENTS, THE TRUST HAS HELPED TO SHAPE THE FACE OF DOWNTOWN

Chicago since the mid-1800s.

The focal point of The Chicago Dock & Canal Trust's real estate portfolio is Cityfront Center, a dynamic 60-acre master-planned waterfront neighborhood with expansive public spaces and esplanades, and residential, commercial, retail, and hotel developments. Cityfront Center is unique because it includes the only expanse of prime undeveloped waterfront land located in the heart of Chicago.

Over the years, the land held by the Trust has been the site of various developments. Lake Point Tower, North Pier Terminal, and Chicago Tribune warehouses were all built on its property. The Lake Shore Drive S-curve and Kraft's headquarters are also a part of its history.

The Chicago Dock & Canal Company, as the Trust was originally known, was created in 1857 by William B. Ogden, the city's first mayor. Ogden, who believed the harbor area could play an important role in helping the city become a trade center, purchased a 45-acre

tract of land along the Lake Michigan shore just north of the Chicago River. With the aid of his attorney, Abraham Lincoln, he established a company to develop the lakefront property.

"Today, The Chicago Dock & Canal Trust is a publicly held real estate investment trust actively engaged in developing a significant piece of downtown Chicago waterfront," says Charles R. Gardner, the Trust's current president. "Our primary asset these days is Cityfront Center, Chicago's newest urban development."

The Trust is listed in the NASDAQ system, with shares traded over-the-counter under the symbol DOCKS. It has paid dividends to shareholders each year since 1887, and reported gross revenues in excess of $20 million in 1992.

REALIZING A VISION

Not long after Ogden made his initial purchase of land in 1857, his vision for a prosperous waterfront

became reality. Within a few decades, Chicago emerged as the world's busiest port, and the 1890s marked a period of extensive construction of factories and warehouses on the land. One of these structures, the North Pier Terminal building, was the largest combined warehouse and docking facility in the world upon its completion in 1905.

Tragically, most of the construction was destroyed in the Great Chicago Fire of 1871. But, like the city itself, Chicago Dock & Canal recovered quickly, declaring its first dividend on July 30, 1872.

After World War I, construction activity throughout Chicago slowed down significantly. Although the company successfully weathered this sluggish period which continued through the Depression, it was apparent that the property would never return to its former status as a center for manufacturing and warehousing. As early as the 1920s, company officials began planning for the redevelopment of the land for resi-

Through its massive Cityfront Center project, the Trust is enhancing downtown Chicago's existing residential, commercial, office, and retail space. According to the master plan (right), one-quarter of the development will be devoted to open spaces, including the River Esplanade (top) along the Chicago River and the 1.2-acre Ogden Plaza Park (bottom).

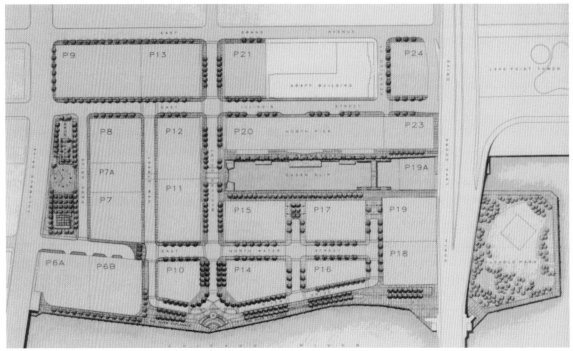

The Cityfront Place Hi-rise and Mid-rise apartment buildings (left) include 900 units.

dential and commercial uses, a focus that remains firmly in place today.

While continuing to prosper from existing rental income, Chicago Dock & Canal spent several decades awaiting the right time to implement the transition. It wasn't until the early 1960s that the face of the company's property really began to change. In 1962, Chicago Dock & Canal converted from a corporation to a real estate investment trust (REIT). The reorganization allowed the company to avoid paying corporate tax on earnings by passing income directly to shareholders. With a slight name change, The Chicago Dock & Canal Trust was finally ready for redevelopment.

CITYFRONT CENTER

In 1982, a new bridge spanning the Chicago River was completed, offering vastly improved access to the Trust's property and fueling the growth of its most exciting project to date, Cityfront Center. Through this massive urban development, the Trust is enhancing the city's existing residential, commercial, office, and retail space. The property earmarked for development lies between Grand Avenue on the north and the Chicago River on the south, and from Columbus Drive on the west to Lake Shore Drive on the east.

Currently, about 25 percent of the master-planned development has been completed, including the recent opening of the 1,200-room Sheraton Chicago Hotel & Towers, the 900-unit Cityfront Place apartments, the 500-unit North Pier

Apartment Tower, and North Pier Chicago, which includes retail, office, and residential space.

Cityfront Place Mid-rise, a two-building, 12-story apartment complex, offers 424 rental units. Since its completion, the property, wholly owned by the Trust, has become its largest income-producing asset. The nearby Cityfront Place Hi-rise, one-third owned by the Trust, climbs 39 stories and includes 425 rental apartments.

As part of Cityfront Center's master plan, one-quarter of the development has been devoted to open spaces—parks, plazas, and promenades—that offer views of the Chicago River, Lake Michigan, and the Ogden Slip. These include Jean Baptiste Point DuSable Park; the River Esplanade, a continuous lighted walkway along the Chicago River; and Ogden Plaza, a 1.2-acre park located directly east of Columbus Drive. Cityfront Center's remaining unbuilt land is the only expanse of prime waterfront land available in the city for development. Pending improvements are expected to be residential in nature, but the current master plan offers flexibility for a variety of uses.

Gardner predicts that while the entire project should take an additional 15 years to build, it will be well worth the wait. "The Chicago Dock & Canal Trust has been around a long time, and the quality and location of our property have stood the test of time," he says. "We are very excited about our location and our position in the heart of

Chicago. We have a continuing commitment to ongoing development and look forward to the successful completion of Cityfront Center."

The 1,200-room Sheraton Chicago Hotel & Towers rises behind Ogden Plaza Park (above).

279

ILLINOIS BELL

T ELECOMMUNICATIONS HAS REVOLUTIONIZED THE WAY PEOPLE LIVE, FROM PROVIDING DIRECT LINKS THAT CONNECT LOVED ONES TO ENABLING COMPUTERS TO TRANSMIT HIGH VOLUMES OF INFORMATION QUICKLY. ◆ FOR DECADES, THE WORLD HAS BEEN DEPENDENT ON THE TELEPHONE, AND AS

technological advances are made, that dependency continues to grow. New time-saving developments are assimilated almost as quickly as they are introduced. Just 10 years ago, few people could have imagined how commonplace much of the emerging technology would be today: fax machines, cellular phones, digital transmission, and Caller ID, a service that lets people know who is calling before they pick up the phone.

Since its inception in 1881, Illinois Bell has been at the forefront of the telecommunications industry. The Chicago-based company continually has kept pace with changing technology over the years. Today, Illinois Bell hopes to jump-start the Information Age through widespread deployment of advanced technology throughout the state.

In 1984, after the breakup of AT&T, Illinois Bell became a subsidiary of Chicago-based Ameritech

Corp., along with the Bell companies of Wisconsin, Indiana, Ohio, and Michigan. Following the transition, Illinois Bell continued to grow and develop. Today, the company provides affordable, reliable telephone service via 2.6 million residential phone lines and 1.5 million business phone lines within the two area codes that serve the Chicago metropolitan area.

A HISTORY OF INNOVATION

Many of the technological advances in telephone service that are taken for granted today throughout the country were introduced first in Chicago and Illinois by Illinois Bell. In 1959, for example, push-button or "Touch-Tone" phones were given their initial product trial in the Chicago suburb of Elgin.

The company has continued its pursuit of innovation ever since. In 1983, Illinois Bell and Ameritech Mobile Communications launched a communications revolution in Chicago by activating the nation's first commercial cellular telephone system.

Likewise, fiber optics, another important development in the modern delivery of telecommunications services, was used first in Illinois. The technology is mind-boggling: Pairs of hair-thin glass fibers utilize pulses of light to transmit up to 24,000 calls simultaneously. In 1977, Illinois Bell installed the world's first fiber-optic cable system to provide a wide range of communications services to its Chicago customers. The half-inch thick cable spanned 1.5 miles under the city's downtown streets and carried customers' voice, data, and video signals. Illinois Bell has now in-

Patty Dalton, support assistant in order administration for Ameritech Services, tests an Ameritech Personal Communications Service (PCS) phone.

stalled more than 100,000 miles of fiber-optic cable.

While fiber-optics technology is still spreading throughout the state, Illinois Bell is now offering such innovative services as Ameritech Integrated Services Digital Network (ISDN). This versatile, economical service allows voice, video, and high-speed data to be transmitted simultaneously through an ordinary pair of telephone wires, thus eliminating the annoying tangle of wires that often results from fax machines, computer terminals, and other nearby office equipment.

In 1992, Ameritech and Illinois Bell began a major communications test project that will give many Chicagoans access to a ground-breaking communication device much like Dick Tracy's fictional telephone wristwatch. Known as personal communications service, or PCS, the trial program employs new, pocket-size portable phones that allow calls to be made anywhere in the world, as well as a prototype digital radio system.

PCS is designed to eliminate the need for separate home, office, and car phone numbers. The system's advantages over existing technology include higher quality sound, reduced power requirements, and the easy transport and use of the equipment.

LEADING ILLINOIS INTO THE INFORMATION AGE

Illinois Bell is looking forward to the day when its network of fiber-optic cable and digital switching systems can provide a new generation of services to consumers and businesses throughout Illinois. One such service would provide students with affordable access to schools within a single school district or thousands of miles away. "Distance learning" would benefit teachers as well as students. Teachers would be able to use laser discs, videos, overhead machines, and old-fashioned face-to-face teaching skills to teach students in their own schools and in classrooms across the state.

Other services would improve health care and increase access to

specialized medical technology by allowing doctors to meet with patients via interactive video and to receive instant visual information, such as X-rays, from distant locations. Additionally, the quality of life would be improved for the elderly and disabled by providing convenient home-based shopping, banking, and security.

The applications for advanced technology are countless. For example, businesses are fast replacing expensive air travel with more affordable teleconferencing, which allows them to utilize interactive video, graphics, data, and voice to conduct a meeting or conversation with someone across the street or around the world.

Through its entry into the Information Age, Illinois Bell is paving the way for an advanced telecommunications network while helping to revitalize education, improve the state's economy, and enhance the quality of day-to-day living for virtually everyone in Illinois.

Roger Frank tests his PCS phone between business meetings in Chicago's Loop (above left).

Susan Colunga (above right) enjoys the portability of her PCS phone en route to work.

MICHAEL REESE HOSPITAL AND MEDICAL CENTER

FOR NEARLY 112 YEARS, MICHAEL REESE HOSPITAL AND MEDICAL CENTER HAS BEEN A VITAL PART OF CHICAGO'S HEALTH CARE INFRASTRUCTURE. FROM ITS EARLIEST DAYS OF SERVING THE JEWISH COMMUNITIES OF CHICAGO, THE HOSPITAL HAS GROWN TO BECOME A LEADER IN MEDICAL

This statue on the medical center grounds honors Michael Reese, the hospital's first benefactor (right).

research and education, and in providing quality care for patients of all backgrounds.

Today, Michael Reese is one of the largest general and specialty medical centers in the United States. The hospital's affiliation with the University of Illinois has fostered its development as one of the largest freestanding teaching programs in the country. Graduates of the Michael Reese program practice medicine in all 50 states and several foreign countries.

Michael Reese continues to thrive and grow in an urban setting, providing care both to residents of the community surrounding the hospital and to those arriving for specialty care from other parts of the metropolitan area and nearby states. The Jewish community's sense of social responsibility, or mitzvah (good

The downtown Chicago skyline rises to the north of the medical center's main campus, located on the near south lakeshore.

work), was the vital force that helped build the hospital and sustain it through difficult times. Today, that spirit of charity, service, and dedication lives on in one of the most well-recognized medical institutions in the world.

FOUNDED IN 1881

The hospital was opened in 1881 by the United Hebrew Relief Association of Chicago and was named for

Michael Reese, a German-Jewish immigrant who made his fortune in real estate in San Francisco during the Gold Rush and the subsequent development of the western United States.

Reese was an independent soul who never married or had children. When he consolidated his estate prior to his death in 1877, he decided to leave his money to several charities in the San Francisco area and to his family, who had settled in Chicago. Following his death, Reese's relatives used his generous bequest to finance the building of a new hospital which bears his name today. Thanks to this funding and the efforts of the United

Hebrew Relief Association, the cornerstone was laid on November 4, 1880. Less than a year later, on October 23, 1881, Michael Reese Hospital opened its doors to the sick of Chicago.

This longtime relationship with the Jewish relief association helped create a strong tradition of caring at Michael Reese. For more than a century, the hospital's physicians, nurses, volunteers, and staff have worked to make Michael Reese a place where patient care is the highest priority. The hospital's primary mission of service to the community lives on today in the form of multispecialty, high-technology medicine being deliv-

ered to urban dwellers and inner-city residents of Chicago in the 1990s.

ALWAYS AT THE FOREFRONT

Michael Reese Hospital and Medical Center has been at the forefront of the medical community virtually since its founding. Education and research have always been a vital part of the institution. For example, the hospital's first staff physicians introduced innovative antiseptic techniques and laboratory procedures that were state-of-the-art for their time.

The medical center was among the first to recognize that the health care needs of children and women are different from those of adult men. As a result, the hospital opened the Annex for Women and Children in 1897. Located across the street from the main facility, the annex housed the departments of pediatrics and women's medicine. Michael Reese physicians encouraged women to have their babies in the hospital rather than at home, emphasizing that the hospital would provide a cleaner, safer environment.

In 1915, Michael Reese scientists and physicians developed the forerunner to the modern incubator for premature infants. Reese researchers also established the first blood bank in 1937 and built the first linear accelerator to fight cancer in 1953.

At the hospital today, physicians are engaged in numerous pioneering research projects. The Division of Nuclear Medicine is the first in the Chicagoland area to offer a remarkable new diagnostic test to detect recurring colon or ovarian cancers. Michael Reese is the only institution in the United States currently performing imaging techniques for pa-

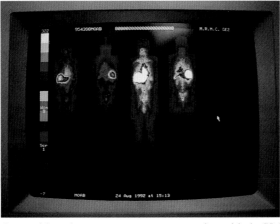

tients with melanomas.

Other pioneering research is under way that would allow for the indefinite storage of blood supplies and for the development of blood extracts and new blood products which would decrease the need for blood transfusions by patients, as well as provide an uncontaminated blood supply. Michael Reese's Autologous Blood Transfusion program currently allows patients to save their own blood for future surgeries.

A COMMITMENT TO EDUCATION

Education has been a priority throughout the hospital's many decades of service. Aspiring physicians receive the highest level of training available on the latest medical equipment and techniques. As part of its commitment to education, the hospital has maintained a long-term affiliation with the University of Illinois schools of medicine, dentistry, nursing, pharmacy, associated professions, and public health. Currently, Michael Reese has about 140 full-time faculty members who work with more than 600 residents and students.

Michael Reese is affiliated with numerous schools of nursing— primarily the University of Illinois. As is the case with the practice of medicine, Reese's nursing program has always been a leader among

Pillar, a sculpture by artist Richard Hunt, graces The Meadow, a parklike area south of Kaplan Pavilion.

Nearly 112 years after its founding, Michael Reese Hospital and Medical Center is a leader in medical research and education, and in providing quality care for patients of all backgrounds.

hospitals nationwide. Individuals who practice clinical nursing at the medical center have authored and co-authored textbooks that are in use worldwide to teach nursing students.

Education is extremely important in other health professions as well. Michael Reese operates the only school of cytotechnology in the state of Illinois. It has the second largest school for radiation technologists in the country. Michael Reese also maintains affiliations with universities across the country to provide clinical experience for those students who want to be trained at one of the busiest and best medical centers in the United States.

This unique blend of academic

medicine with clinical practice is the distinguishing reason why the quality of medical care at Michael Reese has always been and will continue to be outstanding. Clinicians work side by side with the teachers of tomorrow's doctors and researchers, looking for solutions to medical puzzles and working to improve future lives.

COVERING CHICAGO AND SURROUNDING AREAS

The medical center's main campus is located on the city's near south lakeshore. Near major expressways and Chicago's Lake Shore Drive, the hospital is easily accessible to the entire city and suburban area. Because of its strong reputation in the medical community and the multitude of specialty programs it offers, Michael Reese Hospital and Medical Center has also become a major referral center for patients throughout the Midwest.

In addition to the main campus, the hospital operates satellite facilities in two key downtown Chicago locations: Sears Tower and the 900 North Michigan Avenue Annex at the Nathan Cummings Outpatient Center in the Bloomingdale's building. The Sears Tower facility offers access to Michael Reese physicians and dentists for commuters and residents in Chicago's Loop. The 900 North Michigan Avenue Annex facility offers specialty and primary

care services in elegant quarters convenient to both shoppers and Near North Side residents. Services include internal medicine and other specialties, a state-of-the-art outpatient surgery center, and plastic and orthopedic surgery programs. Also located in the 900 North Michigan Avenue Annex is the Michael Reese Fertility Center, which boasts one of the highest success rates in the country for in vitro fertilization.

SPECIALTY SERVICES

Consistent with the hospital's long tradition, Michael Reese's Cardiovascular Institute and Division of Cardiology continue to provide excellence in the full range of modern cardiovascular diagnostic and therapeutic techniques. Reese's clinic for the evaluation and treatment of Marfan's syndrome and other genetic cardiac disorders is unique in the Midwest. Over the years, cardiologists at the hospital have pioneered research in heart disease, including the notable contribution of Dr. Louis N. Katz and his associates in establishing the relationship of high serum cholesterol levels to coronary heart disease; the preeminence as world authorities of Drs. Alfred Pick and Richard Langendorf in the interpretation of complex rhythm disturbances of the heart; and the early demonstration of the relationship of viral infections to subsequent dis-

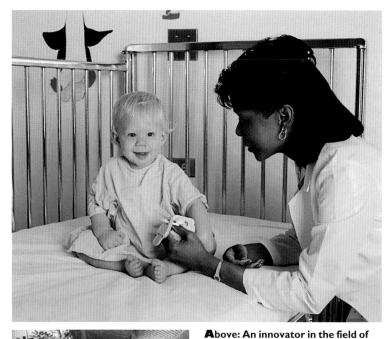

ease in heart muscle. Research in other causes of heart disease is an ongoing commitment at Michael Reese today.

The medical center's comprehensive Cancer Center unites some of the country's top researchers and specialists to advance the diagnosis and treatment of cancer. Patients who come to Michael Reese with advanced cancer gain access to an exceptionally wide range and large number of innovative therapies. Only a handful of other medical centers in the United States offer so many experimental treatment programs.

Medical and surgical oncology, radiation oncology, chemotherapy, and bone marrow transplantation are among the many cancer programs and services available at the medical center. The Reese bone marrow transplant program specializes in sibling donor transplants for the treatment of leukemia, as well as autologous transplants as an adjunct to chemotherapy. The Head and Neck Oncology and Reconstructive

Center offers an innovative combination of chemotherapy and radiation. Similar pioneering therapy is under way for the treatment of lung cancer. Autologous bone marrow transplant and high dose chemotherapy are being used by Reese physicians in the assault on advanced breast cancer.

Rounding out the hospital's list of services are its maternity and child-birth-related facilities and programs. Since it was opened in 1986, the New Life and Maternity Center has set the standard for women's health care in Chicago. It was the first in the city to offer labor, delivery, and recovery suites, which allow mothers to share the childbirth experience with their husbands, family members, and friends in a homelike setting.

The medical center's Special Care Nursery provides high-level intensive care for high-risk and premature infants. The Level III Newborn Intensive Care Unit, a part of the University of Illinois Perinatal Network, offers the latest technology in maternal-fetal medicine. The Center

for Medical and Reproductive Genetics provides genetic evaluation and counseling, ultrasonography for detection of fetal anomalies, and screening and prenatal diagnosis for genetic diseases. This centralized genetics testing facility is run by nationally renowned geneticists and serves both Michael Reese and the University of Illinois. The Pediatric Intensive Care Unit is one of the busiest short-term pediatric care facilities in the state of Illinois.

For more than a century, Michael Reese Hospital and Medical Center has been at the forefront of medical research, education, and patient care. In this unique "laboratory," patients benefit from the hospital's specialized research expertise, facilities and equipment, and the many minds all working together to provide the highest quality patient care. It is this unique blend that has made Michael Reese special for so long.

MONTGOMERY WARD AND CO., INC.

ACROSS AMERICA THE NAME MONTGOMERY WARD HAS BEEN A HOUSEHOLD WORD—SYNONYMOUS WITH QUALITY AND CUSTOMER SATISFACTION—FOR MORE THAN A CENTURY. FOUNDED BY AARON MONTGOMERY WARD IN CHICAGO IN 1872, MONTGOMERY WARD AND Co., Inc. is today the "comeback company" in American retailing after a management-led buyout in 1988. Today more than 350 stores nationwide bear the Montgomery Ward name, as well as a new and successful retailing format.

The retailer has a strong presence in Chicago, with its corporate headquarters located downtown and 23 stores in the area. Of the 75,000 people employed by Montgomery Ward nationwide, about 10,000 work in the Chicago area. The company's overall sales are more than $5.8 billion a year.

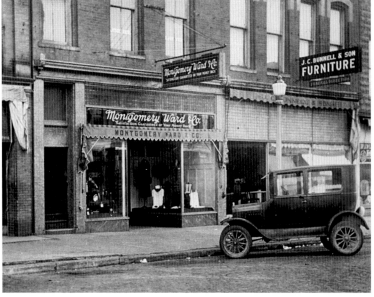

Aaron Montgomery Ward (top) launched the mail-order catalog industry in 1872 in Chicago. After several decades of growth, his company entered the retail business in 1926 (bottom).

LAUNCHING A BUSINESS AND AN INDUSTRY

Aaron Montgomery Ward, a traveling salesman, didn't like the merchandise he saw on the shelves of the stores he encountered in his travels. The goods were of poor quality and over-priced, and he became convinced he could sell superior merchandise at fair prices through the mail.

Although his idea was greeted with derision from "wiser" businessmen of his time, Ward launched both a business and an industry in 1872 when he issued his first general merchandise mail-order catalog.

The publication bore little resemblance to today's mail-order catalogs. It was simply a list with descriptions and prices of the items he had available—"Men's pants, $1," for example.

But for rural Americans, Ward's simple catalog fundamentally changed their shopping habits. Instead of taking occasional trips into town to buy dry goods and household items, they could shop through the mail and buy a wide assortment of goods in the comfort of their homes.

Three years after the company's inception, Ward introduced another innovative concept that made mail-order shopping even more attractive: the money-back guarantee. Until that time, most consumers purchased goods defensively, or by the motto *caveat emptor*—let the buyer beware. Montgomery Ward's money-back guarantee eliminated the customer's risk from the transaction and increased the company's business tremendously. By 1876, company sales exceeded $300,000, and in 1887 they topped $1 million.

In 1926, the company entered retailing, not by design but by consumer demand. Early that year Montgomery Ward opened three display stores—one in Marysville, Kansas, another in Plymouth, Indiana, and a third in Little Falls, Minnesota. Items were not available for purchase but were put on display so that customers could view them before placing orders. When a persistent carpenter convinced a Plymouth store clerk to sell him a display saw, Montgomery Ward officially entered retailing. By the end of 1926 there were 10 retail stores including the Plymouth location.

Retail expansion accelerated rapidly. By the end of 1927 the company had opened 37 retail stores across the country, and by year-end 1928 it boasted 244 stores, with sales topping $200 million. By 1930, Montgomery Ward had 556 retail locations.

In 1941, the company was at the peak of its store expansion, operating 183 catalog stores and 650 retail stores. Sixteen years would pass, however, before Montgomery Ward would open another retail location. Anticipating a nationwide depression after World War II, company management held back on growth in the post-war years. But the 1950s were boom years, and suburban malls sprung up with Montgomery Ward competitors taking anchor positions in the malls. Although the company maintained competitive downtown locations in many cities, a number of stores closed due to the increased competition.

EXPANSION IN THE '60S
The company got back on track in the 1960s with a $500 million expansion program initiated for new stores and distribution centers, and a modernization program for existing operations. In 1960, Ward had approximately 547 retail stores and 594 catalog stores. During the decade of the '60s many older stores were replaced by new stores. By 1969, Montgomery Ward's annual sales topped the $2 billion mark.

The company prospered through the 1960s and into the 1970s. Then in 1974, Mobil Oil Corp. purchased Montgomery Ward, a development that was hailed as further good news and a promising future for the retailer. Run as a subsidiary operation, however, the company lost its competitive edge. Five years into new ownership, Montgomery Ward began to suffer and reported substantial losses. In response, Mobil hired Bernard F. Brennan in 1985 as president of Montgomery Ward to "re-strategize" the company.

One of the first moves under Brennan's management was the discontinuation of the catalog operation. The company also sold off some unprofitable subsidiaries. Then Brennan and the Montgomery Ward management team began reviewing the company's merchandise categories with the goal of determining the areas in which it could be a dominant force. As a result, Montgomery Ward discontinued plumbing and heating supplies, building materials, hardware, and men's suits.

While sales initially decreased, these products were replaced with an innovative and rejuvenating specialty store concept, conceived in 1985 after Brennan's thorough evaluation of the company. In 1988, in the midst of implementing the new program, the management of Montgomery Ward bought the company from Mobil in the largest management-led leveraged buyout to that date. The company has since enjoyed a continuous series of profitable years and has opened or relocated 59 stores.

IMPLEMENTING A DYNAMIC NEW CONCEPT

Under the new strategy, each Montgomery Ward store operates as a group of specialty "stores," integrated under one roof to achieve total customer satisfaction with quality merchandise at competitive prices. These specialty areas, designed to provide an easy-to-shop environment, include Electric Avenue, Home Ideas, The Apparel Store, Gold 'N Gems, The Kids Store, and Auto Express.

By focusing on major merchandise areas instead of all product categories, each Montgomery Ward store has more space for a broader assortment of merchandise and brands in the specialty areas. The highly successful Electric Avenue features TVs, VCRs, stereos, and many major appliances. Brand names include Maytag, General Electric, Sony, Hoover, RCA, Amana, Zenith, Panasonic, Nikon, AT&T, Tappan, and others. In 1987, Electric Avenue was honored as one of the "Top Ten Retailers of the

Year" by *Consumer Electronics* and *TV Guide* magazines.

Home Ideas offers many of the comforts and conveniences of home. A wide variety of brand-name furniture, window treatments, lamps, housewares, accessories, and small appliances are available by Sealy, Simmons, La-Z-Boy, Cannon, Black & Decker, Levelor, Spring Air, Kirsch, Dan River, Burlington, Sunbeam, and Toastmaster, among others.

The Apparel Store is one of the company's most colorful specialty areas, with eye-catching graphics and merchandise displays of quality apparel, shoes, and accessories for men and women. Brands include Bugle Boy, Jordache, Sasson, Bestform, Russ Togs, Playtex, Cotler, Wrangler, Hanes, Gitano, Lee, L'eggs, Burlington, Bill Blass, Totes, Reebok, Puma, Diane von Furstenberg, Sag Harbor, Samsonite, and American Tourister.

The Kids Store is specially de-

signed to provide a fun and easy shopping experience for children and their parents. Clothes, toys, and extras, such as cards and party favors, are offered by Cotler, Hush Puppies, Fisher Price, Bassett, Lee, and others.

Auto Express features state-of-the-art computer diagnostic equipment and 59-minute service on tire

The company is today headquartered in One Montgomery Ward Plaza in downtown Chicago (left).

Bernard F. Brennan (top) joined Montgomery Ward in 1985 to "re-strategize" the company, an effort which has since led to the opening or relocation of 59 stores nationwide (bottom).

Each Montgomery Ward location now operates as a group of specialty "stores" integrated under one roof, with such easy-to-shop specialty areas as The Kids Store (right) and Electric Avenue (below).

All stores are designed to achieve total customer satisfaction with quality merchandise at competitive prices (right).

and battery installations. Brand names include Michelin, Firestone, B.F. Goodrich, General, Bridgestone, Champion, Delco, Monroe, Quaker State, Prestone, and Penzoil.

Outstanding values in diamonds, gold, precious stones, and other fine jewelry items can be found at Gold 'N Gems. Designed to compete effectively with established national jewelers, Gold 'N Gems is a popular section in all Montgomery Ward stores. Customers find trusted names such as Seiko, Sharp, Casio, Citizen, and Benrus in this specialty section.

MOVING TO THE FRONT RANKS

This new retailing strategy is attracting new customers every day as Montgomery Ward rapidly moves to the front ranks of the retailing industry. To further enhance its market position, the company re-entered the catalog business in 1992 with Montgomery Ward Direct, a series of specialty catalogs offering home items, novelties, and fashions.

After more than a century, Montgomery Ward has come full circle. The company that founded the mail-order industry is regaining its position as a retail leader and is entering the specialty catalog business. As it continues to grow and change, Montgomery Ward and Co. will remain a vital member of the Chicago community.

MIDWEST STOCK EXCHANGE

F OR OVER A CENTURY, "EXCELLENCE THROUGH INNOVATION" HAS BEEN THE HALLMARK OF THE MIDWEST STOCK EXCHANGE, THE SECOND LARGEST STOCK EXCHANGE IN THE UNITED STATES. FOUNDED IN 1882 AS THE CHICAGO STOCK EXCHANGE, THE EARLY EXCHANGE OFFERED 52 STOCKS

and 82 bonds for trading. Although it no longer handles bonds, more than 2,600 stocks are traded at the exchange today.

In the early years, securities traded in Chicago were closely tied to the region's economy: railroads, local banks, utilities, and meat packing companies. As cross-country communication improved, stocks listed in other cities could be traded on the Chicago exchange, and its scope broadened significantly. In 1949, the organization merged with its counterparts in St. Louis, Cleveland, and Minneapolis-St. Paul to form the Midwest Stock Exchange. The New Orleans Stock Exchange joined the group in 1959.

Today, the exchange's logo embodies the historic mergers. An arch, representing the entrance to the old Chicago Stock Exchange Building, is crowned by four lines that symbolize the regional exchanges. Though the original exchange building was demolished in 1972, its distinctive archway designed by Louis Sullivan is displayed in the East Garden of the Art Institute of Chicago. The original trading room also has been reconstructed at the Art Institute.

In April 1985, the exchange opened its present trading floor at 440 S. LaSalle Street, directly south of the Chicago Board of Trade and the Chicago Board Options Exchange. Along with the Chicago Mercantile Exchange, these markets form one of the world's most important financial districts.

The exchange is owned by its membership. The 446 members include all of the major brokerage firms in the country, as well as many of the largest firms in Europe and Asia. More than 270 members make up the trading floor community—a 200 percent increase in floor membership in just 10 years. These members compete with other exchanges and the OTC market to give customers the best possible executions and service.

The Midwest has been the most automated of all U.S. exchanges, and its new floor, designed to facilitate information technology, provides cheaper, faster, and quicker service. More than 90 percent of all Midwest trades are received and executed by computer.

Midwest trading technology has attracted the attention of exchanges worldwide. The Midwest was selected to develop automated trading systems for the Amsterdam Stock Exchange and the Stock Exchange of Thailand. In Amsterdam, the world's oldest stock exchange, Midwest systems modernized the existing trading floor. In Thailand, Midwest systems replaced the trading floor with a direct computer match of customer orders. Growing demand for expertise in the development and implementation of automated trading systems led the Midwest to establish a permanent office in Bangkok to address the future needs of stock exchanges in the Pacific Rim.

The Midwest does more than facilitate trading. Its wholly owned subsidiary, Midwest Clearing Corporation, provides the post-trading services necessary for settlement of trading contracts originating from numerous securities markets. In 1973, the exchange reorganized the clearing corporation to include a trust company. The Midwest Securities Trust Company is the second

largest depository for equities, corporate debt, and municipal debt securities in the United States. Together, the two subsidiaries offer a wide range of services, including safekeeping of certificates, collection and payment of dividends and interest, and handling of stock splits and reorganizations.

Another subsidiary, the MBS Clearing Corp., is the nation's only registered clearinghouse dedicated to providing trade comparison and other services for the mortgage-backed securities market. MBS allows financial institutions to pool real estate mortgages and issue securities to reduce risk and maintain liquidity.

When Charles Henrotin, founding president of the Chicago Stock Exchange, witnessed the first trade more than 100 years ago, he could not have imagined the changes the organization has undergone. Nor could he have forseen the volume of trade, the money involved, or the innovative technology that allows it all to run smoothly. Entering its second century in Chicago, the Midwest Stock Exchange is well-positioned to build on its commitment to excellence through innovation.

More than 90 percent of all Midwest trades are received and executed by computer.

In April 1985, the exchange opened its present trading floor (left) at 440 S. LaSalle Street in one of the world's most important financial districts.

289

SEARS, ROEBUCK AND CO.

SEARS, ROEBUCK AND CO. IS MADE UP OF THE SEARS MERCHANDISE GROUP, WHICH CONDUCTS MERCHANDISING AND CREDIT OPERATIONS IN THE UNITED STATES, CANADA, AND MEXICO, AND THE ALLSTATE INSURANCE COMPANY, WHICH SELLS PROPERTY-LIABILITY AND LIFE INSURANCE.

COMPANY HISTORY

Sears traces its roots to a shipment of pocket watches and the imagination and initiative of a young man. While working as a railway station

Sears' corporate headquarters is located in the Sears Tower. The 110-story building, which opened in 1973, is the world's tallest building. It has 4.5 million square feet of space and reaches 1,454 feet into the sky.

agent in North Redwood, Minnesota, Richard Warren Sears noticed a shipment of watches being returned to the manufacturer by a local jeweler. He bought the watches and then sold them at a profit to other station agents.

Sears' success in the venture encouraged him to found the R.W. Sears Watch Company in Minneapolis in 1886. The following year, Sears moved the company to Chicago, where he advertised for a watchmaker. Alvah C. Roebuck, a young Irishman from Hammond,

Indiana, answered the call. In 1893, the firm's name officially became Sears, Roebuck and Co., and the company began its relationship with Chicago that has lasted a century.

Initially, Sears served its customers' needs through the mail. While the earliest catalogs featured only watches and jewelry, the firm was soon producing catalogs offering goods from clothing to wagons, stoves, furniture, musical instruments, saddles, buggies, bicycles, and baby carriages. Through the years, American consumers would come to rely on the catalog for a wide range of products and services.

In 1925, Sears opened its first retail outlet on the site of its Chicago mail order plant. It was an immediate success. Before the year was out, seven more retail stores were opened. Over the next several decades, Sears opened stores throughout the United States and in Canada and Mexico.

SEARS TODAY

Sears today is a highly focused company with a clear direction and purpose: to provide mid-market consumers with superior service and great product values in apparel, home, and automotive categories. Sears continues to address the changing needs and expectations of consumers. Recognizing that today's family cannot afford to spend a lot of time and money shopping, Sears' goal is to become the store that meets the needs of time- and value-conscious customers.

The shopping mall is now the predominant destination for American shoppers, and Sears has one of the best portfolios of mall-based locations in the industry. With 800 stores nationwide, Sears is capitalizing on these locations. The company is bringing together new store design elements—fixtures, coloration,

lighting, wider aisles—to enhance the shopping experience, and expanding its assortment of national brands to complement its well-recognized proprietary brands.

Likewise, Sears is increasing the amount of floor space devoted to its women's, men's, and children's lines of apparel. Driven by fashion, quality, and value, the merchandise is well designed and quality made. The company is also expanding fashion accessories and testing the introduction of cosmetics and fragrances.

In its home business, Sears is building on the foundation of its powerful brands, such as Kenmore appliances and Craftsman tools, which dominate the marketplace through their long-standing reputation for quality, innovation, and value.

Under its Brand Central banner, Sears continues to build its number one appliance outlet share by competing from a price point of view and providing customers with top-notch service before and after the sale. The company is also increasing the number of freestanding Homelife furniture stores and Hardware stores.

Sears plans to leverage its dominant position in products for the home with its superior ability to deliver, install, repair, and finance these goods. The company has a strong national product services organization with more than 17,000 trained technicians meeting customer needs across the country.

In the automotive lines, Sears will focus on the sale of tires, batteries (including its top-selling DieHard brand), and related installation and repair services.

Sears launched a major initiative in 1992 to improve customer service. Called "Pure Selling Environment," it streamlines sales floor

procedures, enabling sales associates to spend more time taking care of customers.

The company is well positioned for the '90s as it continues to refine its merchandising programs to meet the needs of its customers, who represent the strength and diversity of middle America.

ALLSTATE INSURANCE

In 1931, Sears founded the Allstate Insurance Company to sell auto insurance to customers through the catalog. The name was taken from a Sears line of automobile tires. Several years later, the company added fire and other home coverages and began selling insurance through Allstate booths in Sears stores. In 1951, the company launched its slogan, "You're in good hands with Allstate," which has become one of the most famous advertising slogans of all time.

Today, Allstate writes a broad range of insurance for individuals, businesses, and other organizations and is also a reinsurer. It is the second largest property and casualty insurer in the United States. Approximately one out of every

eight insured households in America carries Allstate auto or homeowners insurance. And Allstate Life, one of the 20 largest life insurers in the industry, offers a variety of life insurance, annuity, and pension products.

Allstate meets the needs of its customers from everyday small claims to major catastrophes such as Hurricane Andrew, which resulted in 158,000 claims. In the aftermath of the storm, the com-

pany sent in more than 1,400 employees to service the needs of customers.

Allstate employs more than 51,000 people and has more than 9,400 sales locations and nearly 300 claim service offices throughout the country. While the company sells its products primarily through its agency force of 15,000, nearly 60,000 independent agents and brokers are licensed to sell certain Allstate products.

THE NORTHERN TRUST COMPANY

THE NORTHERN TRUST COMPANY HAS BEEN A PART OF CHICAGO'S FINAN-
CIAL SCENE FOR MORE THAN A CENTURY. SINCE ITS FOUNDING IN 1889,
THIS VENERABLE BANKING INSTITUTION HAS REMAINED A CORNERSTONE
OF THE CHICAGO BUSINESS COMMUNITY. ◆ OWNED TODAY BY NORTHERN

Trust Corporation, a holding company headquartered in Chicago, the bank is the largest member of a growing network of subsidiaries in Illinois, Florida, New York, Arizona, California, and Texas. Since it was incorporated in Delaware in 1971, Northern Trust Corporation has grown to employ more than 6,500 people nationwide. This publicly held organization trades its common stock in the NASDAQ over-the-counter market under the symbol NTRS.

From 42 offices in six states, Northern Trust provides a full spectrum of superior financial services, ranging from private banking, trust administration, and investment management for individuals to commercial banking, master trust, and global securities custody for corporations, foundations, and public funds. The corporation and its subsidiaries also excel in the areas of cash management, futures trading, brokerage, and leasing services.

THE NORTHERN TRUST COMPANY

Headquartered at 50 S. LaSalle Street in downtown Chicago, The Northern Trust Company has distinguished itself from other banks in three primary areas: master trust and global services, commercial banking and cash management, and personal financial services.

In 1974, Congress enacted the Employees Retirement and Income Security Act (ERISA), mandating that assets held in corporate employee benefit funds be overseen by an independent master trustee or custodian. Through advanced accounting and reporting systems already being used for personal trust clients, Northern Trust was able to meet the complex reporting requirements of ERISA. Since that time, substantial investments in people, technology, and marketing have kept Northern Trust on the cutting edge of this segment of the financial services industry. In fact, the bank currently ranks among the top five trustees/custodians in the nation and has developed an equally prominent reputation for its global custody services.

In less than two decades, the bank's master trust and custody business has expanded from a single market—large corporate employee benefit funds—into a highly diversified environment serving several markets with varying needs. Today, the bank administers pension plans and funds for universities, corporations, public retirement funds, foundations, endowments, and insurance companies, among others. Staff members in the trust and custody division utilize the bank's custody capabilities, comprehensive analytical tools, and innovative information delivery systems to provide accounting, reporting, safekeeping, automated cash management, global custody, on-line data systems, investment, and securities lending services.

Northern Trust's commercial banking activities are focused on the large corporate market and the middle market, which includes companies with less than $125 million in annual sales. In addition, Northern Trust provides traditional banking services for domestic banks and for brokers/dealers of securities and commodities. Administered through the Chicago office, branches in London and the Cayman Islands, and an Edge Act subsidiary in New York, the company's international banking business is focused on the financing of trade flows and dollar clearing activity.

Northern Trust is also a leader in corporate cash management, ranking in the top 10 nationally in market share. A major provider of wholesale lockbox, controlled disbursement, and automated clearinghouse services, the bank specializes in the design and implementation of customized cash management strategies for major corporations.

Northern Trust has developed a highly successful corporate money market account business as well. This service allows employees, dealers, and stockholders of major

Northern Trust's headquarters is located at LaSalle and Monroe streets in the heart of Chicago's financial district.

corporations such as GMAC and Ford to invest in their company's commercial paper programs.

For more than a century, Northern Trust has been a major factor in the personal trust market and today is known throughout the Chicago area as a high-quality provider of personalized private banking and asset management services. The bank has attained this premier position by developing close relationships with individual clients through an emphasis on personal attention and sophisticated services.

To build on this leadership position, Northern Trust Corporation has expanded into the strong growth regions of Florida, California, Texas, Arizona, and suburban Chicago. In these areas, subsidiaries are providing a combination of private banking, trust, and investment management services to high net worth individuals. In fact, the company is renowned as a top investment manager and as one of the country's largest bank managers of personal assets.

SERVICE THROUGH TECHNOLOGY

At Northern Trust, superior technology always has played a major role in enhancing the bank's competitive advantage. In 1990, Northern Trust further confirmed its commitment to technology by opening Canal Center in Chicago. At this 500,000-square-foot central operations facility, located at Canal Street between Polk and Taylor streets, state-of-the-art technology plays a major role in Northern's ability to provide a broad range of sophisticated services to meet trust and banking clients' increasingly complex needs.

Newly installed imaging equipment for check processing makes Northern Trust an industry leader in the use of this technology. Among the other technology-based services currently offered by the bank are multi-currency reporting, international securities lending, and a highly advanced electronic communication system that allows clients

on-line, interactive access to account information.

COMMUNITY INVOLVEMENT

Over the years, Northern Trust also has nurtured its relationships with the communities in which it operates. Its ties to community-based organizations, both in Chicago and in subsidiary locations, continue to grow and broaden as Northern Trust pursues innovative solutions for affordable housing and economic development. The expertise of its lenders and other staff in govern-

ment finance, real estate, and taxation helps the bank address the increasingly complex credit needs of its communities.

Throughout the decade of the 1990s, Northern Trust plans to concentrate on three themes: quality, growth, and productivity. But none of these terms are new to this 104-year-old company. Since its founding before the turn of the century, Northern Trust has pursued these corporate ideals to become an important force in the financial world of Chicago and beyond.

Northern Trust's commitment to Chicago is exemplified by Canal Center, its state-of-the-art trust and commercial banking operations center located southwest of the Loop.

SEARLE

BREAKING NEW GROUND IS IMPORTANT IN ANY BUSINESS, BUT IN THE PHARMACEUTICAL INDUSTRY, INNOVATION IS THE ONLY WAY TO SURVIVE, LET ALONE THRIVE. FOR MORE THAN 100 YEARS, SEARLE HAS BEEN A WORLDWIDE INNOVATOR IN THIS CHALLENGING FIELD.

Gideon Daniel Searle was just 22 years old when he purchased a Fortville, Indiana drugstore. The products he prepared there proved to be so popular with local physicians and druggists that Searle gave up the retail business to become a full-time manufacturer. In 1888, he established a manufacturing business in Omaha, Nebraska, but relocated the company to Chicago in 1890 because the city offered better opportunities for expansion. G.D. Searle & Co. was incorporated on April 10, 1908.

Today, Searle ranks 21st among U.S. manufacturers of prescription pharmaceuticals, but the company is not complacent even in this enviable position. "Our goal is to break into the top 15 worldwide," says Charles Fry, corporate vice president for public affairs.

Over the years Searle has developed many products that consumers take for granted today. Metamucil®,

◀ BACHRACH

Chairman of the Board and CEO Sheldon G. Gilgore, M.D. (right) has streamlined Searle's management structure to focus on the pharmaceutical business and to achieve more rapid communications and decision-making on a worldwide basis.

The company's history as an innovator of new drugs extends back to the 1800s.

the world's first modern bulk laxative, was introduced in 1934. Dramamine® (dimenhydrinate), which helps control motion sickness, was made available by prescription in 1949. Searle also introduced the first birth control pill, Enovid® (norethynodrel with mestranol), in 1957.

A major source of the company's sales and growth in the early 1980s was aspartame, an artificial sweet-

ener marketed under the brand name NutraSweet®. Although NutraSweet was developed in a Searle research-and-development lab in 1965, it was not approved until 1981 by the U.S. Food and Drug Administration for use in tabletop sweeteners and other dry food products. In July 1983, NutraSweet was authorized for use in carbonated beverages, and by 1985 the product was in use in various forms in 48 other countries.

ACQUIRED BY THE MONSANTO COMPANY

In 1985, Searle was acquired by the Monsanto Company, a large, diversified organization based in St. Louis, Missouri, with leadership positions in high-quality chemical and agricultural products and industrial process controls. The addition of Searle capped a decade-long effort by Monsanto to enter the international pharmaceutical industry.

To help Searle become one of the top-tier pharmaceutical companies by the year 2000, Monsanto merged its health care research operations with Searle's, increasing the acquired company's research-and-development capability by nearly 50 percent. In addition, Monsanto sold Searle's consumer products group to Proctor & Gamble Co. in order to focus solely on producing prescription drugs; formed the NutraSweet Company as a separate Monsanto subsidiary; and hired Sheldon G. Gilgore, M.D., a 23-year veteran of the pharmaceutical industry, as Searle's new chairman of the board and chief executive officer.

Dr. Gilgore has brought a new vitality to the management of Searle. He believes that three factors are critical to the company's success: efficient management of the discovery, development, manufacture, and marketing of new prod-

ucts; the ability to market Searle products in the top seven world markets; and a steady flow of new products that have medical or cost advantages over existing therapies.

Dr. Gilgore streamlined the company's management structure to focus on the pharmaceutical business and to achieve more rapid communications and decision-making on a worldwide basis. An executive committee was formed to develop objectives and strategies aimed at reaching Searle's goal of becoming a worldwide industry leader and to oversee their implementation. Among these objectives are achieving annual worldwide sales of $2.5 billion to $3 billion by the middle to late 1990s and launching at least one important new product in a key country every year.

CONTINUING INNOVATION AND GROWTH

Monsanto's resources and the strategy of Searle's new management have resulted in a dramatic expansion of new pharmaceuticals in development, with emphasis on the high-growth areas of cardiovascular, immunoinflammatory, and infectious diseases.

One of Searle's recent success stories is Cytotec® (misoprostol), the first medication proven to prevent stomach ulcers caused by nonsteroidal anti-inflammatory drugs (NSAIDs). Although NSAIDs are the standard therapy for arthritis

patients, it is estimated that at any one time, ulcers are present in up to 31 percent of users. Cytotec has been uniquely effective in preventing gastric ulcers caused by NSAIDs. First approved for overseas use in 1985, the drug was cleared for U.S. marketing in 1988.

Searle's track record in introducing new treatments for patients' ailments is continuing. In 1992, the company launched Maxaquin® (lomefloxacin), the only once-a-day quinolone antibiotic. And in 1993, Searle expects to launch three other new products in the United States or abroad: Arthrotec® (diclofenac 50 mg/ misoprostol 200 mcg), an NSAID that offers built-in protection against medication-induced ulcers; Daypro™ (oxaprozin), a once-a-day NSAID for the treatment of osteoarthritis and adult rheumatoid arthritis; and Ambien™ (zolpidem tartrate), the first in a new class of prescription sleep aids.

Searle's innovation has not been limited to medical treatment. The company also has been a pioneer in social responsibility programs that reach out to patients who are in economic distress or in need of education about their medication. These programs include Patients in Need®, which provides free medication to people who could not otherwise afford it; the Patient Promise® program, which offers refunds to patients if a Searle product does not achieve its desired therapeutic benefit; and Patients in the Know®,

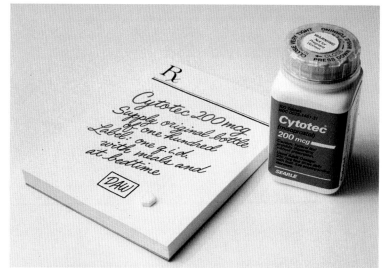

which supplies easy-to-understand consumer information materials on Searle medications.

Searle's world headquarters and its largest research-and-development facility are located in Skokie, a suburb just north of Chicago. The company employs about 3,000 people in the United States. Searle also has subsidiaries or joint ventures in more than 119 countries and employs nearly 10,000 people around the world.

The company has seen tremendous growth and success in its century-long history, and it is using its significant resources to push ahead. Says Fry, "Our commitment to joining the ranks of the top pharmaceutical companies in the world is backed by strong management, an innovative team of employees, financial strength, and a wealth of experience in the marketplace."

Searle's world headquarters (top) and its largest research-and-development facility are located in Skokie, a suburb just north of Chicago.

One of the company's recent success stories is Cytotec® (above), the first medication proven to prevent stomach ulcers caused by NSAIDs.

A MERE 20 YEARS AFTER THE GREAT Chicago Fire, the World's Columbian Exposition of 1893 marked the city's breathless rise from the ashes. Some 27.5 million visitors viewed the fair's famed White City as it glowed in the night, thanks to that new invention, electricity. One building alone, the Manufacturers Building, was the size of five baseball fields. The exposition featured the world's first Ferris wheel, 250 feet high, invented by George W.G. Ferris.

1891

SARGENT & LUNDY

1891

WM. WRIGLEY JR.
COMPANY

1893

DRAPER AND KRAMER,
INCORPORATED

1893

EVANSTON AND GLENBROOK
HOSPITALS

1893

INLAND STEEL
INDUSTRIES, INC.

1894

ERNST & YOUNG

1894

HOUSEHOLD
INTERNATIONAL, INC.

1894

SAINT MARY OF NAZARETH
HOSPITAL CENTER

1896

SCOTT, FORESMAN
AND COMPANY

1896

THE UNIVERSITY OF ILLINOIS
AT CHICAGO

1897

CNA INSURANCE
COMPANIES

1897

LUTHERAN GENERAL
HEALTHSYSTEM

1898

THE BERGHOFF
RESTAURANT

1898

DEPAUL UNIVERSITY

1901

WALGREEN CO.

1904

CHICAGOLAND
CHAMBER OF COMMERCE

EVANSTON AND GLENBROOK HOSPITALS

DURING A TIME WHEN RISING HEALTH CARE COSTS AND HIGHLY SPECIALIZED MEDICAL TREATMENT ARE LEAVING MANY AMERICANS DISILLUSIONED AND CONFUSED, THE EVANSTON HOSPITAL AND ITS SISTER FACILITY, THE GLENBROOK HOSPITAL, ARE RESPONDING BY

controlling costs while delivering excellent, compassionate care.

The Evanston Hospital, a 500-bed teaching hospital located in Evanston, Illinois, celebrated its centennial in 1993. It is a Level I Regional Trauma Center, the highest level designated by the state. The hospital offers all medical specialty and sub-specialty services.

The Glenbrook Hospital, a 125-bed teaching hospital located in Glenview, Illinois, observed its 15th anniversary in 1992. A Level II Regional Trauma Center, Glenbrook provides the same sophisticated level of technology and expert care that is found at The Evanston Hospital. Together, they have annual patient admissions of more than 24,000 and outpatient/emergency room visits totaling more than 180,000 a year.

Scientific investigators at Evanston and Glenbrook Hospitals conduct research in areas including immuno-biology, molecular biology, oncology, cardiovascular disease, and the neurosciences (right).

COMMITTED TO EDUCATION AND RESEARCH

The hospitals share a professional staff of 800 doctors, virtually all of whom are board-certified or board-qualified in their specialty areas and hold faculty appointments at Northwestern University Medical School. Evanston and Glenbrook physicians train more than 150 medical residents annually. Thirty percent of those who graduate from the residency program later join the hospitals' medical staff.

This university relationship has also been important to the focus on research at Evanston and Glenbrook. For example, in April of 1993 Northwestern University Medical School was selected as one of 16 sites across the nation to participate in the NIH Women's Health Initiative, the largest clinical trial ever held, which will examine heart disease, cancer, stroke, and osteoporosis in post-menopausal women. The

Evanston Hospital is the primary hospital site for this study.

In addition, Evanston and Glenbrook are the only hospitals in the Chicago area to participate in the National Institutes of Health Community Clinical Oncology Program, which gives patients access to many new cancer treatments.

The hospitals treat more patients with breast cancer, colon cancer, and malignant melanoma than any other institution in Illinois. They treat the second largest number of patients in the state with non-Hodgkin's lymphomas; the third largest number with brain cancer and cancer of the pancreas; and the fourth largest number with leukemia and cancers of the prostate, bladder, and rectum. Evanston and Glenbrook also have the Midwest's largest brain tumor program, which has been funded continuously by NIH since 1970 and receives referrals from all over the country.

Additional research in immunobi-

ology, molecular biology, oncology, cardiovascular disease, and the neurosciences is conducted by about 50 scientific investigators throughout the hospital. The new Center for MR Research at Northwestern University/Evanston Research Park recently opened. As the first center of its kind in Chicago and one of a few in the United States, it brings together physicians and scientists to study the power of imaging techniques to diagnose disease.

The leadership of the hospitals in clinical research was enhanced in 1992 by the opening of the new 24-bed Searle/Evanston Hospital Clinical Pharmacology Unit, which conducts clinical trials on the latest drug therapies.

"It is vital to carry out research today to strengthen the chances of survival for the patients of tomorrow," says Nicholas A. Vick, M.D., head of neurology at Evanston Hospital and professor at Northwestern University Medical School.

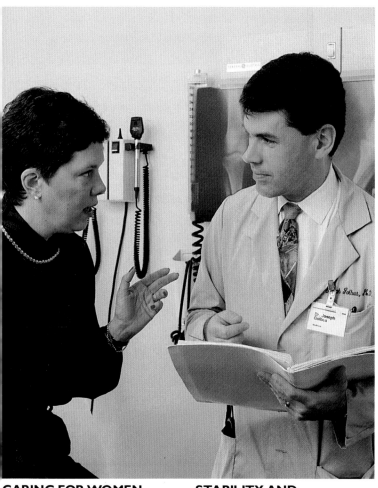

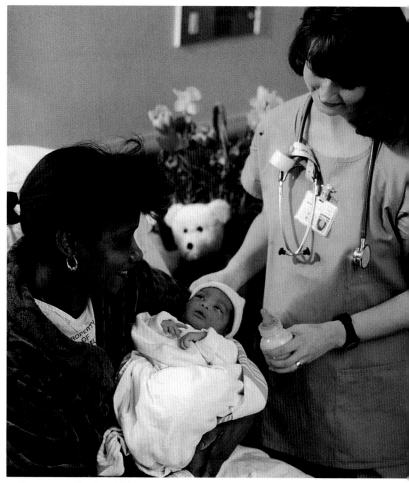

CARING FOR WOMEN AND INFANTS

The Evanston Women's Hospital offers a full range of care for women and children. It is a Level III Perinatal Center, the highest level designated by the state, for high-risk mothers and infants. With a comprehensive team of experienced obstetricians and specially trained nurses, it is a wonderful place to have a baby. The women's hospital has one of the highest survival rates in the city for extremely premature babies, and one of the lowest rates for cesarean sections.

The Fertility Center of Evanston and Glenbrook is nationally recognized for its success in combating infertility factors in both men and women. Thousands of babies have been born as a result of this highly acclaimed program.

STABILITY AND COMMUNITY SUPPORT

Over the years, extraordinary management stability and leadership have made a significant contribution to the strength of the Evanston and Glenbrook Hospitals. The average tenure of top administrators at both facilities is 15 years, compared to an average of three at most other hospitals in the country.

Mark R. Neaman, president and chief executive officer of the Evanston Hospital Corporation, which owns and operates Evanston and Glenbrook, has been with the system for 18 years. Raymond Grady, Evanston's president, and Jeffrey H. Hillebrand, Glenbrook's president and senior vice president of Evanston Hospital Corporation, have each been with the corporation for more than 12 years.

The Evanston and Glenbrook Hospitals are good neighbors to their communities. Emergency care is provided to more than 53,000 patients annually. In 1992, about $15 million in subsidized care was provided to low-income families. Educational classes, seminars, support groups, and preventive screenings are also offered throughout the year.

The hospitals are also a major source of employment. In fact, The Evanston Hospital is the second largest employer in Evanston. Both hospitals work closely with local youth programs and high schools to provide training and jobs in health care.

With a century-long heritage of caring, the Evanston and Glenbrook Hospitals are looking forward to another 100 years of health care excellence. A commitment to superior patient care, enhanced by renowned medical education and research programs, will continue to inspire the physicians and staff of both hospitals into the future.

Doctors at Evanston and Glenbrook Hospitals not only care for patients but also hold faculty appointments at Northwestern University Medical School (above left).

With a comprehensive team of experienced obstetricians and specially trained nurses (above), Evanston Women's Hospital is a wonderful place to have a baby.

WM. WRIGLEY JR. COMPANY

W HEN A TALENTED YOUNG SALESMAN NAMED WILLIAM WRIGLEY JR. ARRIVED IN CHICAGO IN THE SPRING OF 1891, HE HAD $32 IN HIS POCKET AND A LOT OF AMBITION. TODAY, THE WM. WRIGLEY JR. COMPANY IS THE LARGEST CHEWING GUM ENTERPRISE IN THE UNITED

States, employing more than 2,000 people in the Chicago area and more than 6,200 worldwide.

DETERMINING THE WINNING PRODUCT

Manufacturing and selling gum was not how William Wrigley originally planned to make his mark on the world. He started out in Chicago selling Wrigley's Scouring Soap, a product his father manufactured in Philadelphia. To encourage merchants to buy his stock, he offered them a selection of premiums. Eventually, one of them, baking powder, proved to be more popular than the soap, so Wrigley switched the focus of his efforts to selling baking powder.

A master marketer, Wrigley saw the company's early brands (above) achieve international recognition.

William Wrigley Jr. (above right) founded the Wm. Wrigley Jr. Company in Chicago in 1891.

In 1892, Wrigley began offering two packages of chewing gum with each can of baking powder. Once again, the premium seemed more promising than the product it was supposed to promote. As a result, Wrigley began marketing chewing gum under his own brand names: Lotta and Vassar. In 1893, the now familiar Juicy Fruit and Wrigley's Spearmint brands were introduced.

Getting a foothold in the chewing gum business was not easy; existing companies offered better known products, and the competition was fierce. Around the turn of the century, Wrigley's enterprise almost failed, but the determined businessman forged ahead, using his many talents to keep the company afloat. Wrigley did much of the selling himself, traveling widely and meeting with wholesalers and retailers across the country. He had a gift for seeing his customers' point of view and accommodating their needs, and the company grew under his leadership. His use of premiums as sales incentives continued to be so popular that he published a catalog of items for merchants to choose from.

A MASTER MARKETER

A pioneer in promoting brand recognition, Wrigley saw that consumer acceptance of his gum could be built faster by telling people about the benefits of his product through newspaper and magazine ads, posters, and other forms of advertising. As consumers began asking for Wrigley's gum, storekeepers would naturally want to keep a sufficient supply on hand.

In 1906, Wrigley put his faith in advertising to the test with a modest campaign in Buffalo, Rochester, and Syracuse, New York to promote Wrigley's Spearmint gum, at that time a slow seller. The results of the campaign were encouraging. As his competitors cut back on their advertising budgets, Wrigley seized the opportunity with a campaign for Wrigley's Spearmint in New York City where two previous campaigns had failed. This time, the effort was so successful that he expanded it to other cities. By 1910, Wrigley's Spearmint was America's favorite chewing gum. Doublemint gum was introduced in 1914 and quickly became another nationwide favorite.

The Wm. Wrigley Jr. Company rapidly grew into an international

business, and its brands became known the world over. The first Wrigley factory outside the United States was built in Canada in 1910. A second opened in Australia in 1915, and a third began operations in Great Britain in 1927. Additional factories were opened as the Wrigley Company expanded its global market.

BUILDING AN ARCHITECTURAL LANDMARK

In addition to its extensive manufacturing operations, one of the company's most important contributions to Chicago is its headquarters, the Wrigley Building. Located at Michigan Avenue and the Chicago River, the structure has become one of the city's most famous skyscrapers.

Construction began in 1920, and the 30-story south section with its well-known clock was completed in 1921. The 21-story north section was completed in 1924, and in 1931 a walkway was added at the 14th floor to connect the ornate Renaissance-style sections. The nighttime floodlighting of the Wrigley Building makes it one of the most easily recognized features of Chicago's skyline.

THE NEXT GENERATION

When William Wrigley Jr. died in 1932, his son, Philip K. Wrigley,

took command of the business. The younger Wrigley soon demonstrated the same resourcefulness and business sense of his father.

During World War II, for example, Philip Wrigley led the company in an unusual move to protect the reputation of its brands. Because of the war, supplies of top-grade ingredients used to produce the gum were limited, while demand for the product had increased. The company shipped large quantities to the Armed Forces, but eventually had to take Wrigley's Spearmint, Doublemint, and Juicy Fruit off the civilian market. Because the company felt these products were not quite up to the standards of the Wrigley label, in their place, Wrigley developed a wartime product for civilians called Orbit.

Not long after that, top-grade ingredients became so scarce that the company completely halted production of its established brands and began supplying Orbit, its only product, to the Armed Forces. A unique advertising campaign was developed to keep the Wrigley name fresh in consumers' minds during its absence from the market. The ads featured a picture of an empty Wrigley's Spearmint gum wrapper with the slogan, "Remember this wrapper!"

Following the war, the company was again able to purchase high-quality ingredients and resumed production of the established brands. Wrigley's Spearmint was back on the market in 1946, Juicy Fruit followed later that year, and Doublemint reappeared in 1947. The three brands quickly regained and then exceeded their pre-war popularity.

Once Wrigley's regular brands were re-established, the company began concentrating on global expansion. Sales offices were opened throughout Asia and Europe. Factories were built in the Philippines in 1965, France in 1967, Austria in 1968, Kenya in 1971, and Taiwan in 1978. In the spring of 1991, 100 years after its founding, the Wrigley Company broke ground for a factory in Guangzhou, China.

During 1961, in the midst of market expansion, Philip Wrigley was elected chairman of the board, and his son, William Wrigley, became president, marking the third generation in the Wrigley family to lead the business. Philip Wrigley passed away in April 1977, and since then his son has continued as president and chief executive officer of the company.

MEETING CONSUMER NEEDS

To meet changing consumer tastes in the U.S. market, the company introduced non-tack Freedent gum,

Big Red cinnamon gum, and Hubba Bubba bubble gum in the mid-1970s. Extra sugarfree gum was introduced in 1984. Today, Wrigley brands make up approximately one-half of the chewing gum market in the United States. "About 50 percent of Americans chew gum, and 50 percent of those consumers chew Wrigley's," says Vice President-Corporate Affairs and Secretary William Piet.

Throughout its history, the Wrigley Company has maintained high product standards and applied innovation, creativity, and determination to every facet of its operations. After more than 100 years as an American pioneer, the Wm. Wrigley Jr. Company still upholds one basic principle: "Even in a little thing like a stick of gum, quality is important."

This advertisement (above) was used to keep the name and quality of Wrigley's gum in consumers' minds during World War II.

On May 8, 1991, the Wrigley Company displayed an eight-story by four-story flag (left) to honor the U.S. troops returning home from the Persian Gulf War.

DRAPER AND KRAMER, INCORPORATED

C ELEBRATING ITS CENTENNIAL IN 1993, DRAPER AND KRAMER, INCORPO-
RATED IS ONE OF THE OLDEST REAL ESTATE FIRMS IN CHICAGO AND THE
UNITED STATES. IN A CONSTANTLY CHANGING INDUSTRY WITH NEW
CHALLENGES AT EVERY CORNER, DRAPER AND KRAMER HAS SURVIVED

Developed, leased, and managed by Draper and Kramer, 33 West Monroe has served as the firm's headquarters since 1980 (below).

the economic ups and downs and is beginning its second century of serving the real estate needs of Chicago and the country.

Today, more than 500 people, including 350 in the corporate head-quarters at 33 West Monroe Street, are employed by the firm in the Chicago area. Draper and Kramer oversees an additional 2,000 project-specific employees nationwide.

The privately-owned firm pro-vides a full spectrum of property and financial services. Property services include management, marketing, leasing, sales, and development and construction management for resi-dential, office, industrial, and retail properties. Financial services in-clude mortgage financing, pension fund advisory, financial consulting, appraisal, receivership, real estate tax, and insurance services. Draper and Kramer's diverse client base includes corporations, private and institutional owners and investors, government agencies, condominium associations, and foundations.

FOUNDED IN 1893

The company has experienced tre-mendous growth since its founding in the late 19th century, a time of economic hardship for the entire nation. As American businesses struggled through a devastating depression, Chicago staged the World's Columbian Exposition on the city's South Side in 1893 in hopes of encouraging a recovery.

That same year, two ambitious

Chicagoans, Arthur W. Draper and Adolph F. Kramer, defied the odds and formed a small real estate brokerage and mortgage company. By the turn of the century, the business was enjoying success, and Draper and Kramer eventually grew to become one of Chicago's most important real estate management, brokerage, and mortgage firms.

100 YEARS OF FAMILY OWNERSHIP AND EXPERIENCE

A century after its founding, the firm is still owned and managed by the Kramer family. Ferdinand Kramer, the son of founder Adolph Kramer, serves as chairman of the board. His son Douglas is president of the firm, and son Anthony is executive vice president and treas-urer. With three generations of fam-ily ownership, Draper and Kramer's depth of experience and consistency of management are virtually un-matched. Family ownership has also simplified the decision-making pro-cess, allowing the firm to act quickly when important decisions are required.

Draper and Kramer's longevity has given it a level of expertise that serves both the company and its clients well today. The experience that only a century of service can bring is among the attributes most

HEDRICH-BLESSING

Right: Draper and Kramer in the 1910s: Founders Arthur W. Draper (foreground at desk) and Adolph F. Kramer (at right, giving dictation), as well as current chairman Ferdinand Kramer (in knickers and cap).

Far right: Draper and Kramer is still family-controlled today. From left: Douglas Kramer (president), Ferdinand Kramer (chairman), and Anthony Kramer (executive vice president and treasurer).

valued by the firm's clients. The systems and methods that Draper and Kramer has developed over the years contribute to efficiency and add value to every service the company provides.

Sound judgment is another quality the firm's clients have come to appreciate. Its depth of experience is a strong foundation for making recommendations, providing the right solutions, and knowing what's important for clients.

Although "teamwork" has become a buzzword in recent years, it's no cliche at Draper and Kramer. In fact, the team approach is the foundation of the firm's commitment to customer service. A team of experts, each certified in his or her respective field, can be assembled to address most any client need. Because all of Draper and Kramer's team members are employed in-house, they often have worked together before, resulting in a level of efficiency that is rarely possible with outside consultants.

Draper and Kramer is highly compartmentalized to ensure the specialized expertise and focus of each department. For example, residential and commercial property management services are provided by separate divisions. The residential management staff is further divided into rental and condominium groups, and the commercial

management division is divided into office, industrial, and retail groups. By applying this philosophy of specialization throughout its practice, the firm is able to assign qualified people with specific experience to each project or client need. Property managers, architects, certified public accountants, attorneys, financial analysts, appraisers, and other professionals are among the experts available in-house.

DEVELOPING CHICAGO
After World War II, the company moved into real estate development. The firm's first postwar endeavor was a faculty housing project for the University of Chicago at 56th Street and Dorchester Avenue, completed in 1948. Two years later, Draper and Kramer started constructing the 1350-60 North Lake Shore Drive apartments on the site of the old Potter Palmer mansion. The twin towers were the first apartment high-rise buildings to be constructed on Lake Shore Drive during the postwar years.

Other successful developments followed, including 4800 Chicago Beach Drive (728 units) in 1963, the 43-story building at 1130 S. Michigan Avenue (656 units) in 1967, 2626 Lake View (492 units) in the Lincoln Park neighborhood in 1968, and 1700 E. 56th Street (369 units) in 1969. Completed in 1990, The

Chicagoan (221 units) at 750 N. Rush Street is one of Draper and Kramer's most recent residential developments.

The 1980s marked a peak in the company's development activities, beginning with the completion of its corporate headquarters at 33 West Monroe in 1980. The 842,800-square-foot building, which contains three atriums, is noted as one of the first multi-atrium buildings constructed in the United States. Other notable projects in the Chicago area in which Draper and Kramer played

Above left: 1350-60 North Lake Shore Drive (740 units) were the first apartment high-rises to be constructed on Lake Shore Drive following World War II.

The Chicagoan (above), located just off Michigan Avenue, is Draper and Kramer's most recent residential development.

Completed in 1990, Bradley Place Business Center (above) is believed to be the first new industrial park built within city limits in over 20 years.

Right: 33 West Monroe is one of the first multi-atrium buildings constructed in the United States.

a development role include Regent Business Center in Elk Grove Village, Oakmont Circle in Westmont, and award-winning Bradley Place Business Center in Chicago.

To date, the firm has developed or provided development consulting services for over 10 million square feet of office, industrial, retail, and residential properties nationwide, including approximately 7.5 million square feet in the Chicago metropolitan area.

Since its inception, Draper and Kramer has also been a leader in mortgage financing. Notable projects for which the company arranged financing include the first new postwar town in suburban Chicago, Park Forest, and Chicago's landmark shopping mall, Water Tower Place. In addition, Draper and Kramer has financed, leased, and managed five of the largest shopping centers in the Chicago area, including Old Orchard in Skokie, Oakbrook Center in Oak Brook, River Oaks in Calumet City, Hawthorn Center in Vernon Hills, and Fox Valley in Aurora.

COMPANY SERVICES

Draper and Kramer provides a wide range of real estate and financial services, including development, mortgage financing, property management, leasing, sales, real estate tax, insurance, appraisal, and advisory services.

Draper and Kramer's professional

property management group employs highly skilled specialists who recognize the complexity of property management and accept the challenge with enthusiasm. Successful management requires an attention to detail and an understanding of the personal element of the business. Whether managing an office, industrial, retail, or residential property, the firm's professional staff knows how to deal with the array of legal, financial, operational, and technical aspects of management. They are also skilled at maintaining a pleasant working or living environment for the tenants of the buildings they manage.

The firm currently manages approximately 41 million square feet of office, industrial, retail, and residential space, including more than 25,000 residential units in Chicago and other major urban areas.

Draper and Kramer's real estate brokerage (sales and leasing) staff utilizes the firm's longtime experience and state-of-the-art information and communications resources to

provide complete, centralized national real estate brokerage services. With a solid knowledge of property values and locations, the company can help its clients relocate, locate a suitable site, or find a compatible tenant or buyer for any property. In addition, Draper and Kramer maintains a separate residential brokerage office on Chicago's Near North Side where its staff represents both buyers and sellers of residential property.

Another Draper and Kramer division, mortgage financing, is divided into two groups—residential and commercial. This structure allows the firm to offer its clients specialized guidance and service, from origination to closing to servicing of the loan. Each group is staffed with trained, experienced professionals who are capable of providing all types of real estate financing, from single-family home loans to the complex financial requirements of a multi-use complex. The company currently services a portfolio valued at $2 billion.

304

The firm's real estate tax division is a recent addition to the broad spectrum of services offered through Draper and Kramer. Established in 1984, the division now administers more than 10 million square feet of office, retail, industrial, and multi-family properties for a select group of institutional clients. The tax division's services include research, property inspection, compliance preparation, representation, and tax planning to establish long-term tax minimization.

In response to volatile conditions in the real estate industry, D&K Realty Advisors, Inc., a wholly owned subsidiary of Draper and Kramer, was formed in 1987 to provide additional specialized real estate services for pension funds, investment trusts, and partnerships with real estate holdings. These services may include investment services, market evaluation, physical assessment or appraisal, operational review, and financial feasibility analysis.

A GOOD CORPORATE CITIZEN

Draper and Kramer has been very civic-minded throughout its history. In the early 1950s, for example, when Michael Reese Hospital considered moving from the deteriorated neighborhood that surrounded it, Ferdinand Kramer, a former member of the Reese board of directors, proposed and helped implement plans to revitalize the area through slum clearance and redevelopment. The first residential project of the South Side Planning Board—a coalition of business and community interests including Draper and Kramer, Michael Reese, Mercy Hospital, and the Illinois Institute of Technology—was the 2,009-unit Lake Meadows complex built on a 70-acre tract at Martin Lutheran King Drive between 31st and 35th streets. Kramer also spear-headed the development of Prairie Shores, a complex of five 19-story residential buildings adjacent to the hospital that provided 1,678 apartments to the area. The project was

completed in 1962.

A more recent example of the firm's community involvement is Dearborn Park, a project which Draper and Kramer helped launch. The residential development is situated on 51 acres of abandoned south Loop railway land just south of the long-closed Dearborn Street train station. Since the project was begun in the mid-1970s, it has revitalized the economy of a blighted area, provided a new anchor for south Loop businesses, and significantly increased tax revenues for the city. Phase I of the project produced over 1,000 units, including three mid-rise buildings, three high-rise buildings, a 192-unit apartment building for the elderly, and 166 townhouses. Phase II, still under development, will include approximately 800 individual homes and townhouses.

As Draper and Kramer begins its second century in the real estate industry, this family-owned Chicago business will continue to build on its traditions of service, experience, and hard work. The firm looks forward to continuing its record of steady growth and community involvement, as it has since its founding in the tough economic times of the 19th century.

Prairie Shores (left), a five-building residential project, helped revitalize the city's South Side.

Not since the original Burnham-Wacker Plan was promulgated at the turn of the century has any one project had as profound an effect on the city's development as the creation of Dearborn Park (above).

305

INLAND STEEL INDUSTRIES, INC.

THE YEAR 1893 WAS NO TIME TO LAUNCH A NEW BUSINESS. THERE WAS A DEPRESSION, AND MONEY WAS SCARCE. YET JOSEPH BLOCK, A CINCINNATI DEALER IN OLD RAILROAD MATERIAL VISITING THE COLUMBIAN EXPOSITION IN CHICAGO, RECOGNIZED THE OPPORTUNITY FOR A NEW

enterprise. Along with his son, Philip, and six others, Block raised $130,000 to start the Inland Steel Company, which was incorporated on October 30. By the end of January 1894, machinery purchased from a bankrupt Chicago steel works was rolling reheated rails into fencing, plow beams, and other agricultural implements in suburban

Located near South Bend, Indiana, I/N Tek is the most advanced cold-rolling mill in the world, a successful blend of sophisticated technology and commercial and industrial leadership.

Robert J. Darnall serves as chairman of the board for Inland Steel Industries, Inc. (right).

Chicago Heights, 27 miles south of the city.

Today, as the nation's fifth largest steel producer, Inland is celebrating its 100th anniversary with the theme, "Beginning a Second Century of Progress." Headquartered in Chicago, Inland has had a long and rewarding association with the city and the Midwest. As the nation's primary manufacturing region developed, Inland grew along with it, contributing to and benefiting from the development of the Midwest manufacturing base.

Seven years after Inland was established, the company's founders envisioned the future of American steelmaking on the shores of Lake Michigan and accepted a new challenge. Fifty acres of duneland in nearby East Chicago, Indiana, was offered in exchange for a commitment to invest $1 million to build a steel plant there. In July 1902, an Inland open-hearth furnace crew

poured the first ingots ever teemed in what is now the nation's largest steelmaking region.

Today, Inland's Indiana Harbor Works covers more than 1,900 acres and can produce up to 6 million tons of raw steel a year. One of the nation's largest steel plants, the complex has poured more than 310 million tons. Throughout its history, Inland has accepted risks and made investments enabling its employees to produce the materials used in manufactured products—such as automobiles and appliances—that have improved America's quality of life.

In 1986, Inland Steel Industries, Inc., was formed as a holding company for Inland Steel Company and the Inland Materials Distribution Group, Inc., the nation's largest steel service center network. A new business unit, Magnetics International, Inc., began manufacturing high-quality iron oxide in 1991. Inland Steel Industries employs some 17,000 people nationwide at its steel facilities, mines, and service centers. The company has assets of more than $3.1 billion and annual sales of $3.5 billion.

INLAND STEEL COMPANY TODAY

Inland Steel Company operates two divisions: Inland Steel Flat Products Company and Inland Steel Bar Company. The flat products division accounts for 80 percent of the steel company's total assets. It manufactures sheet, strip, and plate principally for the automotive, appliance, office furniture, electrical motor, and service center industries. The bar division manufactures high-quality bar products for the transportation industry, forgers, heavy-equipment manufacturers, cold finishers, and service centers.

Over the years, Inland has been a pioneer in steel manufacturing tech-

nology, anticipating and meeting the changing needs of the marketplace. The latest examples are two joint ventures with Japan's Nippon Steel Corporation, the world's largest steel producer. Through a combined investment of $1.1 billion—the largest American-Japanese partnership in the United States—the companies have built two state-of-the-art steel

finishing facilities, I/N Tek and I/N Kote, near South Bend, Indiana.

Completed in 1990, I/N Tek is the most advanced cold-rolling mill in the world, a successful blend of sophisticated technology and commercial and industrial leadership. I/N Tek reduces the production time of the five-step cold-rolling and finishing process from 12 days to less than one hour, and its products far exceed the industry's quality standards.

I/N Kote, which began production in late 1991, was designed to make Inland the nation's premier producer of coated sheet steel. The plant supplies automakers in the United States—both American and Japanese—with the finest corrosion-resistant steel.

Combined, I/N Tek and I/N Kote are capable of annually producing 1.9 million tons of the highest quality cold-rolled and coated sheet products in the United States.

INLAND MATERIALS DISTRIBUTION GROUP, INC.

Inland's strategic thinking, during a time when corporate strategies were not yet in vogue, brought the company together with Joseph T. Ryerson & Son in 1935. At the time, the 93-year-old Ryerson was already the world's largest steel warehouse organization, while Inland, at 42, was becoming a leading steelmaker in the Midwest.

Ryerson's 10 warehouses, located throughout the East and Midwest, had become good customers of Inland, which in turn had developed with Ryerson a reputation for providing quality products and a steady supply of materials. In September 1935, the stockholders of both Chicago-based companies approved a merger plan in which Ryerson became a wholly owned subsidiary of Inland.

Ryerson, which marked its 150th anniversary in 1992, and J.M. Tull Metals, founded in 1914 and acquired by Inland in 1986, comprise the Inland Materials Distribution Group, which has 56 plants nationwide. During the 1980s, Inland expanded its service center business to dampen the cyclical effects of the steel business.

Today, IMDG is the nation's largest service center organization and the third largest buyer of steel products after General Motors and Ford. In addition to carbon steel,

IMDG merchandises a variety of metals, including stainless steel, aluminum, nickel, copper, brass, and bronze. It also provides customers with many first-stage processing operations.

LOOKING TO THE FUTURE

With the most modern facilities in both of its business segments, Inland Steel Industries is well positioned to achieve its strategic vision of being the nation's premier producer and marketer of high-quality industrial materials.

In the company's long association with Chicagoland, Inland people have been partners in building and maintaining a vital community. Celebrating its first 100 years, Inland stands ready to meet the challenges of its second century.

Inland's Indiana Harbor Works (top) covers more than 1,900 acres and can produce up to 6 million tons of raw steel a year.

A member of the Inland Materials Distribution Group, Chicago-based Joseph T. Ryerson & Son (bottom) has been a wholly owned subsidiary of Inland since 1935.

Throughout its history, Inland has invested in new equipment (left), enabling its employees to produce materials that have improved America's quality of life.

ERNST & YOUNG

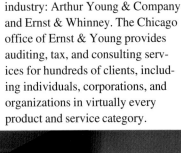

ERNST & YOUNG, ONE OF THE LARGEST PROFESSIONAL SERVICES FIRMS IN THE WORLD, HAS BEEN A LEADING MEMBER OF THE CHICAGO BUSINESS COMMUNITY FOR NEARLY A CENTURY. ◆ TODAY'S ERNST & YOUNG WAS CREATED BY THE HISTORIC MERGER OF TWO GIANTS IN THE ACCOUNTING

industry: Arthur Young & Company and Ernst & Whinney. The Chicago office of Ernst & Young provides auditing, tax, and consulting services for hundreds of clients, including individuals, corporations, and organizations in virtually every product and service category.

Clients and visitors to Ernst & Young's new Chicago headquarters enter through an impressive lobby (below) and attend meetings in conference rooms overlooking the busy south Loop area.

Information systems consultants lay plans before moving out to client sites to design and implement cutting-edge computer systems.

TURN-OF-THE-CENTURY BEGINNINGS

Arthur Young was a Scotsman who came to the United States near the turn of the century to seek his fortune. In 1894, he founded an accounting firm in Chicago with C.U. Stuart, a business associate at the banking and investment firm where Young was first employed. Young was drawn to Chicago because of its enterprising and vigorous business community and the geographical prominence of Lake Michigan.

With $500 in capital and one stenographer, Stuart & Young opened its doors in the Monadnock Building, then the tallest structure in Chicago. After 12 years in business, the firm was dissolved, and Young formed Arthur Young & Company with his brother, Stanley Young.

Meanwhile, A.C. Ernst opened the Chicago office of Ernst & Ernst in 1908 in the First National Bank Building downtown at Clark and Washington streets. Ernst, who had founded his firm in 1903 in Cleveland, sought to better serve his clients and expand his Midwestern base. Since 1923, the firm had maintained a working agreement with Whinney, Murray & Co. of England, and the two firms had conducted their international business under a third name—Whinney, Murray, Ernst & Ernst. In 1979, the entire operation merged to become Ernst & Whinney, establishing a single business name worldwide.

Ten years later, Ernst & Whinney and Arthur Young & Company merged to form Ernst & Young. The new firm consolidated its three Chicago Loop offices in the Sears Tower in 1992, making its home once again in the tallest building not only in Chicago, but in the world.

ORGANIZING TALENT TO SERVE CLIENTS

While the involvement of many accounting firms with their clients begins and ends with the audit, Ernst & Young offers a host of consulting services as part of its mission to be a preeminent business advisor. The firm's Great Lakes Management Consulting Group, which serves the Great Lakes and North Central regions of the United States through consultants in a number of Midwest cities, is headquartered in Chicago.

More than 450 information systems and performance improvement consultants are based in the city. The information technology practice provides solutions in all phases of systems—planning, analysis, design, construction, and implementation. Performance improvement consultants focus on reducing client operating costs while improving quality and customer satisfaction. Also based in Chicago are consultants in health care, compensation and employee benefits, actuarial services, reorganization, insolvency, mergers and acquisition, due diligence, international tax, state and local tax, and corporate finance.

The audit, tax, and consulting professionals at Ernst & Young also work side by side within distinct industry/functional groups—health care, manufacturing, consumer products, insurance, financial services (including real estate and mutual funds), and entrepreneurial services. This industry specialization allows the firm to serve clients' needs more efficiently and comprehensively by concentrating talent and focusing the experience, knowledge, and skills of its professionals on the industries they know best. Consequently, the in-depth solutions Ernst & Young provides are based on a thorough understanding of the special variables affecting a client's particular industry or business segment.

With an effective organizational structure in place, the Chicago office has become a leader in numerous industries. The local office reflects the status of Ernst & Young's international organization, whose

manufacturing specialists have made it the leading audit, tax, and consulting firm for the Fortune 500's largest industrial companies.

Ernst & Young has the largest health care practice among professional services firms in Chicago, where the firm has served virtually all of the larger hospitals in the metropolitan area.

In financial services, Ernst & Young Chicago is one of the leading professional services firms serving banks, thrifts, insurance companies, mutual funds, and the real estate industry. In addition to audit and tax work, the firm advises banks and thrifts in capital deployment, profitability, and new product development. Ernst & Young also provides audit, tax, and consulting services to leading Chicago-area developers, brokers, and managers.

Responding to needs in the marketplace, Ernst & Young established

an entrepreneurial services group in 1981 to provide private companies with the same caliber of financial and tax services that the firm has for years offered to publicly held companies. Members of the group must demonstrate a sophisticated knowl-

edge of the unique financial and tax requirements of private companies and also possess a dedication to establish long-term relationships with company executives.

Ernst & Young has long been Chicago's leading professional services firm for tax-exempt organizations. The firm audits many of the largest Chicago-based trade associations and civic, charitable, religious, educational, and cultural organizations.

With a century of experience to shape and refine its performance, Ernst & Young Chicago offers its clients a superior level of service, knowledge, and commitment. One of the largest and oldest professional services firms in the world, this venerable organization is also an industry leader with the vision and resources to offer the innovative solutions demanded by an ever-changing marketplace.

In mid-1992, Ernst & Young consolidated its Chicago personnel from three downtown locations into newly designed and constructed offices in the Sears Tower, the world's tallest building (above).

Ernst & Young's Chicago auditors, tax professionals, and management consultants are integrated into industry and functional groups (top left) whose leaders meet regularly to share ideas on how best to provide total business solutions to the firm's clients.

The firm's new offices (bottom left) provide many open areas where teamwork and idea sharing are fostered.

HOUSEHOLD INTERNATIONAL, INC.

N BUSINESS, SOME COMPANIES SUCCEED WITHIN WELL-DEFINED ENVIRONMENTS, BUT A FEW ACTUALLY CREATE AND SHAPE FOR THE BETTER THE WORLD IN WHICH THEY OPERATE. HOUSEHOLD INTERNATIONAL, INC., THE NATION'S OLDEST AND LEADING CONSUMER FINANCE COMPANY, IS ONE OF THESE FEW.

Household International is known primarily as the parent of its largest subsidiary, Household Finance Corp. (HFC), which has offered financial services and products to consumers and small businesses for 115 years. Household International was created in 1981 as the parent company for HFC and a number of other companies that had been acquired by the organization.

ORIGINS OF HFC

The enterprise that would become Household Finance Corp. was started by Frank S. Mackey in the back of a Minneapolis jewelry store in 1878. In 1894, HFC, which at that time had 14 offices in the Midwest, relocated its corporate headquarters to Chicago. The company moved again in 1978 to its current headquarters facility in northwest suburban Prospect Heights.

Today, Household International is the parent company of several financial services firms in addition to HFC, and serves more than 10 million customers in the United States, Canada, the United Kingdom, and

Australia. In 1992, the corporation, with over $30 billion in total assets, was ranked by *Forbes* magazine as the 59th largest public company in the United States.

A progressive organization, Household International takes pride in the fact that it offers its 15,500 employees child and elder care, parental leave, and even adoption benefits. Following a tradition established early on by HFC, company executives and staff participate in countless charitable and volunteer activities. In 1992, the company's matching gift program for direct employee donations netted approximately $2.5 million for over 2,000 organizations.

PROMOTING HIGH INDUSTRY STANDARDS

Household International's founding organization, HFC, was an early leader in developing fair and consistent practices and regulatory policies for the consumer finance industry. These efforts lessened the loan-sharking that hurt American consumers during the early part of the 20th century and helped draw more ethical businesses into the industry.

In 1916, for example, HFC began working with the Russell Sage Foundation, a philanthropic group, to develop the first Uniform Small Loan Law, which established customer lending procedures for brokers of small personal loans. This

Household Finance Corporation is the country's oldest consumer finance company. For many decades, HFC operated from small neighborhood offices, but suburban growth dictated the development of larger customer service centers in communities such as Buffalo Grove, Illinois (right).

Household International has been a Chicagoland company since 1894, when HFC came to the area from its Minneapolis birthplace. The firm moved to its present headquarters in Prospect Heights in 1978 (below).

legislation made great strides in protecting consumers from unfair lending practices. HFC also pioneered development of the monthly installment payment plan for consumer loans in 1905.

In 1928, HFC was the first consumer finance company to offer stock and be listed on the New York Stock Exchange. In the 1930s and '40s, HFC expanded its operations to Canada and adopted the HFC company logo that remains a unifying corporate symbol.

After spending much of its early history charting the realm of consumer finance, HFC embarked on an ambitious diversification program in 1961 when it purchased the Coast-to-Coast chain of retail stores. Numerous other acquisitions of retail and manufacturing firms followed during the 1960s.

RETURNING TO FINANCIAL SERVICES ROOTS

In the mid-1980s, Household refocused its growth and acquisition efforts on its origin in financial services. The companies subsequently developed were Household Bank, FSB, a federally chartered savings bank with assets of approximately $9 billion; Household Mortgage Services, a unit of Household Bank and one of the five largest thrift mortgage services in the nation; Household Credit Services, the eighth largest issuer of Visa and MasterCard bank cards; Household Retail Services, the second largest issuer of retail credit cards for merchants nationwide; and Alexander Hamilton Life Insurance Co., which offers a variety of universal life insurance, annuity, and credit/specialty insurance products and has been rated A+ Superior by the A.M. Best Company every year since 1978. Household also is the parent of Hamilton Investments, a Midwestern investment banking and brokerage firm, and Household Commercial Financial Services, which

provides a variety of commercial and corporate finance services.

During the 1980s, the company also pursued a goal of divesting itself of its manufacturing and retail concerns. The last of those entities was sold in 1989.

Continuing its focus on financial services, Household International joined with Ameritech Corp. in 1991 to issue a combination credit and calling card, which brought in nearly 500,000 new customer accounts. Another more recent credit card effort involves a partnership with General Motors Corp. to manage the automaker's new credit card. Launched in September 1992, this venture will significantly increase Household International's 4 million credit card customers and $4 billion

in credit card receivables. The General Motors credit card has already enjoyed one of the most successful introductions ever for a credit card, having attracted about 3 million new accounts as of January 1993.

A pioneer as well as a giant in the world of financial services, the organization that is today Household International has thrived for more than a century by setting high standards for its industry, by being proactive rather than reactive, and by intelligently seizing opportunities for growth. The company's primary goal for the future is to continue on its course of serving the financial needs of customers in the four countries in which it operates.

Household International's program for automating and centralizing account administration has resulted in significant productivity gains while improving customer service. Household companies help each other develop processing technology and share processing facilities such as this regional center in Wood Dale, Illinois.

SAINT MARY OF NAZARETH HOSPITAL CENTER

FOR 100 YEARS (1894-1994), SAINT MARY OF NAZARETH HOSPITAL CENTER HAS STOOD AS A KEY MEDICAL RESOURCE FOR RESIDENTS OF CHICAGO'S NORTHWEST SIDE. ♦ THE "COMMUNITY" HOSPITAL WAS ESTABLISHED IN 1894 BY BLESSED FRANCES SIEDLISKA, A POLISH NUN WHO FOUNDED THE

Congregation of the Holy Family of Nazareth. Mother Mary of Jesus the Good Shepherd (Siedliska's religious name) commissioned her order to build a hospital in Chicago that would provide care for Polish immigrants in a familiar religious and cultural setting.

The original hospital building, formerly a private home, was a modest, three-story brownstone located near Noble and Division streets. By 1901, the building could no longer accommodate the hospital's growing patient load, and the Sisters opened a new facility at 1120 N. Leavitt Street. Several additions were made over the years at that location, increasing the hospital's capacity to 300 beds.

In 1975, a new 16-story, 458,460-square-foot facility opened at 2233 W. Division Street, just 15 minutes from downtown Chicago and about one mile from the Kennedy Expressway. The hospital, with 485 licensed beds, has remained in that location ever since, undergoing several expansions and renovations to update its services. Satellite facilities in Chicago's West Town, Logan Square, and Cragin communities have also been opened and include primary care medical offices, an outpatient testing facility, and an accredited home health care service.

A BROADENING SCOPE

Saint Mary of Nazareth Hospital Center enjoys a century-old tradition of caring for the poor, a mission that remains an important part of its operating philosophy today. While Polish immigrants still make up a significant percentage of the hospital's patient load, its scope has broadened to include Hispanic, Ukrainian, and African-American residents of the neighborhood it serves. From emergency care and surgery to ambulatory care and at-home recovery, the hospital's comprehensive health care services and multi-language capabilities are designed to meet the diverse needs of its patients.

The dedicated staff at Saint Mary of Nazareth makes every effort to provide the kind of attentive service that helps promote patient progress and recovery. Although it is licensed for 485 beds, the hospital currently staffs 285 single-occupancy rooms, guaranteeing privacy for every patient at rates that are competitive with semi-private room rates at other hospitals. Research has demonstrated that single-room care actually improves the speed of recovery. In addition, the admissions process is streamlined because rooms are not held out of service while patients are matched as compatible roommates.

Regardless of the number of beds or cost of service, a hospital's reputation really rests on the skill and compassion of its physicians and support staff. Saint Mary of Nazareth's medical staff of 260 dedicated men and women represents a wide range of training and talent. About 80 percent of its physicians are board-certified in their specialty areas.

The hospital maintains a solid reputation as a leader in applying advanced medical technology to community health needs. From state-of-the-art Magnetic Resonance Imaging services to cardiac diagnostic equipment usually found only in major university medical centers, Saint Mary of Nazareth Hospital Center brings each patient a number of options for conquering disease

Founded in 1894 and celebrating 100 years of community service in 1994, Saint Mary of Nazareth Hospital Center dedicated its third building, a 16-story, 485-licensed-bed facility in 1975 (above).

Saint Mary of Nazareth's medical staff of 260 dedicated men and women represents a wide range of training and talent. About 80 percent of its physicians are board-certified in their specialty areas.

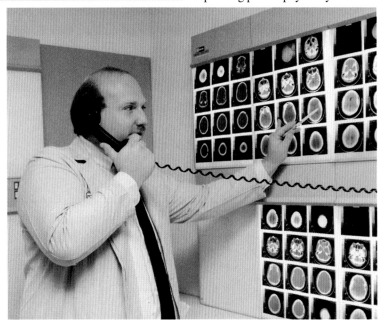

and disability. The hospital's advanced diagnostic treatment technology, combined with the professionalism of its staff, provides the comfort, convenience, and reassurance that patients want from their community hospital.

In addition, the Congregation of the Holy Family of Nazareth, which still operates the hospital today, is dedicated to the promotion of family life and has applied this theme to health care by establishing a unique approach to serving the sick and injured. The hospital's emphasis on the family transforms the routine delivery of medical services to include the intimate involvement of patients and their families in the healing process.

CORE SERVICE AREAS

Saint Mary of Nazareth's approach to community health care on Chicago's northwest side focuses on several core service areas that mirror the major health and medical needs of the local population. For 18 years, the Cardiovascular Center has offered diagnostic and therapeutic services, ranging from open-heart surgery and cardiac rehabilitation to a community heart club.

Established in 1968, the hospital's Mental Health Center is a major community resource for emergency, adult, adolescent, and child

psychiatric services. Its staff is bilingual and bi-cultural in English/ Spanish and English/Polish, reflecting the diverse ethnic backgrounds of the patients it serves.

The five-year-old Cancer Care Center offers a full range of diagnostic and therapeutic services such as surgical oncology, radiation therapy, and chemotherapy provided in both inpatient and outpatient settings.

The hospital's Diabetes Center offers state-of-the-art diagnostic and therapeutic services to diabetics. Opened in 1987, the center emphasizes family-oriented education aimed at coping with the lifestyle changes that are necessary for patients with this condition.

The hospital is also affiliated with 19 managed care organizations, 11 educational institutions, and 16 training programs.

Saint Mary of Nazareth Hospital Center has served the immigrant communities on Chicago's northwest side for 100 years, catering its health care offerings to the unique needs of its neighbors. As it begins a second century of service, the hospital continues that tradition as a modern medical center with a community focus.

Saint Mary of Nazareth is sponsored by the Sisters of the Holy Family of Nazareth (top left), a Roman Catholic congregation of religious women whose foundress, Blessed Frances Siedliska, established the hospital to care for Chicago's Polish immigrants.

A 75-foot stained-glass window (top) stands outside Saint Mary of Nazareth's Chapel of the Holy Family.

Each patient care unit features a central nursing station (bottom) surrounded by single-occupancy patient rooms.

SCOTT, FORESMAN AND COMPANY

SCOTT, FORESMAN AND COMPANY HAS BEEN HELPING EDUCATORS TEACH THE CHILDREN OF AMERICA FOR NEARLY 100 YEARS. SINCE ITS FOUNDING IN 1896, THIS PUBLISHER OF HIGH-QUALITY EDUCATIONAL MATERIALS HAS WORKED IN PARTNERSHIP WITH THE TEACHING PROFESSION TO PROVIDE THE

Scott, Foresman moved to its present Glenview headquarters in 1966. The campus-like setting includes a mile-long walking path in a wooded area and courtyards for outdoor dining and relaxation.

High-tech publishing now replaces traditional design and page layout methods, allowing editors to review textbook pages on the computer screen.

best possible materials for instruction—with a longtime commitment to innovation.

According to Richard E. Peterson, president and chief executive officer, the company's relationship with educators has long been a key to its success. "Scott, Foresman and Company continues its tradition of developing the primary tools used by the teacher in the classroom to facilitate learning," he says.

That tradition is firmly rooted in the beliefs of the company's three founders: Erastus Howard Scott, Hugh A. Foresman, and his brother William Coates Foresman. The trio built the business on a fundamental creed: "We believe we are partners with the teaching profession. That the essence of our product is education itself: the learning that results when the materials we create are used. That our goal is to offer to educators constantly improved programs for teaching and for learning. That courage to pioneer in education is our obligation for our future success."

By adhering to that philosophy, Scott, Foresman has become one of the nation's largest publishers of instructional materials for elementary and high school students, with more than 10,000 books in print. Its products offer 13 levels of instruction for children ages five to 18, including academic courses in reading, literature, mathematics, science, social studies, language arts, foreign language, health, and driver education. The company also is a major publisher of materials used to teach English as a second language, which it markets to schools in the United States and overseas.

With the advent of technology in the classroom, Scott, Foresman once again took an aggressive role in developing, marketing, and distributing related state-of-the-art technol-

ogy such as software, videotapes, cassettes, interactive videos, compact discs, and audio materials.

Headquartered on a 44-acre tract in north suburban Glenview, the company employs about 800 people. It has been wholly owned by Harper-Collins Publishers since 1990 and has annual revenues in excess of $200 million. Regional offices in Oakland, New Jersey; Dallas, Texas; Atlanta, Georgia; and Sunnyvale, California help support its nationwide marketing efforts. The company also maintains a major distribution center in Pinola, Indiana.

AN INNOVATOR IN EDUCATIONAL PUBLISHING

Throughout its history, Scott, Foresman has made publishing history

with many impressive "firsts" in the educational field. One momentous first was the 1935 publication of a dictionary designed especially for children, the *Thorndike-Century Junior Dictionary*. The company also published the first arithmetic text (1911) for students in the primary grades; the first reading primer (1914) with stories based on recognized children's literature; and *The Curriculum Foundation Series* (1932), the first integrated curriculum based on the student's basic reading level. The elementary series included textbooks in the various content areas: health, language arts, mathematics, science, and social studies. The company also published the first instructional materials in the field of modern math (1948) and the first high school driver education text (1954).

One of the company's significant contributions to education occurred in 1930 when it published *The Elson Basic Readers*, the series that introduced the Dick, Jane and Baby (later to be named Sally) characters, who for four decades taught countless individuals to read. The series was created by Dr. William S. Gray, a legend in reading research at the University of Chicago. Dr. Gray's concept proved effective because the story content was based on actual family situations, the vocabulary was strictly controlled, and four-color illustrations were used for the first time in a basic reader.

"Oh, see it work," said Dick.
"See it come up, up, up.
Up comes Tim to Baby Sally."

"Up, up," said Sally.
"Up comes my little Tim.
Up comes Tim to Sally."

That milestone forged a lasting relationship with the University of Chicago that continues today. In 1990, Scott, Foresman teamed up with the university to create a highly successful math series, *The University of Chicago School Mathematics Project, Secondary Component Materials (UCSMP)*. This six-book series, written for the vast majority of students, updates the mathematics content and incorporates real-world applications, among other things.

"*The University of Chicago School Mathematics Project, Secondary Component Materials* series is a bold step forward in the way math is taught at the junior and senior high levels," Peterson says. Thus far, the program's success has exceeded company expectations by 100 percent.

WORKING WITH THE TEACHING PROFESSION

Collaboration with teachers is an ongoing commitment at Scott, Foresman. In fact, teachers are an important part of the decision-making process in product development. "Our employees spend time with America's teachers—in the classrooms and at professional meetings," says Peterson. "They maintain a constant dialogue and a healthy exchange of ideas."

Employees, many of whom have taught in classrooms themselves, also are active in national educational organizations, including the International Reading Association, National Council of Teachers of Mathematics, National Council of Teachers of English, and National Science Teachers Association. Likewise, many of the company's authors hold leadership positions in these groups. To bolster this crucial input from teachers, the company earmarks $15 million to $50 million for the development of each of its elementary instructional programs.

These efforts have led to other ongoing successes in the educational field. One recent example is *Celebrate Reading!*, an advancement in reading instruction that incorporates elements of the Whole Language and Real Literature educational theories. Its components represent innovation in content, teaching methodology, and packaging. "Nobody else has a package like the one we offer," adds Peterson.

It is this constant commitment to innovation that has driven the success of Scott, Foresman and Company for nearly a century. Says Peterson, "There is a real commitment here to education. Our whole success today and tomorrow depends on how well our materials help teachers achieve their goals and mission."

Keeping ahead of the changing times, the new *Celebrate Reading!* offers teachers a wide array of materials, from multi-volume reading books of literature to technology to posters and puppets (above left).

Using a wide range of instructional options—from textbooks to CD-ROMs—*Discover the Wonder* invites students in grades K through 6 to find out how science relates to the world around them (above right).

A textbook page from *The New Way We Come and Go*, 1956 Edition, shows a favorite episode: Sally's teddy is rescued by a steam shovel (left).

THE UNIVERSITY OF ILLINOIS AT CHICAGO

T HE UNIVERSITY OF ILLINOIS AT CHICAGO, THE LARGEST UNIVERSITY IN THE CHICAGO METROPOLITAN AREA, IS BOTH A VERY OLD AND VERY YOUNG INSTITUTION. ♦ UIC TRACES ITS ROOTS BACK TO 1896 WHEN THE UNIVERSITY OF ILLINOIS, FOUNDED 29 YEARS EARLIER IN URBANA-

Champaign, took over private pharmacy and medical schools in Chicago. It absorbed a private dental school in 1901 and added a nursing school in 1943.

After World War II, the University of Illinois opened a two-year undergraduate program on Chicago's Navy Pier to educate returning veterans. The public, however, demanded a four-year campus, so the University of Illinois at Chicago Circle was opened in 1965, just southwest of Chicago's Loop. In 1982, the colleges and schools of the Chicago Circle campus and the University of Illinois Medical Center campus consolidated to become the University of Illinois at Chicago.

A QUALITY UNIVERSITY WITH DIVERSE OFFERINGS

Today, UIC has an enrollment of more than 24,000 students, including more than 8,700 graduate and professional students. The university offers bachelor's degrees in 98 fields, master's degrees in 89 fields, and doctoral degrees in 52 specialties. UIC's 15 colleges make up a diverse university that provides a quality education for many people in the Chicago area and beyond. Approximately 65,000 UIC alumni live in the Chicago area alone.

UIC is one of only 70 higher education institutions in the United States to receive the prestigious Research I designation from the Carnegie Foundation for the Advancement of Teaching, placing it in the same category with the University of Chicago, Northwestern University, and the University of Illinois at Urbana-Champaign.

The campus also boasts a major teaching hospital, the University of Illinois Hospital and Clinics, which has 414 beds and more than 100 outpatient diagnostic and specialty clinics. Built in 1980 to house the most advanced technology available, it provides clinical training for students in the university's colleges of medicine, nursing, pharmacy, dentistry, and associated health professions and the School of Public Health.

The hospital's facilities include the Eye and Ear Infirmary and the Lions of Illinois Eye Research Institute. Located in separate buildings, the programs offer patients both ambulatory services and hospitalization. The Department of Ophthalmology and Otolaryngology-Head and Neck Surgery is internationally recognized for its research and patient care activities.

The University's numerous clinics, many known worldwide for their excellence, provide ambulatory care to patients from the Chicago metropolitan area and across Illinois. The hospital's state-of-the-art emergency facilities see an average of 45,000 patients yearly.

IMPROVING THE QUALITY OF LIFE IN CHICAGO

UIC plays a major role in community-wide efforts to tackle the problems and challenges that Chicago faces as one of the country's largest urban areas. The university has been particularly active in community programs to improve education in public schools and health care for the poor.

"UIC is contributing in many ways to the community, not only because we feel the responsibility to do so," says UIC Chancellor James J. Stukel, "but also because the future of UIC and the future of the city of Chicago are, in a real sense, dependent on one another."

UIC's College of Education contributes to the Chicago public school system's reform efforts by operating a wide range of programs to aid students, teachers, administrators,

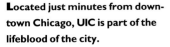

Located just minutes from downtown Chicago, UIC is part of the lifeblood of the city.

and the system's Local School Councils. One such program is the Nation of Tomorrow, which seeks to improve the lives of more than 4,000 children in four low-income neighborhoods in Chicago, primarily in African-American and Latino communities. Funded by a $4 million grant, this comprehensive project addresses the children's academic, health, and social needs.

Project Flame helps Latino parents learn to read, first in Spanish, then in English. The program also teaches the parents how to use their new language skills to help their children improve their academic performance.

In addition, the College of Education runs Early Outreach, one of UIC's oldest and most successful community service programs. Over the past 10 years the program has given academic assistance to more than 1,000 junior and senior high school students, most of whom have since graduated from high school and a majority of whom have gone on to college. Also sponsored and operated by UIC is the Remedial Reading Research Clinic, which offers free tutoring to children and adults with reading difficulties.

UIC provides primary health care, in partnership with the city of Chicago, at the Mile Square Neighbor-hood Health Center on the city's Near West Side. UIC physicians, nurses, pharmacists, and public health professionals staff the clinic. UIC also provides services at the Austin Health Center in the underserved Austin neighborhood on the far West Side of Chicago.

In addition, UIC operates the Reach Future program at the Teen OB Clinic on Chicago's West Side. With the goal of reducing infant mortality, UIC nurses, as well as nurse-midwives, nutritionists, social workers, and community health advocates, assist teenagers through their pregnancies and give follow-up support.

As the 17th largest Chicago area employer, with almost 11,000 employees, UIC is an important force in the city's economy. The university receives more than $60 million a year in federal support for research and other activities. That money in turn circulates through the local economy. In addition, UIC purchases an estimated $250 million a year in goods and services, mostly from Chicago area businesses.

UIC researchers assist Chicago area businesses in many other ways, including development of computer software, micromachining technologies, and computer imaging.

UIC is also dedicated to providing a quality college education for minority students. Eleven percent of UIC's undergraduate student population is African-American, and more than 14 percent is Latino. The medical school graduates more African-American and Latino physicians than any other institution in the United States.

As it nears the end of its first century, this venerable Chicago institution is committed to continuing its mission of quality education and community service, and to increasing its impact on the metropolitan area.

CNA INSURANCE COMPANIES

CNA, HEADQUARTERED IN CHICAGO, IS ONE OF THE 10 LARGEST INSURANCE ORGANIZATIONS IN THE UNITED STATES, AS MEASURED BY PREMIUM VOLUME. CNA IS A MULTILINE INSURER OFFERING A BROAD RANGE OF QUALITY PRODUCTS INCLUDING PROPERTY-CASUALTY, ACCIDENT AND

health, life, and pension. CNA also provides services such as loss cost management, claims administration, and benefits administration. The company sells its products and services through independent agents and brokers to individuals; small, medium-size, and large businesses; associations; professionals; and groups.

"At CNA we've worked hard to build a tradition of long-term commitment to those we serve," says Dennis Chookaszian, chairman and CEO.

In mid-1992, CNA's total assets were $36 billion. Surplus, an indicator of an insurance company's ability to cover unusual fluctuations in claims or investment results, was $3.8 billion for property-casualty operations and $1 billion for life insurance.

"At CNA we've worked hard to build a tradition of long-term commitment to those we serve," says Dennis Chookaszian, chairman and CEO. "We believe that financial integrity is an insurer's most important responsibility."

Chookaszian was named chairman and CEO of CNA in October 1992 as part of a long-term succession plan. Previously, he had served the company for 17 years as a key member of the management team, most recently as president and chief operating officer.

STRENGTH AND STAYING POWER

"We recognize that even our strength and stability will not serve a customer's needs unless they are accompanied by every employee's full-time commitment to giving the quality of service that a person or organization wants and deserves," says Chookaszian. "More than 15,000 strong nationwide, our employees deliver that quality every day—whenever, wherever, and however it's needed.

"We believe in maintaining the utmost integrity in our dealings. We value long-term relationships with agents, customers, and employees and do all that we can to foster these relationships.

"CNA emphasizes long-range rather than short-term profits. This long-term focus allows CNA to remain a stable presence in the market, and that's good for our policyholders. They can enjoy the peace of mind that comes from knowing their insurance company has the resources and resolve to overcome economic volatility and to be there when they need us.

"We also believe we have a long-term responsibility to help control the underlying cost of insurance. We don't see CNA as simply an intermediary—collecting premiums and paying claims. We have long been active in efforts not just to pay our customers' claims but to control the factors that increase costs—such as medical costs, disability costs, legal costs, fraud, and automobile repair costs—and drive up insurance rates."

HISTORY AND HERITAGE

CNA has achieved a reputation for longstanding dependability and service dating back to the last century. CNA's flagship firm—which was to become Continental Casualty Company—was born in Hammond, Indiana in 1897 and moved shortly afterward to Chicago.

The company grew rapidly by offering health and accident coverages and soon established a life insurance affiliate, Continental Assurance Company. The burgeoning organization diversified into other insurance lines and new types of coverages, and acquired a variety of other carriers during the first half of the 20th century.

During the 1960s, the company changed its name to Continental National American Group, which was later simplified to CNA. The organization also created CNA Financial Corporation, a holding company registered on the New York Stock Exchange. Loews Corporation bought a controlling interest in CNA Financial Corporation in 1974 and now owns about 83 percent. In the 1970s, CNA moved into its current home, also known as "the big red building," at 333 Wabash Avenue in downtown Chicago.

As it nears its 100th anniversary, financially strong and solidly positioned in the markets it serves, CNA and its new leadership are confident that the company will remain an industry leader. "CNA's corporate theme is 'For All the Commitments You Make,'" Chookaszian says. "We take our commitments seriously. Living up to them will continue to be our highest priority."

SARGENT & LUNDY

F OR JUST OVER 100 YEARS, ELECTRIC ENERGY PRODUCERS ACROSS THE UNITED STATES AND AROUND THE WORLD HAVE DEPENDED ON SARGENT & LUNDY TO DEVELOP GENERATING STATIONS AND DISTRIBUTION SYSTEMS THAT HAVE POWERED THE 20TH CENTURY. ◆ FOUNDED IN CHICAGO IN 1891, THE FIRM

designed many of the city's first power plants and went on to become one of the nation's most highly regarded engineering firms. Sargent & Lundy undertook its first international project in 1917, a bold step in those days. Today, the firm and its 2,500 employees design power projects for companies throughout the world. In all, Sargent & Lundy has designed more than 700 electric generating units.

PUTTING INNOVATION TO USE

Before starting the firm, Frederick Sargent and Ayers Lundy worked on some of the industry's earliest landmarks, from Thomas Edison's Pearl Street Station in 1882 and the World's Columbian Exposition that lit up Chicago in 1893 to the electrification of railroads. Together, the experience and reputation gained with each new client propelled Sargent & Lundy to the forefront of the power industry—a position that it has never relinquished.

Over the decades, the firm has engineered pioneering projects that implemented improvements in station economy and efficiency. Advances have included successive generations of "the world's largest plant," which introduced significant economies of scale, and industry firsts, such as the first U.S. utility

use of combined-cycle operation.

Sargent & Lundy was instrumental in helping harness nuclear power to generate electricity. Early projects included the world's first boiling water reactor power plant, the Argonne National Laboratory EBWR, in 1954. Since then, the firm has continued its leading role in the field with each new generation of nuclear power plant.

COMMITMENT TO CLIENTS AND PROGRESS

Sargent & Lundy's longtime success can be attributed to a commitment to progress that has kept the firm on the cutting edge, combined with an equally strong commitment to earn each client's respect and repeat business. As a result, the firm continues to work for many of its earliest customers, including its first utility client, Commonwealth Edison.

Central to Sargent & Lundy's management and project philosophy is a companywide emphasis on quality improvement. The firm was one of the first non-manufacturing companies to embrace quality improvement, training all employees in quality improvement techniques. Formal and informal teams throughout the firm are actively encouraged to search for ways to improve results for client projects, develop better internal tools and methods, and

sustain a high quality of professional life.

As for the future, Sargent & Lundy is focused on innovation that can serve clients into the 21st century. Projects include fluidized-bed combustion and integrated gasification combined-cycle plants, U.S. Department of Energy clean coal projects, and gas-insulated substations that are taking the industry to new levels of efficiency and environmental soundness. In the nuclear arena, projects include the next generation of nuclear power plant—a series of evolutionary PWR units in Korea.

Sargent & Lundy also is a leader in renovation and repowering of older plants, helping clients optimize the use of the existing infrastructure. Overall, work for operating facilities encompasses a diverse range, from scrubber retrofits and transmission line upgrades to developing enhanced plant operation and maintenance techniques.

In keeping with its long tradition of innovation in the power generating industry, even more exciting developments are expected in Sargent & Lundy's future. From its Chicago base, this engineering pioneer is prepared to continue working with its longtime clients and new clients for another century.

Far left: The evolutionary Yonggwang Units 3 and 4—a state-of-the-art Sargent & Lundy nuclear power project for the Korea Electric Power Corporation—will begin operation in 1995 and 1996.

The firm developed the award-winning Shidongkou Second Power Plant (left) for the Huaneng International Power Development Corporation and the Shanghai Municipal Government, People's Republic of China.

Sargent & Lundy's longtime success can be attributed to a commitment to progress that has kept the firm on the cutting edge, combined with an equally strong commitment to earn each client's respect and repeat business.

LUTHERAN GENERAL HEALTHSYSTEM

LUTHERAN GENERAL HEALTHSYSTEM (LGHS) TRACES ITS ROOTS IN CHICAGO BACK NEARLY 100 YEARS. NOW BASED IN SUBURBAN PARK RIDGE, LGHS IS A COMPREHENSIVE HEALTH CARE PROVIDER OPERATING A DIVERSE MULTIREGIONAL NETWORK OF MORE THAN 55 HEALTH AND HUMAN SERVICE

organizations in 18 states. "LGHS is focused primarily on creating and managing a patient-centered, integrated continuum of care in the greater Chicago metropolitan area," says Stephen L. Ummel, president and CEO. "Furthermore, we have embraced continuous quality improvement as our central operating strategy into the next century."

Lutheran General HealthSystem was founded in 1897 when Norwegian Lutheran Deaconess Hospital began caring for patients in a two-flat brick building near Chicago's northwest side. Over the years, the system has grown to include 9,100 employees, 1,600 volunteers, and more than 800 physicians who are affiliated with its medical staffs.

Guided by the healing and teaching mission of the Evangelical Lutheran Church in America, LGHS practices a philosophy of Human Ecology. This holistic approach to healing seeks to understand and care for patients as whole persons, acknowledging their spiritual and emotional needs, as well as their medical needs.

A DIVERSE, GROWING SYSTEM

On Christmas Eve 1959, ground was broken for Lutheran General Hospital, the system's flagship facility in Park Ridge. Since then, the 742-bed hospital has become the fifth largest in the Chicago area and number one in total occupancy. As an affiliated teaching hospital of the University of Chicago Pritzker School of Medicine, Lutheran General Hospital provides clinical training annually for 200 medical students, 230 assigned and rotating residents, and 15 fellows.

Special emphasis is placed on services for children. In fact, the hospital is the state's second largest children's medical center and one of only three pediatric trauma centers in the Chicago area. When completed, the new Victor Yacktman Children's Pavilion will house a comprehensive range of general pediatric and subspecialty clinics. Lutheran General Hospital is also home to one of Chicago's busiest obstetrics programs. Each year, its physicians deliver approximately 5,000 babies and provide state-of-the-art care to high-risk pregnant women.

In addition, the hospital operates the highest level trauma center in the area for adults and children. Its cardiac and cancer care programs are also renowned.

Another affiliate of Lutheran General HealthSystem is Lutheran General Behavioral Health (LGBH), formerly Parkside Medical Services Corporation. LGBH is the largest private, not-for-profit provider of addiction and behavior health treatment in the nation. The organization owns, operates, or manages facilities in 14 states and in Sweden, which are dedicated to the treatment of alcohol and chemical dependence, eating disorders, and psychiatric illnesses.

A broad range of tapes, books, and other educational materials are available through LGBH's Parkside Publishing Corporation. Likewise, LGBH operates the Parkside Outdoor Wilderness Experience in Recovery (POWER) adventure-based programs for people in recovery. The innovative POWER program is also used by corporate human resource departments as a management training tool.

Lutheran General Senior Services (LGSS), another system affiliate, offers a broad range of services geared toward improving the quality of life for seniors. Services range from acute care, nursing care, assisted living, retirement housing, and adult day care to community-based assistance. Ranked among the four largest not-for-profit managers of senior facilities in the country, LGSS owns and operates more than 4,600 independent living units in 26 retirement communities and 1,700 beds in 16 long-term care facilities in eight states. Among these facilities is The Moorings, a 291-unit continuing care retirement center located in northwest suburban Arlington Heights.

The Park Ridge Center for the Study of Health, Faith, and Ethics is among the nation's foremost centers for medical ethics. It is regarded as the preeminent institute engaged in critical research on topics where health, faith, and ethics intersect.

The Newborn Intensive Care Unit (below) is the second largest facility of its kind in Illinois. Each year, more than 700 critically ill infants are cared for in the NICU.

Lutheran General Hospital's In Vitro Fertilization Program is the busiest such program in the Chicago metropolitan area (bottom) and the first in the country to be affiliated with the Jones Institute of Norfolk, Virginia.

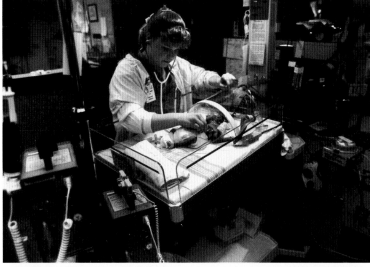

The Park Ridge Center is located near downtown Chicago, close to several large hospitals, universities, and headquarters of national health care associations. The center implements an active program of research, publication, and education, addressing such concerns as euthanasia and other termination-of-life issues, AIDS public policy, abortion and reproductive rights, genetic engineering, and access to health care by the poor.

HEALTH DIRECT, Inc. (HDI), formerly Parkside Health Management Corp., is the managed care joint venture between LGHS and Evangelical Health Systems. HDI contracts with municipalities, business employers, and other organizations to offer fully integrated, high-quality services and cost-containment programs designed to reduce unnecessary or inappropriate health care expenses. The fully accredited HEALTH DIRECT PPO is the 12th largest preferred provider organization in the Chicago area. Behavioral HEALTH DIRECT, a division of HEALTH DIRECT, offers self-insured employers direct contracting for behavioral health and substance abuse treatment—the fastest growing portion of an employer's health care package.

Another major component of LGHS is the Lutheran General Medical Group (LGMG), one of the largest group practices in Illinois, with 193 physician members and 550 non-physician employees. It is the only multispecialty group practice in the state to maintain an ongoing accreditation by the Joint Commission on Accreditation of Healthcare Organizations.

LGMG offers both primary care and specialty care at its 10 practice sites, which also include a fertility clinic, a pain management clinic, multiple pediatric subspecialty clinics, and outpatient mental health services. In addition, LGMG physicians serve as faculty for the training of medical students, residents, and fellows. Many are also involved in ongoing research projects and other scholarly activities.

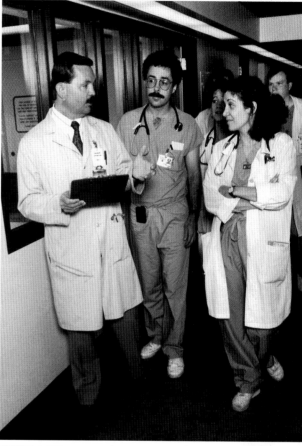

Lutheran General Foundation is the fund-raising arm of LGHS. The organization is committed to working with individuals, corporations, and foundations interested in making philanthropic investments in LGHS programs and services.

LOOKING TO THE FUTURE

As a religiously sponsored, not-for-profit institution, LGHS recognizes its moral and legal responsibility to share its resources with the community. Returning to its origins in Chicago in 1991, LGHS launched the Chicagoland Health Initiative to improve the quality and accessibility of health care in the city's medically disadvantaged communities.

Working in partnership with community groups, governmental agencies, the private sector, religious organizations, other health care providers, and educational institutions all over the city, LGHS continues its century-old mission, demonstrating its social accountability and ensuring comprehensive, high-quality, well-managed health services.

The POWER Program (top left) allows participants to push personal limits, confront fear, and gain confidence as part of their recovery from alcohol and drug dependency.

Lutheran General Hospital is the primary teaching site of the University of Chicago Pritzker School of Medicine (top right).

The Intergenerational Program offered through Lutheran General Senior Services (above) brings together children and older adults from the day care programs for special activities and events.

DePaul University

F OUNDED ALMOST 100 YEARS AGO IN A THREE-STORY BUILDING HOUSING
70 STUDENTS AND SEVEN FACULTY MEMBERS, DePaul University has
GROWN TO BECOME A DOMINANT FORCE IN Chicago. It is an institution
THAT HAS HELPED TRANSFORM TWO OF THE CITY'S NEIGHBORHOODS: THE

DePaul offers classes in two suburban locations: Oak Brook (left) and near O'Hare International Airport. The William E. O'Neil Reading Room (right) is located in the university's new freestanding library on the Lincoln Park campus.

In July 1993, the Rev. John P. Minogue, C.M. (standing), became president of DePaul. His predecessor, the Rev. John T. Richardson, C.M. (seated), now serves as chancellor.

Lincoln Park area, the location of its residential campus, which is now called the "DePaul area," and its downtown campus in the south Loop, which provides a more urban setting. Today, DePaul is poised on the brink of the 21st century with seven colleges and schools, and ranks as the largest Catholic university in the Midwest and the second largest in the country. The university has four campus locations, as well as international programs and partnerships with governments and institutions around the globe.

TREMENDOUS GROWTH IN THE 1980S

The Rev. John P. Minogue, C.M., president, credits his immediate predecessor, the Rev. John T. Richardson, C.M., with the success of the "DePaul Decade." In 1981, enrollment was 13,300; by 1992, it had reached nearly 16,500 students. Similarly, the faculty has grown to over 950 full- and part-time instructors.

"Planned growth has helped the university meet a number of objectives to support that growth," says Herbert E. Newman, vice president for development and university relations, noting that one goal was to increase DePaul's endowment. By the end of fiscal 1992, the endowment had reached $51.9 million.

Another aspect of planned growth is the university's master plan, transforming what was once a random assortment of buildings near Lincoln Park to a full-scale residential campus with architectural integrity and a Chicago flair. In 1992, DePaul opened its first freestanding library, a 190,000-square-foot building with advanced technology and generous study space, augmented by a landscaped quadrangle.

The university will soon capitalize on its distinctly urban setting when DePaul Center (formerly the historic Goldblatt's building) opens in September 1993. Located in the heart of Chicago's downtown, the 650,000-square-foot center serves as an anchor at the south end of fabled State Street and provides an unparalleled mixed-use facility combining retail and commercial space with university offices and classrooms. Ken McHugh, vice president for business and finance, notes that DePaul Center will be a one-of-a-kind building owned and operated by a university. "We're proud of the synergy we are creating between an educational institution and its business partners," he says.

OUTSTANDING ACADEMIC PROGRAM

DePaul's academic reputation has also kept pace with its enrollment. "We've grown, particularly in the last decade, from being a lesser known school to a much more visible institution with a highly regarded academic program," says Father Richardson, now chancellor. In 1992, *U.S. News & World Report* ranked DePaul number one among the Midwest's finest regional universities.

Provost Gladys Styles Johnston points out several particularly renowned schools and departments that have distinguished themselves. "The Charles H. Kellstadt Graduate School of Business is the second largest school of its type in the nation. It received a $9 million pledge in 1992 from the Charles H. Kellstadt Foundation, which is the largest single gift in DePaul's history," she says. "In addition, the College of Law was the only school in the nation in 1992 to be inducted into the Order of the Coif, an honorary scholastic society of the

Although DePaul is primarily a commuter school, about one-fifth of its students live on campus. More than half are full-time working professionals who attend classes at night. In addition to the Lincoln Park and Loop campuses, classes are offered in suburban Oak Brook and near O'Hare International Airport.

DePaul's men's basketball team has been a source of pride for the university, its alumni, and all of Chicago for many years. The Blue Demons, headed by Joey Meyer, son of longtime DePaul coach Ray Meyer, have earned 15 consecutive post-season tournament bids and continue to be a national contender. The DePaul women's basketball team has appeared in three consecutive NCAA tournaments.

The tougher economic times of recent years have challenged the school, but the enthusiasm and resourcefulness of its students, staff, alumni, and other supporters have helped it continue to flourish. DePaul University, recognized as a valuable community institution and resource, is a place with tremendous optimism, a clear sense of its academic mission, and vision for its role in the future of Chicago and its place in the international sphere.

DePaul offers one of the finest performing arts programs in the nation. Each year, its theatre and music schools stage a full-scale opera (above).

Among the university's architectural gems are O'Malley Place (left) and the Hayes/Healy Athletics Center (below).

top law schools in the country."

Other outstanding programs include the School of Music, which counts among its distinguished faculty 18 members of the world-renowned Chicago Symphony Orchestra and the Lyric Opera Orchestra; the School for New Learning, a pioneer in the development of adult degree programs that combine life experience with academic study; the School for Education, which is a national leader in fostering positive change in America's inner-city schools and is currently working with more than 100 Chicago public schools; the Theatre School, a leading theatre conservatory staging eight productions annually in the Merle Reskin Theatre; and the heart of the university, the College of Liberal Arts and Sciences, offering instruction in 10 languages and foreign study opportunities in 12 countries.

DEPAUL AND THE COMMUNITY

With more than 50,000 graduates living and working in the Chicago metropolitan area, the university has a major influence on the local business and cultural environment. DePaul alumni also are among the most influential leaders in business and government nationwide.

Among them are former Chicago Mayor Richard J. Daley and his son, Mayor Richard M. Daley, as well as Benjamin Hooks, the former executive director of the NAACP. Other graduates include Sam Skinner, White House Chief of Staff and U.S. Secretary of Transportation in the Bush administration; H. Laurance Fuller, chairman, president, and CEO of Amoco Corp.; William D. Smithburg, chairman, president, and CEO of the Quaker Oats Company; and actors Joe Mantegna and Elizabeth Perkins.

WALGREEN CO.

I N CHICAGO AND ACROSS MUCH OF THE COUNTRY, "WALGREENS" HAS BECOME SYNONYMOUS WITH THE LOCAL DRUG STORE. AND THAT'S NOT SURPRISING SINCE NATIONWIDE, THE WALGREEN CO. IS THE LARGEST PHARMACIST AND THE BIGGEST DRUG STORE CHAIN IN TERMS OF SALES.

Charles Rudolph Walgreen opened his first pharmacy in Chicago in 1901.

A RELUCTANT FOUNDER

Charles Rudolph Walgreen, who founded the company in Chicago at the turn of the century, had to be persuaded to take his first drug store job.

At the age of 17, Walgreen worked in a shoe factory in Dixon, Illinois. One day, while manning a stitch machine, Walgreen caught his left hand in the contraption and lopped off the top joint of his middle finger. The doctor who treated the wound cautioned him not to use his hand for anything, and to avoid sports in particular. The following afternoon the doctor spotted his young patient on a baseball diamond. When scolded for not obeying the doctor's orders, Walgreen complained that he no longer had a job to occupy him and that he couldn't stand to be inactive.

The doctor offered to find his patient a job in a local drug store, but Walgreen was not interested. After several meetings with the doctor, Walgreen finally relented and took a position in the largest pharmacy in Dixon. After spending 18 months as an apprentice, Walgreen moved to Chicago, seeking a better opportunity for himself. Over the next eight years he worked in a number of different drug stores learning the business. In 1897, he passed the exam given by the Illinois State Board of Pharmacy and became a registered pharmacist.

In 1901, Walgreen bought his first pharmacy from his employer at the time, and in 1909 he purchased a second drug store from another former employer. By 1939, Charles Walgreen, who continued to demonstrate his distaste for idleness, had built a chain of 500 stores. Today, the Walgreen Co. operates 1,750 stores in 29 states and Puerto Rico, including 100 in Chicago.

SUCCESS THROUGH INNOVATION

Energetic and ambitious, Walgreen was also an innovative entrepreneur. "Charles Walgreen broke new ground in retailing and the pharmacy business by taking the basic concept of a successful drug store in a good location and multiplying it, thus creating the first drug store chain," says Edward King, director of Government and Corporate Relations for the Walgreen Co. "Under his leadership, the company was also the first drug store chain to employ national advertising, and early on relied heavily on newspaper advertising. The Walgreen Co. today is still known for its spirit of innovation."

Though Walgreen died in 1939, his tireless efforts and the dedication of other company leaders and employees nationwide have led to tremendous growth for the Walgreen chain over the years. "Although some other companies have more stores than we do, we're the biggest in the country by quite a bit in terms of sales," King says. "We're number one in a dozen major markets, including St. Louis, San Francisco, Milwaukee, Cincinnati, Memphis, and, of course, Chicago."

While the chain has expanded steadily for years, it has enjoyed particularly brisk growth during the past decade. "Only 10 years ago, we were fourth among drug store chains

From left: C.R. Walgreen III, chairman, and L.D. Jorndt, president, perpetuate the spirit of energy, ambition, and innovation that has made Walgreens the nation's largest pharmacist.

With 100 locations across the area, Walgreens is number one in Chicago (far right).

CAGNEY McDOWELL

in the United States. Now we're number one," King comments. "In fact, 1992 marked the 18th consecutive record year in sales and earnings for the chain."

As the largest pharmacist in the nation, the Walgreen Co. fills 7 percent of all prescriptions written in the United States each year. Its pharmacy business accounts for 37 percent of total annual sales. During a recent nine-year period, the company's prescription business grew at an impressive rate of 20 percent.

STAYING AHEAD TODAY

The typical Walgreens store is 9,000 square feet and carries approxi-

mately 16,000 different items, including over-the-counter drugs, cosmetics, housewares, food, paper goods, stationery, and sundries.

Walgreens is the nation's most technologically advanced drug store chain, say company officials. Of great convenience to customers is the "Intercom" program, a computerized prescription information system that links all pharmacies in the chain and allows Walgreens pharmacists across the country to refill a customer's prescription at any store. Also, all Walgreens locations are equipped with time-saving UPC scanners.

For several decades the Walgreen

Co. diversified its activities by purchasing and operating retail stores and restaurants in Mexico, buying interest in other businesses in St. Louis, and operating the Wag's restaurant chain in Chicago and other areas of the country. But by the late 1980s, the company had divested itself of these holdings and began refocusing all its efforts on the drug store chain.

"We've come full circle," says King, "back to what Charles Walgreen originally started: a free-standing, street-corner drug store with a good parking lot and the best products and technology to keep our customers satisfied."

CHICAGOLAND CHAMBER OF COMMERCE

FOR NEARLY 90 YEARS, THE CHICAGOLAND CHAMBER OF COMMERCE HAS SERVED THE DYNAMIC BUSINESS COMMUNITY OF CHICAGO AND ITS SUBURBS. ESTABLISHED IN 1904 BY THE MERGER OF FOUR AREA TRADE ASSOCIATIONS, THE CHAMBER HAS GROWN DRAMATICALLY FROM 93 MEMBER COMPANIES TO more than 2,000 today.

The primary goal of the Chamber's founders was to create a strong, unified voice to promote the diverse and changing needs of local businesses and the Chicagoland communities they serve. In so doing, the young organization acknowledged the crucial role of business in civic affairs and assumed an unprecedented position of leadership in the community.

Over the years, the Chamber has operated under a variety of names. It was founded as the Chicago Commercial Association, but changed its name the following year to the Chicago Association of Commerce to avoid confusion with another local organization. As the Chamber's role in the community ex-

Past Chamber chairmen gathered at a 1993 Executive Committee meeting. From left: James J. McDonough, president and CEO of McDonough Associates Inc.; Kenneth L. Block, chairman emeritus of A.T. Kearney, Inc.; E. Stanley Enlund, of counsel, Chadwell & Kayser, Ltd.; and Maynard P. Venema, chairman of Mid-America Legal Foundation.

James J. O'Connor, chairman and CEO of Commonwealth Edison Company, has served as the Chamber's chairman since 1990 (right).

panded, it underwent a second name change in 1947, this time to the Chicago Association of Commerce and Industry. In 1992, it adopted its current, all-encompassing title, the Chicagoland Chamber of Commerce.

DECADES OF SERVICE

The Chamber has long been a partner in the civic, governmental, and business life of the city and its suburbs. In 1904, the Chamber launched one of its first programs, the "Way to Ship" package car service. Through this plan, Chicago shippers became the only shippers in the nation to enjoy daily fast-freight service to 1,500 communities without a transfer and to 60,000 other destinations with just one transfer.

In 1905, the Chamber created the

Chicago Convention Bureau and began to promote the city nationwide as a good destination for business and tourism. In 1908, the Chamber helped Northwestern University establish its School of Commerce and raised funds to ensure the school had adequate financing in its early years. And in 1911, less than a year after the South Side Stockyards Fire, the Chamber instituted Fire Prevention Day, which is now observed nationwide.

During its early years, the Chamber helped establish numerous vital organizations which remain in existence: the Chicago Chapter of the American Red Cross, the Community Fund, the Chicago Crime Commission, the Chicago Safety Council, the Chicago Better Business Bureau, and the Chicago Plan Com-

mission, among others. The Chamber continues to address the civic and business needs of the eight-county metropolitan area—Cook, DuPage, Lake, Kane, McHenry, and Will counties in Illinois, and Lake and Porter counties in Indiana. The organization maintains a strong working relationship will all levels of government and is an influential and highly respected voice.

STRUCTURED FOR SERVICE

The Chamber's primary purpose is to serve its members, a goal advanced through a variety of programs, seminars, and member-driven committees. This structure allows the organization to respond quickly when issues surface in the public or private sector.

For example, the Chamber's five geographically focused world trade committees strive to increase trade opportunities for small and medium-size businesses in increasingly competitive foreign markets such as Mexico, Eastern Europe, and the Pacific Rim. The committees regularly host visiting trade delegations

from such countries as China, Bulgaria, and Argentina.

The Small Business Division works to increase business opportunities for members. The Chamber hosts the Chicago Small Business Expo, a two-day trade show held annually since 1983, which features exhibits, products, and services exclusively for small business, topical workshops, and a small business counseling center.

The Management Development Division holds professional seminars for participants from all levels of management who want to improve their personal and workplace performance. New seminars are added each year in response to workplace demands, such as "Hiring and Firing: What Employers Need to Know" and "You and the Media: Showcase or Showdown?"

Many area companies recognize the consequences of substance abuse for business and the community, so the Chamber has developed a Drug Free Workplace Program to assist companies in developing effective and legally viable substance abuse prevention policies. The Chamber's Brown Bag Lunch seminars address groups of virtually any size, from five to more than 500 people, who have made a commitment to maintaining a drug-free workplace.

The Criminal Justice and Fire Prevention committees work to protect the community at large. When Chicago was threatened by a historic flood in the spring of 1992, the Fire Prevention Committee hosted a two-hour seminar called "Disaster Recov-

ery for Small Business," which addressed both flood issues and the full realm of natural and man-made disasters that could threaten a business and its employees.

The Crime Prevention Committee works closely with the region's law enforcement agencies. Each year, committee members award outstanding law enforcement officers and private citizens with prestigious Crime Prevention Awards for extraordinary contributions to community safety.

Another Chamber program that serves greater Chicago is the Youth Motivation Program. Volunteers from member companies visit the classrooms of nearly all of Chicago's 65 public high schools and speak to students about the importance of education. These professional role models share their own stories about overcoming obstacles and achieving success and, in the process, inspire thousands of inner-city kids to strive for success in their own lives.

The Transportation Division focuses on everything from infrastructure to downtown parking to the ease and affordability of mass transit in the region. The Chamber has been a key player in maintaining Chicago as the nation's transportation hub and has advocated the building of first-class airports, expressways, and rail lines for both shippers and commercial passengers. .

The Chamber sponsors an endless array of luncheons, seminars, and special programs, all of which are geared toward advancing the inter-

CRAIG SKORBURG

ests of business and the understanding of issues that affect business. Members meet regularly at these functions, including Business Over Breakfast and Business After Hours, which serve as effective networking forums.

Throughout every Chamber function, one thing is constant: the quest to address the civic, business, and governmental needs of Chicago and the eight-county metropolitan area. The Chicagoland Chamber of Commerce was the country's first regional chamber, and as it has for nine successful decades, the organization today stands as a vital force and a community partner striving to foster economic growth and a strong, healthy Chicagoland.

THE BERGHOFF RESTAURANT

N TODAY'S EVER-CHANGING SOCIETY, IT IS COMFORTING TO KNOW THAT SOME THINGS ENDURE THE PASSAGE OF TIME. CHICAGO'S BERGHOFF RESTAURANT, FOUNDED NEARLY 100 YEARS AGO, HAS NOT ONLY SURVIVED, BUT THRIVED. TO WHAT DO THE PROPRIETORS OF THIS FAMILY-OWNED ESTABLISHMENT ATTRIBUTE

its longevity? Herman Berghoff, grandson of the restaurant's founder, says, "We offer high-quality food, reasonable prices, wonderful ambience, a great location, and a rich history of tradition."

To serve over 1 million customers a year, the 750-seat restaurant (above) employs a staff of hundreds, including in-house bakers and butchers.

Herman Berghoff, grandson of the founder, and his wife, Jan, (far right) operate the restaurant today.

Today, Herman and his wife, Jan, operate the popular restaurant, and their son, Peter, is manager. Daughter Carlyn Berghoff has branched out and owns a successful Chicago catering business.

COMING TO AMERICA

The history of the Berghoffs is much like the stories of other 19th century immigrant families across America. Patriarch Herman Joseph Berghoff left his native Dortmund, Germany and came to the United States in 1870. He settled in Fort Wayne, Indiana, where he worked to build up enough capital to establish a small brewery. In 1887, the Herman Berghoff Brewery Co. and Berghoff beer were born.

In 1893, Herman traveled to Chicago to sell his beer outside the

grounds of the Columbian Exposition. The brew was so well-received that he hoped to continue offering his product in Chicago. Unfortunately, city authorities prohibited out-of-town breweries, so Herman struck a compromise by opening three cafes where he gave away sandwiches with five-cent steins of beer. Eventually two of the cafes closed so that Herman could devote his time to the most successful establishment at 17 West Adams Street in the heart of downtown Chicago.

Still operating out of the original Adams Street location with its dark wood interior and grand mahogany bar, The Berghoff entertains today's patrons with turn-of-the-century charm. To serve over 1 million customers every year, the 750-seat restaurant employs a staff of hundreds, including in-house bakers and butchers.

HEARTY GERMAN FARE AND MORE

Although known primarily for its authentic German fare, traditional ethnic dishes account for only one-third of the menu offerings. "People like a change from tradition," says Herman Berghoff. He notes that regular clients actually prefer fish and other lighter items, while tourists, conventioneers, theater-goers, and other non-regular customers seem to come to The Berghoff for hearty German dishes.

"We change the menu on a seasonal basis," says Jan Berghoff. Highlights include a special game menu in the winter and many Lenten fish specials. There are always at least five daily specials to round out seasonal offerings.

On average, The Berghoff serves 1,500 pounds of potatoes, 150 pounds of creamed spinach, 22 half-

barrels of beer, 350 loaves of homemade bread, 250 wiener schnitzels, two barrels of sauerkraut, and two barrels of pickles daily. The bar serves about 600 sandwiches a day, usually accompanied by a stein of

Berghoff beer. Brewed by the Berghoff-Huber Brewing Co. in Monroe, Wisconsin, the beer has proven so popular that it is now available at various stores, restaurants, and taverns in the Chicago area. The Berghoffs also brew a flavorful root beer which is served in the restaurant.

The Berghoff Restaurant has built its reputation on a continuous commitment to quality and service that began nearly a century ago and continues today. "We will be celebrating our 100th anniversary in 1998," says Herman Berghoff. "The fourth generation of Berghoffs has already begun to carry on the traditions that will see us into the next century."

1912
ILLINOIS TOOL WORKS INC.

1924
GRANT THORNTON

1927
W.W. GRAINGER, INC.

1913
ANDERSEN CONSULTING

1926
AMERICAN AIRLINES

1927
LaSALLE NATIONAL BANK

1914
INTERNATIONAL BUSINESS
MACHINES CORP.

1926
THE JEL SERT COMPANY

1928
NALCO CHEMICAL COMPANY

1914
JENNER & BLOCK

1926
POWER CONTRACTING AND
ENGINEERING CORP.

1929
CHICAGO SUN-TIMES

1919
CHICAGO MERCANTILE
EXCHANGE

1926
UNITED AIRLINES, INC.

1919
CONSOER, TOWNSEND &
ASSOCIATES

PRIOR TO THE ADVENT OF THE airplane, Union Station was something like a Midwestern Ellis Island, a cavernous gateway to a big American city and perhaps a whole new life. Bored farm kids hopped a train and headed for Chicago—first stop, Union Station. Immigrants, weary from weeks of travel, straggled into Chicago—final stop, Union Station. Completed in 1924, it was the largest and most modern railroad station in the world, built at a cost of $65 million and covering six city blocks.

"**A**LL I EVER DID WAS TO SELL BEER and whiskey to our best people," Al Capone once said. "All I ever did was to supply a demand that was pretty popular." Poor Al. So misunderstood. Scarface Al remains America's most infamous Prohibition era gangster and, alas, one of Chicago's most enduring black marks. At one time, before Elliot Ness, The Untouchables, and a good tax accountant took him down, Capone was worth $100 million. All the same, if you believed his business card, he was nothing more than a "Second-hand furniture dealer."

ILLINOIS TOOL WORKS INC.

FROM NAILS AND SCREWS TO FILTERS AND ADHESIVES, FROM PACKAGING AND CONSTRUCTION TOOLS TO SPRAY FINISHING AND GEARS, ILLINOIS TOOL WORKS INC. AND ITS 18,000 EMPLOYEES WORLDWIDE MAKE IT ALL. VIRTUALLY EVERY CAR IN THE WORLD LEAVES THE ASSEMBLY LINE WITH

ITW parts. ITW is also the world's largest producer of plastic buckles, the inventor of the plastic-loop device that holds cans together, and the creator of customized parts for Parker Pen's collection of writing instruments.

Headquartered in north suburban Glenview, ITW is a diversified, public company with approximately 200 operating units worldwide. The firm, which produces components, assemblies, and systems for virtually all sectors of business and industry, is organized into two seg-

ments: Engineered Components, and Industrial Systems and Consumables.

ITW has always been a market-driven company that strives to develop new products in response to customer needs and to design improvements into existing products—all with the goal of helping customers become more productive and competitive.

In December of 1911, Byron L. Smith ran an ad in a local financial journal, offering to invest in a Chicago-area manufacturing operation

that could be made into "a large, profitable, permanent business." He sought entrepreneurial types who shared his philosophy of providing innovative, quality products. The four men who answered the ad convinced Smith of a demand within the industrial market for precision metal-cutting tools. In 1912, a partnership was formed and Illinois Tool Works was born.

Since then, the company has expanded into a $3 billion international manufacturer of much more than tools. Recently, *Fortune* magazine recognized ITW's diversity by calling it "The Ultimate Nuts and Bolts Company."

With business units in 33 countries, ITW operates under a very decentralized structure. Its production facilities are located near individual markets, allowing close communication with customers. This flexibility has allowed ITW to enter new industry niches and increase penetration in existing markets.

That is how the Shakeproof fastener, a patented twisted-tooth lock washer, was developed in 1923. The product's immediate success made ITW the leader in a new industry segment, engineered metal fasteners. Today, several ITW units produce fasteners for appliance, automotive, construction, general industrial, and other applications.

Subsequent innovations in plastics, electrostatic spray finishing, and strapping have allowed ITW to become a world leader in other fields. For example, ITW revolutionized the packaging industry in the early 1960s when its Hi-Cone business developed the plastic multipak ring carrier. These photodegradable, recyclable carriers are now commonly used to package beverage, food, medical, and petroleum products.

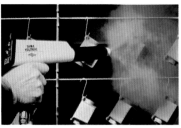

This 1923 twisted-tooth lock washer patent (right) was ITW's first engineered metal fastener. Since then, the company has entered diverse markets through products (from top) such as the Impulse™ airless, cordless power nailing tool, various fluids and adhesives for consumer and industrial uses, and Gema Volstatic electrostatic powder spray finishing systems.

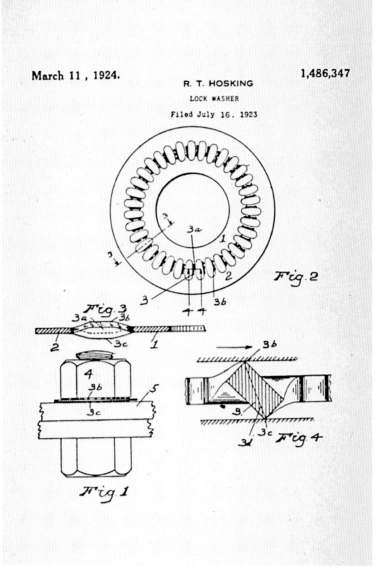

March 11 , 1924. R. T. HOSKING 1,486,347

LOCK WASHER

Filed July 16. 1923

INNOVATION—THE KEY TO SUCCESS

ITW's legacy of innovation continues more than 80 years after its founding. Business units often spring from new product development, and engineers within the company share breakthroughs whenever possible. To extend the capabilities of its operating units, ITW maintains a Technology Center to assist in improving technologies and developing new products and processes.

For example, an automotive truck and hatchback hinge developed by ITW Proffitt in Europe is now being modified for use in the United States. In the mid-1980s, a researcher at ITW Fastex invented a durable plastic life-jacket buckle that dramatically increased safety. That product was the foundation for ITW Nexus, which manufactures and sells an entire product line of fasteners.

The company is also committed to improving established products. Signode Packaging's general purpose strapping machines, manufactured in Glenview, Illinois and around the world, have been refined to meet the specialized needs of the corrugated materials, paper, steel fabrication, and can and bottle industries. Likewise, the revolutionary Impulse™ airless, cordless power nailing tool produced by ITW Paslode in Lincolnshire, Illinois is already used in many construction applications. Sister unit, ITW Ramset/Red Head in Wood Dale, Illinois, now offers the technology to users of its Trakfast™ drywall track installation system.

With this kind of success in product development and improvement, it is no surprise ITW now holds more than 4,400 active patents worldwide.

CONCERN FOR THE ENVIRONMENT

As part of the company's commitment to environmental responsibility, ITW engineers design products to minimize pollution and waste.

For example, Accu-Lube, a vegetable oil-based lubricant manufactured by ITW Fluid Products of Norcross, Georgia, significantly reduces customers' disposal costs. Gema Volstatic of Indianapolis, Indiana, a leading supplier of electrostatic powder spray finishing systems, has developed a spray booth that allows users to recycle virtually all powder residue. ITW has also ventured into the fields of hot-melt adhesive application equipment through its Dynatec unit, and glueless labeling systems for beverage, food, and other PET containers through its Automated Label Systems joint venture.

In an effort to expand existing recycling programs, ITW recently acquired the Chicago-based Plastics Recycling Alliance (PRA) from Du Pont. "We realize the importance of industry becoming proactive on environmental issues, and we're pleased to be assuming a leading role," says John Nichols, ITW chairman and chief executive officer. "PRA is a sound business option that makes practical, economic sense for our company and permits us to increase the volume of post-consumer, recycled plastic materials that are used in our packaging products."

Adapting modern technologies to new products and systems, maintaining close customer relationships, developing environmentally responsible products, and improving manufacturing processes are all proven methods destined to ensure ITW's success for decades to come.

Hi-Cone Carriers

Are lighter than the page this ad is printed on • Are one of the best examples of minimal packaging • Are ten times more material-efficient than paperboard • Photodegrade on land and on water • Are 100% recyclable • Can be recycled with non-degradable plastics • Are being collected on vending routes by scores of beverage companies • Are included in a growing number of curbside and drop-off programs • Are being recycled back into new carriers • Are a highly efficient source of energy when properly incinerated • Are non-toxic to the environment • Take up minimal space in landfills • Now come with easy-opening Tear-Tabs™ to reduce wildlife entrapment concerns • Are America's most responsible form of secondary packaging.

ITW Hi-Cone
1140 West Bryn Mawr Avenue • Itasca, IL 60143 • 708-773-9300

ITW Hi-Cone, manufacturer of recyclable, photodegradable plastic multipack ring carriers, offers assistance to schools, offices, and communities interested in establishing carrier collection programs (left).

From top: ITW Proffitt's constant-force trunk hinges for the automobile industry, Nexus' engineered thermoplastic closures and components, and plastic and metal strapping systems from Signode.

333

ANDERSEN CONSULTING

SINCE ITS FOUNDING IN CHICAGO IN 1913, ANDERSEN CONSULTING HAS GROWN TO BE THE LARGEST MANAGEMENT CONSULTING FIRM IN THE WORLD. WITH AN INTERNATIONAL NETWORK OF 151 OFFICES IN 47 COUNTRIES AND MORE THAN 26,000 EMPLOYEES, ITS GLOBAL RESOURCES ARE VAST.

The organization applies its expertise in information technology, systems integration, strategic planning, business process management services, change management services, and application software products to help clients—from small businesses to Fortune 500 giants—manage the complex process of change to be more successful.

TOTAL BUSINESS SOLUTIONS

Headquartered in downtown Chicago, Andersen Consulting offers a strong blend of industry knowledge and technology expertise to clients

F. Dean Taylor is managing partner of Andersen Consulting's Chicago office, the largest of the firm's 151 offices worldwide.

The Center for Professional Education, a 151-acre campus facility located in St. Charles, Illinois, demonstrates Andersen Consulting's commitment to the continuous education and training of its consultants (above right).

in myriad industries, including aerospace and defense, airlines, automotive, chemicals, electronics, energy, financial services, food processing, government, health care, insurance, manufacturing, retail/wholesale distribution, telecommunications, and utilities. With over 1,600 professionals in the Chicago area, the firm is uniquely capable of providing clients with total business solutions that integrate the four components of an organization—strategy, processes, people, and technology.

The firm has been a leader in technology management since 1952 when it installed the first computer

system for commercial use at General Electric. Andersen Consulting also pioneered the use of artificial intelligence, image processing, relational data base management systems, designer and programmer workbenches, productivity tools, and open systems architectures.

Complementing its technology management capabilities, the firm has built a solid reputation in systems integration. As organizations invest in new computer hardware and software, they often discover that technology produced by different vendors is incompatible. The firm's systems integration practice links these disparate components and helps manage the smooth delivery of information throughout an organization.

Being a systems integrator also means offering clients change management skills that ensure the successful assimilation of technology. Andersen Consulting's change management professionals help educate and train personnel who are dealing with organizational change.

Strategic planning is another area of expertise. Andersen Consulting's strategic services practice helps clients respond to changes in the marketplace by developing and exe-

cuting winning business strategies. The right strategy can help a company steer in a new direction, adapt to new technology, align business processes, and create new links to customers.

Over the years, Andersen Consulting has distinguished itself with the philosophy of "partnering" with its clients. "As consultants, we are more than 'advisers' to our clients. We are their partners, and in that capacity we are both 'doers' and 'thinkers,'" says F. Dean Taylor, managing partner of the Chicago office. Demonstrating that point, Andersen Consulting has long-standing client relationships with many of Chicago's top companies.

PUTTING THEORY INTO PRACTICE

Through several initiatives, the firm strives to maintain its leadership position. Its business integration centers in Chicago, Dallas, and Atlanta display state-of-the-art technologies in work environments ranging from supermarkets to hospitals. These unique research and development facilities illustrate how technology, when integrated with a business vision and management sense, can change the way business is done.

In Chicago, SMART STORE is a prototype supermarket that showcases Andersen Consulting's vision of how technology will be applied by food retailers. The facility integrates technologies such as robotic check-out counters and order-entry devices to show how food retailers and manufacturers can work together to adapt to a changing consumer market.

THE RETAIL PLACE, also in Chicago, highlights a consumer-driven retail organization from storefront to distribution center to corporate office. The facility demonstrates how integrating technology, chang-

Professionals at Andersen Consulting combine general business knowledge with technology expertise to help clients change to be more successful (left).

Below: The firm's Chicago office management team includes (from left) Stephen L. Farmer, F. Dean Taylor, Carla J. Paonessa, and Steven M. Freeman.

ing business processes, and realigning a retail organization can improve profits.

In 1988, the firm established the Center for Strategic Technology Research (CSTaR) in Chicago. CSTaR's mission is to create solutions to diverse problems, from basic business operations and systems development to leveraging the work force. The center is developing the concepts, design methods, and tools to create high value-added systems that improve effectiveness by integrating decision making across business functions.

Andersen Consulting is also the founding sponsor of the Institute for Learning Sciences at Northwestern University. Established in 1989, the Institute researches and designs software applications that reflect how people think. The firm's primary goal is to create innovative approaches to training which utilize artificial intelligence, case-based reasoning, and other state-of-the-art technologies.

COMMITTED TO EMPLOYEE TRAINING

In all of its efforts, Andersen Consulting relies on a solid base of creative, well-trained professionals. Each year, about 6 percent of the firm's revenues are spent on training—a considerable sum since 1992 revenues totaled $2.7 billion. "As a firm, we are committed to hiring and

training the best and the brightest. We hire people who will make a difference to our clients and to our organization. Our business is delivering service, and to be successful, we must develop and nurture our resources—our people," Taylor explains.

To make this possible, Andersen Consulting operates the Center for Professional Development in suburban St. Charles. This campus facility occupies 151 acres and has 135 classrooms to accommodate more than 2,000 participants. The firm also operates training centers in Singapore, the Philippines, and the Netherlands.

COMMUNITY INVOLVEMENT

The firm's tradition of investing in its people carries over to its spirit of investing in its hometown. "In Chicago, being a leader in the civic community goes hand in hand with being a leader in the business community. This responsibility we accept and act on with pride," Taylor adds. "One of the most important ways we invest in Chicago is through the hours of volunteer time our people give. We demonstrate our financial support by contributing to the United Way's Crusade of Mercy, Cubs Care, The Boys and Girls Clubs of Chicago, and many other worthy organizations."

As a leading management consulting firm with vast global resources, Andersen Consulting is well positioned to tackle the challenges of change into the future.

INTERNATIONAL BUSINESS MACHINES CORP.

NTERNATIONAL BUSINESS MACHINES CORP., A GLOBAL INFORMATION SYSTEMS GIANT, HAS BEEN A MAJOR PLAYER IN CHICAGO FOR NEARLY 80 YEARS, CONTRIBUTING TO ITS COMMUNITY AND BUSINESS LIFE IN COUNTLESS WAYS. WITH APPROXIMATELY 300,000 EMPLOYEES IN SOME 130 COUNTRIES, THE COMPANY

Hundreds of students in five suburban school districts and one city high school participate in Project Homeroom, IBM's joint effort with Ameritech and Illinois Bell that links students, teachers, and schools through a sophisticated educational network.

develops, manufactures, markets, and services information processing systems, as well as related software, telecommunication products, storage devices, printers, supplies, and educational materials. It is also a major provider of business solutions through consulting services.

IBM has had a presence in Chicago since 1914, and its nearly 3,000 local employees today market and service computer equipment and systems, and provide consulting services for information systems, executive management, and disaster recovery. "We are a major partner in this community," says John W. Thompson, vice president and general manager of IBM's Chicago-based Midwestern Area. "Our office is the headquarters for an eight-state region that includes Illinois, Indiana, Iowa, Minnesota, Nebraska, North Dakota, South Dakota, Wisconsin, the city of St. Louis, Missouri, Michigan's Upper Peninsula, and western Kentucky."

Most people know IBM as the corporate giant that revolutionized information processing the world over. But in Chicago and the other communities where it operates, IBM dedicates millions of dollars each year in equipment, personnel, and financial assistance to support education/social programs and the arts. That level of involvement has helped strengthen the company's partnership with the communities in which its employees and customers live and work.

COMMITTED TO EDUCATION IN CHICAGO

Because harnessing the power of information is one of IBM's primary businesses, it is no surprise that the company has committed itself to applying computer technology to one crucial human task—learning to read. To that end, support of education has become an important goal for IBM throughout the Chicago area.

Through its three Chicagoland Adult Learning Centers located in northwest suburban Rolling Meadows, at One IBM Plaza in downtown Chicago, and in suburban Oak Brook in DuPage County, IBM reaches out to adults with limited reading skills and gives them an opportunity to improve their abilities and, therefore, their job prospects. Since 1988, more than 300 IBM employee volunteers have undergone intensive training to serve as tutors.

The Chicago Public School System and IBM worked together to develop Project QUEST, which allows students as young as kindergartners to use IBM personal computers in the classroom.

Adults who enter the program participate in three four-hour sessions each week in which they work in small groups led by a professional instructor. These "students" also spend time working independently on IBM's innovative program, the Principle of the Adult Literacy System (PALS), and one-on-one with IBM volunteer tutors. This approach enables the students to progress at their own rate, and individual progress is carefully monitored.

To celebrate its 75th anniversary in Chicago, IBM commissioned artist John David Mooney to create "LIGHTSCAPE '89." The transformation of the Ludwig Mies van der Rohe-designed IBM building, a four-day event, involved more than 200 IBM employees and friends who volunteered some 6,000 hours and used 7,000 special lamps and 11 miles of paper. It is believed to be the only project of its kind undertaken anywhere in the world.

IBM also supports Project Quest, a collaborative effort with the Chicago Public Schools' Guggenheim School. Launched in 1991, the program was designed to create a working model kindergarten through 12th grade educational setting that integrates today's computer technology with a traditional curriculum and instructional management. Each classroom has six personal computer systems plus one teacher's workstation. Under the teacher's direction, the students use the workstations for class work in virtually all subjects. A computer laboratory is available for large assignments and group projects. Parents from the surrounding Englewood community can also use the lab, which offers a PALS program.

Several other educational programs in the Chicago area receive much-needed support from IBM. Launched in 1991, Project Homeroom extends the learning process beyond the classroom in one Chicago and four suburban high schools and one suburban elementary school. A computer network links students and teachers at home to vast information resources through IBM personal computers and Ameritech communications services from Illinois Bell.

IBM has also "adopted" 10 Chicago public high schools, making it the largest corporate Adopt-A-School sponsor in the city. IBM employees work with their adopted schools to develop programs and projects that help prepare students to enter the work force. As part of this business-education partnership, employees spend time at the schools and students visit IBM's offices. In addition, IBM supports the Golden Apple Awards for Excellence in Teaching.

AN AVID SUPPORTER OF THE ARTS

In Chicago, IBM has also made its mark as an avid supporter of the arts. This longtime commitment dates back to the 1930s, when Chairman Thomas J. Watson Sr. authorized the purchase of works of art from each of the 79 countries where IBM was then doing business.

Today, IBM's support is broad-based and includes matching grants of employee contributions to arts organizations. The company also underwrites major cultural projects in virtually every area of the visual and performing arts. Nationwide, IBM provides support to approximately 2,500 cultural organizations. In 1992, the company sponsored an exhibition of European masterpieces from the National Gallery of Ireland at the Art Institute of Chicago. In 1993, IBM is a major contributor to

LEE BALTERMAN

the production of a new play undertaken by the city's critically acclaimed Steppenwolf Theatre Company.

Even as IBM has become a world leader in information processing, the company has remained closely involved with the communities where it does business. That policy has been successfully carried out in Chicago, where IBM's generous contributions in funding, equipment, and human resources have helped address some of the most important problems facing society today and have generally helped improve the quality of life in the community.

Residents of the Cabrini-Green housing project work with IBM volunteer tutors to improve their reading skills in the Adult Learning Center at IBM's Midwestern Area headquarters in downtown Chicago.

JENNER & BLOCK

JENNER & BLOCK IS ONE OF CHICAGO'S PREMIER FULL-SERVICE LAW FIRMS, WITH MORE THAN 350 ATTORNEYS OFFERING EXPERTISE IN VIRTUALLY EVERY AREA OF THE LAW. ◆ THE FIRM WAS ESTABLISHED IN 1914 BY A GROUP OF SEASONED ATTORNEYS WHO HAD BEEN PRACTICING AT OTHER WELL-ESTABLISHED CHICAGO

law firms. Each brought special talents and abilities to the new venture. None, however, could have envisioned the prominence the firm would come to achieve in the decades that followed.

The firm underwent several name changes until 1969, when it finally became the namesake of partners Albert E. Jenner and Samuel W.

Jenner & Block's headquarters office features a mock trial room.

Block, both prominent local attorneys. Headquartered today in Chicago, the firm is housed on nine floors of the 47-story One IBM Plaza. Jenner & Block maintains additional offices in north suburban Lake Forest, Miami, Florida, and Washington, D.C.

The firm's attorneys are supported by a staff of highly trained professionals, including more than 100 paralegals, skilled project assistants, and technical experts in data and information processing. These individuals provide specialized litigation assistance and transactional support. Likewise, Jenner & Block's state-of-the-art technology support

center offers attorneys and staff access to computer equipment and networking capabilities around the clock.

A BROAD CLIENT BASE

Jenner & Block's broad client base includes Fortune 500 companies, such as Tenneco Corp., MCI Communications Corp., and General

Dynamics Corp., as well as a wide range of small and medium-size business enterprises. Industrial and commercial concerns, telecommunications companies, research and development firms, public utilities, and state and local governmental bodies are a few of the clients the firm has served in Chicago and beyond. Jenner & Block has also developed a unique expertise in representing railroad companies and trade associations.

Jenner & Block is widely regarded as the nation's preeminent litigation firm. Clients from across the country rely on the firm's expertise in the most complex and chal-

lenging civil cases, as well as in a broad range of criminal matters. Jenner & Block's litigators have won impressive victories before federal, state, and administrative tribunals and have argued matters before the United States Supreme Court, all 13 circuits of the United States Circuit Court of Appeals, and dozens of other federal and state courts nationwide. The firm's extensive criminal practice has included the defense of corporations and individuals in many high-profile cases.

Jenner & Block represents clients in disputes involving accountant and attorney defense, antitrust matters, appeals, construction, employment, labor, environmental issues, domestic relations, futures, insurance, intellectual property, communications, media, First Amendment rights, product liability, negligence defense, securities, corporate control, transportation, unfair competition, white collar crime, and criminal litigation.

Attorneys in the firm's transaction practice have handled major corporate reorganizations and bankruptcies, mergers, acquisitions, tax matters, financing, patents, and real estate transactions for clients of virtually every size. In recent years, Jenner & Block has been involved in many highly publicized matters, including representing MCI in its successful antitrust actions that lead to the break-up of AT&T, obtaining the dismissal of fraud indictments against General Dynamics, representing debtors in nationally significant Chapter 11 proceedings, and representing management-led groups in leveraged buy-outs.

In all of its diverse areas of expertise, Jenner & Block strives to serve its clients on a timely, cost-efficient basis in accordance with the highest professional standards. The firm is proud of its long-

The firm is today housed on nine floors of the 47-story One IBM Plaza building.

standing reputation as an aggressive advocate for its clients' interests.

SERVING THE LEGAL PROFESSION

As a longtime member of the local legal community, Jenner & Block is committed to serving and improving the legal profession. The firm's lawyers contribute at many levels, holding local government posts and serving on federal and state court committees and on numerous bar association committees.

Likewise, members of the firm hold positions on the advisory committee for Federal Rules of Civil Procedure; on the state rules, criminal, and civil jury instruction committees; and on the permanent editorial board for the Uniform Commercial Code. On three occasions, Jenner & Block attorneys have been appointed to serve as Special Counsel to Judiciary Committees of the House of Representatives and the U.S. Senate.

A firm partner chaired the Special Commission on the Administration of Justice in Cook County, which was charged with recommending changes in the wake of judicial scandals. In 1992, a firm partner was appointed to the Illinois Supreme Court Commission on the Administration of Justice. Other partners include a former judge of the U.S. Court of Appeals for the Seventh Circuit, a former justice of the Illinois Appellate Court for the Second District, and two former U.S. Attorneys for the Northern District of Illinois. Jenner & Block was also named counsel to the City of Chicago in its investigation of municipal corruption.

In addition, the firm's attorneys participate in professional associations and continuing legal education seminars, and serve as instructors for area law schools. They also frequently write articles for a variety of legal and business publications.

COMMUNITY COMMITMENT

This level of enthusiasm for the legal profession is equaled only by the firm's enthusiasm for the many charities, community organizations, and public interest groups it supports. Jenner & Block's attorneys are committed to helping such organizations achieve their objectives through generous donations of time, legal expertise, and resources.

Further illustration of the firm's concern for the community is its long tradition of involvement in socially significant cases and in the representation of indigents in civil and criminal matters. In fact, Jenner & Block is one of the only private law firms in the state to receive the Illinois Public Defender Association's award for representation of indigents in criminal cases at trial and in the appellate courts.

After nearly eight decades of outstanding legal service, the firm is well positioned to build on its impressive past. The attorneys and staff of Jenner & Block look forward to continuing their strong commitment to clients, to the profession, and to the community in the decades to come.

CHICAGO MERCANTILE EXCHANGE

FROM BUTTER AND EGGS TO EURODOLLARS AND JAPANESE YEN, THE CHICAGO MERCANTILE EXCHANGE (CME) HAS GROWN DRAMATICALLY IN THE PAST TWO DECADES. ONCE STRICTLY A MARKET FOR AGRICULTURAL PRODUCTS, THE EXCHANGE IS TODAY THE WORLD'S LEADER IN THE TRADING

of financial futures and options, used for risk and asset management by many of the largest financial institutions in the world.

The vibrancy and energy emanating from the trading floor of the Merc, as it is affectionately called, reflects the real character of Chicago itself. What looks to be a chaotic frenzy of shouting and hand signals is actually the efficient, fast-paced buying and selling of futures and options in a worldwide financial arena.

The CME has its origins in the old Chicago Produce Exchange, which opened in the 1870s as a cash market for farm produce. In 1898, the Chicago Butter and Egg Board was created. That organization changed its name in 1919 to the more inclusive Chicago Mercantile Exchange.

When the CME officially opened on December 1, 1919, three futures contracts were traded in the first 45 minutes, and memberships, required for trading-floor privileges, sold for about $100. Today, futures contracts and options trade at the rate of 20 per second and memberships, commonly called "seats," sell for more than $600,000.

Over the years, the Exchange has evolved into the global leader in financial futures trading, boasting the greatest variety of financial contracts of any exchange in the world. These include foreign-currency, interest-rate, and equity-related prod-

ucts. Average daily trading volume now exceeds 500,000 contracts.

A PIONEER IN FINANCIAL FUTURES

Throughout its history, the CME has been a pacesetter. In the 1960s, bucking futures industry traditions, the Exchange introduced contracts on live animals. Today, the CME is the world's largest futures-trading center for non-storable commodities. But the greatest display of innovation by the Exchange came in 1972 when it pioneered financial futures and created the International Money Market (IMM). CME leaders had the foresight to believe that the principles that applied to the trading of agricultural commodities could be applied successfully to financial instruments.

The first financial futures transaction in history occurred in May 1972 with the launch of CME trading in seven foreign currencies, among them the British pound, Canadian dollar, Japanese yen, and Swiss franc. This breakthrough led to futures trading in short-term interest-rate instruments such as U.S. Treasury bills, certificates of deposit, and Eurodollars. Prior to unveiling Eurodollar futures, the CME initiated the concept of cash settlement, applying it subsequently to stock-index futures contracts, some additional interest-rate contracts, and several agricultural commodities.

The CME created another division, the Index and Options Market (IOM), in 1982. It trades stock index futures and options on futures. The IOM has made futures trading available to participants in the equity market.

Recognizing a global need to manage financial risk around the clock, the CME and the Chicago Board of Trade (CBOT) developed the GLOBEX® trading system in conjunction with Reuters, an interna-

Since 1983, the CME Center on Wacker Drive has housed the world's leading center for risk and asset management. In 1992, the 73-year-old Merc set a trading volume record, as 134,238,555 futures and options changed hands.

JESS SMITH / PHOTOSMITH

tional communications organization. Launched on June 25, 1992, GLOBEX is an around-the-clock, around-the-world automated electronic trading system.

The advent of GLOBEX is just one more indication of the growing acceptance globally of futures and options for risk and asset management. Jack Sandner, chairman of the CME Board of Governors, says, "Not so long ago, it would have been considered malfeasance for a portfolio manager or corporate treasurer to contemplate trading futures and options. Now, in an era of risk and asset management, it would be considered malfeasance to ignore them. Futures and options are fast becoming an asset class unto themselves."

CONTRIBUTING TO CHICAGO'S FINANCIAL PROMINENCE

The CME's prominence has helped make Chicago a world-class financial center. More than 80 foreign bank branches and representative offices have a presence in the city. Many have come to Chicago because of the CME's importance in the worldwide foreign-exchange market.

Each year, the Exchange welcomes dignitaries from around the world. Financial representatives from various countries travel to Chicago to study the market, then frequently return home to create their own. In addition, more than 100,000 tourists visit the CME each year.

The Exchange has in recent years set up offices outside the United States. In 1980, with the opening of a London office, it became the first U.S. exchange to establish such a presence in Europe. Similarly, the CME's Tokyo office, opened in 1987, was the first of its kind in Asia. Early in 1992, the latter office was combined with the CBOT's Tokyo branch.

At home, this explosion of growth has resulted in overcrowding on the CME trading floor—not an altogether unfamiliar occurrence. In

1919, trading was initiated in an office building at Lake and LaSalle streets. Just two years later, the CME relocated to larger quarters at Wells and Lake streets. In 1928, the Exchange relocated again to a new 14-story building at Washington and Franklin streets, where it remained for 40 years. Another move, over Thanksgiving of 1972, sent CME traders to 444 W. Jackson, where another 23,000 square feet of trading space was eventually added. In 1983, the Exchange settled into its current home, a 40-story, twin-tower building at 10 and 30 S. Wacker Drive.

The CME's 40,000-square-foot main trading floor is the world's largest futures trading facility. In 1993, the trading floor will be expanded by more than 30,000 square feet by incorporating the floor above it, which was designed in anticipation of future needs.

Prospects for the continued growth and development of the Chicago Mercantile Exchange are unlimited, according to Exchange officials. Building on more than seven decades of innovation, the Exchange expects to remain at the forefront of the futures industry by continuing to develop and market new products that address the present and future needs of investors worldwide.

When the Chicago Mercantile Exchange opened for business on December 1, 1919, three contracts were traded during the first 45 minutes of that day's session. Today, contracts trade at a rate of more than 20 per second.

CONSOER, TOWNSEND & ASSOCIATES

THE CHICAGO-BASED ENGINEERING FIRM OF CONSOER, TOWNSEND & ASSOCIATES HAS PLAYED AN IMPORTANT ROLE IN THE DEVELOPMENT OF CHICAGO AND ITS SUBURBS FOR 75 YEARS. ◆ THE COMPANY WAS FOUNDED IN 1919 BY GEORGE AND A.W. CONSOER, BROTHERS WHO HAD

served in the Army Corps of Engineers during World War I. Their early commissions included municipal improvement plans for sewer, water, and paving projects in Chicago and in suburbs like Mount Prospect, Niles Center (Skokie), Park Ridge, Calumet City, and Burnham.

The firm's first offices were in a single room, but within two years, growth forced relocation to larger quarters atop the Marquette Building. Since the elevator did not reach the top floor, staff and clients had to walk up, engendering the nickname "Attic Engineers."

The Roaring '20s were busy times for the young firm. Within six years, the staff had grown to 100. The firm's name changed to Consoer, Older & Quinlan, reflecting the addition of two new partners who brought expertise in bridge and highway engineering.

By 1929, Consoer, Older & Quinlan had become the largest municipal engineering firm in the Chicago area. Although the Great Depression decimated the engineering industry, the firm survived by participating in FDR's reconstruction programs. During this time, Darwin Townsend Sr. left a position as Acting Chief Engineer of the Milwaukee Sewage Commission to join the firm. Townsend, who pioneered the activated sludge treatment process, brought instant credibility in wastewater treatment to the firm.

Military projects dominated the World War II years. In recognition of the role played by the firm's younger engineers, the company adopted its current name in 1944. CT&A played an important role in post-war reconstruction, focusing on municipal infrastructure and transportation projects.

Throughout the 1970s and '80s, environmental engineering became increasingly important. CT&A com-

pleted work from coast to coast and overseas, developing many innovative procedures. At Duluth, Minnesota, for example, the firm met the challenges of energy conservation, wastewater pollution control, and solid waste disposal by developing the first wastewater treatment plant to burn sewage sludge and municipal refuse for energy production.

A FULL RANGE OF CLIENT-ORIENTED SERVICES

Entering the 1990s, Consoer, Townsend & Associates became an independently run, employee-owned company.

As a multi-discipline engineering firm, CT&A offers state-of-the-art environmental, transportation, municipal, and energy engineering; architecture; building systems; and construction phase services. Still headquartered in Chicago's downtown, the firm maintains offices in more than a dozen cities across the United States and ranks among the top engineering firms in the country. Of its more than 350 employees nationwide, over half are based in Chicago.

"Consoer, Townsend & Associates is proud of the vital role it has

played in the development of its hometown," says Bill Townsend, CT&A vice president. The firm helped establish one of the most comprehensive transportation systems in the world, including major parts of Chicagoland's expressways and tollways. CT&A has undertaken more than 25 assignments at O'Hare International Airport, including

design of the nation's first taxiway bridge, and is a partner in developing the new international terminal. Recently, the firm designed a specialized traffic signal system which will keep traffic moving along Michigan Avenue's Magnificent Mile. CT&A is also working with both the Metropolitan Rail Authority and the Chicago Transit Authority to upgrade station facilities and make them accessible to disabled residents.

According to Chicago native Robert Fischer, CT&A's president, being headquartered in Chicago offers advantages the firm might not find in another community. "Being based in one of the largest cities in the United States gives us an understanding of the importance of a sound infrastructure system," he says. "We've worked with virtually

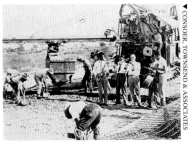

One early project, completed in 1928, was the Howard-Keeler Sewer System in suburban Skokie (top).

Today, Consoer, Townsend & Associates is an independently run, employee-owned company (bottom).

Right: CT&A has completed more than 25 projects at O'Hare International Airport.

Recently, CT&A designed a specialized traffic signal system which will keep traffic moving along Michigan Avenue's Magnificent Mile (left).

every branch of city government and most neighboring municipalities. We've continued to be a major part of Chicago's growth."

ENVIRONMENTAL ENGINEERING

Over the years, environmental engineering has emerged as a growing specialization in the design industry. CT&A has responded to challenges as diverse as developing the Busse Woods Reservoir in Elk Grove Village, which provides stormwater detention and recreational facilities for hiking, boating, and nature preservation; developing a closure and post-closure plan for Chicago's Stearns Quarry municipal landfill; designing a system to bring Lake Michigan water to the northwestern suburbs; and designs and expansions to wastewater treatment plants in DuPage County and for the Metropolitan Water Reclamation District of Greater Chicago.

CT&A's expertise has had worldwide impact as well. The firm created a solid waste plan for metropolitan Manila in the Philippines. In Antarctica, CT&A is involved in a variety of environmental projects, including removal of more than

6 million tons of waste material and the development of a comprehensive waste management program for the U.S. Antarctic Program.

COMMUNITY INVOLVEMENT

"Our engineering achievements are only part of the story," Fischer points out. "Just as important are the contributions we make to the local community."

CT&A maintains an active program in which students from area engineering schools gain professional experience. On both the corporate and individual levels, the firm and its employee-owners contribute to the social fabric of the community. Employees volunteer their time for activities ranging from the Scouts and Camp Fire programs, to religious institutions, to drug abuse and child care programs, to community boards and planning commissions.

CT&A's employees have developed and participated in technology transfer and exchange programs with engineering societies in South America, Ireland, Japan, and Eastern Europe. Through organizational involvement, CT&A has helped

bring a variety of professional conventions and meetings to the city.

The firm's past pioneering work is indicative of its future in Chicago. CT&A is on the cutting edge of environmental cleanup techniques, finding creative solutions to existing problems and helping to prevent them. As a leading engineering firm with a 75-year history of growth and excellence, Consoer, Townsend & Associates looks forward to remaining a vital part of Chicago's future development.

The firm has helped establish one of the most comprehensive transportation systems in the world, including reconstruction work on the John F. Kennedy Expressway (top right).

The Chicago-based firm supplies environmental remediation and management services for the U.S. Antarctic Program (bottom).

AMERICAN AIRLINES

TO THE MORE THAN 12,000 CHICAGO-BASED EMPLOYEES OF AMERICAN AIRLINES AND ITS REGIONAL AIRLINE AFFILIATE, AMERICAN EAGLE, "WE MEAN BUSINESS IN CHICAGO" IS MORE THAN JUST A SLOGAN. IT'S A DECADES-OLD COMMITMENT TO PROVIDING EXCELLENT SERVICE TO THE passengers who travel through O'Hare International Airport each year.

A LONG LIST OF "FIRSTS"

April 15, 1926 marked the beginning of a series of "firsts" for American Airlines in Chicago. On that day in aviation's infancy, a young pilot named Charles Lindbergh flew mail aboard a single-engine bi-plane from Chicago to St. Louis for Robertson Aircraft Corporation. After stopping in Peoria and Springfield on the way, Lindbergh arrived in St. Louis nine minutes early. This mail run marked the first flight for an outfit that grew to become American Airlines. (It was little more than a year later that Lindbergh made his historic transatlantic flight from New York to Paris.)

American made history again in 1936 when it flew the world's first commercial DC-3 flight from Chicago's Municipal Airport to New York. In 1955, American's Flight 715 from Detroit was the first scheduled passenger plane to land at what was the new O'Hare Airport. In 1959, the airline introduced the first jet service in Chicago.

By the early 1990s, more than 10 million American and American Eagle passengers a year were taking advantage of the more than 900 flights into and out of O'Hare each day, including nonstop service to more than 100 destinations. And from its "GAAteway to the World" mid-continent hub, American flew nonstop to more international cities from O'Hare than any other carrier.

The Admirals Club Executive Center at O'Hare (right) has 19 conference rooms that are specially equipped with state-of-the-art audiovisual equipment and other amenities.

More than 10 million passengers flowed through American's "GAAteway to the World" hub at O'Hare in 1992.

CONTINUING SERVICE IMPROVEMENTS

As the nation's largest air carrier, American has an extensive route system and operates the world's largest commercial aircraft fleet.

American has repeatedly won awards for its domestic air carrier service and International Flagship Service. Publications such as *Air Transport World*, *Financial World*, *The Wall Street Transcript*, *Business Traveler International*, and *Corporate Travel Magazine* have ranked the airline as "best" in business and leisure travel, or named it "Airline of the Year."

VIP AMENITIES

In 1939, American became the first airline to establish a VIP lounge to accommodate leisure and business travelers on layovers between flights. Today, American's Admirals Club is synonymous with comfort and elegance at the world's major airports. The 33,000-square-foot Admirals Club at O'Hare is the largest airport lounge in the world.

Also located in the Admirals Club complex, between Terminal 3's H and K concourses, is the unique Executive Center with 19 fully

equipped conference rooms. The rooms can function as a branch office for business travelers needing a quiet place to hold meetings or make presentations.

The Executive Center, opened in 1991, is just one example of the improvements that American Airlines has undertaken since O'Hare was designated as a hub in 1982. Since then, American has spent more than $500 million on upgrades and expansion projects at its O'Hare facility.

Another substantial investment in Chicago is the American Airlines Maintenance Academy located near Midway Airport on the city's south side. Established in 1990, the school has graduated hundreds of qualified students who have received their airframe and power plant licenses, and are not only trained jet engine mechanics but also highly skilled maintenance technicians ready to join the local work force.

American's commitment to the city is further evidenced in its sup-

port of institutions such as the Lyric Opera of Chicago, the Museum of Contemporary Art, and the Museum of Broadcast Communications. American also has been actively involved in Chicago's neighborhood festivals, the Jazz in June perform-ances at Ravinia Music Festival, the annual Chicago-Mackinac Island

sailboat race, and the North Ameri-can Challenge Cup race for sailors with disabilities.

American has a long-standing commitment to providing high-quality passenger service in Chicago and is pledged to continue that tradition for decades to come.

American Airlines and its regional airline affiliate, American Eagle, operate more than 900 flights into and out of O'Hare International Airport each business day (above).

The American Airlines Maintenance Academy (left) is the leading school in the country offering students the technical, academic, and practical training needed to prepare them for careers in the ever-changing large jet transport industry.

THE JEL SERT COMPANY

T HE JEL SERT COMPANY, A NATIONAL LEADER IN THE REFRESHMENTS-FOR-CHILDREN MARKET, KNOWS TO FOCUS ON THREE INGREDIENTS: FLAVOR, FUN, AND VALUE. THE COMPANY SPECIALIZES IN DESIGNING PRODUCTS THAT ARE GREAT TASTING AND FUN FOR KIDS, WHILE MAINTAINING A

good value for the consumer.

With this marketing truism guiding the company, Jel Sert has successfully competed against the giants of the food industry for more than 65 years. Children of all ages across the United States and the globe enjoy Jel Sert products, including Fla-Vor-Aid and Aunt Wick's powdered drink mixes, Fla-Vor-Ice and Pop-Ice freezer bars, and Mondo Fruit Squeezers.

A HISTORY OF GROWTH

A family-owned business since the beginning, The Jel Sert Company has grown by providing the highest quality products at the lowest possible prices.

Mr. and Mrs. Charles T. Wegner Jr. founded the company in 1926 on Chicago's West Side. Charles Wegner had gained industry experience working for the Cracker Jack Company, and the couple borrowed a small amount of money from their

parents to launch the firm. The first product the company manufactured was a gelatin dessert called Jel Sert, a name derived from combining "jelly" and "dessert."

In 1929, the company introduced Fla-Vor-Aid powdered drink mixes and a number of other products, including a powdered syrup mix called Makamix. Of these early products, only Fla-Vor-Aid is still made by the firm.

Even through the Great Depression, Jel Sert grew. The extremely low prices of the company's products helped keep sales steady. Later, it was Jel Sert's new line of sweetened and unsweetened powdered drink mixes that inspired further growth. These mixes, which bore the name "Aunt Wick's" (Mrs. Wegner's nickname), became quite popular in the 1950s and 1960s. Jel Sert still markets Aunt Wick's unsweetened lemonade and root beer flavored drink mixes.

"Our powdered drink mixes have been the foundation of the company since the 1920s, and they are sold at

Jel Sert's plant in West Chicago produces more than 10 million freezer bars per day (above).

The company's product list includes Fla-Vor-Ice and Pop-Ice freezer bars and Fla-Vor-Aid powdered drink mixes (right and above right).

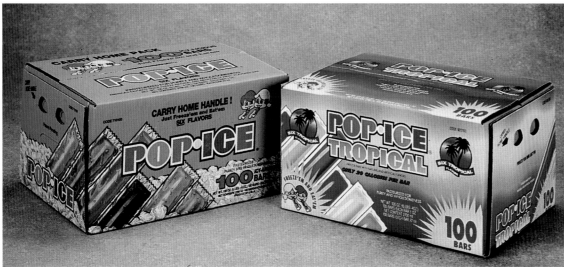

To complement its existing products, Jel Sert recently introduced Mondo Fruit Squeezers (top left), which is made with 10 percent fruit juice and is available in five flavors.

half the price of the leading competitor," says Charles T. Wegner IV, grandson of the founder and president of the company today. It was, however, Jel Sert's acquisition of the Pop-Ice Company in 1963 that led to the introduction of its biggest seller, freezer bars. Today, Jel Sert is number one in the country in the freezer bar market.

In 1969, Jel Sert introduced a second freezer bar brand called Fla-Vor-Ice. The demand for Fla-Vor-Ice and Pop-Ice bars was so great that the company relocated the following year from a plant it had occupied in Bellwood for eight years to a larger facility in west suburban DuPage County where it remains today. With updated equipment and more efficient production, Jel Sert was able to compete more effectively in the freezer bar market. Aggressive marketing and selling efforts by Jel Sert paved the way for the Fla-Vor-Ice and Pop-Ice brands to corner more than 50 percent of

the freezer bar category in the United States. The bars now come in 12 flavors, including a tropical variety, and in packages of varying sizes, from 20 to 150 bars.

Jel Sert's plant in West Chicago is the world's largest freezer bar manufacturing facility. The company produces more than 10 million freezer bars per day there and outsells its closest national competitor by more than three to one. The facility currently supplies freezer bars to the entire United States and 25 foreign countries.

The company also has licensing agreements with manufacturers in other countries, including Haiti, Jamaica, New Zealand, Chile, Venezuela, and Mexico, to produce freezer bars under the Jel Sert name.

A PROMISING NEW PRODUCT

Mondo Fruit Squeezers is Jel Sert's exciting new entry in the growing aseptic juice drink market. Made

with 10 percent fruit juice, the product is available in five flavors, "Outstanding Orange," "Legendary Berry," "Chillin' Cherry," "Global Grape," and "Primo Punch." The eight-ounce bottles, made from the same recyclable material as plastic milk jugs, are packaged in colorful and attractive six-pack cartons. The bottles also are designed with a wide base so they can stand alone and will fit easily into lunch boxes.

For more than six decades, The Jel Sert Company has responded to market changes intelligently and with innovation—creating products that have proven popular with generations of kids. Complemented by the strong commitment of both the Wegner family and company employees worldwide, Jel Sert will continue to flourish by making products that meet the highest standards of flavor, fun, and value.

POWER CONTRACTING AND ENGINEERING CORP.

**M**ORE THAN JUST A STRUCTURE, A BUILDING REPRESENTS A LONG-TERM INVESTMENT FOR WHICH THE OWNER MUST CONSIDER INITIAL COST, OPERATING COST, AND FUTURE VALUE. NO ONE APPRECIATES THE AMBIVALENT FEELINGS OF EXCITEMENT AND APPREHENSION

connected with the start of a building project better than the people at Power. Since 1926, Power has been shaping the metropolitan Chicago landscape by constructing hundreds of health care, commercial, industrial, residential, and institutional facilities.

Headquartered in northwest suburban Rolling Meadows, Power is one of the Chicago area's oldest and most respected builders, providing construction management and general contracting services. Proud of its history of financial strength and stability, Power today completes an annual volume of work in excess of $190 million. In 1992, Power was

chairman of the board. Thomas D. Settles was appointed president in 1991.

AN INDUSTRY LEADER IN CHICAGO

For more than 30 years, Power has been successful at penetrating and, in many cases, dominating various segments of the Chicagoland construction market. In the 1960s, Power became the leader in the construction of educational buildings, including multiple projects for the University of Chicago, Northwestern University, and the Illinois Institute of Technology. Power also built Quigley Preparatory Seminary,

Memorial Hospital, four major hospitals for Evangelical Health Systems, Alexian Brothers of America, Highland Park Hospital, Evanston Hospital, and Loyola University Medical Center.

Today, Power continues to increase its presence and stature in the institutional and health care markets with major projects for the University of Chicago, Loyola University, Good Samaritan Hospital, and Lutheran General Hospital. In 1991, Power was selected as construction manager for the Northwestern Memorial Hospital Redevelopment Program, a $550 million, eight-year program and the largest privately

The Loyola Cancer Center at the Medical Center campus in Maywood is the eighth project Power has built for Loyola University (above).

Good Samaritan Hospital in Downers Grove was built by Power in 1976 (right). Today, Power is construction manager for a multi-year, phased expansion to the hospital.

ranked as the seventh largest construction company in Chicago by *Crain's Business Week*. It is the only firm among the top seven that does business exclusively in the Chicagoland area.

The privately-held company has maintained family ownership and management since its founding by Jerome Goldstein. In the beginning, the firm focused on designing and building power plants, a specialty from which the company took its name. Early on, however, the firm shifted its emphasis to general building and began expanding its experience base on an almost decade-by-decade basis. This trend has continued under the direction of Alvin L. Gorman, who became company president in 1962 and is now

Latin School of Chicago, St. Louise De Marrilac High School, Proviso West High School, and New Trier West High School, among many others.

Beginning in the late 1960s and continuing today, Power emerged as the major builder of hospital and health care facilities in the Chicago area. In fact, no other local firm can match either the number of facilities or the dollar volume of health care construction completed by Power. Some examples of new facilities or major additions constructed by the firm include projects for MacNeal

funded development in Chicago history.

During the 1970s, Power added prominent corporate buildings to its portfolio of project experience, including major projects for Fortune 500 corporations such as United Airlines, Motorola, Honeywell, and Allstate Insurance Company. By the 1980s the company's workload was equally divided among institutional, corporate, and developer projects. During that decade, Power constructed 25 suburban office buildings totaling over 5 million square feet of space.

Designed by Loebl Schlossman & Hackl, One Overlook Point in Lincolnshire Corporate Center is a 250,000-square-foot office building developed by Van Vlissingen & Company (left).

The Marriott Suites Hotel in Rosemont was the first of six projects built for Marriott in the Chicago area (below).

Another important milestone for the company during that period was the construction in 1984 of the 550-room Westin O'Hare Hotel, which led to Power's emergence as the number one builder of first-class hotel facilities in Chicago. Since then, the firm has completed the Compri Hotel, the Hotel Sofitel, three Hyatt Hotels, five Marriott Hotels, the 40-story City Place office/hotel (Hyatt Suites) building, the Guest Quarters Suite Hotel, and the Stouffer Riviere Hotel.

High-quality tenant buildout projects are also a significant part of Power's workload. Representative interior projects are the new 98,000-square-foot headquarters for Marsh & McLennan; 470,000 square feet of tenant improvements for Hewitt Associates; and 240,000 square feet for Benefit Trust Life Insurance Company.

DIVERSITY AND FLEXIBILITY FOR THE FUTURE

Indicative of the firm's continuing commitment to diversification are several projects currently under construction, including the University of Chicago Biological Sciences Learning Center and Jules Knapp

Medical Research Building, the 1.9 million-square-foot United Parcel Service Chicago Area Consolidation Hub, two United States Post Office facilities, and a new 175,000-square-foot corporate headquarters building developed by Van Vlissingen & Company for Washington National Insurance Company.

Power attributes a large part of its success to its willingness and ability to respond to change, whether in the marketplace or on the job. The company has adapted to change through diversification of its work portfolio and an awareness of and appropriate response to market trends. Together with its commitment to total client satisfaction, this philosophy has maintained Power's leadership position in the Chicagoland construction industry.

Another significant factor in the firm's success is a lack of change; that is, in the employee roster. Many employees have been with the firm for more than 20 years. Power's average length of employment of all salaried staff is over 10 years.

Recently, the company's longtime commitment to outstanding work was recognized by the Illinois

Institute of Technology. Power was chosen as the 1991-92 Vendor of the Year from a field of 5,000 companies for its performance in building IIT's new Downtown Center/Kent School of Law. Service-driven, with a reputation for performance, integrity, and client satisfaction, Power Contracting and Engineering Corp. is dedicated to serving the future construction needs of Chicago institutions, corporations, and other commercial enterprises.

UNITED AIRLINES, INC.

THE FRIENDLY SKIES HAVE NEVER COVERED SO MUCH OF THE GLOBE. TODAY, UNITED AIRLINES' WINGS SPAN 33 COUNTRIES ON FIVE CONTINENTS. THIS GLOBAL AIRLINE WITH STRONG CHICAGO ROOTS HAS ITS WORLDWIDE HEADQUARTERS IN THE AREA AND OPERATES ITS LARGEST

Three United flight attendants (right) show their support for the Chicago Cubs at Wrigley Field. United is the team's official airline.

Right: On the ground and in the air, United employees are key to the airline's success.

hub at Chicago's O'Hare International Airport.

Chicago's hometown airline, United traces its history to 1926 and the early air mail routes that paved the way for commercial aviation. United today is one of the largest passenger and cargo airlines in the world, offering more than 2,000 flights each day. Hubs in Chicago, Denver, San Francisco, and Washington, D.C. anchor the carrier's domestic route system and provide efficient access to United's global network.

United is the largest international carrier among all U.S. airlines and the world's largest carrier across the Pacific. International flights account for roughly one-third of the airline's capacity. United operates international hubs in London and Tokyo, as well as major connecting complexes in Mexico City and Paris.

With more than 81,000 employees worldwide and a fleet of more than 500 aircraft, United serves an average of 180,000 passengers daily. As the world's leading cargo airline among combination passenger/cargo carriers, United each day carries more than 4.5 million ton-miles of freight and mail to destinations around the world.

A HISTORY OF INNOVATION

The first chapter in United Airlines' history was written on April 6, 1926, when a Swallow biplane took off from an open field in Pasco, Washington to deliver U.S. mail for the first time on a private-contract basis.

Since those early days, the airline has introduced numerous industry innovations that have contributed to customer convenience, comfort, and safety. In 1930, United introduced the world to flight attendant service. The airline served up another winner

in 1936 when it delivered the first in-flight meal from its first flight kitchen facility in Oakland, California.

The airline also introduced the first coast-to-coast commercial flights, the first automatic baggage-conveyor system, the first radar equipped fleet, and the first nationwide computerized reservations system. In 1987, United pioneered personalized concierge service for its international first-class passengers.

Throughout its history, safety has remained United's number one priority. The company's most recent contribution to improved air travel safety was its assistance in developing the Traffic Alert and Collision Avoidance System (TCAS). This highly sophisticated aircraft equipment not only informs pilots of the location of nearby aircraft but also

advises them on how to avoid a mid-air collision in threatening circumstances.

United operates an industry-leading flight training center in Denver and one of the world's largest aircraft maintenance facilities in San Francisco. In 1993, a second maintenance base will open in Indianapolis, Indiana.

CHICAGO HEADQUARTERS ESTABLISHED IN 1931

United, which established its corporate headquarters in Chicago in 1931, takes great pride in its extensive operations in the area and its contributions to the local economy. The airline's headquarters complex relocated in 1961 to suburban Elk Grove Village near O'Hare International Airport and today employs more than 3,000 people in several

United unveiled a stylish new blue and grey paint scheme for its aircraft in January 1993.

About 43,000 passengers arrive and depart each day on United flights at the airline's 48-gate Terminal One at O'Hare International Airport.

facilities. Its Inflight Training Center, housed at the complex, trains all of the airline's flight attendants, who currently number 18,000. In 1991, more than 2,600 flight attendants graduated from the program.

United's state-of-the-art System Operations Control Center at the complex keeps track of all the airline's flights around the clock and across the globe. The control center's 250 employees communicate with pilots in flight and with field stations, schedule flight crews, plan aircraft maintenance, and develop flight plans. Staff meteorologists at the center gather weather information from U.S. government weather satellites and from the company's Doppler Radar system, which is so sophisticated that the Federal Aviation Administration often calls on United for the most up-to-date weather information.

The airline's 48-gate Terminal One at O'Hare International Airport and 11,800 employees welcome visitors to Chicago with the world's largest light sculpture, designed by artist Michael Hayden and installed in 1987. About 43,000 passengers arrive and depart on United flights at the award-winning terminal each day. United operates more than 425 daily weekday departures from O'Hare to more than 100 non-stop markets in the United States and around the world. Behind the scenes at Terminal One are three flight kitchens where 1,200 employees prepare 43,000 meals a day.

United's largest regional reservations office is located near O'Hare. This $25 million, 120,000-square-foot facility is equipped with nearly 1,000 workstations and has the capacity to handle more than 7,000 calls per hour.

Throughout its history, United Airlines has strived to be an international leader in the airline industry. By not only meeting but exceeding industry standards of safety, convenience, and comfort, the airline that's uniting the world has secured its place for the future in Chicago and in the skies across the globe.

W.W. GRAINGER, INC.

I N BUSINESS FOR 65 YEARS, W.W. GRAINGER, INC. BEGAN AS A SMALL FAMILY BUSINESS AND CONTINUES TO BE SUCCESSFUL BASED ON THE HIGH STANDARDS ESTABLISHED BY ITS FOUNDER, WILLIAM W. GRAINGER. A COMMITMENT TO THE TRADITIONAL VALUES OF HONESTY, FAIRNESS, TRUSTWORTHINESS, QUALITY, AND

dedication to work and service is what has helped the company grow into the $2.4 billion nationwide supplier it is today.

Headquartered in north suburban Skokie, W.W. Grainger, Inc. is a low-profile, highly successful wholesale distributor of equipment, components, and supplies. Grainger especially targets the commercial, industrial, contractor, and institutional markets in the United States.

In 1927, William W. Grainger, a University of Illinois electrical engineer, recognized the need for a wholesale electric motor sales and distribution business. The company he founded that year was incorporated in 1928. The timing for Grainger's new business was perfect: Factories were in the process of converting from single direct current (DC) motors powering whole factories to individual alternating current (AC) motors at each

workstation. Every changeover meant new motors were needed. Grainger and his sister, Margaret, who were the company's only employees in the beginning, worked hard to meet that demand.

Today, David Grainger, son of the founder, serves as chairman of the board and president of the company, which employs 10,000 people nationwide. Employees say W.W. Grainger, Inc. has a "family feel," which is bolstered by the long tenure of many of its people. It is not uncommon for employees to dedicate their entire careers to Grainger.

In 1967, W.W. Grainger, Inc. became a public company. Its common stock is now traded on the New York and Midwest stock exchanges under the ticker symbol GWW.

THE GRAINGER DIVISION

The Grainger Division, which composes a major part of the company's

operations, distributes equipment, components, and supplies to the commercial, industrial, contractor, and institutional markets in the United States. It has about 45,000 products in its line, ranging from air conditioners and ventilation equipment to drills, motors, and pumps. All of these items are featured in the division's principal marketing tool, the 3,000-page *General Catalog*, which has been printed continuously since 1927. Known as the "bible of the industry," it was recently made available on CD-ROM compact disc for quick computer screen access for product selection and technical information.

The division relies heavily on its nationwide team of more than 1,000 sales representatives who personally call on existing customers and prospects. This sales force is backed by fast and convenient service through a comprehensive network of more than 300 branch locations throughout the 50 states. In fact, a Grainger branch is located within a 20-minute drive of a large percentage of the company's more than 1 million customers.

EXPANDING COMPANY HOLDINGS

Within the past several years, Grainger has added six distribution business units to its corporate fold through acquisitions and new business start-ups. They are Allied Safety, a distributor of personal and environmental protection products and equipment; Ball Industries, a West Coast distributor of sanitary equipment and supplies; Bossert Industrial Supply, a distributor of cutting tools, abrasives, and other supplies used in manufacturing; Jani-Serv, a nationwide provider of

This Grainger Division branch in downtown Chicago is one of more than 300 located throughout the 50 states.

sanitary equipment and supplies; Lab Safety Supply, a leading national direct marketer of safety products; and Parts Company of America, a distributor of spare and replacement parts for commercial and industrial equipment.

AN OUTSTANDING RECORD

In its more than six decades of existence, Grainger has never had an unprofitable year, and in only four years—1932, 1938, 1943, and 1982—have sales fallen below the previous year's figures.

The company attributes its success to a solid management philosophy and to high ethical and moral standards. Employees are committed to superior service and customer satisfaction, and to establishing mutually fair and responsible partnerships with suppliers.

"Grainger's everyday emphasis on business ethics has helped make this an outstanding company," says Jere D. Fluno, vice chairman of the company. "I am very proud to say that in my 24 years at Grainger, I have never lost a night's sleep worrying about the company having done something illegal, immoral, dishonest, or unethical."

Richard L. Keyser, president of the Grainger Division, notes, "The company's commitment to others has been particularly evident during crisis situations, such as natural disasters." During 1992's Hurricane Andrew, Grainger provided disaster support by quickly making available a desperately needed supply of power generators, chain saws, and other critical items, often extending credit on faith. Grainger also donated food supplies and material to the communities affected. The company's community activities are conducted for the good of the community, frequently anonymously and always without fanfare.

A BRIGHT FUTURE

In the future, as it has in the past, W.W. Grainger, Inc. will continue to add modern technology to its network of computerized facilities in order to help employees serve their customers faster and more efficiently.

Upgrading facilities regularly and maintaining good employee relations will combine to provide the company with a secure foundation for growth and a promising future. Through its core business activities, Grainger is committed to being the preeminent broad-line distributor of equipment, components, and supplies to the commercial, industrial, contractor, and institutional markets in the United States. With its additional business units, W.W. Grainger, Inc. is striving to attain leadership positions as a distributor in other selected markets.

LASALLE NATIONAL BANK

FOUNDED MORE THAN 65 YEARS AGO TO SERVE THE NEEDS OF THE LOCAL BUSINESS COMMUNITY, LASALLE NATIONAL BANK HAS ESTABLISHED ITSELF AS A LEADER AMONG THE CITY'S COMMERCIAL BANKS. FROM ITS HEADQUARTERS IN THE HEART OF THE FINANCIAL DISTRICT IN DOWNTOWN CHICAGO,

"We strive to be second to none, to be the premier bank meeting the commercial banking needs of businesses in Chicago," says Norman R. Bobins, president and chief executive officer.

LaSalle National Bank is headquartered at 120 South LaSalle Street (right), one of the bank's four downtown locations.

LaSalle offers a full range of commercial banking services to mid-size companies throughout the greater Chicagoland area. "We strive to be second to none, to be the premier bank meeting the commercial banking needs of businesses in Chicago," says Norman R. Bobins, president and chief executive officer.

LaSalle has grown to operate four banking offices to serve its customers in downtown Chicago. It is a subsidiary of LaSalle National Corporation, and affiliated with eight other financial institutions in Chicago: LaSalle Northwest National Bank, LaSalle Bank Lake View, LaSalle Bank Northbrook, LaSalle Bank Westmont, LaSalle Bank of Lisle, LaSalle Bank Matteson, LaSalle National Trust, N.A., and LaSalle Talman Bank, FSB. The LaSalle organization has a strong presence in the Chicago area and works hard to maintain its leadership position.

DECADES OF GROWTH

LaSalle has grown steadily but rapidly through the decades. It was established in 1927 as the National Builders Bank of Chicago to serve the unique needs of business and industry and to provide banking services to working people in the city. Building a strong commercial business has remained a priority for LaSalle. As a leader in the city, however, the bank also has taken commanding roles in meeting the needs of the community, whether through its charitable generosity, by developing bank products and services that help smaller, but proven, businesses, or by working with the government and nonprofit organizations to help revitalize Chicago.

National Builders Bank of Chicago became LaSalle National Bank in 1940, and the 42-member staff moved to new, larger quarters in the Field Building at 135 South LaSalle

Street. In 1969, the headquarters was renamed the LaSalle Bank Building.

The 1940s and '50s were prosperous for LaSalle. By 1960, the bank employed 430 people and boasted $177 million in assets. A second lobby, located on Clark Street, was opened soon after. LaSalle purchased the Mutual National Bank at 79th and Halsted in 1967, and in 1968 the General American Transportation Corporation (GATX) bought controlling interest in the bank. Yet another banking facility was opened two years later at Jackson Boulevard and Wacker Drive.

Not long after GATX's acquisition, new federal banking laws were passed that required the company to

divest itself of LaSalle by 1981. The organization sold a small portion of its interest to four Chicago area bank holding companies in 1973, and in 1978 agreed to sell the remainder to an Amsterdam-based holding company, now known as ABN AMRO Holding N.V. The total transaction, valued at $82 million, was concluded in 1979.

It is the support of ABN AMRO Holding N.V., one of the 20 largest banks in the world with more than $250 billion in assets, that allows LaSalle to maintain higher lending limits than most commercial banks. "Our customers will never outgrow us," says Bobins. "LaSalle can handle virtually any Fortune 1000 company. Most of our customers have

LaSalle Street—in the heart of Chicago's downtown financial district.

$15 million to $75 million in sales, but they extend up to $250 million."

Always looking for new growth opportunities, LaSalle merged with Exchange National Bank in 1990. Exchange was a direct competitor, serving entrepreneurs and middle-market businesses in the Chicago area. The new, expanded LaSalle National Bank is doubly able to meet the needs of the Chicago middle market. More than 700 people and $7.1 billion in assets are working to assure success for the bank's customers.

COMMITTED TO THE CUSTOMER

Given the many years LaSalle has served Chicago, the bank knows that survival depends on a commitment to its clientele. Outstanding service, long-term vision, creativity, competitiveness, responsiveness, and sound judgment are just a few of the ingredients that go into successfully meeting the needs of the customer.

In many respects, says Bobins, a bank is a bank, offering products that are generally standard throughout the industry. While LaSalle has had its share of innovative products

and services, where banks really compete is at the service level. How can LaSalle better serve a client than the bank down LaSalle Street? "Someone who opens a checking account with us," explains Bobins, "isn't, to us, a new checking account customer. That person is a customer who has broader needs and who could benefit from some of our other services—if not now then in the future. Our bankers are trained to make our customers comfortable and to express LaSalle's genuine interest in helping them succeed by finding out how else we can serve them."

LaSalle also understands the importance of vision, as demonstrated by a staff that works hard to anticipate customer needs and cares about closing deals quickly and without a lot of fuss. Whether a customer needs equipment financing to support future growth, a working capital line of credit, or lockbox service for an expanding receivables base, LaSalle has the expertise and the understanding necessary to respond.

Creativity is not just for ad agencies anymore. The bank considers its staff members to be "creative

craftspeople" who have the experience and talent to find innovative solutions to their customers' individual challenges. In order to develop long-term relationships with its clientele, LaSalle keeps informed about their unique businesses and changing needs. Creativity can make the difference between a deal's success or failure, especially when it requires special expertise in commercial real estate lending, treasury products, asset-based financing, or banking for other financial institutions.

Chicagoans thrive on competition, and LaSalle bankers are equipped to survive in that environment. They recognize that effective competition relies on training and study, both before joining the bank and throughout their careers. As a result, LaSalle is home to commercial lenders who understand the unique needs of businesses in wholesale, retail, health care, service industries, and real estate.

Responsiveness is another priority at LaSalle National Bank. Getting the job done right, the first time, is the goal of each relationship manager. Whether responding to a loan request, transferring funds, tailoring cash management services to the customer's specific business needs, or simply answering the phone quickly and politely when a customer calls, LaSalle employees are trained to satisfy the customer.

Without sound judgment, LaSalle could not have survived in the sometimes volatile business environment throughout the years. Its dedication to the long-term view, careful consideration of risks, and avoidance of hasty decisions has made the bank a strong institution through more than a few boom and bust cycles, includ-

LaSalle's ability to look to the long term is central to the success of many middle-market customers. Left to right: Frank L. Corral, president of Chicago Heights Steel; Larry Richman, LaSalle National Bank executive vice president; and Nancy Corral, secretary of Chicago Heights Steel.

ing the Great Depression.

The versatility and sound judgment of LaSalle's bankers are crucial to the well-being of both the bank and its clientele. For example, retail, wholesale, and manufacturing customers who are involved in the import and export business find this versatility and experience critical. LaSalle's trade specialists offer sound advice and direct trade financing backed by a full range of foreign documentary services and the resources of parent company ABN AMRO Bank, with its more than 1,850 offices in more than 55 countries.

Likewise, LaSalle's strong capital base and sound financial condition provide the resources its customers

need when they are expanding and a secure depository for their money when they are waiting for the business climate to improve.

The bank has traditionally served the middle-market businesses of Chicago, which to LaSalle means those with more than $5 million in annual sales. Recognizing that some smaller customers had special needs LaSalle could satisfy, the Business Banking Division, staffed by seasoned commercial lenders, was created in 1992. In the tradition of all other LaSalle divisions, employees in the Business Banking Division

are trained to meet the unique needs of their clients. They are skilled at working with the Small Business Administration, a branch of the federal government that actively tries to help small businesses succeed. The division is backed by LaSalle's ability to lend what the client needs, without the "red tape" those businesses are trying to avoid by turning to LaSalle. These customers can also rely on the talented and resourceful LaSalle staff to develop specialized products that can make a big difference to a small business.

A LARGER ROLE IN THE COMMUNITY

In addition to its banking activities in Chicago, LaSalle has made a

pledge to help improve the community it serves. "While LaSalle has traditionally been a middle-market bank, we recognize the need for an institution like ours to play a larger leadership role in the community," says M. Hill Hammock, executive vice president. Through its Community Development Department, LaSalle is dedicated to supporting the credit needs of Chicago's diverse neighborhoods.

An example of the department's work is a $1.2 million line of credit that is funding the Local Initiatives Support Corporation's Chicago Home Ownership Program, a joint project of LISC, the City of Chicago, Neighborhood Housing Services, and community development corporations in six Chicago neighborhoods. Under the innovative program, community development corporations purchase and rehabilitate abandoned and deteriorated single-family homes and sell them at affordable prices to low- and moderate-income families.

LASALLE: SECOND TO NONE

LaSalle National Bank knows what it takes to survive seven decades in the banking industry: commitments. LaSalle is committed to the customer, committed to making business decisions that maintain the bank's financial strength, and committed to the community. LaSalle has the extensive knowledge of the financial markets that help shape its clientele's business and goals. The people at LaSalle are skilled at creating and maintaining long-lasting relationships with customers and possess the knowledge and ability to use the bank's extensive resources to meet the needs of customers and the community time and time again.

In the fast-paced, high-energy financial services industry in Chicago, LaSalle stands out with its history, strength, and commitments. LaSalle National Bank, like Chicago, is second to none.

For fast-growing companies, success depends on bankers who understand the dynamics of the customer's business and its markets. Left to right: Sheldon Sternberg, president of Bessin Corp., and David Rudis, LaSalle National Bank executive vice president.

Small businesses in the community need bankers who can offer ideas and a sense of direction. Left to right: Kristin Faust, vice president, Community Development, LaSalle National Bank; Karl Bradley, loan officer, LaSalle National Bank; and Heriberto Diaz, owner of Valencia Services, Inc.

PROFILE

NALCO CHEMICAL COMPANY

NALCO CHEMICAL COMPANY, THE LARGEST MARKETER OF WATER TREATMENT CHEMICALS IN THE WORLD, TRACES ITS CHICAGO ROOTS TO 1928. THAT YEAR, TWO LOCAL BUSINESSMEN—HERBERT A. KERN OF CHICAGO CHEMICAL CO. AND P. WILSON EVANS OF ALUMINATE

The Nalco Corporate and Technical Center (right), located in Naperville, Illinois, is the company's worldwide headquarters and major research installation.

Early sodium aluminate products for boiler water treatment were produced in Bedford Park, Illinois (below). Today, this facility is Nalco's largest manufacturing plant.

Nalco is the world's leading boiler water treatment specialist, offering a variety of treatment programs to improve boiler cleanliness, reduce operating costs, and extend boiler life (above).

Sales Corporation—joined forces to create the National Aluminate Corp., just as the country was heading into the Great Depression.

The company's first product was sodium aluminate, a water treatment chemical used in steam engines. From a small manufacturing site in the Clearing Industrial District on Chicago's Southwest Side in the suburb of Bedford Park, the young organization supplied the chemical primarily to railroads to treat boiler feedwater.

More than six decades later, Nalco is a leading producer of specialty chemicals used in many applications of water, waste, and process treatment. Its customers come from all industries, including paper, automotive, steel, utility, mining, oil production and refining, petrochemical, food and beverage, electronics, and transportation.

The company provides chemical programs to treat water both before it is used in industrial processes and before it is released back into the environment. Nalco specialty chemicals help customers improve water quality, reduce pollution, and enhance their products. Its chemical programs and services also enable customers to reduce costs through improved operation of their heating and cooling systems as well as their manufacturing processes.

WEATHERING THE GREAT DEPRESSION

Although founded during a time of general economic hardship, Nalco not only survived the Great Depression but experienced significant growth in the 1930s. In fact, the Clearing plant underwent two expansion projects during that decade to accommodate the increasing demand for water treatment chemicals.

During World War II, Nalco received a significant boost when it was designated by the U.S. govern-

ment as an "essential industry." The company's boiler feedwater treatment chemicals helped railroads at home and abroad keep running so they could transport troops and goods that were vital to the war effort. To meet this steady demand, Nalco constructed additional manufacturing space at the Clearing site in 1940, 1941, and 1944.

In the post-war years, as diesel engines began to replace steam locomotives throughout the railroad industry, Nalco lost 50 percent of its business in just a few years. During this difficult time, the company developed a philosophy of operation that it still follows today: Find the customer's need and fill it.

Under this new philosophy, Nalco moved into new markets such as crude oil treatment, which led to rapid domestic and international growth over the next two decades. The Clearing plant underwent another major expansion in the 1950s and added a facility for testing new products in the 1960s.

Nalco relocated its corporate offices to downtown Chicago in 1966 and to suburban Oak Brook in 1974. In 1979, the company consolidated its Chicago area research operations to a "campus" site in the western suburb of Naperville in DuPage County, and in 1986 moved its

headquarters to that location.

The original manufacturing plant in Clearing continued to expand during the 1980s. Through the purchase of adjacent properties, the site grew to an impressive 43.3 acres. The plant was also significantly updated with the addition of new computerized equipment.

Today, Nalco is a leader among specialty chemical manufacturers worldwide, with nearly $1.4 billion in sales in 1992. The company has approximately 7,000 employees providing products and services to more than 100 countries. Its three Chicago area locations—the Clearing plant, the Naperville Corporate and Technical Center, and a small manufacturing site on Chicago's South Side—employ over 1,500 people.

ENVIRONMENTAL RESPONSIBILITY AND EMPLOYEE SAFETY

Nalco is committed to improving safety and environmental performance as a member of both the Chicago community and the Chemical Manufacturers Association. Through the Responsible CARE® program and by working with government agencies, Nalco strives to meet or exceed applicable laws and government regulations at all of its worldwide operations. Likewise,

358

Nalco produces and sells only chemicals that can be manufactured, used, and disposed of in a safe manner. One recent environmental improvement is the PORTA-FEED® system of refillable chemical containers designed to replace traditional drums used to distribute chemicals. PORTA-FEED containers are returned to Nalco to be cleaned, refilled, and delivered to another customer.

As part of the company's environmental health and safety effort, all employees who will handle products undergo extensive safety training and participate in follow-up instruction throughout their careers. Nalco strives to maintain a safe environment for personnel by reviewing work practices and monitoring the workplace for employee exposure to harmful vapors, noise, and heat. Additional precautions are taken throughout the plant, including protective equipment for workers and highly visible warning signs.

Once every three years, the entire plant undergoes a thorough review of its safety and production procedures by a Plant Operations Review Team. The team includes Nalco management, engineering, and safety personnel, with at least three members who do not work at the plant. During the past decade, Nalco's efforts at ensuring safety have paid off with three plant safety milestones. In 1982, 1989, and 1993 employees at the Clearing facility worked 1 million hours without a lost-time injury. In addition, the South Chicago plant has operated for six years without a lost-time injury.

For more than six decades in Chicago, Nalco Chemical Company has taken its responsibility to its employees, the community, and its customers very seriously. As the world's largest water treatment chemical company, Nalco looks forward to continued growth and a prosperous future by following its 40-year-old philosophy: Find the customer's need and fill it.

SOUTHERN PACIFIC LINES

F OR MORE THAN A CENTURY, THE PIONEERING RAILROADERS OF SOUTHERN PACIFIC LINES DREAMED OF REACHING CHICAGO—A TRANSPORTATION CROSSROADS WITH MORE RAIL FREIGHT VOLUME THAN ANY OTHER LOCATION ON THE CONTINENT. ♦ IN 1989, SP'S DREAM CAME TRUE. THE COMPANY,

which has had a sales agency in the city since the last century, now operates two major routes into Chicago, one from Kansas City and another from St. Louis. These routes help complete a system linking Chicago, Southern Pacific, and its customers together in the most comprehensive rail network in North America.

SP Lines is the last major rail system to reach Chicago and brings with it the most efficient through route to Los Angeles, connections with most major West Coast ports, unequaled access to Mexico through SP's six ports of entry, and interline connections with the other major railroads in the country. "We now maintain more east-west gateways for transcontinental traffic than any other carrier west of the Mississippi," says Pete Rickershauser, managing director of sales.

"Direct access to Chicago has given SP Lines unmatched competi-

tive strength," he adds. "Chicago is now the only American city served by all major U.S. and Canadian rail carriers and is truly the rail crossroads of the nation."

A FULL-SERVICE NETWORK

Southern Pacific Lines is a full-service transportation network providing national and international carload, container, and trailer distribution services across 15 states and over 15,000 miles of track. With a fleet of about 2,000 locomotives and 53,000 freight cars, the company carried nearly 2 million carload shipments in 1992. An average of 16 Southern Pacific trains enter Chicago each day, and the company estimates 80,000 freight cars and 200,000 intermodal loads will be handled locally by Southern Pacific in 1993.

"Intermodal service is the fastest growing segment of SP's business,"

says Rusty Radloff, managing director of intermodal sales. "Intermodal transportation—truck trailers, railroad-owned or leased trailers, and steamship containers transported on flatcars or doublestack cars—gives shippers unmatched flexibility in moving their freight."

Southern Pacific pioneered the new technology in 1977 that ushered in the doublestack era. Today, the flowering of that technology is SP's new doublestack Spirit Service running daily between Chicago and Los Angeles. Business has increased over 500 percent on this route, and the service has been extended to St. Louis and El Paso. "SP's access to Mexico and our reach to the rest of the country and Canada through Chicago has created a true comprehensive intermodal rail network," says Radloff.

The upshot of SP's developing carload and intermodal capabilities through Chicago is the creation of a

In 1989, Southern Pacific burst onto the Chicago skyline when it began operating two major routes into the city (above).

Chemical traffic from SP's Texas service area is one of the major commodities that move via the company's Gulf Coast Corridor to Chicago and beyond (right).

network that provides customers potentially the most efficient rail distribution network to all major domestic and international markets in Mexico.

Railroads promote regional economic growth through their service capabilities. An important component of SP's business plan in the Midwest is an aggressive industrial development program. The company places a high priority on working with business leaders to expand their industries or locate new ones in areas served by SP rail lines. Southern Pacific also provides warehousing for key industries and other important forms of industrial development assistance.

FOUNDED IN THE 1850s

The San Francisco-based company traces its roots to 1851 when its oldest link, the Buffalo Bayou,

Brazos & Colorado Railway, was established near Houston, Texas. Southern Pacific's next major boost came in 1855 when construction began on the Sacramento Valley Railroad, the first steam railroad in the far West. Its builder, Connecticut-born civil engineer Theodore Judah, became a driving force in the quest for a transcontinental rail line.

Eventually, Judah found four businessmen who shared his vision: Collis P. Huntington, Leland Stanford, Charles Crocker, and Mark Hopkins. Known as the "Big Four," these men helped win support in Washington for a transcontinental railroad. With the backing of President Abraham Lincoln, the Pacific Railroad Act was signed in July 1862, and the Big Four formed the Central Pacific Railroad to lay track toward the East Coast. This resulted in the famous "meeting of the rails"

at Promontory, Utah on May 10, 1869—the completion of the nation's first transcontinental railroad. In 1884, the organization was reincorporated as the Southern Pacific Company, bringing numerous individual rail lines under one banner.

For more than a century, SP has served the nation's freight shippers and passengers as the premier western railroad. A new era began for the company in 1988 when Denver businessman Philip Anschutz purchased Southern Pacific and joined it with his Denver & Rio Grande Railroad. The route strength the combination brought to Southern Pacific also created strategic advantages for SP's many customers. And SP's entry into Chicago in 1989 is not the end of the story. Analysts project the '90s as the decade of the railroad—good news for Chicago and the entire Midwest.

From left: The International Bridge between Piedras Negras, Mexico and Eagle Pass, Texas is one of SP's six Mexican gateways.

This Golden West Service boxcar is part of SP's massive equipment rebuilding program.

The SP513300, the industry's first doublestack intermodal car, underwent test runs in 1977. SP pioneered this important technology.

A doublestack train makes the daily run to Los Angeles from Chicago.

The SP 9725 is one of the new GP-60 locomotives at SP's doublestack facility in Chicago.

CHICAGO SUN-TIMES

DURING ITS COLORFUL HISTORY, THE *CHICAGO SUN-TIMES*, ONE OF THE 10 LARGEST DAILY METROPOLITAN NEWSPAPERS IN THE UNITED STATES, HAS CULTIVATED A RICH JOURNALISTIC HERITAGE. ◆ THE *SUN-TIMES* CAN TRACE ITS ROOTS TO THE FALL OF 1929 WHEN THE FIRST AFTERNOON

The *Chicago Sun-Times* management team includes Sam S. McKeel, publisher; Dennis A. Britton, editor and executive vice president; and Michael J. Veitch, general manager and executive vice president.

Above: Sam S. McKeel (right) and Michael J. Veitch enjoy a downtown view of the city and Chicago River from the Sun-Times Building.

Above right: Dennis A. Britton checks the quality of the newspaper as it comes off a press, one of 10 in the two-story pressroom.

edition of the *Chicago Daily Times* rolled off the presses. In December 1941, just days before the bombing of Pearl Harbor, Marshall Field III introduced a competing morning newspaper, the *Chicago Sun*. Six years later, in 1947, Field purchased the *Daily Times* and merged it with the *Sun* into one around-the-clock newspaper called the *Chicago Sun and Times*. By the spring of 1950, the *Chicago Sun-Times*, as the newspaper is still known today, had officially become a morning daily.

GROWTH FROM 1950 TO THE PRESENT
Field's son, Marshall Field IV, served as publisher of the *Sun-Times* from 1950 to 1965. During his tenure, the newspaper grew to one of the largest in the country, boasting the highest daily circulation within the city of Chicago. Today, the *Sun-Times* still enjoys the largest circulation of any newspaper within the city boundaries, with a daily total of more than 550,000.

In 1959, Field also purchased the *Chicago Daily News*, an afternoon newspaper that published its last edition in 1978. Together the *Sun-*

Times, the *Daily News*, and the *Chicago Times* have been awarded 23 Pulitzer Prizes.

The Field family sold the *Sun-Times* in 1984 to Rupert Murdoch's News America, Inc. Under pressure from the Federal Communications Commission, News America, which also owns WFLD-TV, Channel 32 in Chicago, sold the newspaper in 1986 to a group of private investors who formed The Sun-Times Company Inc., a holding company that continues to operate the newspaper and two suburban chains.

Today, the holding company is directed by Sam S. McKeel, a veteran Knight-Ridder executive and publisher who joined The Sun-Times Company as its chief executive officer in mid-1989. In November of that year, Dennis A. Britton, former deputy managing editor of the *Los Angeles Times*, was named editor and senior vice president of the *Sun-Times*. Under Britton's leadership, the holding company's flagship publication has received numerous honors, including 22 Illinois Press Editors Association awards for excellence in 1991.

In late 1986, The Sun-Times Com-

pany purchased Star Publications, a group of 19 community newspapers serving the Chicago area's south and southwestern suburbs. In early 1989, the company acquired Pioneer Press, which at that time published 38 community newspapers serving the north and northwest suburbs. Those acquisitions enabled the company to form the Sun-Times Newspaper Network in July 1989.

Other expansions and innovations have followed, including the November 1989 introduction of Final Markets Plus, a 16-page evening wrapper for the *Sun-Times* that includes closing market information, as well as local, national, and international news updates. In the last several years, the *Sun-Times* also has endeavored to increase its regular coverage of national, international, and business news.

According to Sam S. McKeel, publisher of the *Chicago Sun-Times* and president and CEO of The Sun-Times Company, the *Sun-Times* is a "scrappy" newspaper. "Because we're small, lean, and aggressive, we can turn around quickly, reacting well to news and to changes in the market," he says.

"We also use an extensive network of wire services for the most comprehensive, up-to-date foreign news."

The *Chicago Sun-Times'* daily circulation is 553,355, according to the March 1993 report from the Audit Bureau of Circulation. For the six months ending March 28, the *Sun-Times* recorded the largest percentage daily gain among the nation's top 10 metropolitan daily newspapers.

"One of the reasons the *Chicago Sun-Times* has been so successful in recent years has been its market-driven focus on serving its readers and advertisers," says Michael J. Veitch, general manager and executive vice president.

AGGRESSIVE PRODUCT ENHANCEMENT

"In 1992, the *Sun-Times* kicked off an aggressive product enhancement campaign that began with the introduction of more news pages and the addition of a 'Celebs' page, Nation and World Business Briefs, and the Metro Report," says Dennis A. Britton, editor and executive vice president.

The paper introduced Moneylife to replace its existing Sunday business section. While readers can still find the usual weekly financial markets round-up, the new section places a greater emphasis on consumer finance. For example, Moneylife features one story each week to spotlight a particular issue that's important to the general reader's pocketbook. The section also includes a consumer tips column, "Your 2 Cents' Worth," and a financial workshop page, which challenges readers to solve a variety of financial problems. "One Family's Finances" is a unique column that analyzes real-life financial situations and includes advice from a professional financial planner.

Earlier in 1992, the *Sun-Times* introduced MedLife, a weekly pull-out section that brings its readers a compelling combination of news and feature stories of interest to both

The *Chicago Sun-Times* (above) targets sections to readers' special interests. The Sun-Times Company reaches suburban communities through its 41 Pioneer Press newspapers (top right) and 19 Star Publications (bottom right).

health-conscious consumers and health care professionals. Stories in the section have included advice on how to find a physician and how doctors choose a physician for themselves and their families. MedLife features a career column for the professional audience, as well as updates and "digest" items on current medical research. Since its introduction, MedLife has proven to be an effective vehicle for health care advertisers to reach their audience.

Another 1992 *Sun-Times* addition was AUTO*Times*, a pullout section dedicated to the automotive interests and needs of readers and advertisers. Stories are written for both the car and truck enthusiast and the general consumer, with helpful, in-depth information about buying, selling, and maintaining an automobile.

WeekendPlus, a weekend entertainment guide, was revamped in 1992 as well. The comprehensive pullout section features more editorial pages, an expanded restaurant section, and more music features and entertainment listings than ever before. WeekendPlus also includes information on live entertainment, dining, fairs, and festivals; a personal ad section; movie reviews and listings; home entertainment

news; and schedules for galleries, museums, and theaters.

SERVING SUBURBAN CHICAGO

In addition to its flagship publication, The Sun-Times Company is proud of its community newspaper groups; it has operated Star Publications since 1986 and Pioneer Press

since 1989. Each brings a unique personality and a long history of service to the businesses and residents of suburban Chicago.

Together, the *Sun-Times*, Star Publications, and Pioneer Press organized the Sun-Times Newspaper Network, which allows advertisers to make a single "buy" of any combination of the three newspaper

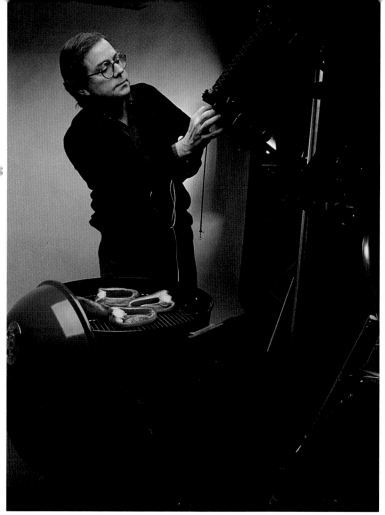

organizations. They cover the city and suburbs with a circulation of more than 804,256 and a reach of more than 2.5 million readers throughout the Chicago metropolitan area.

Star Newspapers was founded in 1901 as the *Chicago Heights Star*. Over the years, the newspaper group has grown and flourished. Through its 19 twice-weekly community newspapers, the Star group today serves 51 cities and villages in Chicago's south and southwest suburbs. Star Newspapers has expanded aggressively since its purchase by The Sun-Times Company in 1986, adding seven editions and two new weekly sections. Likewise, its circulation has reached more than 66,000.

As part of the organization's strong community focus, each Star newspaper is carefully crafted to meet the interests and needs of the particular area it serves. Through an array of attractive, well-designed sections geared toward each community's day-to-day needs and interests, an experienced staff of more than 100 editors, reporters, feature writers, and photographers combines forces to produce an award-winning group of newspapers.

In fact, Star Newspapers has been recognized throughout the industry as a pacesetter in suburban journalism, noted for the quality of its writing, the overall appearance of its publications, and its technical expertise. In 1991, the Illinois Press Association awarded Star the Will Loomis Trophy, its highest honor for exemplary quality among large-circulation, non-daily newspapers.

Another member of the Sun-Times family of newspapers is Pioneer Press. Founded in 1879, this dynamic group of community papers has enjoyed a unique vantage point from which to observe and chronicle the evolution of the suburbs of Chicago. Over the years, the growth of Pioneer Press, both in the number of newspapers it publishes and in its editorial sensitivity to changing community needs, has more than kept pace with the expansion of suburbia. Today, the organization serves more than 75 communities through a diverse network of 41 papers blanketing the north, west, and northwest suburbs of Chicago.

Throughout its history, Pioneer Press always has pursued the goal of being the major information source for each of the communities it serves, striving to reflect in its individual newspapers the expectations and aspirations of its readers and advertisers. While each newspaper maintains a strong local focus, the individual staffs have access to the broader resources of Pioneer Press. This central bank of talent allows editors to enhance and broaden coverage through the use of timely, Pioneer-generated graphics and regional perspectives on local stories of importance.

By adhering to this successful community-oriented philosophy for more than a century, Pioneer Press has become the largest suburban news-gathering operation in America and the third largest among all Illinois newspapers. With a circulation of nearly 185,000, the Pioneer group reaches more than 700,000 readers each week, from the youngster to the senior citizen.

Throughout more than six decades of service to the Chicago area, the *Chicago Sun-Times* and its sister publications of Pioneer Press and Star Newspapers have played a vital role in bringing their readers the news that's important to them—whether from around the corner or around the world. Looking to the

future, the publications of the Sun-Times Newspaper Network will continue to deliver quality, award-winning journalism to the diverse communities of Chicago and its suburbs.

Photographer Jim Frost captures delectable images for Thursday's "Food" section (left).

▶ KEN GOLDMAN

Above: Dick Mitchell (center), deputy metro editor, dispatches reporters Mary A. Johnson and Mark Brown from the City Desk, the hub of activity in the newsroom.

GRANT THORNTON

GRANT THORNTON, ONE OF THE WORLD'S LARGEST INTERNATIONAL ACCOUNTING AND MANAGEMENT CONSULTING FIRMS, HAS BEEN PART OF THE CHICAGO BUSINESS SCENE SINCE 1924, WITH A PRACTICE AS DIVERSE AS THE CITY ITSELF. ♦ "OUR CLIENT BASE COVERS A WIDE RANGE OF

industries with concentration in manufacturing, distribution, banking, real estate, government, health care, and tax-exempt organizations," says John C. Burke, managing partner of the Chicago office.

The Chicago office is one of 45 U.S. locations of Grant Thornton, which is headquartered in One Prudential Plaza. The firm has offices in 76 countries and serves clients worldwide through Grant Thornton International.

A unique aspect of Grant Thornton is that while it serves clients of every type and size, it is the only international accounting firm primarily serving growing mid-size companies, both private and publicly held. Says Burke, "We help companies meet the challenges of the marketplace through our experience, the structure of our organization, and the talent of our people."

Grant Thornton recruits, trains, and promotes employees who can reach the firm's expectations of professional excellence, superior service, and technical competence (far right).

Right: Chicago Area Managing Partner John C. Burke, Management Consulting Department Head Joseph L. Goodman Jr., and Audit Department Head Michael C. Hall.

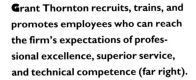

A BROAD RANGE OF PROFESSIONAL SERVICES

Grant Thornton has long enjoyed a reputation for excellence in accounting and auditing, but the firm's hallmark is its ability to look beyond the accounting records to the operations and environment that create an organization's culture. Grant Thornton offers clients a comprehensive range of professional services, including tax and business planning, information systems and operations management, acquisition and financing assistance, litigation support, and international consulting. These services, which help clients reduce

costs, increase efficiency, and enhance growth, are delivered by teams of professionals who specialize in specific areas of an industry to ensure the highest level of expertise.

Through a client-centered approach called "Distinctive Service," the firm prides itself on providing a level of service that is unmatched. The central feature of the service is a partner-client dialogue in which clients define the standards they expect Grant Thornton to meet and then assess how well the firm has performed. To enhance this high level of service, partners in the firm establish relationships with their clients that promote regular, open communication.

In further striving for excellence, Grant Thornton maintains a ratio of partners to staff that is among the highest of all major accounting firms. Grant Thornton's partners work with clients to provide the level of experience they prefer. "Even in a recession, it is often possible to find imaginative busi-

ness solutions that increase profits and generate growth," says Burke.

Demonstrating that technical excellence is another fundamental ingredient in providing top-level service, the firm leads the accounting profession in using microcomputer technology to maximize efficiency and provide clients with the information they need to make effective business decisions.

Grant Thornton also recruits, trains, and promotes employees who can reach the firm's expectations of professional excellence, superior service, and technical competence. Likewise, the Chicago partners contribute to the accounting profession and the community through active participation in professional and civic associations.

Over its 68-year history, Grant Thornton has earned a reputation for distinctive service. Its commitment to the highest professional standards ensures continued success and an important presence in Chicago and around the world.

1931
BAXTER
INTERNATIONAL, INC.

1936
BLUE CROSS AND BLUE
SHIELD OF ILLINOIS

1948
COTTER & COMPANY

1931
CHECKERS, SIMON & ROSNER

1936
CULLIGAN INTERNATIONAL
COMPANY

1948
KEMPER FINANCIAL
SERVICES, INC.

1933
CONTINENTAL DISTRIBUTING
COMPANY, INC.

1936
SKIDMORE, OWINGS
& MERRILL

1952
EDELMAN PUBLIC
RELATIONS WORLDWIDE

1934
BOZELL WORLDWIDE

1945
SARA LEE CORPORATION

1965
EASTMAN KODAK COMPANY

1934
CHICAGO PARK DISTRICT

1946
TATHAM EURO RSCG

1965
KMART CORPORATION

1934
MCDERMOTT, WILL
& EMERY

1947
WMAQ-TV, CHANNEL 5

CHICAGO'S SECOND WORLD'S FAIR was the 1933 Century of Progress, an extravagant party in the middle of the Great Depression. The fair celebrated Chicago's first 100 years and also, as its name implies, a host of recent inventions that had transformed the nation—the telephone, the automobile, and the airplane. More than 39 million people visited the fair, which featured a full-scale re-creation of Fort Dearborn.

BENNY GOODMAN, THE "KING OF Swing," grew up on Chicago's Maxwell Street and borrowed his first clarinet from a neighborhood synagogue. And if his two older brothers hadn't grabbed the tuba and trumpet first, the history of jazz might have been very different. Goodman learned to play his instrument in a band sponsored by Jane Addams' famous settlement house, Hull House. He went on to become the first jazz musician to play Carnegie Hall.

BAXTER INTERNATIONAL, INC.

BAXTER INTERNATIONAL, BASED IN NORTH SUBURBAN DEERFIELD, HAS A PRIMARY OBJECTIVE OF BEING THE LEADING GLOBAL HEALTH CARE COMPANY. THE ORGANIZATION IS GUIDED BY THREE STRATEGIES: TO PROVIDE THE UNDISPUTED BEST SERVICE TO HOSPITALS, TO BRING TO MARKET A

continuous stream of innovative products, and to increase its penetration of global markets.

Baxter divisions manufacture or distribute thousands of different products—enough to address 75 percent of the supply needs of the modern hospital. The company's Hospital Business also offers an

ment because this dialysis technique is relatively inexpensive and very accessible.

Expansion in the Far East is a current priority, and new manufacturing plants, as well as potential joint ventures and shared technology, are planned throughout that vast region. In particular, the company will man-

& Johnson. The company's self-manufactured products are distributed through its own network and through other distributors.

Baxter has developed several cost-reduction programs for U.S. hospitals. The Corporate Program offers price incentives for volume purchasing and also provides a

Baxter International is headquartered at One Baxter Parkway in north suburban Deerfield.

BELLINI DESIGN

array of services that substantially reduce hospital operating costs. Baxter has strong positions in virtually all of its U.S. hospital supply and distribution businesses, including intravenous solutions, renal therapy, diagnostic equipment, blood therapies, and many basic hospital supply categories.

Baxter's Global Business—defined both geographically and by type of product—holds large and growing market shares in most developed markets of the world, including Western Europe, the Pacific Rim, Japan, and South America. Currently, the company serves hospitals and other health care providers in 100 countries.

Baxter's international expansion has accelerated in the 1990s as a number of regions have opened to increased use of the most modern medical techniques. Often, the first Baxter product initiative in a new geographical area is focused on continuous ambulatory peritoneal dialysis (CAPD) supplies and equip-

ufacture CAPD products in China. Baxter is also proceeding with manufacturing and sales opportunities in Russia, Eastern Europe, and South America.

COMMITTED TO COST REDUCTION

In all of its businesses, Baxter is focused on finding ways to reduce the cost of health care worldwide. Says Vernon R. Loucks Jr., chairman and CEO, "Far more than any other company, we have the skill and capacity to become a true partner with our hospital customers. No one can match our breadth of distribution or our product line. We help customers achieve our shared cost-reduction goal because we can influence every part of the process of working with the hospital, from raw materials through patient care."

As a full-line distributor of hospital supplies, Baxter offers its own complete line of products as well as products from 1,000 other manufacturers, including 3M and Johnson

range of unique consulting services. Through its Access program, the company helps hospitals increase efficiency and reduce cost and risk in waste management, asset management, information processing, systems management, and real estate management.

Enhanced Distribution Services is a new program that delivers supplies to hospitals in a manner tailored to the individual customer's needs for labels, packaging, and storage. This program has permitted some hospitals to reduce associated costs by more than 90 percent.

The ValueLink® "stockless inventory" program allows electronic ordering and delivery of supplies by Baxter personnel, as needed, directly to the area of the hospital where the supplies are used. ValueLink is a working partnership between Baxter and its hospital customers.

Together, these efforts—bolstered by a long-term program to build the most modern and efficient

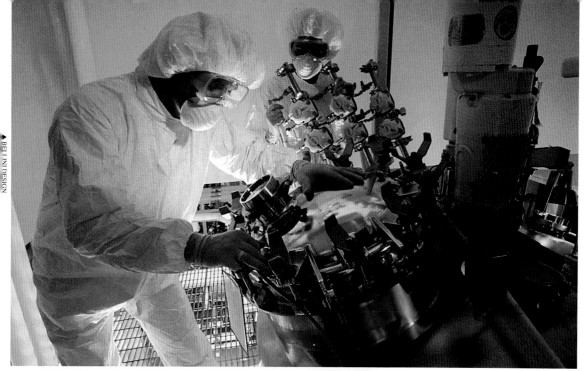

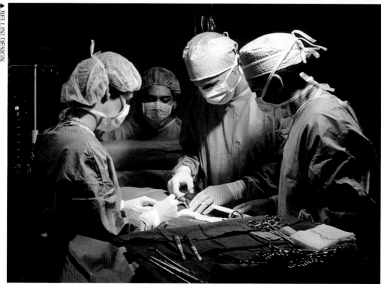

plans to test a version of the device that operates independent of a power and control console, permitting patients complete freedom of movement through the use of an external battery supply.

COMPANY VALUES

Baxter bases its business on a prescribed set of values and seeks leadership through quality and innovation. The company strives to reduce health care costs by relating to customers along the entire "value chain," from product design to patient care. Baxter also works for the personal development of all members of its diverse, productive, and highly committed work force and embraces the principle of continuous improvement.

Since its founding in 1931, the company has built a work force of 61,300 that mirrors the diversity of its worldwide markets and customer base. Managers are encouraged to further the company's diversity goals and are rewarded for their progress. The company has implemented work-and-family programs, including flexible working hours, that permit employees to care for children or other family members. Baxter also has a progressive environmental program and lends financial support to international relief efforts, medical research, and the volunteer activities of its employees.

"We believe our strategies give us a unique and sustainable competitive advantage," Loucks says. "Our prospects have never been greater."

The company's products are used worldwide throughout the health care industry, from cutting-edge genetic research to basic hospital supply needs.

warehouse facilities—saved Baxter's hospital customers nearly $200 million in 1992. Savings per hospital range as high as $1.5 million a year.

FROM RESEARCH TO MARKET

Baxter has been very proficient at converting its research and development into successful new products. In recent years, the company has created an advanced biotechnology capability, as well as major advances in blood therapy and immunotherapy, diagnostic techniques, anti-rejection medicine, and the search for a device to supplement a diseased or failing heart. With annual research and development expenditures of more than $300 million, the company employs 2,000 researchers in 17 facilities in the United States, Japan, Germany, Switzerland, and Belgium. In 1992,

products introduced during the previous five years accounted for 34 percent of total sales of Baxter-manufactured products.

One of Baxter's most important developments expected to reach market in the mid-1990s is anti-CD45, a drug that reduces the incidence of organ rejection in kidney transplants to 18 percent from the usual 63 percent. The drug is part of a larger program to develop a number of products useful in organ transplants.

Baxter has also developed a hemoglobin-based blood substitute that is of use in medical situations, such as emergency response to hemorrhagic shock. The Baxter blood substitute does not have to be typed or cross-matched before it is administered.

Yet another Baxter milestone is the Novacor® left-ventricular assist device, which has been implanted in more than 100 individuals awaiting heart transplants. The company has

CHECKERS, SIMON & ROSNER

FOR MORE THAN 60 YEARS, THE CERTIFIED PUBLIC ACCOUNTING FIRM OF CHECKERS, SIMON & ROSNER HAS HELPED THOUSANDS OF ENTREPRENEURS IN THE CHICAGO METROPOLITAN AREA BUILD AND MAINTAIN VIABLE, PROFITABLE BUSINESSES. ◆ THE FIRM WAS FOUNDED IN 1931 DURING THE GREAT

Depression by Joseph M. Checkers and Nate Simon as Checkers, Simon & Company. The need for certified public accountants was especially strong then, as many businesses were failing and modern accounting practices were beginning to evolve. In 1945, Manuel Rosner joined the partnership, and the firm adopted its current name.

The firm employs more than 260 people, including 150 certified public accountants and 70 other professionals. Above: A final review of the work.

Over the years, Checkers, Simon & Rosner has experienced steady, managed growth by maintaining a limited client base and paying meticulous attention to quality. By the 1960s, the firm's employee roster included five partners, 19 professionals, and six other staff members. Checkers grew to more than 200 employees during the 1980s through

mergers with three local accounting organizations: B.L. Rosenberg, Berman & Berman, and Doherty & Zable. Most recently, the firm of Goldberg Geiser & Co. Ltd., with an extensive practice in long-term health care, merged with the Checkers family. Each of these firms brought a tradition of excellence in product quality and a commitment to the highest standards of client service.

COMPREHENSIVE SERVICES FOR THE ENTREPRENEUR

Today, Checkers is among the top 10 accounting firms in Chicago. The full-service organization employs more than 260 people, including 150 certified public accountants and 70 other professionals, such as attorneys, certified management consultants, property appraisers, and private investigators. Together they offer a comprehensive range of accounting and business services. The firm's traditional tax and audit expertise is complemented by significant resources in technology consulting, management advisory services, real estate services, business consulting, and forensic accounting.

According to Managing Partner Jerome A. Harris, the practice serves primarily middle-market, privately held entrepreneurial businesses with annual sales of $5 million to $75 million. "An entrepreneurial business requires a high level of hands-on service delivered by professionals who can become involved in the financial affairs of their clients," Harris says. Within that framework, the firm's clients include financial services firms, manufacturers and distributors, real estate developers, members of the hospitality industry, publishers, broadcasting companies, hospitals

and extended-care facilities, wholesalers, and leaders in the construction industry.

"We are a full-service firm to those industries in which we've chosen to work," says Harris. "We perform certified audits and reviews of financial statements, and we provide assistance in tax planning. For manufacturing clients, we assist in developing cost accounting and quality management systems."

Adds Harris, "Our approach is to adapt our services to the unique personality of the entrepreneur. We want to know what makes our clients tick, so we can customize our approach to each individual."

One way Checkers serves its clients is by providing information systems services. Because technology changes almost daily, many companies must look to an outside advisor to help them keep pace and know what combination of computer equipment and software is best for their business. Checkers professionals lead clients through the technological maze to ensure they get the most from the programs and equipment that are available.

For example, staff members analyze and document existing computer systems, help the client identify needs, and design a new system accordingly. The firm also helps plan and implement information systems projects, formulates short- and long-range plans, offers an objective opinion on proposals, carries out feasibility studies, and provides training for the client's staff once a new system is in place.

Checkers also offers an investigative accounting service known as Checkmate Consulting. According to the American Management Association, employee theft accounts for about 20 percent of the nation's business failures. To address that

problem, the firm introduced Checkmate Consulting in 1989 to help companies protect themselves against embezzlement and employee theft. The service also helps victimized companies discover and investigate losses.

Under the Checkmate program, a team of certified public accountants, MBAs, PhDs, experienced business valuators, and former FBI and government agents handle everything from corporate embezzlement, insurance proof-of-loss claims, fraud investigations, and mergers and acquisitions, to due diligence and pre-employment investigations. The team also provides expert witness and litigation accounting support.

A CHICAGO FIRM WITH INTERNATIONAL RESOURCES

During more than six decades of managed growth, Checkers has proudly remained a Chicago firm.

"Most of our clients are located in the Chicago metropolitan area, and most of our employees have roots in the Midwest and Chicago," says Harris. "In fact, we recruit our staff right out of college, mostly from Midwestern schools with strong reputations in business and accounting. Currently, about 40 percent of our partners are alumni of DePaul University."

But as strong as its roots are in Chicago, Checkers recognizes the growing importance of the international marketplace to its clients. In 1981, the firm established a relationship with BKR International, a worldwide affiliation of accounting firms based in New York and London. Says Harris, "This forward-looking affiliation gives our clients the worldwide access they need to compete in the ever-expanding global economy."

Looking to the future, the firm will continue to serve the needs of

entrepreneurs throughout the Chicago area. From traditional audit and tax services to management consulting, information services, and investigative accounting, Checkers, Simon & Rosner is a full-service firm with a commitment to each client's success.

CONTINENTAL DISTRIBUTING COMPANY, INC.

WHEN THE U.S. CONGRESS REPEALED PROHIBITION ON DECEMBER 5, 1933, IT ENDED ONE OF THE MOST COLORFUL AND CONTROVERSIAL ERAS IN AMERICAN HISTORY. TO THIS DAY, IMAGES OF THE TIME STILL INFLUENCE POPULAR PERCEPTIONS OF CHICAGO.

While these perceptions have been slow to change, the city itself recovered quickly from the effects of the era. Previously unmarked doorways were opened to the public, and shadowy vans were replaced by the trucks of legitimate liquor distributors. Some of those trucks belonged to Continental Distributing Company, Inc.

Founded in 1933 by husband and wife Abe and Ida Cooper, Continental has grown along with the city as both overcame their gritty beginnings. In the process, Continental has embraced modern management techniques and technology. Its ultra-modern 235,000-square-foot warehouse in northwest suburban Rosemont mirrors the city's skyline just a few miles to the east.

Continental's main warehouse facility is located in suburban Rosemont, Illinois. From left, front row: Laren Ukman, corporate development; Fred Cooper, president and CEO. From left, back row: Howard Rappin, CFO; Barry Labovitz, general sales manager; and Charles Margolis, general manager.

IN TOUCH WITH CHICAGO'S NEIGHBORHOODS

Continental believes that to know Chicago, one must know its neighborhoods and streets. That philosophy has helped the company become one of the largest liquor distributors in America, covering the entire state of Illinois.

Staying in touch with the streets is vitally important, considering there are more than 23,000 liquor licenses in Illinois. Each establishment—from the chic watering holes of Chicago's River North area to the package stores and corner taverns of downstate Illinois—has a unique mix of clientele, each with its own tastes.

Accordingly, Continental has divided its thousands of accounts into ethnic categories as complex as the globe itself—from Middle Eastern to Italian to Greek to Chinese. But the company also is sensitive to demographic changes in established neighborhoods. For example, Continental's salespeople will work with

stores in an Eastern European neighborhood that's gradually becoming more Hispanic to make sure they carry the right selection of tequila alongside the slivovitz.

While Continental strives to understand what people are drinking today, it's just as important to understand what they're likely to be drinking next year. Working closely with distillers and vintners, Continental has helped establish a number of brands that were unknown 10 years ago but are now available statewide. This orientation to the future is one way Continental adds value to distillers' and vintners' sales—and one reason it continues to prosper while dozens of competitors have fallen by the wayside.

Over the years, Continental has built its reputation on premium brands and today distributes such highly regarded spirits as Stolichnaya, Finlandia, and Absolut vodkas, Bombay Gin, Jim Beam, J&B Scotch, Christian Brothers

Brandy, Bailey's Irish Cream, Amaretto di Saronno, Frangelico, Remy Martin Cognac, Kahlua, Courvoisier Cognac, Grand Marnier Liqueur, and dozens of aperitifs.

Continental distributes an impressive portfolio of wines ranging from Mogen David to Mumm Champagne and everything in between, including Kendall-Jackson, Blossom Hill, Sutter Home, Mouton Cadet, Chateau Ste. Michelle, Almaden, and Clos Du Bois. Continental also has pioneered the fine Italian wine business in Chicago.

Getting these brands and many others out of the warehouse and into the right restaurants and taverns is the nitty gritty of the liquor distribution business. Continental's facility in Rosemont can store about 600,000 cases at any time and, over the course of a year, loads and ships more than 2 million cases. During the Christmas season, more than 20,000 cases a day may leave the facility via a fleet of 55 trucks.

John Barry (left), sales manager, chain store wine sales, and Fred Greenfield, sales manager, fine wines, sample the goods in the company's massive, temperature-controlled wine room.

MANAGEMENT CONTINUITY

Continental has satellite operations in other areas of Illinois and is in the midst of an aggressive statewide expansion. Unlike many other wholesalers, it is Continental's policy to keep the current management team in place in each of its acquisitions, realizing that no outsider could understand the local market as well.

Maintaining management continuity is a tradition at Continental. In fact, Fred Cooper, Abe and Ida's son, has served as president of the company since 1979. Amazingly, some of the people who worked alongside Abe and Ida in the firm's early years continue to work with Fred Cooper today.

Continental's current manage-ment has strived to add a high-tech dimension to the company's heritage of personal service. Using the most sophisticated computer network in the industry, the Continental team can access sales analysis, inventory control, order processing, and purchasing reports and use the information to develop detailed marketing strategies for suppliers. The system also helps Continental communicate with its satellite facilities and with a market that has been described as the toughest in the United States.

But on Friday at 5:45 p.m., a computer system is not much help when a restaurant asks for a case of hard-to-find premium cognac or fine vintage wine for a private party later that evening. Often enough, one of Continental's executives will walk into the warehouse, pick an order, load it into his or her car, and drive it to the restaurant personally.

While such special orders represent a minuscule fraction of Continental's sales, they offer great insight into the company's success. Continental Distributing Company has advanced immeasurably over the past six decades in terms of facilities and computer systems. But its orientation to personal service hasn't changed at all—because today, more than ever, companies like Continental succeed one customer at a time.

BOZELL WORLDWIDE

I N 1921 LEO BOZELL, A NEWSPAPER EDITOR, AND MORRIS JACOBS, A NEWSPAPER REPORTER, FOUNDED AN ADVERTISING AGENCY IN OMAHA, NEBRASKA. ♦ THE SMALL OFFICE THEY RENTED HAD ONLY ONE DESK, AND THEY COULDN'T AFFORD A TELEPHONE OR EVEN A SIGN ON THE DOOR. THE PAIR KEPT THEIR DAY JOBS FOR a while. They really had no choice; they needed the money.

Early on, however, the agency began creating its history of success stories. During the 1920s Bozell and Jacobs created the name "Boys Town" for Father Flanagan's home for boys in Omaha and later devel-

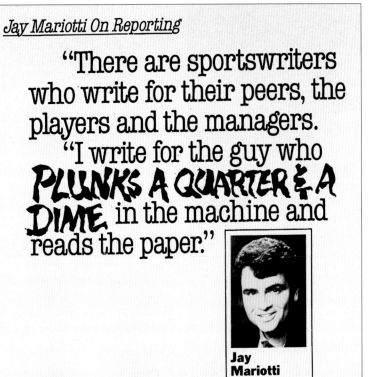

As the 14th largest advertising agency in the world, Bozell does work for diverse clients, including the *Chicago Sun-Times* (above).

Tom Hayden (above right), executive vice president and general manager of Bozell Chicago.

oped the organization's famous slogan, "He ain't heavy, Father...he's my brother."

From these humble, grass-roots beginnings, Bozell Worldwide has grown to be the 14th largest advertising agency in the world. With billings of more than $1.7 billion in 1992, Bozell is also the fourth largest privately held advertising

agency. Employee-owned, the agency considers its independence one of its greatest assets.

Responsible only to itself and its clients, Bozell maintains seven U.S. offices and an additional 46 offices in 44 countries. Offices serving Europe, Asia, the Pacific, Latin

America, the Caribbean, and the Middle East produce work for clients in consumer products, food, retail, business and industry, and agriculture.

BECOMING AN INTERNATIONAL AGENCY

The company's transition to Bozell Worldwide began in 1986, when the agency was purchased by Lorimar-Telepictures of Los Angeles. Lorimar in turn merged Bozell and Jacobs (which had moved its headquarters to New York in 1975) with Kenyon & Eckhardt, a New York-based ad agency with roots dating back to 1899.

Each half of the newly formed agency brought a strength to the merger and gained new strength through it. Over the years, Bozell and Jacobs had developed a reputation for being a solid, well-managed, and talented organization, while Kenyon & Eckhardt was regarded as

a sophisticated, international agency with panache. Bozell, Jacobs, Kenyon and Eckhardt became one highly competitive firm with a strong domestic and international presence.

In 1988, two years after the merger, the agency's management bought back the organization and changed its name to Bozell Worldwide. Long ago, the agency came to afford its own telephone, and each of the more than 50 offices has a sign on the door. But much of the attitude shared by the founders back in Omaha has become a part of the corporate culture today.

A MIDWESTERN ORIENTATION

International presence and New York headquarters notwithstanding, Bozell Worldwide has retained a strong Midwestern orientation and work ethic. The agency still believes that producing quality work is the key to success for its clients and itself. And that quality work has been a part of Chicago since 1934.

That year, Nathan Jacobs (Leo's brother) moved to Chicago to head the public relations and advertising programs for The National Job-Saving Bureau of the Coal Industry. At the time, coal companies and coal miners were losing business and jobs as hydroelectric power was being developed and launched by the federal government. A group of coal mine owners, coal jobbers, and the United Mine Workers' Union decided to work together to oppose federally financed hydroelectric projects, and they selected Bozell and Jacobs to represent their interests.

The program developed for this first Chicago client was so effective that President Franklin Delano Roosevelt soon met with John L. Lewis, head of the United Mine Workers' Union and co-chairman of

The National Job-Saving Bureau of the Coal Industry. The result of that meeting was a letter from Lewis, in which he resigned as co-chairman of the coal group and withdrew all coal union affiliations with the movement, thereby ending Bozell's first client relationship in Chicago. But the Chicago office kept its doors open and, over the years, has serviced accounts ranging from Alberto-Culver, Thomas J. Lipton, J I Case, and Inland Steel Company to Hush Puppies, Yardley of London, and Jim Beam Brands. More recently, the agency has produced some of the most noteworthy advertising seen in Chicago—for the Illinois State Lottery.

Bozell helped launch the lottery in 1974 and worked tirelessly during the next 17 and a half years as the lottery grew into a $1.5 billion operation. Countless Bozell commercials helped sell billions of Lotto, Little Lotto, Daily Game, and Instant Game tickets. The lottery's advertising and marketing success also became the model for other lotteries across the United States.

Today, Bozell Chicago and its client, the National Pork Producers Council, are teaching America to think of pork as "The Other White Meat." The phenomenal success of this marketing and advertising effort, launched in 1987, has inspired Dr. Stephen Greyser of the Harvard Business School to call it the product repositioning success story of the '80s. *Forbes* magazine has called the campaign "just the thing to dispel the bugaboos that have long surrounded pork." And even though the "bugaboos" may be disappearing quickly, Bozell and the National Pork Producers Council plan to make "The Other White Meat" a success story of the '90s too.

The agency will also be servicing a blue chip roster of Chicago clients.

As the base of Bozell's Midwest organization, the Chicago office currently works for clients such as Abbott Laboratories, Ace Hardware Corporation, the *Chicago Sun-Times*, Continental Baking Company, Gingiss Formalwear, the Hong Kong Tourist Association, Monsanto, Pizza Hut, Speedy Muffler King, Valvoline, and Weber Grills.

Bozell Chicago employs over 100 professionals who specialize in advertising, public relations, direct marketing, sales promotion, marketing research, media planning and placement, and event marketing. Gone are the days when Nathan Jacobs had to fill all those needs for the agency's first clients. Gone too is the Jacobs name from the door. But Bozell Worldwide maintains the drive for quality and the focus on results that Jacobs first brought to the world of Chicago advertising nearly 60 years ago.

Above left: Since 1987, Bozell has been helping the National Pork Producers Council teach America to think of pork as "The Other White Meat."

Above right: The agency's current list of Chicago area clients includes Weber Grills.

CHICAGO PARK DISTRICT

N A CITY WHOSE OFFICIAL SLOGAN IS "URBS IN HORTO" (CITY IN A GARDEN), IT'S NO SURPRISE THAT CHICAGOANS ENJOY MORE THAN 7,400 ACRES OF PARK-LAND. WITH 23 MILES OF SCENIC LAKEFRONT PROPERTIES, MANY OF THEM JOINED BY TREE-LINED BOULEVARDS, AND MORE THAN 550 NEIGHBORHOOD

parks, Chicago has an abundance of green space.

In 1934, the Chicago Park District was created from 22 smaller park commissions to manage this vast urban resource. Today, it is the nation's largest recreational system, employing over 3,800 full-time workers and nearly 3,000 people on a seasonal basis. Over the years, the parklands have become known as the "Emerald Necklace" because of the patches of green dispersed through the concrete jungle. Among the largest and best known of Chicago's 550-plus parks are Lincoln Park (1,200 acres), Jackson Park, (542 acres), Washington Park (366 acres), Grant Park (319 acres), Humboldt Park (206 acres), Garfield Park (184 acres), Douglas Park (174 acres), and Columbus Park (134 acres).

"Leisure means different things to different people," says General Superintendent Robert C. Penn, "so

we strive to provide something for everyone. The Chicago Park District is at the heart of everything in this city—from the world-renowned museums, to the lesser known petting zoo at Indian Boundary Park, to the Garfield Park Conservatory, the largest garden under glass in the country."

Many of Chicago's most important tourist attractions are part of the Park District family: the Art Institute of Chicago, Field Museum of Natural History, Adler Planetarium, Chicago Historical Society, John G. Shedd Aquarium, Chicago Academy of Sciences, the Museum of Science and Industry, Soldier Field, and the world-class Buckingham Fountain. Add to that list the District's cultural facilities which reflect the rich ethnic diversity of the neighborhoods: the DuSable Museum of African-American History, the Mexican Fine Arts Center Museum, the South Shore Cultural

Center (a former 65.5-acre country club on the lake), and the new Emiliano Zapata Recreational and Cultural Center.

RESPONDING TO COMMUNITY NEEDS

During the late 1980s, the Park District implemented a new, more effective governing system based on citizen input. The more than 250 advisory councils that resulted from the system are made up of community members who work with the District to define and articulate what

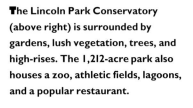

The Lincoln Park Conservatory (above right) is surrounded by gardens, lush vegetation, trees, and high-rises. The 1,212-acre park also houses a zoo, athletic fields, lagoons, and a popular restaurant.

The 184-acre Garfield Park (right) has one of the nation's foremost conservatories, which features four annual flower shows. Recreational areas include athletic fields, a swimming pool, and tennis courts.

they need from their neighborhood parks to create the best possible recreational environment.

"We don't take a cookie-cutter approach to facilities or parks," explains Park District Board President Richard A. Devine. "We believe Chicago's beauty and strength are intimately linked to our ethnic and cultural diversity. The councils tell us what they want, and we work with them to help define the leisure activities and environment suitable for their individual communities."

Thanks to the advisory council concept, the Park District has made significant progress in responding to community needs. For example, a media arts center was developed at Fuller Park on West 45th Street, where teen talk programs and music video productions originate. Likewise, the grounds surrounding a former tuberculosis sanitarium at Peterson Park on West Ardmore were transformed into a retirement village, which features a summer senior day camp. In 1993, the District completed renovation of its 550 playlots, making each recreation center safer, environmentally responsible, and handicap accessible.

MAKING THE CITY MORE LIVABLE

The Chicago Park District strives to offer all the amenities that make a city livable. "Passive" parks, renowned for their beauty and historical significance, are reserved for walking, jogging, sitting, and pic-

nicking, while "active" parks offer opportunities for softball, baseball, football, soccer, volleyball, frisbee throwing, and kite flying, to name a few.

Currently, there are 720 tennis courts at over 128 sites, including an indoor facility. Golfers can take advantage of one 18-hole and five 9-hole courses, two driving ranges, and a 48-trap course in Lincoln Park. For those who are more interested in team sports, there are nearly 530 baseball diamonds, 185 gymnasiums, and more than 1,145 basketball backboards. Rounding out the recreational offerings are more than 100 winter ice skating facilities, 19 bicycle paths totaling more than 24 miles, and eight harbors with slips for nearly 5,000 boats.

Unlike others, the Park District also offers various programs at its myriad facilities, parks, and community centers. They include traditional arts and crafts classes, seminars on parenting skills, and a variety of activities for the physically challenged, such as sailing and sledge hockey.

One recent addition to the District's extensive recreational offerings is the "Swim Blitz," which provides swimming lessons to school-age children in an effort to ensure that every child in Chicago knows how to swim. Free classes are available at many of the Park District's 58 indoor and outdoor pools, as well as additional locations throughout the city.

The District is also involved in a unique recycling program called "POP," or Plastic on Parks. Empty plastic containers collected in neighborhood parks are sent to recycling plants where the discarded material is formed into wood-like timbers that are used to build new playlots.

In addition to comprehensive recreational offerings, the Park District sponsors various cultural, entertainment, and special events programs year-round. About 120 pieces of sculpture, many by well-known artists, are displayed throughout the system. The South Shore Cultural Center offers theatre, cultural events, and music. Collectively, Theatre on the Lake and the Grant Park Music Festival have provided popular summertime entertainment for more than 100 years. Chicagoans can also enjoy outdoor summer concerts and mini-festivals at the James C. Petrillo Bandshell, in Grant Park, and in neighborhood parks throughout the city.

"What we have to offer spans the whole scope of leisure activity," says Director of Communications Shawnelle Richie. "Under the careful direction of the Chicago Park District's board and general superintendent, there will always be parks, both large and small, that will serve as a welcome oasis amid the concrete jungle of Chicago's urban environment."

A former private country club, the South Shore Cultural Center (above left) features a 2,903-yard nine-hole golf course, tennis courts, and a beach.

Holes on the Sydney A. Marovitz Golf Course (above right) are modeled after some of the most challenging holes at different courses around the country. Its 48 bunkers represent the states of the Union at the time the course was laid out.

McDERMOTT, WILL & EMERY

THE U.S. TAX CODE HAS UNDERGONE COUNTLESS CHANGES AND REVISIONS OVER THE YEARS, BUT ONE CONSTANT IN FEDERAL TAXES HAS BEEN MCDERMOTT, WILL & EMERY, ONE OF CHICAGO'S PREMIER LAW FIRMS. ALTHOUGH BEST KNOWN AS A LEADER IN TAX LAW, IT OPERATES AS A full-service firm representing thousands of clients in eight offices across the country and around the world.

McDermott, Will & Emery's 500 attorneys, 247 of whom work in Chicago, provide their clients with expert legal services in tax law, employee benefits, estate planning, corporate law, health law, real estate, litigation, and more.

FOUNDED IN 1934

When the firm was established in 1934, its original focus was tax law. Founders Edward H. McDermott, a former chief counsel to the Joint Committee on Internal Revenue Taxation of the U.S. Congress, and William M. Emery, a tax attorney who had worked with McDermott, began a tradition of legal excellence now approaching its seventh decade.

"It was a boutique firm at first," says John S. Pennell, a retired partner who joined the practice in 1941, about the same time as Howard A. Will, the third attorney to become a partner. "Originally, all they did was federal taxes, and their reasoning was that other lawyers would bring their tax problems to the firm with no fear of losing their clients to us."

That policy changed, however, after the firm's attorneys realized they were wasting their clients' money, Pennell says. For example, the firm's staff would address the tax questions pertaining to a will, only to discover that the referring attorney had not completed the final draft of the will to McDermott, Will & Emery's satisfaction. "We were practically drafting the wills ourselves," Pennell says. Thus the firm's Corporate and Estate Planning departments were born in 1941, when Will (Corporate) and Richard J. Frankenstein Jr. (Estate Planning) joined the firm.

The 1940s was a period of tremendous growth for McDermott, Will & Emery. "The firm exploded during that period," Pennell says. "The practice broadened beyond the tax field, but taxes remained the largest part of the practice."

EXPANDING BEYOND CHICAGO

In the late 1970s, McDermott, Will & Emery began its expansion to other cities. The first office outside Chicago was established in 1977 in Miami; the second opened a year later in Washington, D.C., where for years the firm's attorneys had traveled to meet with the IRS on behalf of their clients.

The firm then opened offices in Boston in 1981, in Los Angeles and Newport Beach in 1987, and in New York City in 1988. In 1991, after the breakup of the Soviet Union, McDermott, Will & Emery established the first U.S. law office in Lithuania's capital, Vilnius, where the firm represents Lithuania's Ministry of Transport and numerous other local clients. The firm also advises United States-based and multinational clients on opportunities in Eastern Europe.

From left: Attorneys E.H. McDermott, Howard A. Will, and William M. Emery practiced law together from the 1940s to the 1960s in the firm that bears their names. Today, McDermott, Will & Emery ranks as one of the nation's largest law firms, with nearly 500 attorneys.

This formal notice (opposite) announced the newly founded law firm in 1934. Since 1990, McDermott, Will & Emery's Chicago office has occupied several floors in the AT&T Corporate Center at 227 West Monroe Street.

In its U.S. offices, McDermott, Will & Emery serves a broad range of clients, from Fortune 100 corporations to small businesses and individuals. By virtue of its multi-office structure, the firm is able to efficiently represent the legal interests of its clients throughout the country. The range of services provided to these clients encompasses almost all of their possible legal needs. "The depth and scope of our practice is really quite amazing," says Larry Gerber, the firm's managing partner. Gerber joined McDermott, Will & Emery in 1965 and became a partner in 1971. Prior to his 1991 election as managing partner, he headed the firm's Health Law Department.

McDermott, Will & Emery is known for its expertise in a number of areas other than tax law, such as the rapidly growing field of health law. Clients of the firm's Health Law Department include hospitals, alternative delivery systems, physicians and other health care providers, medical device and drug manufacturers, and professional associations of the health care industry.

For these clients, McDermott, Will & Emery attorneys handle mergers, acquisitions, and other formal and informal affiliations; joint ventures; and financing of all kinds. The firm's attorneys also provide extensive regulatory representation, lobby Congress and other agencies on health care issues, and advise clients about proposed administrative regulations and legislation. Attorneys counsel clients on health care cost containment and patient care issues. In addition, they advise on obtaining payment from Medicare, Medicaid, or third-party payers for new technology, medical devices, and drugs. Health law attorneys also provide counsel on EPA, USDA, and FDA regulations.

The firm tackles all aspects of real estate law, corporate law, public finance, mergers and acquisitions, private finance, and project finance. It enjoys a national reputation in the area of employee benefits, with a particular emphasis on pension benefits.

Litigation is another important aspect of the firm's work, representing about two-fifths of its activity. Its trial lawyers practice in areas of law ranging from bankruptcy, workouts, and restructurings to environmental work to intellectual property.

The Chicago office, which also serves as the firm's administrative headquarters, occupies 14 floors of the AT&T Corporate Center. McDermott, Will & Emery's Chicago library, one of the largest law firm libraries in the country, houses more than 47,000 volumes, periodicals, and other research tools. While each office maintains its own library, all have access to the vast resources in the Chicago headquarters.

McDermott, Will & Emery takes pride in the fact that it is one of the nation's leaders in hiring and promoting women attorneys. In 1957, the firm was the first in Chicago to elect a woman partner, which was a bold move at that time. Today, more than half of the 112 associate attorneys in Chicago are women; moreover, 10 percent are members of a minority group.

The firm's distinguished history, outstanding attorneys and support staff, and commitment to the highest standards of the profession have contributed immeasurably to Chicago's legal infrastructure for almost 60 years now. Nevertheless, McDermott, Will & Emery has kept a surprisingly low public profile. "We haven't done a lot of self-promotion," Gerber says. "We let our work—and our clients—speak for us."

EDWARD H. McDERMOTT

ANNOUNCES THE REMOVAL OF HIS OFFICES TO

1111 HARRIS TRUST BUILDING, CHICAGO, ILLINOIS,

WHERE HE WILL CONTINUE THE PRACTICE OF LAW.

WILLIAM M. EMERY WILL BE ASSOCIATED WITH HIM.

CENTRAL 4543   FEBRUARY 2, 1934

BLUE CROSS AND BLUE SHIELD OF ILLINOIS

THE ORGANIZATION THAT IS TODAY KNOWN AS BLUE CROSS AND BLUE SHIELD OF ILLINOIS WAS INCORPORATED IN CHICAGO IN LATE 1936 AND BEGAN ITS FIRST HOSPITAL CARE COVERAGE IN 1937. THE COMPANY'S FIRST MEMBER WAS FRED MCNALLY, A VICE PRESIDENT OF RAND MCNALLY &

Company. He was one of a committee of 30 Chicago business leaders, hospital officials, and physicians who were the driving force behind the prepaid health care movement and who provided financing for the endeavor.

Just after World War II, the original Blue Cross hospital prepayment plan was augmented by the Blue Shield Plan for physician services. Both grew exponentially. Over the years, smaller Blue Cross plans around Illinois, such as in Peoria and Danville, were merged with the Chicago operation. The final merger, with the Rockford Plan, was completed in 1982.

COVERING ILLINOIS
Today, Blue Cross and Blue Shield of Illinois, whose official title is Health Care Service Corporation, insures more than 2.4 million Illinois residents. With annual reve-

nues of $2.5 billion and reserves of more than $500 million, the firm has earned an "AA" excellent rating from Standard & Poor's.

Illinois Blue Cross also serves as the Medicare intermediary for the state, processing nearly 25 million claims a year and paying beneficiaries upwards of $4.5 billion on behalf of the federal government.

Locally and statewide, Blue Cross is a major employer, with some 2,500 people at its corporate headquarters on Michigan Avenue in Chicago. Another 2,000 employees are spread among its claims processing offices in Springfield, Marion, Jacksonville, Champaign, Danville, and Rockford, and its sales offices in Springfield, Rockford, Peoria, and Fairview Heights.

A PIONEERING SPIRIT
The spirit that led Blue Cross to pioneer the health insurance concept

in Illinois has remained an essential part of its corporate ethic ever since.

HMO Illinois, the Blue Cross health maintenance organization subsidiary, was founded in 1973 and quickly became the largest in the state. Today, it is still the largest, with a network of more than 5,000 physicians serving more than 350,000 members in more locations than any of its competitors.

In 1985, recognizing not only that managed care was a key element in

Raymond F. McCaskey (far right), president and CEO of Blue Cross and Blue Shield of Illinois.

The company's Illinois headquarters occupies more than half of the 30-story 2 Illinois Center building in downtown Chicago. Branch offices are located from one end of the state to the other.

keeping health care costs under control, but also that HMOs aren't for everyone, Blue Cross launched the state's first preferred provider organization (PPO). Initially, the Blue Cross PPO included only hospitals throughout Illinois. The key cost-saving element coupled with the PPO network was the Medical Services Advisory system, under which registered nurses working at Blue Cross pre-approve non-emergency hospital stays.

The PPO plan proved so popular with employers and employees alike that PPO Plus was launched. This enhanced program gave patients access to a network of some 15,000 physicians throughout the state. As was the case with the original plan, benefit levels were higher for using a PPO Plus provider, and were substantial, but considerably lower, for going outside the network.

With such a large list of providers to choose from, most patients found that their personal physicians were already members of the network. By the fall of 1992, the program had proven so popular that membership in the Blue Cross PPO topped the 1 million mark.

However, the Blue Cross pioneering spirit didn't stop there. In 1991, yet another cost-saving managed care initiative was launched: Point of Service (POS). Like an HMO, the POS product requires that a member choose a primary care physician who then handles all referrals to specialists and hospitals. Similar to a PPO, the patient can still go outside the network if he or she is willing to settle for a lower level of benefits.

Several major employers have already embraced the POS concept. Ameritech (parent company of Illinois Bell) and American Stores (parent company of Jewel/Osco) were among the first to enroll.

"Point of Service is our newest product, but it certainly won't be our last," says Raymond F. McCaskey, president and chief executive officer of Blue Cross and Blue Shield of Illinois. "The health insurance business keeps evolving, and we're going to be out where we've always been—on the leading edge of the evolution."

The public service office (above) on the concourse level of the headquarters building is equipped to handle all of a policyholder's needs, from accepting premium payments to providing quick answers to questions on claims or coverage levels.

The special inquiries section (left) is geared to provide solutions to complicated claims problems.

CULLIGAN INTERNATIONAL COMPANY

FOR MILLIONS OF PEOPLE AROUND THE WORLD, THE NAME CULLIGAN HAS BECOME SYNONYMOUS WITH HIGH-QUALITY WATER AND WATER TREATMENT PRODUCTS. ESTABLISHED IN 1936 BY EMMETT J. CULLIGAN, CULLIGAN INTERNATIONAL COMPANY IS TODAY AN UNDISPUTED LEADER IN WATER

treatment for home and commercial establishments. By drawing upon its expertise in water treatment, the company has successfully positioned itself as a force in the bottled drinking water market as well.

It was in a blacksmith's shop in suburban Northbrook, Illinois that Emmett Culligan first conceived the idea of marketing soft water on a service basis through franchised dealers. Since then, faith, integrity, hard work, and a lasting entrepreneurial spirit have paved the way for this industry leader that invented the first automatic water softener. Thanks to the efforts of Emmett Culligan and his associates, the company has evolved into a full-service organization committed to customizing water treatment equipment and methods for businesses and consumers worldwide.

A GROWING PRODUCT LINE

Still located in suburban Northbrook, the company's corporate headquarters occupies a 42-acre plot north of Chicago. Culligan also operates five manufacturing plants located in Spain, Italy, Canada, Belgium, and the United States.

Supported by these facilities, the company develops innovative solutions for everything from complex municipal treatment plant problems to producing a delicious bottle of Culligan drinking water. Organized into two areas—Household and Commercial/ Industrial—Culligan offers a line of products and services to all types of customers that includes bottled water; drinking water treatment products such as filters for improved taste and odor or lead reduction; water conditioning products used as softeners and whole house filters; and desalination equipment.

Culligan's water conditioning products and services are distributed by more than 1,350 independently operated dealers and licensees in the United States and Canada, and throughout more than 90 countries in Europe, Latin America, Africa, Asia, and Australia.

Over the years, Culligan has been a leader in the development of technically advanced water treatment devices. In the early 1980s, the company pioneered the use of reverse osmosis technology for the treatment of drinking water in the home. Culligan's advanced reverse osmosis filter systems reduce undesirable contaminants such as lead and nitrate. The company's newest product, a water vending machine called the Fresh Water Station™, uses this advanced filtration technique to produce high-quality drinking water that is 98 percent free of total dissolved solids.

Since it entered the desalination field in 1978, Culligan has become a worldwide leader in sea and brackish water treatment techniques. An example of its leadership in this industry is marked by a $10 million contract to produce equipment for a series of desalination plants to be built along the Red Sea and the southern Sinai Peninsula.

Senior executives note that many people don't realize the great potential the sea presents in regard to potable water. The sea does in fact provide a virtually endless supply of water, which when treated properly, can provide high-quality water for consumption or any other use.

Building on its expertise, technology, and worldwide reputation for quality, Culligan launched a line of premium packaged water products in 1986. Through this growing facet of its operations, the company offers several sizes of bottled drinking water for home and office use.

"We have some of the most advanced water treatment capabilities in the industry. As such, we feel that we have the ability to produce superior packaged water products," say Culligan officials. "We offer the consumer a quality domestic prod-

For millions of people around the world, the name Culligan has become synonymous with high-quality water and water treatment products.

uct with a premium image."

It is this longtime commitment to quality that has made Culligan a leading force in the industry. In fact, many Culligan products are certified by the National Sanitation Foundation (NSF), an independent, non-profit testing organization. Products that carry NSF certification meet some of the most stringent performance standards in the industry. Many Culligan products also have undergone rigorous testing and received certificates from Underwriters Laboratories, the Water Quality Association, and the International Association of Plumbers and Mechanical Officials.

ENHANCING PUBLIC AWARENESS

Beyond its manufacturing and distribution focus, Culligan strives to bring the vital issue of water quality to the public's attention. Each August, the company sponsors National Water Quality Month. Culligan began sponsoring the month-long campaign to help increase public awareness of water as a precious resource. During the month, Culligan encourages the public to examine and increase their

knowledge about the quality of the community water supply, and if concerned, to have it tested.

Year-round, Culligan operates a toll-free water quality hotline. Known as the Culligan® Water-Watch™ Information Bureau, the service offers consumers a free resource for reliable information about water.

As public concern about the environment continues to grow, the need for a constant source of potable water is becoming increasingly ap-

parent. With extensive research and development capabilities, Culligan International is prepared to face this challenge.

As a world-renowned water quality expert, the company plans to build on its history of success and further its reputation for excellence. By developing and marketing innovative new products and by bringing the complex issue of water quality to the public's attention, Culligan International Company is prepared to remain an industry leader.

Located in suburban Northbrook, Culligan International Company's corporate headquarters occupies a 42-acre plot north of Chicago (above).

Culligan operates its own truck fleet, known as Culligan Distribution System (left).

385

SKIDMORE, OWINGS & MERRILL

FOR MORE THAN FIVE DECADES, TALENT AND TEAMWORK HAVE EARNED SKIDMORE, OWINGS & MERRILL A GLOBAL REPUTATION FOR SUPERIOR PLANNING, ARCHITECTURE, AND ENGINEERING. ♦ FOUNDED IN CHICAGO IN 1936 BY NATHANIEL OWINGS AND LOUIS SKIDMORE, WHO COLLABORATED

on the planning of the 1933 Chicago World's Fair, the firm quickly garnered respect for its ability to tackle large, complex projects within a

The award-winning Rowes Wharf mixed-use complex (above) in Boston exemplifies SOM's capacity for contextually responsive civic design.

The firm applied its visionary approach to the design of Arlington International Racecourse (right) located just outside of Chicago. Specifically geared toward creating a family entertainment environment, the design has set a new quality standard for the racing industry.

creative architectural framework. Since then, SOM has left its imprint on Chicago in many ways. Perhaps the most recognized are the Sears Tower and the John Hancock Center, two major features of the city's modern skyline. "[The firm's] distinguished reputation rests largely on its technical virtuosity and a determination to stay in the mainstream of corporate taste," wrote the late Chicago architecture critic Paul Gapp.

In 1937, the founding partners launched a New York City office and took on a third partner, engineer John Merrill. Today the firm is one of the largest architecture/engineering firms in the world, with offices in Chicago, New York, San Francisco, Los Angeles, Washington, D.C., and London.

A MULTI-DISCIPLINARY TEAM APPROACH

Over the years, Skidmore, Owings & Merrill has won hundreds of architectural and engineering awards, including the first ever American Institute of Architects (AIA) firm award for excellence. The firm's unique multi-disciplinary practice and team approach have enabled it to succeed at architectural challenges as diverse as airports, race tracks, museums, and corporate

headquarters. "What separates us from other firms is that we can deliver quality and added value to a city or an environment rather than simply employing a cookie-cutter approach," says Partner Thomas Fridstein.

Among the firm's best-known projects are the U.S. Air Force Academy in Colorado Springs, the Inland Steel Building, Northwestern University Main Campus, the Hancock Center, and the Sears Tower. In addition to over 50 projects completed in Chicago in the past decade, the firm has recently worked on the massive Canary Wharf development in London, the Rowes Wharf mixed-use complex in Boston, Hotel de las Artes (part of the Vila Olimpica complex in Barcelona), and the Spiegel Corporate Headquarters in suburban Chicago.

The diverse SOM staff includes architects; civil, electrical, mechanical, plumbing, and structural engineers; landscape architects; urban planners; and interior designers. A team consisting of members from each discipline remains with a project from the initial marketing call until after the building is completed, providing consistency and maintaining project integrity. The SOM project manager coordinates this team and ensures that the client's interests are realized by utilizing the firm's resources.

DEDICATED TO PROBLEM-SOLVING

While other firms may specialize in a particular market, SOM emphasizes problem-solving. This focus enables the firm to excel at the large-scale, complex ventures that have garnered accolades worldwide.

For example, in 1987 SOM designed its first equestrian center and racecourse, the Arlington Park International Racecourse located just outside Chicago. That project has since set the standard for the horse-racing industry in terms of design quality and the realization of a vision.

The firm's problem-solving expertise has also attracted corporations, governments, and city planners who are faced with large-scale, potentially controversial projects. According to Jerry Roper, president and CEO of the Chicago Convention and Tourism Bureau, Skidmore, Owings & Merrill has always made sure that its building designs fit in with the fabric of the rest of the city. "People turn to them as protectors of the city," says Roper.

Indeed, the firm sees that as one of its primary goals. "A lot of people think of architects as people who just design buildings, but we have always viewed ourselves as designers of cities," says partner Kim Goluska.

In the 1990s and beyond, the firm expects to be involved in more urban revitalization projects worldwide, much like its recent work on London's successful Broadgate redevelopment of the Liverpool Street Station and the revitalization of the Canary Wharf docklands. Completed in 1991, the Canary Wharf project challenged SOM to transform 70 acres of devastated industrial property into a new commercial area. The firm is currently working on projects in Europe, Eastern Europe, the Middle East, and the Far East, reflecting its ability to maintain a leadership position in an ever-increasing global marketplace.

STRONG TIES TO CHICAGO

Despite its international scope, Skidmore, Owings & Merrill has always maintained strong ties to Chicago. As part of its commitment to the community, the firm encourages all employees to be involved in civic work, and its partners sit on boards ranging from the Field Museum of Natural History and the Chicago Film Festival to the Chi-

cago Central Area Committee, among others.

One example of the firm's local efforts is the rebuilding of the Holy Angels Church, a Chicago landmark that was destroyed by fire in the 1980s. SOM employees helped in fund-raising efforts and donated design work and construction oversight on the project.

SOM has historically placed importance on civic involvement. Among the firm's noted civic contributions is its widely recognized role in convincing Pablo Picasso to design the sculpture that now stands in front of Chicago's Richard J. Daley Center. SOM Partner Bill Hartmann initiated and led a successful delegation to approach the artist, who agreed to donate the sculpture to the city in 1966.

POSITIONED FOR THE FUTURE

With over 50 years of rich heritage and a strong civic reputation as its foundation, Skidmore, Owings & Merrill intends to carry on its tradition of community involvement and its legacy for excellence in architecture and engineering into the next century. The firm is positioned and committed to approach each future challenge, both locally and abroad, as it always has: with vision, freshness, and unsurpassed expertise.

Among SOM's designs are two of Chicago's most prominent contemporary architectural landmarks: the Sears Tower and the AT&T Corporate Center (left).

The renovation of the 1904 Murray Theatre at Ravinia Festival (top) has been recognized with several historic preservation awards and illustrates SOM's depth of commitment to quality architecture, engineering, and interior design on small-scale and specialty civic projects.

The firm designed the state-of-the-art Spiegel Corporate Headquarters (above) in suburban Chicago.

TATHAM EURO RSCG

TURNING CONSUMER PRODUCTS INTO HOUSEHOLD NAMES HAS BEEN THE LEGACY OF TATHAM EURO RSCG SINCE 1946. ♦ THE CREATOR OF MR. CLEAN, FLINTSTONES VITAMINS, AND IKE THE LUCKY DOG, TATHAM TOUTS ITS BRANDS AS IF THEY ARE LONG-LOVED, BEST FRIENDS. A VISIT TO

the North Michigan Avenue agency prompts a quick lesson in the difference between products and brands. One learns that products occupy physical space on a shelf or in a showroom, whereas a brand leaps out and talks to a consumer. In fact, Tatham has proven time after time that consumers have feelings and emotions about a brand, and those come from one place: advertising. Effective advertising.

While Tatham has continued to live up to its brand-building heritage, in recent years it has branched out, diversified, and expanded its client base, making it one of the city's fastest-growing advertising agencies. Over the past decade, the firm has nearly tripled in size and today represents 13 key clients, 10 of whom are Fortune 500 companies and five that rate among the country's top-spending advertisers. Such rapid growth has been accomplished through a strong, experienced management team known for its strategic thinking and an award-winning group of creatives who are recognized for their ability to come up with business-driven creative solutions as well as memorable TV and print campaigns.

Tatham has always occupied somewhat of an individual niche among advertising agencies. The firm prides itself on being small enough that clients consistently applaud their day-to-day access to top management, yet its client roster includes some of the biggest names in the business: Procter & Gamble, Miles Inc., Ralston Purina, Ameritech, Stouffer Foods, and Adolph Coors, to name a few. Procter & Gamble, the number one packaged goods advertiser in the United States, first knocked on Tatham's door in 1956. One of the agency's first assignments was to introduce a revolutionary all-purpose household cleaner, Mr. Clean, followed by a new shampoo, Head & Shoulders. Tatham not only named both of the products, but has been solely responsible for making them two of the best-selling and most-recognized brands of the past few decades.

Ralph Rydholm, Tatham's chairman, CEO, and chief creative officer, explains that the agency was founded on the premise that advertising is outstanding only if it helps build brand strength and recognition. "What I call 'inventing the brand' and then building brand equity are the most important things our agency does," says Rydholm, who has been with Tatham since 1987 and at the helm since mid-1992. "The characters we've created, such as Mr. Clean, almost become living things. And Ralston Purina's dog Ike strikes a cord in people. This, of course, helps motivate consumers to continually buy the product."

THE EVOLUTION OF TATHAM EURO RSCG

Rydholm is one of a select few "brand loyalists" who have led the agency. It was founded in 1946 by Art Tatham and Ken Laird, who had one key account, the Bendix washing machine, and a clear vision—that they would build brands out of products.

Ralph W. Rydholm, Tatham's chairman, CEO, and chief creative officer, has been with the agency since 1987 and at the helm since mid-1992 (below).

Tatham was founded in 1946 by J. Kenneth Laird and Arthur E. Tatham (above).

MOO. **AND IMPROVED.**

DEAN FOODS

Easy 2%

Easy to Digest Lowfat Milk.

"DON'T WORRY, I NEVER GET LOST."

Phone First.

AMERITECH @ Illinois Bell

© 1993 A

The Tatham-Laird agency grew from the start, and it quickly gained in national stature when it earned its first assignment from Procter & Gamble in the early '50s. By the mid-1960s, the firm saw a chance for even greater expansion and teamed up with The Kudner Agency of New York to form Tatham-Laird & Kudner.

A Chicago-based agency at heart, Tatham nonetheless was quick to eye the trend toward globalization in the 1980s. The agency knew it never wanted to become an office of a multinational network. Instead it sought a partner who shared its own vision and goals and who could provide the international resources Tatham sought for its clients. A prolonged search for the right partner produced a marriage in 1988 with Paris-based Roux, Seguela, Cayzac & Goudard (RSCG). Then in 1992, RSCG and Tatham joined forces with another Paris-based agency, forming EURO RSCG. Tatham changed its own name to Tatham EURO RSCG shortly thereafter.

The seventh largest agency network in the world, EURO RSCG has offices throughout Europe, North America, Asia, Africa, and the Middle East. Top multinational clients include Nestle, 3M, Cadbury Schweppes, Jacobs Suchard, Cartier, Citroen, Kraft General Foods, Tambrands, and Procter & Gamble.

THE PHILOSOPHY REMAINS

In addition to a shared love of brands, Tatham and its new partners hold a common belief that the most successful businesses are built by people who have a stake in their company. Tatham has always believed that its managers must be active partners in business with their clients, never simply figureheads whose only function is to run an office. Throughout the EURO RSCG network, this structure prevails. The managers in different countries for the most part have invested in their companies directly to build the business and as such are hands-on managers who share in the profits directly.

RECENT WINS AND FUTURE GROWTH

Tatham's dramatic, double-digit growth over the past few years has been fueled by a string of new business wins as well as growth from existing clients. Old Spice, Metamucil, and Vidal Sassoon are just a few of its Procter & Gamble accounts today. The agency also has responsibility for the Brown & Williamson Tobacco Corporation, Dean Foods, The Hoover Company, and Fould's Inc., among others.

Ameritech, the Midwest's largest telecommunications company, along with Tatham's two newest clients, Kemper Financial Services

and Zenith Data Systems, are helping the agency fulfill one additional goal—to increase its local prominence and diversify its client base by attracting more service-oriented accounts.

Founded on and still guided by a time-tested philosophy, the agency is enjoying success on a national as well as global basis. With a management team and staff recognized for creative talent and sound advertising concepts, Tatham EURO RSCG is an industry leader poised and prepared for continued growth.

❶ver the years, Tatham has established a strong brand-building heritage, including its introduction in the 1950s of Procter & Gamble's Mr. Clean all-purpose household cleaner (top right). More recently, the agency created Ike the Lucky Dog for Ralston Purina (opposite) and spearheaded new product introductions for Dean Foods (top left) and Ameritech (above).

WMAQ-TV, CHANNEL 5

NICK MERRICK / HEDRICH-BLESSING

WMAQ-TV, CHANNEL 5 HAS BEEN A VIBRANT PART OF CHICAGO FOR MORE THAN 45 YEARS. IN ONE OF AMERICA'S GREATEST CITIES, THIS NBC OWNED AND OPERATED STATION HAS DEMONSTRATED A STRONG COMMITMENT TO SERVING THE ENTIRE NORTHERN ILLINOIS

and northwest Indiana community.

As early as 1930, experimental television broadcasts were being conducted, but the station did not officially begin commercial operations until 1947. Channel 5 began its first test signal in September 1948 and initiated full-time operation in January 1949. The station's original call letters, WNBY, were changed to WNBQ in 1948, and then to WMAQ in 1964. The station is wholly owned by the National Broadcasting Company, which became a division of General Electric in 1986.

AN INDUSTRY LEADER

Because television was a medium in its infancy, the original pioneers were professionals working in related fields—film, theatre, or even vaudeville. The station's early staff members were out to make a splash, so they treated television as a whole new endeavor, not just as "radio with pictures." They attempted to create a new look for their programming—a "Chicago style" of broadcasting, which utilized innovative camera work and a visual style that separated the city from others finding their way in this new electronic medium.

As this newest household appliance gained in popularity, WMAQ became important as a supplier of network shows. Among those programs were "Garroway at Large" with Dave Garroway, "Studs' Place" starring Studs Terkel, "Zoo Parade" hosted by Marlin Perkins, "Mr. Wizard" starring Don Herbert, and "Ding Dong School" with Dr. Frances Horwich.

For a period of time in the early 1950s, about half of NBC's programming originated in Chicago. The

station's first network entry was the legendary "Kukla, Fran and Ollie" starring Burr Tillstrom, Fran Allison, and the Kuklapolitan Players.

But for a long time, the "heart and soul" of Channel 5 has been its news department. Its number one commitment to Chicago was, is, and always will be news. In fact, more than half of the station's 250 employees today work in the news department.

Outstanding news and information programming has been produced for much of the station's history. It all began with "Five Star Final," a unique combination of news, weather, sports, household hints, and musical nostalgia. The program featured the news team of Clifton Utley, Clint Youle, Tom Duggan, Dorsey Connors, and Herbie Mintz. In 1952, Channel 5 premiered "City Desk," which still runs on the station. Over the years, guests on that program have included George Bush, Dan Quayle, Mike Ditka, Malcolm X, and numerous congressional, state, and local officials.

Since the 1980s, WMAQ-TV's news department has been led on air by Ron Magers, Carol Marin, Joan Esposito, Warner Saunders, weatherman Jim Tillmon, and sports director Mark Giangreco. WMAQ also boasts an outstanding investigative journalism team, Unit 5, which has been honored with Peabody and Columbia-DuPont awards, along with numerous Emmy, Associated Press, United Press International, Ohio State, and other industry awards.

WMAQ-TV also has been a launching pad for many of the best-loved and most influential news personalities on television. Dave Garroway left the station to become

the first host of "Today" in 1952. Later station staff members to join the legendary morning show were Hugh Downs, Deborah Norville, and Jane Pauley, who was a co-host for 13 years and is still with NBC News. Longtime NBC Nightly News anchor and commentator John Chancellor also worked at WMAQ-TV.

ROLLIN' DOWN THE RIVER

In 1989, WMAQ-TV moved into its new home, the 40-story NBC Tower, located on Columbus Drive near the Chicago River and Lake Michigan. Its previous home was upriver in the world-famous Merchandise Mart.

In addition to its executive offices and newsroom, NBC Tower is also the home of NBC Tower Productions, the most advanced studio and production facility in the Midwest. It includes two fully equipped sound-stages: Studio A, boasting 11,400 square feet, is currently home to the nationally syndicated show, "Jenny Jones," and Studio B, with its 4,180 square feet, houses "The Jerry Springer Show." Both programs utilize state-of-the-art control rooms and equipment.

WMAQ-TV is making plans for the introduction of high-definition television (HDTV) later in the 1990s, which will take viewers into a whole new world of entertainment. After more than 45 years in Chicago, WMAQ-TV and NBC will continue to lead the way in broadcasting quality entertainment and news programs well into the 21st century.

State-of-the-art control rooms and equipment are an important part of WMAQ-TV's commitment to broadcasting quality entertainment and news programs well into the 21st century (above).

In 1989, WMAQ-TV moved into its new home, the 40-story NBC Tower (opposite), located on Columbus Drive near the Chicago River and Lake Michigan.

COTTER & COMPANY

ALTHOUGH THE NAME COTTER & COMPANY MAY NOT BE A HOUSEHOLD WORD, THERE IS HARDLY A CONSUMER WHO HASN'T USED THE HARDWARE COOPERATIVE'S PRODUCTS OR SHOPPED IN ONE OF ITS AFFILIATES—THE LOCAL TRUE VALUE HARDWARE STORE.

Cotter & Company, the world's largest dealer-owned wholesaler of hardware and related products, reported sales of over $2.3 billion for 1992. Its more than 6,800 member stores are located in all 50 states and in 27 foreign countries.

John Cotter (left), founder and chairman of the board, and his son, Dan, president and CEO, in 1986.

The company's entire business life has been centered in Chicago, and its commitment to the community goes back to its origins. For example, Cotter & Company has been one of the strongest supporters of Boys and Girls Clubs, starting with the Lathrop Boys and Girls Club just three blocks from Cotter & Company National Headquarters.

Through the efforts of President Dan Cotter, who has been involved in automobile racing since he was in high school, one of the premier

events on Chicago's sports social schedule is a banquet recognizing champion auto racing drivers. This annual affair alone has contributed well over $1 million to Boys and Girls Clubs in Chicago, while bringing to the city famous drivers like Richard Petty, Mario and Michael Andretti, Dale Earnhardt, A.J. Foyt, Emerson Fittipaldi, and many others.

FOUNDED IN 1948
The company was founded in 1948 by John Cotter, who, though only 44 years old, had 32 years of experience in the hardware business. As a boy, Cotter worked after school in a hardware store in his hometown of St. Paul, Minnesota. Later he became a salesman and then a buyer for a hardware wholesaler. For three years, he owned and managed his own hardware store in Eau Claire, Wisconsin.

In 1948, Cotter founded the Cotter & Company hardware cooperative in Chicago with just 25 member stores. Business grew quickly, and by the end of 1950, there were 133 members. Cotter & Company's gross sales had reached $7.5 million by 1955, making it the third largest wholesaler in the hardware industry. In 1961, the company became the number one hardware wholesaler in the country with gross sales of $25 million.

Many in the industry give John Cotter credit for almost single-handedly providing the leadership that ultimately kept the threatened independent retailers alive, allowing them to thrive.

In 1963, Cotter & Company acquired the True Value trademark, along with 400 True Value members, through consolidation with Hibbard, Spencer, Bartlett and Co. of Chicago, a former rival and one-

time industry leader. John Cotter considered the merger one of his finest achievements.

Cotter was active in the day-to-day management of the company until only a few weeks before his death in 1989 at the age of 85. His son, Daniel Cotter, president since 1978, heads the organization today.

"What John Cotter brought to this company and that still lives on is enthusiasm and great salesmanship," says Dan Cotter. "He had determination, too. People advised him to stay within 200 miles of Chicago, but through his efforts, there are member stores all over the world."

MEMBERSHIP BENEFITS
Cotter & Company members are independent, and in most cases family-owned, retail operations. A neighborhood hardware store can become a member by buying stock in Cotter & Company; the store then has access to more than 60,000 items that can be purchased at low prices made possible only by large-scale cooperative buying.

In addition to the merchandise, Cotter & Company provides programs and services that allow the independent retailer to maximize profits and financial stability. Most members choose to use the True Value store name because it has worldwide recognition reinforced by advertising campaigns with popular spokespeople like Willard Scott. Cotter & Company also operates its own insurance company to provide health and hospitalization insurance, property and casualty coverage, life insurance, and other protection for True Value Hardware members. Finally, because the company is owned by its members, profits of Cotter & Company go to them.

"This is a company that was founded on a dream and a principle rather than on a money-making scheme," says Cotter. "Our purpose is to serve independent retailers and help them thrive in a business world that's becoming more and more controlled by chains."

Cotter & Company makes available to its members the products of more than 10,000 manufacturers from around the world, but the company also owns several manufacturing facilities to produce its exclusive national brands. Among them is General Power Equipment Co. in Harvard, Illinois, which manufactures outdoor power equipment, including Lawn Chief lawn mowers and tractors, Snow Chief snow removal equipment, and Ultra-Comfort ceramic heaters. Always socially conscious and alert to consumer wants and needs, General Power also offers a very successful line of chippers and shredders.

The well-known Tru-Test quality paint line is produced for members at Tru-Test Manufacturing Co. plants in Chicago and Cary, Illinois. Also located in Cary is the Baltimore Brush Co., which manufac-

tures paint brushes, rollers, and other application tools.

Likewise, Master Mechanic tools, Master Plumber plumbing equipment, and Master Electrician electrical products are made exclusively for True Value stores by some of the best-known manufacturers in the world.

Cotter & Company members order their products through 15 distribution centers located throughout the country in Allentown, Pennsylvania; Atlanta, Georgia; Cleveland, Ohio; Corsicana, Texas; Denver, Colorado; Harvard, Illinois; Henderson, North Carolina; Indianapolis, Indiana; Kansas City, Missouri; Manchester, New Hampshire; Kingman, Arizona; Mankato, Minnesota; Ocala, Florida; Portland, Oregon; and Woodland, California.

To better serve and inform its members, Cotter & Company hosts national dealer markets each spring and fall. Known as Red Carpet Markets, they are held at the company's national headquarters facility on Clybourn Avenue in Chicago. Representatives from more than 6,800 True Value stores attend the markets to view and purchase the

products and programs offered by thousands of manufacturers.

For over 50 years, thousands of independent hardware dealers have benefited through their affiliation with Cotter & Company. The competitive prices, quality products, and other benefits of membership in the cooperative have helped the neighborhood hardware store remain a viable force in today's marketplace.

393

SARA LEE CORPORATION

WHEN PEOPLE HEAR THE NAME SARA LEE, CHEESECAKE MOST LIKELY COMES TO MIND. BUT SARA LEE CORPORATION MEANS MUCH MORE THAN QUALITY FROZEN BAKED GOODS. ◆ THE CHICAGO-BASED MANUFACTURING GIANT IS A GLOBAL, BRAND-NAME CONSUMER

packaged goods company with 128,000 employees in more than 30 countries. Sara Lee manufactures and markets a wide variety of well-known products, including *Jimmy Dean* meats, *Champion* activewear, *L'eggs* and *Hanes* hosiery, *Kiwi* shoe care products, *Coach* leatherware, *Isotoner* gloves, *Sara Lee* frozen baked goods, and many, many more. Sara Lee's business is concentrated in two areas, Packaged Foods and Consumer Packaged Products, and includes a variety of products from coffee and toothpaste to shampoo and hosiery. Both segments of business have major operations in North America, Europe, Asia, and the Pacific Rim.

BALTIMORE BEGINNINGS
In 1939, Nathan Cummings began his acquisition of the Baltimore-based C.D. Kenny Company, a small wholesale distributor of sugar, coffee, and tea. He completed the acquisition in 1941, and in 1945 moved its headquarters to Chicago and changed its name to Consolidated Grocers Corporation. The company's name changed again in 1954 to Consolidated Foods Corporation, and in 1956, its portfolio of businesses also included Kitchens of Sara Lee.

Consolidated Foods' growth continued into the 1960s with the acquisition of a small canned goods company in Holland and such prominent regional food processors as Kahn's Meat Company and Bryan Foods (originally named Bryan Brothers Packing Company).

John H. Bryan, who sold the family-owned and -operated meat business, Bryan Foods, to Consolidated Foods in 1968, became chief executive officer in 1975 and the following year assumed the chairman's post. He continues to serve as chairman and chief executive officer.

The Sara Lee Packaged Meats and Bakery line of business includes such brands as *Hillshire Farm*, *Ball Park*, *Jimmy Dean*, and *Sara Lee* (top right).

The Household and Personal Care line of business includes shoe-care, skin-care, oral-care, and baby-care products, as well as insecticides, air fresheners, and specialty laundry detergents (bottom right).

In 1978, the company fortified its presence in the European market with the purchase of Holland-based Douwe Egberts, one of the world's largest coffee roasters. The 1979 purchase of Hanes Corporation also made Consolidated Foods a major player in the U.S. hosiery, underwear, and intimate apparel markets. During the early 1980s, the company concentrated on expanding its market shares and strengthening its international consumer products business. To that end, Australia-based Nicholas Kiwi was acquired in 1984. The following year, Consolidated Foods was renamed Sara Lee

Corporation.

Since the mid-1980s, Sara Lee's acquisitions have included businesses that fit strategically within existing operations. Some of these acquisitions include Bil Mar Foods, which produces turkey products; Hygrade Food Products, a manufacturer of processed meats; Champion Products, a manufacturer of recreational activewear; Playtex Apparel, an international manufacturer and distributor of intimate apparel; Pretty Polly, a manufacturer and marketer of hosiery in the United Kingdom; Balirny Praha, a leading coffee and tea producer in Czechoslovakia; and Pessi Guttalin, a manufacturer and marketer of shoe-care products in Italy.

SARA LEE PACKAGED FOODS

Sara Lee's Packaged Foods business is grouped into two major areas: Packaged Meats and Bakery, and Coffee and Grocery.

The Packaged Meats business includes many well-established brands. In addition to *Jimmy Dean* meats, brand-name products include *Ball Park* hot dogs and *Hillshire Farm* breakfast and smoked sausage. *Mr. Turkey*, *Bryan*, *Kahn's*, and *Gallo Salami* are also brand leaders in their regional markets.

Flagship brand *Sara Lee* is today the leading line of frozen baked goods sold in the United States. *Sara Lee* brand products are also available in grocery stores in Canada, the United Kingdom, Australia, Hong Kong, Singapore, and Europe.

The company's Coffee and Grocery business, based in the Netherlands, is managed under the name Sara Lee/DE. Through the *Douwe Egberts* brand, the corporation has become a leader in the retail coffee markets of the Netherlands, Belgium, Denmark, and Spain. In addition, Douwe Egberts markets *Pickwick*, the leading Dutch brand of tea, as well as *Van Nelle* tea. Sara Lee/DE also is a leading manufacturer and marketer of nuts and snack foods in several European markets.

CONSUMER PACKAGED PRODUCTS

Sara Lee's Consumer Packaged Products also are grouped in two major areas: Personal Products, and Household and Personal Care Products.

The Personal Products operation has a strong presence in both the United States and Europe. Sara Lee has a major position in the U.S. hosiery market with such brands as *Hanes Silk Reflections*, *Donna Karan*, and *Fitting Pretty*, which are top sellers in department and specialty stores. Underwear for adults and children also is sold under the *Hanes* label. In addition, *L'eggs* is the leading pantyhose brand sold in

The Sara Lee Personal Products line of business (above) includes underwear and activewear, intimate apparel, and hosiery. Major brands are *Abanderado* and *Princesa* (Spain), *King Gee* and *Stubbies* (Australia), and *Hanes, Hanes Her Way,* and *L'eggs* (United States).

Other Personal Products brands include *L'eggs Classic Comfort* and *Sheer Elegance,* as well as Australia's *Razzamatazz* and France's *Dim* (right).

food, drug, and mass-merchandise outlets. In Europe, Sara Lee markets hosiery, women's lingerie, men's underwear, and socks for the entire family under the *Dim* brand, the hosiery market leader in Europe. Intimate apparel items also are sold through this business, including such well-known brands as *Playtex, Bali,* and *WonderBra.*

Sara Lee's Household and Personal Care business, managed by Sara Lee/DE, is represented in markets in Europe, Asia, Australia, Africa, and the Americas. Despite this geographic diversity, Western Europe represents the largest area of concentration for this organization with continued interest in Central Europe, the Pacific Rim, and Latin America. Many of Sara Lee's Household and Personal Care products hold significant positions in their respective markets, including *Sanex* liquid bath and shower products, *Radox* bath products, *Biotex* detergents, and *Catch, Bloom, Ridsect,* and *Vapona* insecticides. The familiar brand-name product, *Kiwi* shoe polish, is sold throughout the world.

CORPORATE LEADERSHIP BY DESIGN

Sara Lee Corporation aspires to hold the leading position in each product category and in each marketplace where it participates. Maximizing shareholder value also is of key importance to the corporation, and its three key financial goals bear this out: Sara Lee strives for real growth in earnings per share of 8 percent annually over time, a return on equity of at least 20 percent, and a total-debt-to-total-capital ratio of no more than 40 percent.

Sara Lee also believes that a responsible corporation gives something back to the communities where its employees live and work. Each year, Sara Lee Corporation contributes at least 2 percent of its U.S. pretax income to nonprofit organizations. The Sara Lee Founda-

tion makes contributions on behalf of Sara Lee Corporation and designates 50 percent of its giving to organizations serving people who are disadvantaged, while 40 percent goes to support cultural activities and 10 percent to other programs. Sara Lee Corporation divisions manage their own giving programs, helping local nonprofit organizations serve the needs of their immediate communities.

With Chicago roots dating back nearly half a century and a proud history of growth and success, Sara Lee Corporation is today a prominent local and global corporate citizen. Thanks to its high standards and aspirations for future growth, Sara Lee will remain a global leader in an increasingly competitive world economy.

KEMPER FINANCIAL SERVICES, INC.

KEMPER FINANCIAL SERVICES, INC. WAS FORMED IN 1948 BY A GROUP OF CHICAGO ENTREPRENEURS WHO DECIDED TO INVEST IN THE FUTURE SUCCESS OF TELEVISION AND TECHNOLOGY. ◆ THE ORGANIZATION, KNOWN AS THE TELEVISION SHARES MANAGEMENT COMPANY, CREATED

its first mutual fund and called it the Television Fund. In 1963, the company was repositioned for broader appeal, and its name was changed to Supervised Investors Services (SIS). By 1969, SIS had established three new equity funds and managed more than $900 million in assets.

Kemper Corporation, a diversified financial services holding company headquartered in Long Grove, Illinois, acquired all of SIS's outstanding stock in 1970. The acquisition combined Kemper's fixed-income expertise with the solid equity management of SIS. In 1976, the firm became Kemper Financial Services, Inc. and today is one of the largest investment management companies in the United States.

INNOVATION AND DIVERSIFICATION

Currently, KFS employs approximately 1,800 people in Chicago and Kansas City. With over $69 billion in assets under its management, including $15 billion in money market funds and $38 billion in mutual funds, Kemper manages more than 57 separate investment portfolios that address a wide range of investment needs. Currently, Kemper provides services to more than 2.3 million mutual fund shareholder accounts. Kemper mutual funds are sold through broker/dealers, banks, and other financial intermediaries.

As one of the nation's premier financial services firms, KFS has been a leader in offering innovative investment alternatives. In 1974, the

Kemper Income and Capital Preservation Fund, a high-quality bond fund, was created. Later that year, Kemper began offering one of the industry's first money market funds—an open-end mutual fund that invests in short-term securities, such as Treasury bills, certificates of deposit, and commercial paper.

In 1976, Kemper developed the nation's first fully managed tax-exempt income bond fund, the Kemper Municipal Bond Fund. This innovative fund invests in bonds issued by states and municipalities to finance public projects such as schools, highways, airports, and water and sewer works. Kemper also offers a full line of fixed-income investment products and was one of the first to expand its retail and wholesale lines to include government securities portfolios.

According to Steven Radis, vice president of corporate communications, Kemper's mutual funds today offer a level of investment diversity and know-how not otherwise available to an individual. "Our mutual funds allow shareholders to pool their financial resources, reducing risk and giving them access to the expertise of top quality money managers," he explains.

HIGH-QUALITY INVESTMENT MANAGEMENT SERVICES

The investment philosophy at KFS is to provide high-quality investment management services based on teamwork, a clearly defined investment style, and thorough research.

In its equity mutual funds, which invest primarily in stocks, Kemper strives for "growth at the right price." Its team of investment professionals use research to identify quality growth companies whose stocks are selling at reasonable prices and whose earnings are growing faster than the market average.

Kemper's fixed-income department emphasizes credit and sector analysis and seeks to balance a competitive current yield with opportunities for total return. Kemper generally selects fixed-income debt instruments with intermediate maturities from among corporate, treasury, and mortgage-backed bond sectors so that each mutual fund portfolio captures a relatively high yield while reducing price volatility.

Through its subsidiaries, Kemper also provides international and pension plan investments. Kemper Asset Management Company is a major player in the institutional investment arena. Offering investment management services to corporate pension and profit-sharing plans, foundations and endowments, corporations, and public institutions, the division manages about $4 billion for these institutional clients.

London-based Kemper Investment Management Company Limited, Inc. manages more than $1.2 billion in international fixed-income portfolios for institutional clients worldwide.

Diversification, top quality money managers, and a well-defined policy of quality investment: This recipe for success has made Kemper Financial Services a leader for more than 45 years.

Kemper's offices are located at 120 S. LaSalle Street in Chicago's bustling financial district.

Kemper Financial Services strives to provide high-quality investment management services based on teamwork, a clearly defined investment style, and thorough research (left).

397

KMART CORPORATION

S INCE ITS BEGINNINGS AS S.S. KRESGE AT THE TURN OF THE CENTURY, KMART HAS SUCCESSFULLY MET THE CHALLENGE OF SERVING THE CHANGING NEEDS OF THE AMERICAN FAMILY. TODAY, THROUGH AN AMBITIOUS RENEWAL AND EXPANSION PROGRAM, KMART CORPORATION IS FURTHER SOLIDIFYING ITS

position as an American retail leader and securing its place as a dynamic force in the international marketplace.

In 1899, Sebastian Spering Kresge opened the first of many stores that attracted shoppers with low prices, open and inviting displays, and convenient locations. S.S. Kresge became virtually an American institution.

In response to changing buying patterns in the marketplace, the company established a division of Kmart discount department stores in 1962. The first Kmart opened in Michigan, where the company is still headquartered (Troy), and other stores followed that year. The first Chicago area location opened in 1965. Today, Kmart has 2,300 stores in the United States and employs more than 350,000 people, with about 7,000 in its 50 Chicago area locations.

"The key to our success is exceeding customer expectations every day," says Joe Antonini, president and chief executive officer. "Kmart does that by offering good value— quality products at low prices."

In an effort to fully satisfy today's consumer, Kmart offers established national-brand goods, as well as innovative private-label products. In addition to a complete inventory of clothing, home improvement, and health and beauty products, Kmart attracts consumers who are both value-oriented and fashion-conscious with Jaclyn Smith apparel, designer jeans for men and women, name-brand athletic shoes, Martha Stewart fashions for the bedroom and bathroom, and national-brand cosmetics and fragrances.

Behind the scenes, Kmart more efficiently delivers customers what they want through a combination of computers, communications technology, and centralized merchandise replenishment. The corporation is fully committed to running a state-of-the-art retail operation.

AN AMBITIOUS RENEWAL PROGRAM

To continually meet and exceed American consumer expectations in the coming years, Kmart is now engaged in an ambitious $3 billion renewal program. Under the program the company is building new stores, and each existing U.S. Kmart store will be evaluated and then refurbished, enlarged, or relocated. By the end of 1995, all Kmart locations will be full-size retail stores, each averaging 85,000 square feet and featuring a modern interior design, fresh color schemes, innovative displays, wider aisles, and bolder graphics. State-of-the-art price scanning systems and a team of store associates will ensure faster check-out and more efficient customer service.

As part of the renewal program, Kmart Corporation recently announced the accelerated development of Super Kmart Centers, which combine the established concepts of general merchandise and grocery

By the end of 1995, all Kmart locations will be full-size retail stores, featuring a modern interior design, fresh color schemes, innovative displays, wider aisles, and bolder graphics.

stores. Kmart may have 400 to 450 of these centers in place by the mid-1990s, including several in the Chicago area.

Another aspect of Kmart's growth plan has been the acquisition of a number of specialty retailers. Among its diverse group of subsidiaries are PACE Membership Warehouse, which offers a complete range of quality merchandise; Builders Square, which features home improvement supplies for the value-conscious shopper; PayLess Drug Stores, one of the nation's largest retail drugstore chains; the Sports Authority, a group of sporting goods megastores; Waldenbooks, one of the largest U.S. book store chains; Borders, a chain of book superstores; and OfficeMax, a national leader in the office products industry.

INTERNATIONAL EXPANSION

Kmart also has bold plans for the expansion and upgrading of its international operations. Recently, the corporation announced it was actively negotiating to launch a joint venture with a major Mexican retailer to build and operate food and general merchandise stores in Mexico following the Super Kmart Center concept. The program calls for opening a series of stores each year beginning in 1994.

Kmart is extending its reach even further by becoming the first American retailer to make a major commitment to the emerging economies of

Eastern Europe. The company is presently refurbishing the 13 stores it acquired in 1992 in the new Czech Republic and Slovakia, with plans to establish a distribution center in the region as well.

Kmart's other international operations include Kmart Canada Limited, which operates 125 stores in Canada; a 22 percent equity in Coles Myer, Ltd., the largest retailer in Australia; and 14 retail outlets in Puerto Rico. In addition, Kmart has buying offices in Germany, Hong Kong, Taiwan, South Korea, Singapore, Japan, the Philippines, and Chicago.

Taking advantage of its financial strength and its presence in neighborhoods all over the country, Kmart has made a corporate commitment to support programs and efforts to improve the environment, education, and family and cultural life in

the various communities it serves. In the Chicago area alone, Kmart is a major supporter of the United Way, March of Dimes, Chicago Symphony Orchestra, Field Museum, Mid-America Legal Foundation, YMCA, Girl Scouts, Big Shoulders Fund, INROADS, the National Safety Council, and Junior Achievement.

As for its future in the marketplace, Kmart is focused on continuing the tremendous impact the corporation has had on retailing in the United States. Says Antonini, "Our renewal program, our leadership in pricing, our substantial investment in information-gathering systems, the continued expansion of our specialty retail and international formats, and our strong financial base have positioned Kmart Corporation as a true world-class retail organization."

The new Super Kmart Centers (above left), which combine the established concepts of general merchandise and grocery stores, will complement the company's program to build new standard stores and refurbish existing ones (above right).

Today's Kmart offers an array of national-brand and private-label goods for consumers who are both value-oriented and fashion-conscious (left).

EASTMAN KODAK COMPANY

FOR MORE THAN A CENTURY, EASTMAN KODAK COMPANY HAS BEEN SYNONY-MOUS WITH QUALITY PHOTOGRAPHY. SINCE 1880 WHEN GEORGE EASTMAN DEVELOPED THE DRY PHOTOGRAPHIC PLATE AND 1888 WHEN HE INTRO-DUCED THE WORLD'S FIRST KODAK CAMERA, THE GLOBAL COMPANY THAT

still bears his name has been a "World Leader in Images."

A DIVERSE PRODUCT LINE

Today, Kodak's catch phrase is "Imaging by all means," signifying that the company's products create images in a variety of different ways. Kodak manufactures photo-copy machines, printing and publishing equipment, microfiche information storage equipment, printers, radiology products, blood analyzers, other medical equipment, and, of course, film and cameras for both consumers and professionals. Based in Rochester, New York where George Eastman himself lived and worked, the company today employs 133,000 people worldwide.

Five hundred of the company's employees work at the Kodak marketing and distribution center in suburban Oak Brook, Illinois.

Opened in 1965, the Oak Brook facility is one of five area distribution centers the company operates in the United States.

The 225,000-square-foot facility supplies film, cameras, chemicals, and photographic paper to retailers and photofinishers in 12 Midwestern states, accounting for 20 percent of Kodak's domestic distribution, says William D. Zollars, vice president and area general manager. In a typical year the facility ships 2.6 million cartons weighing 75 million pounds in aggregate. Kodak also maintains marketing facilities in Oak Brook and in downtown Chicago.

SUPPORTING THE CHICAGO COMMUNITY

"Kodak takes great pride in its support of education programs throughout the country," says Zollars, "and Chicago-area employ-

ees actively support company-sponsored programs in this community." Many employees give volunteer time at Elliott Donnelly Youth Center, which serves Stateway Gardens and the Robert Taylor Homes, two of the city's public housing projects. Kodak volunteers work with children at the center, teaching classes and serving as role models, and with the center's professional staff, giving advice and counsel.

Kodak employees are also involved in a partnership with students at John Marshall High School, a public school on Chicago's West Side. Through the Youth Motivation Program sponsored by the Chicago-land Chamber of Commerce, at-risk students in schools throughout the city are matched with professional role models. Thirty-six Chicago-area Kodak employees are currently

From film to cameras to the new Photo CD, Kodak manufactures a range of products geared toward diverse consumer needs.

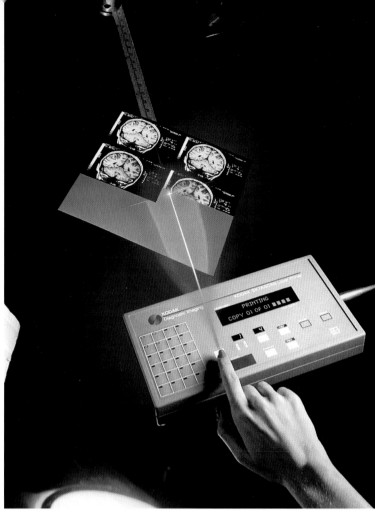

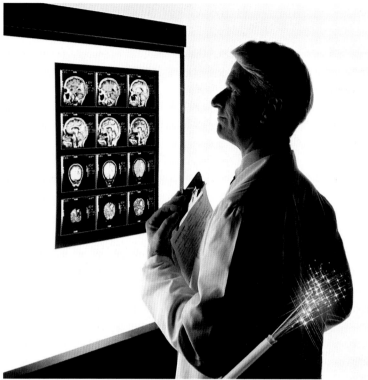

Kodak offers "Imaging by all means," including state-of-the-art radiology products and other diagnostic equipment.

working with John Marshall students, spending time with them and talking to them about making their lives successful.

Other national programs include the Kodak Scholars Program, which awards more than $2.5 million a year to students who have achieved educational excellence and have shown a commitment to studying the sciences. The annual Youth Career and Education Conference recognizes accomplishments in science, while the Inner-Scholarship Mathematics League salutes high school math achievers.

Kodak has promoted the importance of education to 450,000 fourth grade students nationwide through the Kodak/Alan Page Challenge essay contest. Through this annual writing competition, the company and Alan Page, a former Chicago Bears defensive lineman and an NFL Hall-of-Famer, hope to convey an important message: Sports can be a viable career for only a small group of individuals, so students should work at excelling in school as the best preparation for the future.

The understanding that individuals, organizations, and businesses thrive only when the communities they serve prosper is the philosophy

behind the company's commitment to Chicago's diverse communities. Support of diversity initiatives is a Kodak tradition, dating back to the turn of the century, that guides the company in choosing the community efforts and national programs it will support. In 1902, the company, with George Eastman at the helm, made one of its first educational contributions to the Tuskegee Normal and Industrial Institute, now known as Tuskegee University. On a national level, Kodak's contributions have expanded to include a 10-year, million-dollar commitment to the United Negro College Fund. Locally, the company strives to support organizations that serve as advocates for large communities throughout the Chicago area, such as the Latino Institute and Chicago Urban League.

ENVIRONMENTAL RESPONSIBILITY

Kodak is also justly proud of its record on environmental issues and the many steps the company has taken to do its part. Every year, for example, Kodak recycles more than 4 billion pounds of material in its offices and manufacturing facilities in the United States. The company

is committed to a minimum of 25 percent post-consumer recycled plastic in all of its plastic containers, and its steel containers are made of at least 25 percent recycled steel. Kodak Funsavers cameras are "single use" cameras which are recycled up to six times. The company pays photofinishers to send camera bodies back to Kodak to be reused. In 1992, Kodak recycled its 3 millionth camera.

Kodak is also making a company-wide change from new paperboard to recycled paperboard for its consumer film packaging, saving about 6,000 tons of virgin fiber a year. Another of the company's environmental goals is to completely phase out by 1995 emissions of chlorofluorocarbons, which are believed to contribute to the depletion of the ozone layer.

A commitment to providing quality products, improving educational standards nationwide, recognizing and supporting diversity, and actively demonstrating concern for the environment are the hallmarks of the Eastman Kodak Company, an American institution in business for more than a century.

EDELMAN PUBLIC RELATIONS WORLDWIDE

EDELMAN PUBLIC RELATIONS WORLDWIDE IS A PIONEER IN THE FIELD OF PUBLIC RELATIONS. THE FIRM WAS ESTABLISHED BY DANIEL J. EDELMAN IN CHICAGO IN 1952 WITH THREE EMPLOYEES AND THREE ACCOUNTS. THE FIRM IS NOW THE LARGEST INDEPENDENT AND THE FIFTH LARGEST PUBLIC

relations firm in the world. With 26 offices and 650 employees, Edelman Worldwide directs public relations programs for some of the world's leading companies and organizations.

"Throughout the past 40 years, Edelman Worldwide has played an important role in the development and success of many products and companies," says Dan Edelman, chairman and chief executive officer. Among the clients of the firm's Chicago office are Kraft General Foods, H.J. Heinz Company, Con-Agra, G.D. Searle, The NutraSweet Company, Monsanto Company, Inc., Abbott Laboratories, Safety-Kleen, Motorola, Brown-Forman, General Mills, J I Case, and Information Resources, Inc.

A RECOGNIZED LEADER

A PR pioneer, Dan Edelman is considered the "father of the media tour," which is today a marketing and public relations standard. He initiated the concept when he toured the "Toni Twins" around the country as spokespersons for Toni Home Permanents in the late 1940s and '50s.

Recognized as the preeminent leader in consumer marketing public relations, the firm has also become known for expertise in such specialty areas as health care, public affairs, technology, sports and event marketing, corporate and financial relations, and the environment. Edelman's outstanding efforts for its clients have won 24 Silver Anvils, the highest award in public relations, from the Public Relations

Society of America. *The New York Times* has called Edelman Worldwide one of the "most influential" public relations firms in the world.

A STRONG FUTURE

Dan Edelman remains an active and strong leader of the firm he founded. His drive, creativity, and commitment continue to spur the firm's growth and success. A second generation of management is now firmly in place led by son Richard W. Edelman, president and chief operating officer, who spearheaded the growth of the firm's New York headquarters. With solid experience and leadership throughout the world, Edelman Public Relations Worldwide is well positioned to remain an innovative force and to shape the industry into the future.

Established by Daniel J. Edelman (left) in Chicago in 1952, Edelman Public Relations Worldwide is today the largest independent and the fifth largest public relations firm in the world.

A second generation of management is now firmly in place led by the founder's son, Richard W. Edelman (right), president and chief operating officer.

1968

WASTE MANAGEMENT, INC.

1973

CHICAGO BOARD OPTIONS
EXCHANGE

1983

ARIEL CAPITAL
MANAGEMENT, INC.

1969

COMDISCO, INC.

1973

HONGKONG AND SHANGHAI
BANKING CORP. LTD.

1985

CELLULAR ONE

1970

AZTECA FOODS, INC.

1978

NEW DAY CENTER OF
HINSDALE HOSPITAL

1985

FRUIT OF THE LOOM, INC.

1970

IVI TRAVEL

1979

BROOK FURNITURE RENTAL

1985

HABITAT CORPORATE SUITES
NETWORK AND HABITAT
RELOCATION GROUP

1972

FMC CORPORATION

1980

CCC INFORMATION
SERVICES INC.

1985

PRESIDENTIAL TOWERS

1972

HUMANA HEALTH CARE
PLANS

1981

MIDCON CORP.

1987

HOTEL NIKKO CHICAGO

1982

THE PRIME GROUP, INC.

1989

OAKWOOD CORPORATE
APARTMENTS

THE WIDE ANGLE LENS RECREATES
Chicago as an island state encircled
by a freshwater ocean. The island's
castle, appropriately, is the tallest
building the world, the Sears Tower,
jabbing the sky and looming over its
domain.

▲ MARK SEGAL / PANORAMIC IMAGES, CHICAGO

COMDISCO, INC.

COMDISCO, INC., THE WORLD'S LARGEST INDEPENDENT LESSOR AND REMARKETER OF HIGH-TECHNOLOGY EQUIPMENT, HELPS BUSINESSES MANAGE THEIR COMPUTER AND OTHER EQUIPMENT IN MYRIAD WAYS. ♦ HEADQUARTERED IN NORTHWEST SUBURBAN ROSEMONT, THE COMPANY

was founded in 1969 by Kenneth Pontikes, a former IBM salesman who foresaw the rapid growth in computer leasing and seized the opportunity. The son of Greek immigrants, Pontikes started his venture with an investment of just $5,000. After more than two decades in business, the company has grown to over $2.2 billion in annual revenue and $5 billion in total assets.

"Keeping pace with the constant changes in high technology can be a daunting task and a drain on a business' resources," says Neal Lulofs, marketing communications manager for Comdisco. "As a result, 80 percent of Fortune 500 firms lease at least some of their high-tech equipment. Because technology changes so fast, leasing gives a business the needed flexibility to change."

Comdisco was founded in 1969 by Kenneth Pontikes (right), a former IBM salesman who foresaw the rapid growth in computer leasing and seized the opportunity.

Comdisco Medical Equipment Group provides hospitals and other medical facilities with an alternative to the outright purchase of costly, up-to-date equipment.

A WORLDWIDE CLIENT BASE

Comdisco serves a majority of the Fortune 1000 companies, and has equipment installed in more than 60,000 locations around the world. The company leases virtually every kind of high-technology equipment imaginable, including mainframes, PCs and workstations, tape and disk drives, terminals, peripherals, satel-

lite earth stations, CAD/CAMs, point-of-sale equipment, PBXs, modems, automated teller machines and other banking equipment, and much more. The firm carries products manufactured by such industry leaders as IBM, Apple, and Hewlett-Packard.

In addition, Comdisco leases high-tech medical equipment through Comdisco Medical Equipment Group, a subsidiary that provides hospitals and other medical facilities with an alternative to the outright purchase of costly, up-to-date equipment. In the ever-changing field of modern medical technology, leasing allows medical facilities to manage cash flow and avoid technological obsolescence. Despite these advantages, leasing is a fairly new practice for many hospitals, and relatively few have taken advantage of the opportunities. "Whereas about 80 percent of the Fortune 500 currently lease high-tech equipment, only 20 percent of hospitals do," Lulofs says. "But that figure has doubled in the last five years and is expected to double again by 1996."

Comdisco's medical equipment group specializes in therapeutic and diagnostic imaging equipment, in-

cluding X-ray machines, CT scanners, ultrasound equipment, nuclear medicine cameras, and magnetic resonance imaging (MRI) scanners. The firm also leases selected high-tech treatment devices for heart disease and cancer, as well as equipment such as lithotriptors used to treat kidney stones.

COMPREHENSIVE SERVICES

According to Lulofs, leasing represents only a portion of Comdisco's long list of services. "We're consultants, really," he explains. "We have the capability to examine a company's overall equipment needs and advise them on the best, most economical route to take."

In addition to guidance in determining the kinds of equipment a client needs, Comdisco lets a company know what is available now, what is likely to become available in the near future, and whether leasing or buying is more advantageous to them. "It's important for our customers to know what their options are if they wait six months to lease or purchase equipment," Lulofs says.

Comdisco assists its clients further by developing unique strategies for meeting all their high-tech needs, from computers and PCs to telecommunications equipment and medical technology. Hospitals, for example, usually have a basic idea of what kinds of equipment they are interested in having. "We work with them to determine how and when they should acquire it," Lulofs says.

Another challenge Comdisco meets for its clients is understanding ever-changing market conditions. Evaluating market fluctuations and the increasing number of alternatives offered by multiple vendors is just one of the ways Comdisco helps users of high-tech equipment manage their assets. Careful comparisons of new, used, lease, and

purchase alternatives allow the company to determine the best strategy for each customer.

According to Lulofs, users constantly upgrade and replace their high-tech equipment. To address this high turnover rate, Comdisco operates a technical facility in nearby Schaumburg, Illinois that specializes in refurbishing equipment. With access to thousands of installations, Comdisco can offer its customers a ready market and a reliable source for used equipment.

Comdisco is also the world's largest provider of disaster recovery and business continuity services, with a domestic and international subscriber base of more than 2,700 businesses and organizations. The company maintains nine major computer and business recovery facilities in the United States and Canada, which are devoted to equipment replacement and data recovery in case of fire, earthquake, or other disasters. Comdisco also has an interest in three major recovery facilities in Europe and three more in the Pacific Rim.

"Our business continuity services have evolved from an initial focus on the data center in the 1980s to protecting the proliferation of assets our customers now have throughout their organizations," Lulofs says. Quarterly drills help keep Comdisco and its customers ready for the worst. If an emergency does arise, the customer declares an alert and Comdisco responds immediately. With the Chicago flood and Hurricane Andrew, a total of 46 customers needed support in 1992, making it Comdisco's busiest year yet.

Another innovative Comdisco product is CLASS, an integrated asset management software tool. CLASS allows clients to order high-tech equipment, both purchased and leased, directly from any vendor they choose. The software also automatically tracks thousands of equipment assets as they move and change, and it analyzes important financial data on all equipment the customer has on the system.

As more companies downsize and rely on PCs and servers rather than mainframes, it becomes increasingly difficult to manage all the pieces. "Our customers often have no idea who's got what, where they're located, what features are included on the equipment, what's leased, and what they own," says Lulofs. "CLASS is the first system of its kind that allows the client to access

all of this information on-line."

With nearly 25 years of experience in high-tech equipment sales, leasing, and service, Comdisco looks forward to meeting the challenges of the future. The company's size, expertise, and history of innovation will help it maintain a leadership role in the complex and growing field of high-technology planning and management.

AZTECA FOODS, INC.

AZTECA FOODS, INC. IS A FAMILY-OWNED AND -OPERATED BUSINESS STARTED ON CHICAGO'S SOUTHWEST SIDE MORE THAN 20 YEARS AGO. TODAY IT IS ONE OF THE LEADING PRODUCERS OF TORTILLA PRODUCTS IN THE UNITED STATES. ◆ WITH AN INITIAL INVESTMENT OF $80,000,

Azteca's product line (right) has grown to include tortilla chips, flour and corn tortillas, salsa, and a unique salad shell.

the Azteca Corn Products Corporation was established in 1970 as a positive role model for the Hispanic community. The founding group of 10 Mexican-American businessmen were all members of the Azteca Lions Club in Chicago's Pilsen community. "We would meet and talk about community activities," remembers Arthur R. Velasquez, the company's president, owner, and one of the original investors. Two decades later, Azteca's annual sales have reached $30 million, and Velasquez projects that figure will double in the next five years.

In 1984, The Pillsbury Company acquired Azteca as a wholly owned subsidiary. Velasquez and his wife, Joanne, bought back the company in 1989, and it remains a family-run business and a successful role model for the Hispanic community today.

AN INDUSTRY PIONEER

Over the years, Azteca has cultivated an industry-wide reputation as a pioneer. Until the company entered the tortilla business in 1970, tortillas were sold either hot from a bakery or frozen, and targeted almost exclusively at Mexican-American consumers. In a bold marketing move, Azteca went after the general consumer with a refrigerated tortilla product designed to stay fresh longer than its bakery-type predecessors. Although the company does not use a lot of preservatives in its products, Azteca tortillas remain fresh for up to 90 days thanks to modern refrigeration techniques and high-quality packaging designed to keep out air and moisture.

Initially, Azteca concentrated its manufacturing and marketing efforts on corn tortillas. The product line has since grown to include tortilla chips, flour tortillas, and a unique

salad shell available in a variety of sizes. The company adopted its current name, Azteca Foods, Inc., in 1989 to reflect this increased diversity. Its products are currently sold in 45 markets in 35 states east of Oklahoma.

Azteca has been recognized as an industry leader in nutritional labeling and was the first tortilla company to use freshness date codes on its packaging. As part of its long-time commitment to quality, all Azteca tortillas have been produced with kosher ingredients since the early 1970s.

The company is also known for its high-tech manufacturing capabilities, which incorporate the most up-to-date equipment available in a highly automated 61,000-square-foot plant. For example, a single standard press line can make 1,040 dozen flour tortillas per hour, while the company's twin die-cut line can turn out 7,000 dozen per hour. Each day, Azteca's 125 employees produce an impressive 2 million tortillas in the Chicago manufacturing facility.

THE VERSATILE TORTILLA

Velasquez believes Azteca was founded at just the right time. Since

the early 1970s, the tortilla industry has flourished and is currently growing at a rate of about 12 percent a year. Likewise, the popularity of tortillas has spread beyond young consumers to include virtually every age group. Flour tortillas now account for 70 percent of Azteca's sales, and consumers are using this versatile product not only for traditional Mexican dishes, but with other ethnic foods, appetizers, and desserts.

As a result, the company has tailored its marketing efforts to help educate consumers about the versatility of tortillas. All of Azteca's packaging and marketing materials show product applications, and the company urges consumers to write for a free 12-page recipe book. In 1991 alone, Azteca received more than 15,000 requests for the booklet, which includes traditional Mexican dishes such as chicken flautas, chimichangas, and quesadillas, as well as non-traditional fare such as chicken broccoli salad, shrimp and salsa tortilla rounds, and cheesy tuna tacos.

Azteca is currently developing new recipes that use tortillas in an even broader range of foods. Traditionally Italian, Polish, and Chinese

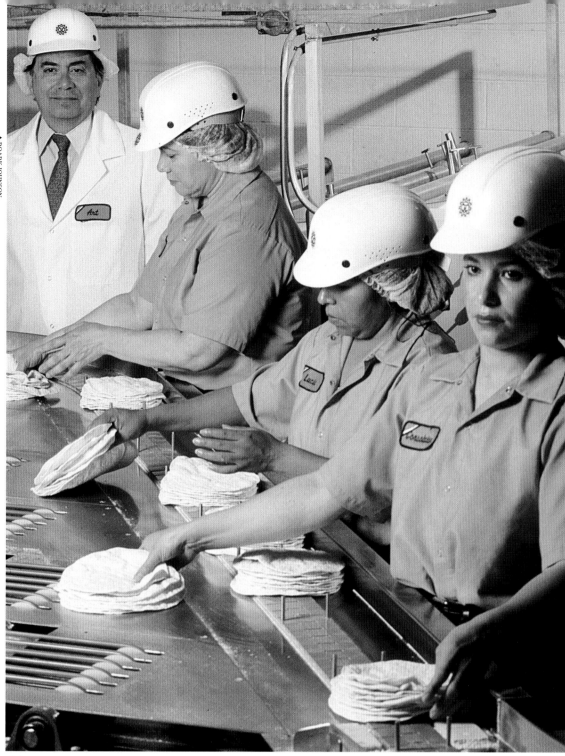

Each day, Azteca's 125 employees produce an impressive 2 million tortillas in the Chicago manufacturing facility.

dishes are being adapted to include Azteca products.

A FAMILY BUSINESS WITH A COMMUNITY FOCUS

Azteca is proud of its strong family orientation and its longtime commitment to the community. Today, Joanne Velasquez, who played an important role in the start-up of administration at Azteca, is the company's vice president. The Velasquez's daughter, two sons, two sons-in-law, and Joanne's brother are also in high-profile company positions.

As an extension of this family atmosphere, the company strives to give back to the community in both time and resources. For example, Arthur and Joanne Velasquez are active in business, civic, and service groups on the local, regional, and national levels. In 1974, Arthur Velasquez became the first Hispanic in Illinois chosen to hold a statewide office when he was named a trustee of the University of Illinois.

Currently, he is a director of Peoples Energy Corp., the Chicago Metropolitan and National Boards of Junior Achievement, and the Economic Club of Chicago. Velasquez also serves on the Board of Trustees of the Museum of Science and Industry, the University of Notre Dame, Saint Xavier University, and many other community organizations in Chicago and across the country.

For more than two decades, Azteca has been a vital part of the Chicago community—as a business, as a role model for Hispanics, and as a producer of high-quality products. An innovative company in a rapidly growing industry, Azteca Foods has enjoyed tremendous success and expects more of the same in the future.

HABITAT CORPORATE SUITES NETWORK AND HABITAT RELOCATION GROUP

MOVING TO A NEW CITY IS NEAR THE TOP OF THE LIST OF STRESS-LOADING LIFE CHANGES, AND EVEN RELOCATING TEMPORARILY TO ANOTHER CITY CAN BE A DAUNTING TASK. BUT WHEN THE MOVE, WHETHER PERMANENT OR TEMPORARY, IS TO A CITY OF MORE THAN

3 million people, albeit the great one of Chicago, the effort can become overwhelming.

The Habitat Company, founded in 1971 and a leader in Chicago real estate, saw that it could fulfill a need for the thousands of individuals who make such moves to the city every year. As a result, it established the Habitat Corporate Suites Network in 1985, and within that division, the Habitat Relocation Group in 1992. The eight-year-old division, which today employs 50 people, not only

The Habitat Corporate Suites Network includes three properties located in the heart of downtown Chicago. From left: Presidential Towers, River Plaza, and Columbus Place.

simplifies the process of relocating for a permanent or temporary stay in Chicago, but strives to make it a pleasant experience.

THE FINEST IN LOCATIONS, AMENITIES, AND RATES

The Habitat Corporate Suites Network is a group of 475 luxury apartments managed by The Habitat Company and located in three buildings in the heart of downtown Chicago. These fully furnished studio, convertible, and one- and two-bedroom units are available to extended-stay business travelers who will be making a temporary visit of at least 30 days to the city. The suites also are leased to corporations for rollover lodging, in which

the client rotates suite guests according to its needs.

The three buildings housing the network's suites are Presidential Towers at 555 W. Madison Street, River Plaza at 405 N. Wabash Avenue, and Columbus Plaza at 233 E. Wacker Drive. Guests at Presidential Towers have access to a concierge, four restaurants, a full-service health club, conference rooms, and a retail center in the main lobby. River Plaza, located alongside the Chicago River, offers two restaurants and a

health club with an indoor pool. In addition to stunning views of the city, residents can enjoy the restaurants, entertainment, and nightlife of Chicago's River North area. A lure for clients considering Columbus Plaza is its prime location next to Illinois Center, an office complex with more than 80 restaurants and shops.

While each of the three buildings is unique, most suites throughout the network feature standard amenities, such as fully equipped kitchens, direct-dial telephones with voice-mail messaging, cable television, parking facilities, and maid service. Even with the many conveniences and extras, the suites are competitively priced. A 30-day stay in a Habitat corporate suite is considera-

bly less expensive than a stay of the same duration in a good downtown hotel.

HABITAT RELOCATION GROUP ENSURES A SMOOTH MOVE

When The Habitat Company created the Habitat Relocation Group in 1992 for the purpose of finding permanent homes for individuals moving to the Chicago area, the company was essentially putting into practice the thorough knowl-

edge of the city that it had acquired over more than two decades as a developer and manager of large-scale residential and commercial projects. The Habitat Relocation Group offers an advanced, comprehensive relocation service with capabilities that go far beyond those offered by other similar firms. The group's full range of services makes it the most logical and cost-efficient resource for corporations, whether they are relocating one executive, a department, or an entire company.

The Habitat Relocation Group guides clients through a four-step process that makes moving to Chicago as easy and painless as possible. First, the client is assigned a relocation consultant who ascertains and evaluates the housing requirements of that client and his or her family. Habitat's consultants are careful to consider every aspect of a family's new home needs, from proximity to the workplace to location of area schools.

In the next step—finding the ideal home—the consultant taps the vast resources that the relocation group has at its disposal. For those who enjoy apartment living, The Habitat Company manages more than 10,000 luxury apartments in choice city locations. The group also has access to thousands of additional apartments located throughout the metropolitan area. For clients who would rather buy a single-family home in the city, The Habitat Company's brokerage division has thou-

sands of listings, from vintage brownstones to high-rise condominiums and spacious lofts. And for those who find the quiet suburban life more appealing, the relocation group can make referrals to The Habitat Company's extensive network of suburban brokers.

The third step, which is optional, involves making arrangements for interim living. The relocation group offers temporary housing through the Habitat Corporate Suites Network to individuals and families who must move to Chicago before they have found a permanent place of residence.

The fourth step is providing the additional assistance that can make a tremendous difference to those who are moving and adjusting to new

homes and lives. Among many other services, Habitat Relocation Group can provide confidential mortgage prequalification, make referrals to reliable moving companies, and even direct spouses to career assistance programs.

Whether to arrange for an extended visit or to help a family put down permanent roots, the Habitat

Corporate Suites Network and Habitat Relocation Group are the best introduction to Chicago for business travelers or transferees. Together, they provide the most complete and professional service in the industry, supported by substantial corporate resources, years of experience, and unparalleled knowledge of the city.

Both elegant and comfortable, Habitat suites are supported by an experienced staff that makes extended-stay business travel easy and convenient (left and below left).

Guests of the Habitat Corporate Suites Network can enjoy many of downtown Chicago's attractions, such as Adler Planetarium (top) and Second City (bottom).

PRESIDENTIAL TOWERS

O N A SITE THAT STOOD BARREN FOR MORE THAN 20 YEARS IN CHICAGO'S WEST LOOP AREA RISES PRESIDENTIAL TOWERS, A COMPLEX OF FOUR 49-STORY TOWERS THAT OPENED IN 1985 AND IS HOME TODAY TO MORE THAN 3,000 PEOPLE AND 30 BUSINESSES. ♦ VIRTUALLY A SELF-

contained residential community, the complex was built and is managed by The Habitat Company, a leader in the development and management of large residential projects in Chicago since 1971.

▼ DAVID CLIFTON

With more than 2,300 studio, convertible, and one- and two-bedroom apartments, Presidential Towers offers the finest in urban living, including such amenities as a beautifully landscaped sun deck (top right).

URBAN LIVING AT ITS FINEST

An ideal location for city dwellers, Presidential Towers provides all the comforts and conveniences for day-to-day living. The complex has more than 2,300 studio, convertible, and one- and two-bedroom apartments. Spacious and well appointed, all apartments include Eurostyle kitchens, mini blinds, dishwashers, and heat and air conditioning.

A number of services and amenities are available to tenants. Among

them are 24-hour doorman, cable television, voice-mail messaging, and regular maid service. The popular concierge service offers residents help with obtaining tickets for entertainment and sporting events, providing travel information, arranging limousine service, making recommendations and reservations for dining, and even locating baby-sitters. In addition, a lobby assistant is available to help tenants with luggage, parcels, and special requests within the Presidential Towers complex.

What adds even greater value to living at Presidential Towers are the many amenities, services, and conveniences that residents enjoy only steps from their doors. The Lyric Opera, the Art Institute, great shopping, and the Loop, Chicago's central business district, are all within

walking distance. Public transportation is available just around the corner. Anchoring the complex is an atrium shopping mall that features stores and services that residents rely on for daily needs. Within Presidential Towers are four restaurants, a complete gourmet grocery store, a dry cleaners, a hair salon, a video rental store, a florist, a car rental agency, a medical clinic, and much more.

Another bonus at Presidential Towers is a full-service health club located within the complex. Membership in the health club gives an individual access to a full line of exercise equipment (including stair-climbers, treadmills, computerized exercise bikes, airdynes, Universal weight equipment, and free-weight equipment), a variety of fitness classes and personalized fitness pro-

grams, and a sky-lit 75-foot-long swimming pool. The spacious men's and women's locker rooms are equipped with showers, steam rooms, and saunas. A beautifully landscaped sun deck is available for lounging and summer fun, including a game of basketball on the adjacent court. Likewise, seven laps around the deck's professional quality running track provides an invigorating one-mile run—without even leaving the complex.

Also provided for residents' convenience is a large, five-level parking garage. For residents' protection, "call for assistance" buttons are strategically located throughout the garage, which is monitored by security cameras. Parking for guests is also available at hourly rates. Adjacent to the parking garage are secure storage areas where residents can

lock up their bicycles.

All of these conveniences mean that after a hard day at work in the city, tenants at Presidential Towers can pick up their dry cleaning and run other errands, take in an aerobics class, and meet friends for dinner, all without leaving the building.

AN ECONOMIC PLUS FOR THE CITY

In addition to providing luxury housing just west of downtown Chicago, Presidential Towers has made important contributions to the city. The complex has been an anchor for the redevelopment of the once-blighted west Loop area. Nearly a dozen new or rehabilitated properties, including major developments such as the Northwestern Atrium Center, Riverside Plaza buildings, and the Trans Union Building, have been com-

pleted since Presidential Towers was opened in 1985.

A delightful place to live, work, or shop, Presidential Towers is an attractive and convenient haven for the urban professional. Through the Presidential Towers development, The Habitat Company has not only created new housing for city workers, but also reinvigorated an important neighborhood in downtown Chicago.

WASTE MANAGEMENT, INC.

WASTE MANAGEMENT, INC. WAS ESTABLISHED IN CHICAGO A LITTLE MORE THAN TWO DECADES AGO BY DEAN L. BUNTROCK, A MAN WITH A VISION. IN 25 SHORT YEARS, BUNTROCK HAS TURNED A SMALL FAMILY-RUN SCAVENGER AGENCY INTO A NEARLY $10 BILLION

publicly owned global environmental services enterprise.

In 1968 Buntrock, then the head of Ace Scavenger Service, spearheaded a merger of that company's resources with several other midsize waste collection agencies in Chicago, Wisconsin, and Florida to create what is now the largest and most comprehensive environmental services company in the world. At

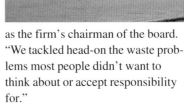

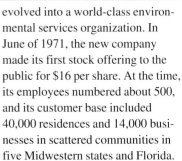

Waste Management is headquartered in west suburban Oak Brook in DuPage County (above). With a massive fleet of 13,000 vehicles, the company still performs its original task of collecting solid waste for nearly 12 million residences and more than 1 million commercial, industrial, and institutional customers worldwide (above right).

the time, interest in environmental issues was evolving rapidly and gaining impetus; solid waste was known as the "third pollution." The Environmental Protection Agency began full operations in 1970, and the first Earth Day celebration was held in April of that year. Simultaneously, the American public was becoming more aware and concerned about the condition of the world's resources.

It was in this conducive atmosphere that Waste Management began to grow and prosper. A major regulatory milestone came in 1976 with passage of the Resource Conservation and Recovery Act (RCRA), the most important piece of waste management regulation ever enacted by Congress. RCRA defined chemical and hazardous wastes and regulated their transportation, treatment, and disposal.

Foreseeing the impact that this and other emerging environmental legislation would have upon the waste management industry and the nation as a whole, Buntrock capitalized on the opportunities. "On the heels of RCRA's passage, Waste Management helped to fundamentally change the way Americans manage and dispose of waste," recalls Buntrock, who currently serves as the firm's chairman of the board. "We tackled head-on the waste problems most people didn't want to think about or accept responsibility for."

During its two-decade history, the company has grown from a regional waste collection firm to a technological enterprise whose services respond to virtually every environmental need of the entire planet. Waste Management collects and disposes of solid waste, recycles cans and bottles, cleans up hazardous waste, provides low-level nuclear waste disposal, turns trash into electricity, and offers water and wastewater treatment as well as clean air technologies. In recent years, the firm has also moved into the areas of environmental engineering, building demolition, building design and construction, and environmental consulting and infrastructure design serv-

ices. Says Buntrock, "In just over two decades, we have made the transition from basic waste services to a comprehensive environmental program."

MORE THAN TWO DECADES OF GROWTH

Headquartered in west suburban Oak Brook in DuPage County, Waste Management has rapidly evolved into a world-class environmental services organization. In June of 1971, the new company made its first stock offering to the public for $16 per share. At the time, its employees numbered about 500, and its customer base included 40,000 residences and 14,000 businesses in scattered communities in five Midwestern states and Florida.

Since then, the company has experienced phenomenal growth. Today, Waste Management employs nearly 70,000 people, including 3,000 in Illinois. Its worldwide service area includes operations throughout the United States and Canada, in Mexico, and in 22 countries overseas. Likewise, an investor who purchased 100 shares for $1,600 in the initial public offering would now own 7,200 shares with a value of approximately $250,000. The firm first reported $1 billion in annual

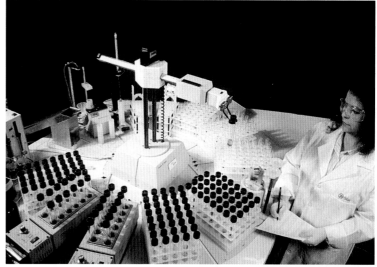

revenues in 1983, 12 years after its organization as a public company. Just one decade later, Waste Management expects to reach the $10 billion mark in 1993.

The company is now organized into five principal operating areas: Waste Management of North America, Inc.; Chemical Waste Management, Inc.; Waste Management International, Inc.; Wheelabrator Technologies, Inc.; and Rust International, Inc. Through these subsidiaries, employees can be found collecting waste in London, cleaning streets in Milan, and constructing a comprehensive chemical waste processing and disposal facility in Hong Kong. When Waste Management first entered the international marketplace with a $240 million contract to serve Riyadh, Saudi Arabia, it doubled in size. Today, through its international division, the company

continues to offer the same comprehensive services it provides in the United States.

Over the years, Waste Management has enhanced its growth and diversification through careful acquisitions, each intended to complement or expand the firm's existing resources. One of the company's primary objectives today is to have all its subsidiaries and acquisitions function efficiently as one comprehensive whole.

"We have an unparalleled opportunity to marshall our diverse resources into a single, seamless, comprehensive package of services to meet all of the environmental and infrastructure needs of our customers," Buntrock says. "Today, we are integrating and coordinating these individual pieces to support the environmental services our customers will demand of us globally, both

now and into the future. In providing these services, we will seize opportunities to build on all of our past achievements."

A LEADER AND PIONEER

Waste Management has been an industry leader and pioneer in virtually all phases of environmental services. It is the nation's largest solid and chemical waste handler, among the largest private water and wastewater treatment companies, one of the largest managers of medical waste, and the most experienced provider of environmental cleanup services in the United States.

With a massive fleet of 13,000 vehicles, the company still performs its original task of collecting solid waste for nearly 12 million residences and more than 1 million commercial, industrial, and institu-

Waste Management's areas of expertise include water and wastewater treatment (above left), environmental research (top), and groundwater monitoring and analysis (bottom).

The company does cleanup work at Superfund sites and other contaminated properties (top) and generates valuable energy by recovering methane gas from decomposing waste in landfills (bottom).

forts—known as Recycle America® and Recycle Canada®—divert for reuse approximately 2 million tons of paper, plastics, glass, and aluminum from residential and commercial customers. The company also generates valuable energy by recovering methane gas from decomposing waste. In fact, its landfill energy programs save 1.5 million barrels of oil every year by harnessing natural gas from decomposing garbage in landfills.

One of its divisions, Wheelabrator Technologies, is the nation's leading developer of trash-to-energy facilities. Through a sophisticated combustion technique, the division processes non-hazardous municipal solid waste to produce clean electricity for industry and local utilities. The electricity generated is used by more than 400 communities and 7.7 million residential customers each year. The combined energy output from the company's 14 generating facilities ranks it among the 10 largest independent power producers in the nation.

Waste Management is also the nation's largest provider of comprehensive hazardous waste services and the only company with a national network of treatment and disposal sites to support this expertise. For example, the firm does cleanup work at Superfund sites and other contaminated properties, disposes of low-level radioactive waste, and provides maintenance services at nuclear power facilities.

In fact, it is the only private provider of low-level radioactive waste disposal east of the Mississippi River.

Across the United States, Waste Management has completed more than 10,000 cleanup projects at contaminated sites, employing the industry's most sophisticated technologies to tackle the complexities of hazardous waste contamination. The company's worldwide mobilization capabilities in the area of hazardous waste were put to the test in early 1991 at the climax of the Persian Gulf War. In early March, just three days after the conflict was over, 100 Waste Management employees traveled to Kuwait to help with environmental cleanup and restoration.

The company also boasts significant water and wastewater treatment capabilities. As a recognized leader in clean water treatment, Waste Management companies have pioneered many of the technologies that are now industry standards. One of its subsidiaries was the first in the nation to offer full wastewater treatment contract operations for municipalities and industries and is among the leading operators of municipal wastewater treatment facilities.

Another area of expertise at Waste Management is environmental engineering. Its capabilities in this field have made the firm a world-class engineering organization and a leader in construction, infrastructure design, and environmental consulting services. Incorporating the latest environmental

tional customers worldwide. The company also provides medical waste disposal.

Waste Management operates the largest and most comprehensive recycling collection program in the world. Annually, its recycling ef-

technology, Waste Management engineers design and construct manufacturing complexes, power plants, major roadways, and transportation systems. The company also acts as a major contractor to various environmental, aerospace, defense, pulp and paper, and industrial clients.

In the Chicago area, the company engineered the rehabilitation of North Lake Shore Drive, and its team of divers plugged the underground tunnel leak during the downtown flood in April 1992. Currently, Waste Management is managing a major expansion of Chicago's McCormick Place, the largest convention center in North America.

Waste Management also offers services in all phases of industrial chimney design, construction, and maintenance. The company has worked on more than 10,000 such projects, including the five tallest chimneys in the world. In addition, Waste Management provides industrial customers with scaffolding services, industrial cleaning and maintenance, dismantling and demolition, and specialty nuclear and marine services. The company is also positioned to play a major role in environmental cleanup projects at U.S. Department of the Army weapons plants, military bases, and other federal government installations.

Waste Management's Environmental Monitoring Laboratories, located in Geneva, Illinois, is the nation's largest and most sophisticated organization dedicated to the

analysis of groundwater. The one-of-a-kind, $30 million facility provides analysis of groundwater sampled regularly from each of the company's 7,500 monitoring points located at disposal facilities throughout the country.

Other divisions of the company specialize in marine construction and diving, dredging, and specialty nuclear and environmental services. The company also provides complete solutions for today's sludge management challenges in hundreds of programs nationwide.

By offering such a complete line of services, Waste Management is moving closer to its ultimate goal of becoming a single-source environmental services company capable of meeting the diverse and changing needs of major corporations, governments, and individuals virtually anywhere across the globe.

A GOOD CORPORATE CITIZEN

While providing the finest in comprehensive environmental services, Waste Management strives to be a good corporate citizen in Chicago and in the other communities where it operates. Over the years, the company has received numerous awards for its work with environmental advocacy groups on policy issues of common interest. Waste Management also operates a two-to-one matching program for employee donations to environmental groups and provides a cash match for em-

ployees and their families who volunteer their time for nonprofit organizations.

In addition, the company's commitment to protecting the world's environmental resources has resulted in the development or sponsorship of more than 1,000 acres of public sanctuary wetlands and habitat near its facilities.

"Waste Management's story is just getting started," says Buntrock. "I am confident that the chapters ahead will be even more exciting and remarkable. No other company in the world has the resources we do to serve the global environmental needs of today and tomorrow."

The company's Wheelabrator Technologies division is the nation's leading developer of trash-to-energy facilities, which utilize non-hazardous municipal solid waste to produce clean electricity (top left).

Waste Management carefully constructs new landfills (top right) and helps convert closed landfills into useful property (above).

FMC CORPORATION

MORE THAN 100 YEARS AGO, THE COMPANY THAT IS NOW FMC CORPORATION WENT INTO BUSINESS WITH A SINGLE PRODUCT LINE: AGRICULTURAL SPRAYERS. OVER THE YEARS THAT FOLLOWED, FMC NURTURED ITS AGRICULTURAL AND FOOD PROCESSING MACHINERY

Chairman Bob Burt (right) meets with FMC's new MBA recruits at company headquarters.

business and expanded into new areas.

Today, the Chicago-based company is one of the world's leading producers and suppliers of chemicals and machinery for industry, government, and agriculture. Once known as the Food Machinery Corporation, the firm has diversified so extensively that FMC is no longer an acronym but stands alone as the company's official name.

FMC ranks as a Fortune 150 company, with multi-billion-dollar annual sales to customers in over 100 countries. Worldwide, the company operates 95 manufacturing facilities and mines in 18 countries with more than 20,000 employees.

HEADQUARTERS MOVE IN 1972

In 1972, FMC moved its corporate offices to Chicago from San Jose,

California. It was thought a Chicago headquarters would make intra-company communications swifter and smoother, since most of the firm's U.S. employees were based east of the Rockies. Other draws included Chicago's central location and its enviable position as both a major financial and cultural center and the hub of an extensive transportation network. Another reason for FMC's move to Chicago was that then Chairman of the Board Robert Malott wanted "employees to be involved in associations, business organizations, luncheons, charitable events—everything that contributes to better, more interesting, and broader-thinking individuals."

During its 20 years in the city, that hope has been realized, as FMC has developed a high profile through employee and corporate activities. For example, the FMC Foundation

and FMC employee volunteers generously support the Chicago Symphony Orchestra, Lyric Opera of Chicago, and Field Museum of Chicago. FMC is a supporter of the Rehabilitation Institute of Chicago and Chicago's Gateway Foundation, a treatment center for alcohol and chemical dependency. FMC was also a founding member of the Illinois Business Roundtable, an association of chief executives of Illinois-based companies, which works with the state legislature on key issues.

Throughout its history, FMC has enjoyed financial strength and strong management. In 1986, it was the first publicly traded company to recapitalize by issuing a cash and stock package to existing public stockholders. The strategy proved successful because it captured the company's entire value for its shareholders and gave employees a major share in the business.

As FMC senior executives note, "Our confidence that recapitalization would enhance shareholder value has been more than justified. Since the beginning of 1986, FMC stock has appreciated at an average annual rate of 27 percent, compared with 12 percent for the Standard & Poor's 500." By the end of 1991, FMC had repaid $1.2 billion in debt, or 60 percent of the debt associated with recapitalization, without selling any assets. The objective to increase

FMC is one of the world's leading producers of chemicals and machinery for industry, agriculture, and government. Clockwise from top left: glass products manufactured from FMC soda ash, energy and transportation equipment, crop protection chemicals, and food machinery equipment.

PHOTOS BY JAMES L. BALLARD

value for its shareholders, say FMC officials, is a constant. Employees today own 30 percent of FMC's shares.

DIVERSE PRODUCTS

FMC's product lines are divided among seven major markets: chemical products, agricultural chemicals, precious metals, defense systems, food machinery, energy, and transportation equipment.

FMC-manufactured chemicals are market leaders, essential in producing an array of consumer goods, from paper and detergents to foods and pharmaceuticals. Some of its products serve as important raw materials in processing other chemicals. The company is also the world's largest producer of natural soda ash, a basic component in the production of glass, and lithium-based chemicals, which are used in batteries, cosmetics, and pharmaceutical products.

FMC plays a vital role in protecting and producing the world's food supply. The company's crop protection chemicals, used on a broad spectrum of food and fibers on four continents, are effective against a range of insects, weeds, and other pests. FMC's agricultural products are instrumental in improving farmers' yields and keeping food costs low.

FMC owns 79 percent of FMC Gold Company, a producer of gold and silver from mines located in the western United States. A public company since 1987, the operation is aggressively pursuing opportunities for reserve expansion in the United States and Central and South America.

For more than 50 years, FMC's defense operations have supplied equipment to the U.S. military, as well as the armed forces of other free-world governments. Recently, FMC ground combat vehicles and naval weapon systems performed with distinction in the Persian Gulf War. Most notable was FMC's Bradley Fighting Vehicle, which

played a key role in the Army's ground force strategy.

In its energy and transportation equipment unit, FMC produces equipment for land or subsea oil and gas drilling, as well as airline, automotive service, and materials handling equipment.

Since FMC began manufacturing its first product, the orchard sprayer, its food production equipment has set the industry standard for excellence. Today's descendant of that original device is the Crop Care System, a high-tech sprayer with electronic sensors that scan the size and shape of trees to provide a concentrated, efficient spray.

FMC chemicals and machinery add quality, flexibility, and speed to the food production process. The company's products are integral to virtually all prepared foods, from baking soda to frozen waffles, from fruit juices to coffee, and from canned soups and microwavable dinners to candy bars and ice cream.

In all its manufacturing and processing activities, FMC is mindful of protecting the environment, and

of the health and safety of employees, customers, and members of the communities where the company has operations.

PLANS FOR THE FUTURE

FMC's plans for the future include global growth by expanding internationally and continuing to capitalize on markets in Europe, Asia, and Latin America. The corporation intends to boost the competitiveness of its main businesses worldwide, and to get closer to customers on both a regional and worldwide basis.

Over the years, FMC has focused on key goals that continue to guide the company toward further success. Increasing shareholder value, better understanding customers' needs, becoming a true worldwide business contender, and developing opportunities for employees are all critical to the continued growth and prosperity of FMC Corporation.

FMC employees volunteer their support to the United Way (bottom right), the Chicago Symphony Orchestra, and a host of other civic and community service organizations.

Customers of FMC's diverse products include the U.S. military (top left), refiners and fabricators of precious metals (top right), and pharmaceutical companies (bottom left).

PHOTOS BY JAMES L. BALLARD

▼ MICHAEL KELLY

HUMANA HEALTH CARE PLANS

ONE BEGAN IN 1972 AS A SMALL GROUP HEALTH PLAN IN THE BASEMENT OF MICHAEL REESE HOSPITAL; IT GREW TO SERVE MORE THAN 240,000 MEMBERS AT 22 HEALTH CENTERS, MAKING IT THE SECOND LARGEST STAFF MODEL HMO IN THE CHICAGO AREA. THE OTHER WAS ONE OF

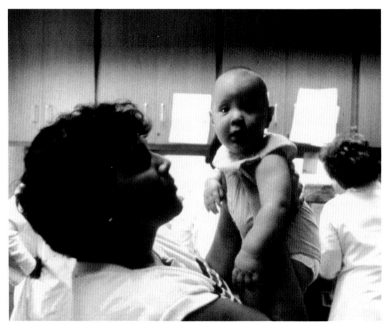

the nation's largest health care and health coverage providers. Their combination in 1991 created a potent force in Chicago health care and insurance.

When Humana Inc. acquired the Michael Reese Health Plan, the company provided resources and financial backing for the plan to expand its product lines, which now include a preferred provider organization (PPO) and the Humana Gold Plus Plan for Medicare subscribers. The growth of Humana Health Care Plans also included the acquisition of the HealthChicago HMO in 1992, adding more than 60,000 members. Today, Humana covers more than 310,000 people in the Chicago area.

Humana's staff model HMO puts an emphasis on infants by covering pediatric exams and immunizations, as well as offering a wide range of classes for new and expectant parents (right).

FLAGSHIP

The flagship of Humana's efforts is the staff model HMO, which continues to serve more than 240,000 people at 22 health centers. In the near future, the plan looks to add at least two more health centers.

When the Michael Reese Health Plan began, HMOs were an untested concept. Today, most health experts point to them as the most affordable option for ensuring quality health care in an era of steadily rising

The 22 health centers of Humana's staff model HMO combine modern medical facilities with attractive, comfortable environments. The Weathers Y. Sykes Center (above) is the plan's largest.

medical costs. By joining the plan, members prepay for the majority of their health care and then receive office visits, check-ups, prescriptions, and even hospital stays for minimal copayments, often as low as $3 to $5.

"In the stormy sea of spiraling health care costs, the HMO is an island of calm," says Associate Executive Director Patrick R. Brady. "In addition, most medical professionals agree that the staff model plan has the greatest ability among HMOs to effectively control costs while providing a high level of quality health care."

Humana operates the 22 health centers and employs the physicians, support staff, and technicians at each, thereby encouraging a team approach to medicine. "Working for Humana is a chance to practice medicine in a group setting without having to worry about overhead, bill paying, and other nuisances that a physician has to be concerned with in private practice," says Associate Medical Director Fred Volkman, M.D. "The plan provides a regular staff, with consistent R.N. and medi-

cal assistant team members, as well as access to lab facilities and contracted specialists. With this support, the physician's energies can be concentrated on the patient and on the practice of medicine."

Dr. Volkman, a pediatrician who has been with the HMO for nine years, has found that the staff model allows physicians a great deal of flexibility in terms of practice style, as well as opportunities for growth. "There is a real emphasis on continuing education and expanding medical horizons here," he says. "Because the plan is so large, we've seen a broad spectrum of patients with diverse needs."

To help ensure member satisfaction with the staff model HMO, Humana recently introduced the Renaissance Project to the health centers. Previously, members had made appointments and requested lab results and prescription refills through a central switchboard. Under Renaissance, members can directly contact their physician or a nurse to ask urgent medical questions, make an immediate appointment, or request test results and

Humana's annual "I Feel Good" run and walk draws Chicagoans of all ages to the lakeshore for a day of fitness and fun.

medication refills.

"Continuous improvement in member services has been our goal for more than 20 years, and it is the key to our future," says Vice President-Illinois for Humana Health Plans Barry Averill. "The Renaissance Project is new, but the commitment behind it has been with us since the beginning."

SERVICES FOR MEMBERS

Key words for any HMO are "preventive health care." With a wide-ranging health education program, the Humana HMO plan far exceeds most others in a commitment to keeping members well.

"From the beginning, the HMO has concentrated on serving the complete health needs of our membership," says Patrick Brady. "We offer a lifetime of wellness opportunities, from new baby care to aerobics for senior citizens."

"Our health education programs are a good reflection of our organization and its philosophy," adds Director of Health Education Kathy Wieland. "One way we've demonstrated a consistent commitment to our

members' wellness needs is through the classes we offer at many of our health centers."

Through the Health Education department, the Humana health centers offer a continuing series of courses in weight loss, smoking cessation, cholesterol reduction, stress management, and aerobics, among others. Classes target working men and women, senior citizens, teens, or expectant parents. Members learning to live with chronic conditions, such as diabetes or asthma, find that classes and one-on-one teaching sessions are an important part of their treatment. The HMO's health education effort also includes an extensive series of patient education pamphlets and a video lending library with more than 40 health care titles.

COMMUNITY OUTREACH

Humana reaches out to the Chicago community with the preventive health message. As a participant in the Chicago Public Schools Adopt-A-School program, the organization has developed a health education curriculum for grade school chil-

dren, covering topics from proper nutrition and substance abuse to preventing pregnancy.

Humana also brings together hundreds of HMO members, physicians, employees, and the general public along Lake Michigan each summer for the annual "I Feel Good" day. Featuring a 5-kilometer run, 2-mile race walk, and half-mile Kids' Fun Run, the event allows participants to break a sweat for a good cause. Over the years, proceeds have benefited local teen living programs, eldercare services, and emergency housing and food providers.

Quality, affordable health care has always been the centerpiece of the HMO plan's "Feel Good" efforts. With a dedication to maintaining excellent medical care, offering the best in preventive education and services, and encouraging a team approach to patient care, Humana's staff model HMO, along with the other Humana health coverage products, looks forward to a successful future as a health care leader in the Chicago area.

CHICAGO BOARD OPTIONS EXCHANGE

WHILE OPTIONS TRADING HAS EXISTED IN ONE FORM OR ANOTHER FOR MANY YEARS, IT WAS THE CHICAGO BOARD OPTIONS EXCHANGE (CBOE) THAT FIRST BROUGHT STOCK OPTIONS TRADING TO A NATIONAL, REGULATED SECURITIES EXCHANGE. ◆ THE CBOE

launched the first listed options market on April 26, 1973, when it began trading call options on 16 underlying stocks. In just two decades, it has become the world's largest options exchange and the second largest U.S. securities exchange after the New York Stock Exchange (NYSE).

As a major worldwide financial institution, the CBOE is subject to the oversight of the Securities and Exchange Commission. There are some 1,700 exchange members, who collectively represent one of the NYSE's largest customers, generating approximately 5 percent of its volume. Additionally, the CBOE employs nearly 800 people from throughout the Chicago area.

technology that have set industry standards.

A GROWING LIST OF OPTIONS PRODUCTS

Options are a risk-management tool, providing investors with a versatile means with which to tailor the risk/reward characteristics of equity investments. Currently, the exchange lists options on more than 375 equities, on the world's most active stock indices, and on short- and long-term interest rates.

In 1983, the CBOE introduced the first option on a broad-based index, known as the Standard & Poor's (S&P) 100 Index. The S&P 100 Index option (ticker symbol OEX) is the most actively traded index op-

index options at the CBOE represents 92 percent of the total U.S. index options market.

In late 1992, three new index options products were introduced to round out the CBOE's index product line: options on the Russell 2000® Index, the CBOE BioTech Index, and the FT-SE 100 Index.

The Russell 2000 Index serves as the benchmark for small capitalization stocks. Of the 3,000 largest capitalized U.S. stocks, this index tracks the smallest two-thirds. The CBOE BioTech Index is a price-weighted, 20-stock index which includes a cross section of biotechnology companies, ranging from highly capitalized firms to smaller emerging companies. The FT-SE (Financial Times-Stock Exchange) 100 Index, introduced in 1984, is the established equity index benchmark for the United Kingdom. Based on the market values of the largest 100 U.K. stocks traded on the London Stock Exchange, this capitalization-weighted index has enjoyed steady growth and worldwide attention.

Forging a new niche in the securities world, the CBOE launched LEAPS® (Long-term Equity Antici-Pation Securities) in 1990 with the introduction of long-term equity options on 14 blue-chip stocks. In response to the success of these long-term options, the CBOE now lists LEAPS on 44 highly capitalized, actively traded equities, as well as on the S&P 100, S&P 500, the Russell 2000, and the CBOE Bio-Tech indexes. Further attesting to the popularity of the LEAPS concept that the CBOE pioneered, LEAPS are available industry-wide on more than 120 equities.

In one of its most significant developments for the future, CBOE launched FLexible EXchange (FLEX) options to capture a portion of the more customized over-the-

In all, some 1,700 CBOE members work on the exchange's bustling trading floor.

Located at the corner of LaSalle and Van Buren streets in one of the world's most important financial districts, the CBOE boasts a 45,000-square-foot, clear-span trading floor, the largest functioning trading floor in the world. From the gallery overlooking this arena, visitors witness the CBOE's market maker system at work, enhanced by product innovation and cutting-edge

tion in the world, trading an average of more than 249,000 contracts per day in 1992. These options are an essential tool for many investors and traders, allowing them to participate in the movement of the market as a whole. The CBOE also lists options on the S&P 500 Index, which many U.S. money managers use as a benchmark for portfolio performance. Together, trading in these two

counter (OTC) segment. FLEX options provide an exchange-traded alternative for institutional users of the OTC market. "Over-the-counter index options have grown into a multi-billion-dollar market," says CBOE Chairman Duke Chapman. "Our new FLEX options will provide institutional asset managers with an alternative to OTC options with the benefits of an exchange setting."

These and other product advances have enabled the CBOE to continually address the needs of its participants and the demands of an ever-changing economy. This ongoing spirit of innovation at the CBOE also can be documented through its cutting-edge technology and its commitment to educating investors.

TECHNOLOGICAL INNOVATION

The CBOE has implemented several technological innovations throughout the years designed to enhance market efficiency and customer service. One of its most successful implementations came in the form of the Retail Automatic Execution System (RAES) introduced in 1985. This innovative system allows public customer orders to be filled automatically at the prevailing bid or offer, with the filled order reported within seconds.

Other recent advances include Autoquote, which provides up-to-the-minute prices from the trading floor, and the Electronic Book, which increases the speed of order execution and fill reporting for limit and market orders that arrive prior to the market's opening.

MEETING THE EDUCATIONAL NEEDS OF INVESTORS

In response to the tremendous growth and versatility of options products in an increasingly complex financial arena, the CBOE established The Options Institute in April 1985 to provide instruction on the use of options for risk management and bottom-line results. Students of the Institute have included retail and institutional customers, investment professionals, bank authorities, the staff of the U.S. Congress, and members of the Securities and Ex-

change Commission. The Institute also serves a growing international clientele from firms throughout Europe, Australia, and the Far East. Recognized as the premier source for options education, the Institute's alumni roster includes more than 15,000 people worldwide.

THE CBOE LOOKS TO THE FUTURE

During 20 years of innovation and growth, the CBOE's listed options markets have served as an integral source of financial management tools for customers ranging from individual investors to pension fund managers and other large institutional investors. The exchange's efforts in the areas of education, product development, market quality, and technology have enabled the CBOE, in an era of accelerated competition, to hold a 60 percent share of the U.S. options market. Upon this foundation, the CBOE's market maker system is poised to meet the competitive challenges of the future with new and sophisticated solutions for risk management.

THE HONGKONG AND SHANGHAI BANKING CORPORATION LIMITED

AS A WORLD-CLASS FINANCIAL CENTER AND THE INDUSTRIAL BASE OF THE MIDWEST, THE CITY OF CHICAGO IS NATURALLY HOME TO INNOVATIVE AND SOPHISTICATED EXCHANGES AND FINANCIAL INSTITUTIONS. IN FACT, MORE FORTUNE 500 COMPANIES ARE BASED IN THE CHICAGO

area than in any other metropolitan area except New York City.

Therefore, it is not surprising that Chicago has attracted the attention of a member bank of the HSBC Group, one of the world's 10 largest international banking organizations. The Hongkong and Shanghai Banking Corporation Limited, a British-managed banking company headquartered in Hong Kong, has been an important presence in Chicago since 1973.

HongkongBank's Chicago branch office is dedicated to serving the operational and financial needs of local companies, while assisting them in the development of international business opportunities. The Chicago office provides a full range of credit, treasury, and trade finance products tailored to the specific needs, cash flow cycles, and foreign markets of its customers.

Founded in 1865 to serve the needs of merchants on the China coast and to finance the growing trade among China, Europe, and the United States, the bank has been an international financial institution from its earliest days.

WORLDWIDE RESOURCES

The staff of HongkongBank-Chicago is committed to using the resources of HSBC Group's worldwide network of branches, affiliates, and correspondents to assist its clients with transactions, projects, and investments from beginning to end. With assets of over $269 billion, the HSBC Group maintains more than 3,300 offices in 66 countries and employs 100,000 people worldwide. As a result, the bank is well-positioned to aid in the expansion and funding of its clients' international business endeavors.

Success in international trade is often based on an institution's ability to provide a competitive financing package. Because it has access to a worldwide group of professionals trained in the structure and delivery of trade finance products and services, HongkongBank-

Chicago can develop the most attractive and economical package for many of its clients.

Customers of HongkongBank-Chicago can be found in many different industries, including manufacturing, retailing, wholesaling, trading, and services. The bank provides these diverse clients with commercial and standby letters of credit, government-supported export program financing, forfaiting, foreign exchange trading and hedging, working capital and term financing, interest rate swaps and hedges, leasing, commercial finance, and property financing.

As evidence of its vast financial resources, HongkongBank's preferred credit relationships begin at $5 million. Its highest priority customers are large private and public corporations, but the bank does provide services to select smaller

firms with annual sales below $100 million who have a continuing demand for the unique expertise of the HongkongBank.

HongkongBank-Chicago can tailor individual service packages to meet the varying needs of its American customers. For one client, the bank furnished transferable documentary credits to provide pre-export financing, which allowed the customer to purchase silk from Korea for assembly in China and importation into the United States. For another client, HongkongBank-Chicago supplied back-to-back documentary credits for the purchase of coal from Australia for power generation in Taiwan. For still another, the bank provided standby letters of credit in favor of British authorities as duty deferment bonds for garments manufactured in Hong Kong under documentary credits and subsequently imported into the United Kingdom.

Another distinguishing characteristic of HongkongBank-Chicago is its dedication to quick operational turnaround of documentary presentations, amendments, discrepancies, and payments. At a time when many of its competitors are de-emphasizing investment in staff and time-saving automation, HongkongBank continues to expand the quality and efficiency of its existing documentary capabilities.

MORE THAN A CENTURY OF EXPERIENCE

The history of The Hongkong and Shanghai Banking Corporation Limited gives it a unique position among the world's top financial institutions. Founded in 1865 to serve the needs of merchants on the China coast and to finance the growing trade among China, Europe, and the United States, the bank has been an international financial institution from its earliest days. In 1875, it also earned the distinction of being the first foreign bank to open an office in the United States.

Today, The Hongkong and Shanghai Banking Corporation Limited is the largest international bank headquartered in Asia outside of Japan, and the scope of its parent company's presence in foreign markets gives the Chicago office the financial resources and expertise to best serve its customers. As the Pacific Rim becomes increasingly important in world trade, a bank with strong ties to that region can play an important role in the success of many international business transactions.

Thanks in part to the presence of organizations like The Hongkong and Shanghai Banking Corporation Limited, Chicago continues to grow as a world-class financial center. After two decades of service to some of the city's largest corporations, HongkongBank-Chicago is poised to serve its customers' growing needs, from corporate banking to international finance and trade, far into the future.

The Hongkong and Shanghai Banking Corporation Limited, a British-managed banking company headquartered in Hong Kong, has been an important presence in Chicago since 1973.

IVI TRAVEL

FROM THE COMPLEX AIRLINE FARE STRUCTURES TO TRACKING TOTAL SPENDING, EFFECTIVE TRAVEL PROGRAMS RELY ON SUPERIOR INFORMATION. THROUGH A SKILLFUL INTEGRATION OF QUALITY TRAVELER SERVICE AND CUTTING-EDGE TECHNOLOGY, IVI TRAVEL HELPS HUNDREDS OF COMPANIES nationwide regulate this information flow to serve their employees' travel and entertainment needs while effectively controlling the expenses involved. Headquartered in suburban Northbrook with over 250 branches throughout North America, IVI has been managing information to serve people for more than 20 years.

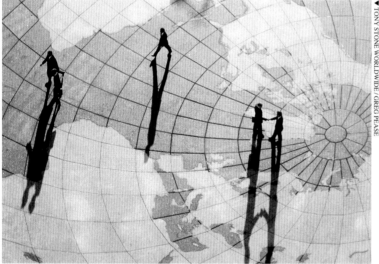

TONY STONE WORLDWIDE/ GREG PEASE

IVI and its partners in Business Travel International have developed a global reporting system that consolidates corporate travel data for all of a company's travelers from every office worldwide.

IVI reservation agents (right) draw from an extensive data base of negotiated corporate rates in offering customers the lowest available airfares. After booking, an automated fare evaluation system continually searches for lower alternatives until actual departure.

REIGNING IN TRAVEL EXPENSES

"Travel is one of the largest controllable expenses for any corporation," says IVI President Walter Freedman. "By consolidating all travel spending with one business travel firm, a corporation can lower its cost substantially. IVI clients can expect to save 15 percent over an unmanaged travel program."

To achieve that level of savings, IVI has developed several innovative strategies. Foremost is COMPASS, IVI's computerized travel management information system. For each customer, COMPASS derives data from corporate travel preferences and spending patterns, supplying the company with current, comprehensive information via paper, computer diskette, or on-line formats. IVI Account Development Managers and customers work together to identify trends and opportunities for reducing travel costs through vendor negotiations and travel policy refinements.

"For example, COMPASS data distinguishes between employees who comply with company travel policy and those who do not. However, it doesn't stop there. Our analysis also tells customers why," Freedman says. "The company can then determine whether to modify policy or enforce existing practices more vigorously."

BIG CONNECTIONS IN A SHRINKING WORLD

As globalization began sweeping the business world, IVI developed another creative strategy to serve the growing international marketplace. In 1990, IVI and several prominent western European agencies cofounded Business Travel International, a unique joint venture that brings together the world's leading business travel companies.

Through this partnership with prestigious members in Europe, Japan, Singapore, Australia, and other major regions, IVI ensures consistently high quality service on a global scale while offering unique tools and techniques for managing travel costs worldwide.

COST-EFFICIENCY IN MEETING PLANNING

One key in IVI's philosophy is helping corporate customers approach familiar travel needs in new ways. The Meetings Management System is a prime example. "We've found that as much as 25 percent of a company's travel can be classified as meeting travel, thus qualifying for substantial discounts," Freedman explains.

IVI's systems approach encourages clients to think of all meetings—whether for conferences, conventions, employee training, or incentive trips—as one segment of business travel with similar requirements, rather than as a series of separate events. From this perspective, customers can anticipate much of their meeting travel far in advance, allowing IVI to negotiate rates with airlines and hotels based on overall volume.

"Many companies rely on us to manage their entire meetings program for them because we can do the job more efficiently and at a lower cost," says Freedman.

A HISTORY OF INNOVATION

IVI's affinity for innovation has its roots in the agency's origins. The company was the first travel firm to focus solely on the needs of corporate travel. During the past two decades, technological leadership and a reputation for traveler service have built a solid customer base that includes Fortune 500 corporations and many other industry leaders.

"Today, we're the sixth largest travel management firm in the country, and we make more than 1 million reservations annually," attests Freedman. "We've accomplished this, first and foremost, by delivering the highest level of traveler services possible, and secondly, by reinvesting in our own resources."

Offering high-quality service, innovative technology, and unique cost-containment programs has made IVI Travel one of the most successful businesses in its field.

NEW DAY CENTER OF HINSDALE HOSPITAL

FOR MORE THAN 15 YEARS, NEW DAY CENTER OF HINSDALE HOSPITAL HAS BEEN TREATING VICTIMS OF ALCOHOL AND DRUG ADDICTION, WITH THE ULTI-MATE GOAL OF HELPING THEM RETURN TO HAPPY, PRODUCTIVE LIVES. ♦ THE OVERARCHING PHILOSOPHY BEHIND THE CENTER, WHICH OPENED IN WEST

suburban Hinsdale in 1978, is that chemical dependency is a progressive and chronic disease that destroys the harmony of human life and brings on spiritual, mental, emotional, physical, and social deterioration. As a result, some level of treatment is the necessary first step toward establishing a foundation for long-term recovery, a process of self-discovery in which the chemically dependent person becomes aware of and accepts the consequences of his or her behavior, finds a solid base of support for abstinence, and surrenders to the care that is offered.

COMPREHENSIVE SERVICES

Since its founding, New Day Center has developed a comprehensive array of services geared toward the unique needs of the chemically dependent and their families. The center's inpatient program offers three to four weeks of intensive treatment for the emotional, mental, social, vocational, and spiritual aspects of addiction. All patients who are admitted on an inpatient basis undergo an initial detoxification process, which involves treatment for withdrawal signs and symptoms, and other medical complications.

A day treatment program was initiated in 1989 to provide a less restrictive, lower cost treatment option for patients who can be successfully treated in an outpatient setting. This more flexible program allows patients to maintain their family and work responsibilities during recovery.

New Day Center recognizes that chemical dependency is not just a disease of the patient; it affects all members of the family. Consequently, the center offers programs designed to educate a patient's fam-

ily and friends about the disease and the often difficult recovery process. For example, assessment and intervention counseling are available to families and prospective patients. Intervention is the process by which the family, friends, or employers of a chemically dependent person present facts about that person's alcoholism or drug abuse in a caring, non-judgmental manner with the goal of motivating him or her to seek help.

Aftercare is another vital service of New Day Center designed to help patients remain drug- and alcohol-free after their initial recovery. All patients who complete treatment at the center are enrolled in a two-year program of continuing support at no additional charge. Nearly 600 New Day Center graduates participate each week in the aftercare program.

QUALITY STAFF AND AN IMPRESSIVE SUCCESS RATE

Housed in beautifully appointed facilities at Hinsdale Hospital, the center employs a highly trained staff of more than 50 counselors and support personnel who can care for up to 34 inpatients and 18 outpatients at one time. During its 15 years in operation, New Day Center has treated more than 7,000 chemically dependent individuals, and its staff have been duly proud of the center's impressive success rate. Close to 90 percent of those who complete the aftercare program actually stay sober.

New Day Center of Hinsdale Hospital was created to treat chemically dependent individuals as people and as members of a family, while helping them and their loved ones combat a potentially devastating addiction. With the understanding that the most difficult step

toward recovery often is acknowledging that a problem exists, New Day Center provides a caring atmosphere in which its patients can recognize and confront their illness and begin a successful journey down the road to recovery.

Housed in beautifully appointed facilities at Hinsdale Hospital, the center employs a highly trained staff of more than 50 counselors and support personnel who can care for up to 34 inpatients and 18 outpatients at one time.

PROFILE

BROOK FURNITURE RENTAL

SINCE ITS FOUNDING IN 1979, BROOK FURNITURE RENTAL HAS GROWN DRAMATICALLY, FROM TWO SHOWROOMS AND A 5,000-SQUARE-FOOT WARE-HOUSE IN THE CHICAGO AREA TO 29 SHOWROOMS, FOUR DISTRIBUTION CENTERS, AND FIVE CLEARANCE CENTERS LOCATED ACROSS THE COUNTRY.

Brook Furniture Rental's dedication to identifying and meeting its clients needs can be credited for a 60-fold increase in revenue in just 13 years. The company's 1992 sales were in excess of $45 million.

"We have established ourselves as pioneers in the furniture rental business," says Robert W. Crawford, CEO. "And we are continuing to set the standard for the industry."

A NEW BUSINESS OPPORTUNITY

Based today in northwest suburban Elk Grove Village, Brook was founded by Bob Crawford, a former Procter & Gamble executive who was looking for a new business opportunity. In 1979, he came across Broyhill Furniture Rental, a small furniture rental business in Chicago. Intrigued by the potential

he envisioned for growth, Crawford purchased the company, changed its name to Brook Furniture Rental, and built the business into an industry leader.

Today, Brook provides a variety of furniture for the home and office, including tables, chairs, sofas, wall units, and bedroom furniture. The company also supplies virtually every other finishing detail for a home or office, such as artwork, dishes, towels, linens, phones, televisions, VCRs, microwave ovens, and even paper towels, bathroom tissue, and other paper goods.

"Our team can go into an apartment or home, and in 48 hours or less it will be completely transformed into a model home," says Crawford. "It's truly amazing."

Brook got its start primarily renting home furnishings to a very

specific customer base: business people on temporary assignment, disaster victims, and recently divorced men and women, among others. Eventually the company's employees, who are referred to as team members, began to receive regular requests for office furnishings. "Those early inquiries are what fueled our growth in office furniture rental, which today accounts for 30 percent of the company's business," says Erling Smedvig, vice president and general manager.

Renting furniture has become a popular option because it gives a business the flexibility to expand and upgrade its furnishings. It is also an inexpensive and relatively simple way for a new company to establish an image of success. "Renting office furniture is more economical than buying it, and it's 100 percent tax deductible," says Smedvig. "Since the growth of the office furniture side of the business, we've been asking ourselves more and more what our clients' needs are."

An outgrowth of that increased attention to customer needs is Brook Relocation Services, an executive relocation division that makes a move less stressful by helping newcomers settle in as quickly as possible. This free service will assist individuals and families new to Chicago in finding a rental apartment or home, guide them to areas of town or residential buildings that meet their needs, and help them find professional services like banks, day care, medical and dental care, and other services that might be difficult to find when relocating to a new city.

"We had been informally collecting and distributing information on apartments and services for years," says Christa Landgraf, manager of Relocation Services. The service was finally formalized as a company

Today, office furniture rental accounts for 30 percent of the company's business.

Brook offers a showcase of exceptional furnishings for the home, including all the finishing touches (left and below left).

division in March 1991 to provide free, unbiased advice and assistance to out-of-state newcomers. "Our referrals are strictly based on the client's needs," adds Landgraf.

In turn, the service helps strengthen relationships with the corporations who refer their new employees to Brook. A percentage of the newcomers also rent furniture from the company.

Serving the convention and trade show market is another aspect of Brook Furniture Rental's expanding business. Exhibit houses or companies participating in or sponsoring trade shows in Chicago and around the country rent office furniture, tables, sofas, and chairs for booths, hospitality suites, and other uses.

NATIONWIDE GROWTH

From its suburban Chicago base, Brook has expanded geographically, primarily through the purchase of other furniture rental operations around the country. The company currently operates showrooms in northern and southern California markets, where it ranks as the largest furniture rental company. Brook also maintains showrooms in Las Vegas, Phoenix, and Milwaukee.

In addition, the company operates five clearance centers nationwide where it sells previously rented furniture and factory overruns at reduced prices.

Throughout its 13-year history, growth has been the norm at Brook Furniture Rental. Currently, the company employs 85 people in the Chicago area and has 350 additional

employees in other parts of the country. According to Smedvig, Brook is today the number one furniture rental company in each market it serves, and number three in the industry overall.

The company has attained this enviable stature by providing the highest level of service possible, offering a broad selection of furniture styles, and remaining committed to identifying and meeting its clients' needs. Whether they are business people on assignment who want to make temporary housing more like home, or a new business trying to keep a tight rein on expenses, Brook Furniture Rental offers its customers unparalleled quality in the growing furniture rental market.

Brook currently operates four distribution centers (above) to serve its customers in the Chicago area and beyond.

CCC INFORMATION SERVICES INC.

ONE OF CHICAGO'S FASTEST GROWING COMPANIES, CCC INFORMATION SERVICES HAS MADE A NAME FOR ITSELF IN THE INSURANCE AND AUTOMOTIVE SERVICE INDUSTRIES. A DYNAMIC AND FAST-MOVING FIRM, THE COMPANY SOLVES ITS CLIENTS' BUSINESS PROBLEMS THROUGH CLOSE

working relationships backed by cutting-edge technology.

When CCC was founded more than a decade ago, the value of a wrecked vehicle was determined by a variety of manual methods. As a result, insurance companies and policyholders were faced with inaccurate estimates and a mountain of red tape to settle "total loss" claims. In 1980, the new company pioneered an alternative approach that offered computerized market valuations based on "real steel"—automobiles located on local franchised new and used car lots.

The idea was accepted readily by consumers, insurance companies, and regulators, as the system was more efficient than randomly calling dealers and more accurate than hypothetical guide book figures. By 1988, CCC had expanded from two customers and two claim offices in Illinois to over 300 property and casualty insurers across the United States and Canada. CCC's state-of-

the-art systems today process an evaluation every 6 seconds, 12 hours a day, totaling more than 1.5 million vehicle evaluations a year.

However, the company delivers much more than technology, says J. Laurence Costin, executive vice president for client services. "The close relationships we've built over the years and our willingness to listen to and learn from our clients have allowed us to play an expanding role in solving their business problems," he explains.

Says one client, "In our view, what separates CCC is its people and how responsive they are. They anticipate difficulties and fix problems before we even know we have them."

EXPANDING INTO NEW MARKETS

This commitment to personal service and state-of-the-art systems applications earned CCC high marks throughout the insurance in-

dustry and led to the development of its second major product breakthrough—PC-based collision estimating. Introduced in 1990 into a market then dominated by two companies that provided mainframe systems to process collision estimates, CCC's EZEst was the first use of the adaptable, portable attributes of personal computers in this labor-intensive, costly segment of the insurance claims arena.

Glen E. Tullman, president of CCC's Insurance Services Division, explains the company's strategy at the time: "The progress in the development of notebook computers and our willingness and ability to move quickly to apply this new technology to collision estimating gave us an opportunity to change the way business was done and decisions were made." With EZEst, appraisers were able to write accurate estimates on-site while viewing the automobile, significantly reducing the time and cost of completing a collision

The company's management team is committed to the personal service and state-of-the-art systems applications that have fueled CCC's growth for more than a decade.

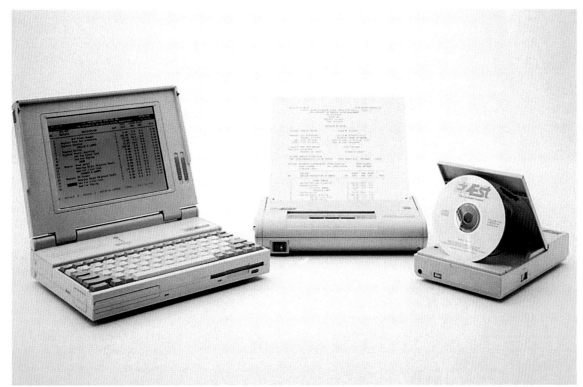

estimate. Within a year of the product's introduction, CCC had become the leading provider of stand-alone collision estimating systems.

On the heels of that success, the company entered another fast-growing business in 1992—providing information to collision repairers. David B. Mullen, now vice chairman and chief financial officer, set up and headed CCC's Collision Repair Division. In the span of just 12 months, the division grew to 125 employees and generated revenue exceeding $6 million by installing EZEst systems in more than 2,000 body shops. Underscoring the strength of its relationship with the insurance industry, the company worked closely with a major insurance client that had an existing relationship with 3,700 collision repairers.

"Our insurance clients wanted body shop estimates to be written on a computerized estimating system that reduced friction costs, i.e., disagreements between appraisers and shop owners over price that typically delay settlement. The insurers also wanted a sophisticated way to communicate with the shops," Mullen explains. CCC satisfied both needs with EZEst and the creation of

EZNet, a unique data communications network that allows insurance companies to electronically dispatch assignments to body shops and body shops to return estimates electronically. The system is also designed to handle other interactive business transactions. Says Eddie Cheskis, president of the Collision Repair Division, "We believe the body shop will be the claims office of the future."

CCC's Insurance Services Division recently took the industry a step further in automating the job of the claims representative. Introduced in 1993, the Integrated Claims Workstation 2000 (ICW2000) offers clients access to all the estimating, communication, and workflow processes that an adjuster performs during a typical day, making it possible for an adjuster to work at home. This workstation concept has extended CCC's reach into property, contents, and salvage estimating services.

POISED FOR FUTURE GROWTH

With more than a decade of innovation and growth under its belt, the company's contribution to the insurance and automotive services indus-

tries has been impressive. In 1983, CCC went public with its initial stock offering, and by 1986, it was recognized by *Inc. Magazine* as the 31st fastest growing company in the United States and first in profitability. David M. Phillips, current chairman and chief executive officer, returned the company to the private sector in 1988.

"My goal was to move CCC from a one-product, entrepreneurial success story to a more broadly based provider of integrated business solutions," explains Phillips. Since then, the company has invested more than $20 million in new products and services. Its 1993 revenues are expected to exceed $90 million and are growing 35 percent a year.

With a young, energized work force of 900, a strong strategic plan, and a continued emphasis on meeting client needs, CCC Information Services is well positioned to continue its record of growth and success. Says Tullman, "Our goal is to work directly with our clients to focus on and improve upon their business processes, reduce their costs, and improve their customers' satisfaction level."

THE PRIME GROUP, INC.

WHAT KIND OF PILLARS SUPPORT A COMPANY THAT IN ITS FIRST 10 YEARS HAS BECOME ONE OF CHICAGO'S LARGEST AND MOST ACTIVE WORLDWIDE REAL ESTATE COMPANIES? IF YOU ASK THE EXECUTIVE TEAM AT THE PRIME GROUP, INC., THOSE PILLARS ARE MADE OF

The Prime Group's diversity is reflected in the projects of its six major divisions. Top to bottom: East Chicago Enterprise Center (Industrial Division), Gulf Coast Factory Shops (Retail Division), and Brookdale Village (Multi-Family Division).

portfolio diversity and an exceptionally high level of professionalism. These two attributes, along with strict adherence to the firm's eight guiding principles, have allowed The Prime Group to adapt and respond quickly to changes within the real estate industry.

Established in Chicago in 1982, the company is today a full-service diversified real estate firm employing more than 650 people worldwide. Its experienced staff members work in the areas of planning, design, construction, marketing, leasing, property management, finance, law, tax, and corporate advisory services. In addition to its downtown Chicago headquarters, Prime maintains eight other offices in North America and Europe (Baltimore, Barcelona, Boca Raton, Chicago, Dallas, Houston, Knoxville, and San Antonio).

The principles that guide Prime's day-to-day operations include a focus on real estate projects in which the company can create or add value; a commitment to excellence and attention to detail that allow quality development at low cost; a team of real estate professionals with significant and diverse achievements; a portfolio of projects that are diverse both in type and location; a knowledge of capital markets to ensure efficient, low-cost

financing; a reliance on traditional values such as honesty, integrity, loyalty, dedication, team effort, and old-fashioned hard work; an ongoing market research program; and a constant application of common sense to all aspects of the firm's business.

SIX OPERATING DIVISIONS

The diversity of The Prime Group's business is reflected in the six major divisions that have evolved over the past 10 years.

The Office Division focuses on developing, building, and managing premier office and mixed-use projects in major urban areas, such as the 50-story office tower at 77 W. Wacker Drive that houses the firm's Chicago corporate headquarters. Prime's success in leasing 77 W. Wacker, despite high office vacancy rates in downtown Chicago, demonstrates its ability to meet the tough challenges of a dynamic and cyclical industry.

The division also buys, renovates, and remarkets major office and mixed-use projects. Two of its most successful ventures are Greenway Plaza in Houston, which includes 10 office buildings containing over 4.2 million square feet of office and retail space, and Plaza of the Americas in Dallas, which boasts 1.1 million square feet of office and retail space. Acquired in 1989, Greenway Plaza experienced an impressive jump in occupancy (from 69 percent to 86 percent) in the two years after an affiliate of The Prime Group acquired a 50 percent interest in the property.

In addition to the work it performs for its own account portfolio, the Office Division provides leasing and marketing, management, tenant consulting, and build-to-suit services for third parties. With increasing focus on the cost and exposure

of a firm's real estate portfolio or needs, Prime expects its services group to play an expanding role within the Office Division.

The Retail Division is involved in developing both traditional retail and manufacturers' outlet centers in the United States and Europe. To aid this effort, Prime formed "The Manufacturers' Forum" in 1989—a trade group of over 125 upscale manufacturers who operate outlet stores that sell merchandise directly to the public at factory discount prices. The company's flagship retail centers include San Marcos Factory Shops (Austin/San Antonio corridor), Gulf Coast Factory Shops (near Tampa-St. Petersburg), Triangle Factory Shops (Raleigh/Durham), Warehouse Row (Chattanooga), and Castle Rock Factory Shops (south of Denver).

The Industrial Division acquires sites for the development or renovation of business parks with flexible industrial, warehouse/distribution, and manufacturing capabilities. One such project is the East Chicago Enterprise Center, formerly an abandoned M-60 tank factory. Acquired by the company in 1988, the 1 million-square-foot facility was renovated and re-leased on a multi-tenant basis, helping to revive the local community's economy.

The Multi-Family Division develops new multi-family homes and acquires, renovates, and manages existing housing. With over 5,000 residential units in its portfolio, Prime has focused on both the Midwest and Southwest markets for long-term growth and stability. Popular amenities such as attached garages, vaulted ceilings, bathroom suites, and large kitchens help ensure tenant stability and bring above-market returns on these developments.

The Senior Housing Division develops and manages housing for the growing elderly population. This division responds to the unique needs of senior citizens by providing functional floor plans, pleasant common areas, helpful services and programs, and an understanding and knowledgeable operating staff. For example, The Devonshire, a 313-unit development in Lisle, Illinois, offers competitively priced rental housing to seniors on a continuum of care basis. Catering to the varied needs of the project's residents, housing options range from congregate living to skilled nursing services.

The Land Development Division assists communities and other clients in creating master plans and in rezoning critical land areas to achieve the best overall use for a site. A major example of the division's work is a recent community plan involving 2,600 acres of land in Huntley, a village located in the path of Chicago's fast-growing Northwest Tollway corridor. The plan involves a variety of housing types, a corporate office campus, a business park, shopping centers, schools, and multiple golf courses and recreational facilities, all complemented by a landscaped network of open spaces, public parks, and lakes. The Prime Group plans to develop the community infrastructure, sell land to home builders, and retain the development and management responsibilities for the office, retail, and business park sites.

The company's International Division, established in 1987, pursues private and public sector real estate opportunities in Europe. In 1988, the division formed subsidiaries Kepro S.A. to operate in Spain and Kepro International B.V. to cover the rest of Europe. In Spain, the division is involved in more than 20 office, retail, and residential projects, including the 110-acre Diagonal Mar mixed-use development on Barcelona's waterfront. Located adjacent to the Olympic Village, Diagonal Mar will feature over 2.2 million square feet of office space arranged in a campus-like setting around heavily landscaped courtyards, a

regional shopping mall with over 900,000 square feet of gross leasable space, a business hotel and conference center, 300 upscale waterfront condominiums, an abundance of underground parking, and several large public parks.

The six operating divisions are supported by six support groups: Finance, Capital Markets, Asset and Development Management, Legal, Tax, and Human Resources. Each group provides support on a cost-efficient basis to assist each operat-

ing division in maximizing the performance of its real estate assets and therefore maximizing returns to owners and investors.

Entering a new decade of worldwide real estate opportunities, The Prime Group is poised to build on its well-established pillars of diversity and professionalism. The firm and its six operating divisions intend to continue to lead the industry as one of Chicago's most diverse and successful real estate companies.

Michael W. Reschke, president of The Prime Group (above).

Prime's Office Division developed, built, and now manages the 50-story office tower at 77 W. Wacker Drive that houses its Chicago corporate headquarters (right).

ARIEL CAPITAL MANAGEMENT, INC.

WHEN JOHN W. ROGERS JR. FOUNDED ARIEL CAPITAL MANAGEMENT, INC. IN 1983, HE WAS ONLY 24 YEARS OLD. THROUGH A STRATEGY OF CAREFUL INVESTING IN SMALLER COMPANIES THAT ARE OFTEN OVERLOOKED BY WALL STREET, ROGERS AND HIS COMPANY HAVE developed an impressive reputation for serving institutional clients and mutual fund investors.

The 18-person firm has grown from managing $500,000 its first year to more than $2 billion a decade later. Today, Ariel Capital Management is known as a solid, stable company that emphasizes patient investing based on in-depth research.

▼ STEVE HALL/HEDRICH-BLESSING

The company employs 18 people at its headquarters on North Michigan Avenue (above).

Above right: After only a decade in business, founder John W. Rogers Jr. and Ariel Capital Management have built an impressive track record in both the community and the financial services industry.

The firm is also well respected in the financial services industry. Currently, Ariel manages $1.5 billion for 50 institutional clients including Ford Motor Company, Mobil Oil, and several public pension funds and universities. The firm also runs two mutual funds: the Calvert-Ariel Growth Fund and the Calvert-Ariel Appreciation Fund. Bethesda, Maryland-based Calvert Group Ltd. handles administration for both mutual funds. Only the Appreciation Fund is open to new investors.

A CONSERVATIVE INVESTMENT PHILOSOPHY

Ariel's motto, "Slow and steady wins the race," reflects a conservative investment philosophy designed to maximize long-term returns for its clients. The firm's five-person research team carefully chooses small- to medium-capitalization companies, frequently with a market capitalization of under $1 billion, that are undervalued or have been overlooked by larger investment houses.

While many firms trade stocks frequently in an effort to produce short-term gains, Ariel sticks with companies for the long haul. Its average portfolio turnover is just 20 to 25 percent a year, compared to a 91 percent industry average for small-company funds. Ariel generally holds each stock for four to five years.

Although its investment strategy is conservative, Ariel Capital Management believes that profitable investments don't have to run contrary to social responsibility. For example, the firm avoids stocks of companies that do business in South Africa or that are involved in the nuclear and defense industries. The Calvert-Ariel Appreciation Fund also screens potential investments for environmental responsibility.

As one of the few African-American-owned money management firms in the United States,

Ariel and its founder understand their responsibilities as a role model to the community. The firm actively supports various organizations, such as Travelers and Immigrants Aid, YWCA of Metropolitan Chicago, and the Better Boys Foundation. In addition, Rogers sits on the boards of several community and social service organizations, including the Chicago Urban League and the Chicago Symphony Orchestra. In 1989, he was appointed to the McCormick Place Navy Pier Board, which oversees the expansion of the McCormick Place Convention Center. His corporate directorships include the Chicago-based AON Corporation, American National Bank and Trust Company, and Burrell Communications Group, Inc.

After only a decade in business, Rogers and Ariel Capital Management have built an impressive track record in both the community and the financial services industry. Looking to the future, the firm believes its conservative investment philosophy and community involvement will make a lasting impact on the city of Chicago.

MIDCON CORP.

PROVIDING ABOUT 10 PERCENT OF THE NATURAL GAS CONSUMED ANNUALLY IN THE UNITED STATES MIGHT SEEM LIKE A BIG JOB FOR AN ORGANIZATION FORMED JUST OVER 12 YEARS AGO. THIS SIZABLE TASK RECKONS, HOWEVER, WITH THE VAST ABILITIES AND RESOURCES OF LOMBARD, ILLINOIS-BASED

MidCon Corp. and the eight decades of combined experience of its major pipeline companies.

Incorporated in 1981, MidCon companies buy, sell, store, and transport natural gas throughout the center of the nation and connect to pipelines serving East and West Coast markets. Each year, the corporation's pipeline companies move more than 2 trillion cubic feet (Tcf) of natural gas. The net sales and operating revenues of MidCon, a subsidiary of Los Angeles-based Occidental Petroleum Corp., are about $2.5 billion.

MidCon gathers natural gas from major producing areas such as the Gulf of Mexico, Texas, Oklahoma, Louisiana, and the Southwest, and from regions as widespread as the Rocky Mountains and western Canada. To transport this large volume of fuel, MidCon maintains a 17,400-mile network of wholly and jointly owned pipelines. MidCon employees also operate field compressor stations and staff a number of underground gas storage fields. These storage facilities can supply up to 3.7 billion cubic feet (Bcf) of natural gas per day.

A MAJOR GAS SUPPLIER

MidCon's largest subsidiary, Natural Gas Pipeline Company of America (NGPL), maintains offices in Lombard and in Houston, Texas. Founded in the 1930s as the Continental Construction Corp., the company was established with the objective of building a 900-mile natural gas pipeline from the Texas Panhandle to Chicago.

Today, NGPL delivers about 1.7 Tcf of natural gas per year, operates 14,022 miles of wholly and jointly owned pipelines in 12 states, and maintains 124 compressor stations and nine subterranean natural gas storage fields. NGPL was a pioneer in the develop-

ment of its underground storage facilities, which consist of huge porous rock formations or depleted oil and gas fields located in Iowa, Illinois, Texas, and Oklahoma. In addition, NGPL's subsidiaries have interest in 1,350 miles of pipelines, including two offshore operations in the Gulf of Mexico and a pipeline that transports natural gas from the Rockies.

MidCon's second largest subsidiary is Houston-based MidCon Texas Pipeline Corp., which was founded in 1969. MidCon Texas' pipelines operate in Texas, including a 2,650-mile system that reaches from Laredo to Louisiana. The subsidiary delivers about 490 Bcf of natural gas per year to utilities, industrial customers, and power plants along Texas' gulf coast region, particularly along the Houston Ship Canal and in the Beaumont-Port Arthur area. MidCon Texas has connections with pipelines reaching other major U.S. markets and runs nine compressor stations. Palo Duro Pipeline Co., a subsidiary of MidCon

Texas, operates a 390-mile pipeline in the Texas Panhandle.

MidCon Corp. manages its businesses through two divisions, one handling the regulated pipelines and the other directing non-regulated businesses. The regulated company operates the pipeline and storage assets of MidCon subsidiaries and markets services of these units to capitalize on their strong competitive positions. The non-regulated company manages gas supply acquisition and sales, as well as product development for markets that offer significant potential for growth in natural gas usage, such as power generation.

MidCon Corp. brings together decades of experience in the natural gas industry. As it has for generations of businesses and residents in Chicago, much of the Midwest, and a large portion of the United States, MidCon is prepared to help gas consumers stay warm and businesses operate efficiently, and to provide a basic fuel source well into the 21st century.

MidCon Delivery Network

An inspector (top) checks the coating on a new pipeline built to increase the capacity and flexibility of Natural Gas Pipeline's transmission network.

MidCon owns and operates a pipeline network which stretches across 12 states and connects to pipeline systems serving markets from coast to coast (bottom).

CELLULAR ONE

SINCE ITS INCEPTION IN THE EARLY 1980S, THE CELLULAR COMMUNICATIONS INDUSTRY HAS UNDERGONE EXPLOSIVE GROWTH, REACHING 10 MILLION SUBSCRIBERS NATIONWIDE IN LESS THAN A DECADE. CELLULAR ONE, FROM ITS HEADQUARTERS IN NORTHWEST SUBURBAN SCHAUMBURG, HAS BEEN A

part of that explosion as the leading cellular service company in the Chicago area. Established by Metromedia TeleCommunications in 1985, Cellular One was acquired by Dallas-based Southwestern Bell Mobile Systems in 1987.

Cellular One's 200-plus cell sites and network of digital switches span more than 7,000 square miles in Illinois and Indiana (above).

Customers can enjoy one-stop shopping to purchase a cellular phone and receive quality installation and service (above right).

GROWING IN SIZE AND TECHNOLOGY

During its relatively short history, Cellular One has become the largest cellular service provider in the Chicago metropolitan area. More than 250 authorized Cellular One distributors can address virtually all customer needs, from providing the basic cellular equipment to acquiring a phone number and installing the service.

To maintain its leading position in the competitive cellular communications industry, Cellular One strives to offer the best, most up-to-date technology available. The company's extensive network of digital switches and 200-plus cell sites cover more than 7,000 square miles in eight counties in Illinois and two counties in Indiana. These cell sites house the radio and control equipment necessary to interconnect a cellular mobile unit with the company's switching offices.

From the start, growth has been a way of life at Cellular One. In 1985, the company had just one digital switching center. Today it operates four. In 1987, Cellular One underwent a major expansion that extended its service area to include northwest Indiana. The company has broadened its reach even further through "roaming" agreements with more than 2,000 cellular networks in the United States and Canada, giving Chicago-area customers the freedom to use their cellular phones while traveling almost anywhere.

In 1993, Cellular One became the first in Chicago and among the first in the nation to launch a digital system. Considered the "wave of the future" in both mobile office and personal communications, the digital system will allow more calls to go through on the first attempt and will enhance privacy by digitizing voice conversations, virtually eliminating static and cross-talk, and reducing dropped calls.

IMPROVING CUSTOMERS' LIVES

Cellular One customers throughout the Chicago area report that their cellular phone systems have brought them a new level of efficiency, productivity, and convenience.

"Cellular technology has dramatically enhanced the lifestyles of our customers," says Bob Nelson, president and general manager. "They appreciate the increased freedom their cellular phones give them."

Over the years, Cellular One has geared its products and services toward people who want to improve the management of their business and personal lives, as well as those who are seeking extra security when they are away from home. A majority of its customers are business people, from top executives to sales professionals and small business owners. Women now comprise the

fastest growing segment of Cellular One's client base.

The company's nine varied rate plans reflect the diversity of its customers' needs. The Cellular One basic service plan provides an affordable option for people who use the phone primarily for emergency purposes. At the other end of the spectrum, the company's top-of-the-line program, "The One Club," is geared toward corporate customers and individuals who spend more than 500 minutes on the phone each month. "The One Club" plan includes three-party conference calling, a voice mail answering service, call forwarding, call waiting, and phone replacement coverage.

As an added bonus to all customers, Cellular One offers live informa-

The company has more than 250 authorized distributors in Chicago and northwest Indiana, where customers can choose from the latest cellular phone models.

program with seminars that are free and open to the public. Led by personal safety experts, the seminars offer potentially life-saving advice on how to avoid becoming a victim of crime. Cellular One also offers Safety-on-Call kits, which contain emergency equipment such as flares and help signs.

Also in 1993, Cellular One introduced the Beyond the Call Awards,[SM] a cellular samaritan program to encourage customers to report accidents and crimes in progress. Customers who go "beyond the call" are honored quarterly and annually.

After less than a decade in business, Cellular One has become one of the fastest growing companies in the Chicago area. Its commitment to comprehensive coverage, unique customer-oriented programs, and cutting-edge technology has fueled its phenomenal success. With the constant goal of improving the lives of its customers, Cellular One plans to continue down the same path and play a key role in developing the next generation of wireless communications.

Headquartered in northwest suburban Schaumburg, Cellular One (left) prides itself on providing cutting-edge cellular technologies to its customers.

tion lines that address a wide range of topics and needs. For example, customers can access up-to-the-minute traffic news and receive local travel directions from operators who literally "talk" them to their destinations. Other information lines provide sports news, weather reports from all over the world, legal advice, winning state lottery numbers, real-time financial informa-

tion, and a professional concierge service that can help with dinner reservations or theatre tickets.

More importantly, Cellular One customers have access to free help lines which link callers with an operator to report emergencies such as traffic accidents, stranded motorists, and crimes in progress. In 1993, the company introduced Safety-on-Call,[SM] a personal and road safety

FRUIT OF THE LOOM, INC.

FOR MORE THAN A CENTURY, FRUIT OF THE LOOM HAS STOOD OUT AS ONE OF THE MOST RECOGNIZABLE NAMES IN UNDERWEAR PRODUCTS FOR MEN AND BOYS AND, MORE RECENTLY, FOR WOMEN AND GIRLS. WHILE THIS BROAD CATEGORY REMAINS A VITAL MAINSTAY OF THE COMPANY'S BUSINESS, THE

world has discovered that Fruit of the Loom is much more than just underwear. Today, Fruit of the Loom is a leading international manufacturer and marketer of basic family apparel that is known for comfort and value—and "unconditionally guaranteed" for quality.

Fruit of the Loom is one of the

than 8 million total square feet of production space and state-of-the-art equipment at a cost of $870 million.

Fruit of the Loom employment has grown from 13,000 workers in 1985 to more than 32,000 workers at over 60 locations in the United States, Canada, Mexico, and Eu-

duced a full line of branded casual and activewear products, including T-shirts, sweatshirts, and other fleecewear for retail markets. Today, Fruit of the Loom Casualwear® features more than 30 styles of T-shirts and fleece in 28 coordinated colors, and is available in a full range of sizes to fit the entire

Right: In 1992, Fruit of the Loom manufactured and sold more than 1 billion pieces of apparel in North America, Europe, and other markets through its own stores, as well as other retail outlets.

Above (from left): William Farley, chairman and CEO, and John B. Holland, president and COO.

largest knit apparel companies in the world, with principal brands that include Fruit of the Loom®, BVD®, Fruit of the Loom Best®, and Munsingwear®. The company also manufactures and markets underwear and knit apparel through major licensing agreements that include Wilson Sporting Goods, the Walt Disney Company, Warner Bros., and Warnaco.

A CHICAGO COMPANY SINCE 1985

In 1985, Fruit of the Loom was acquired by Chicago-based Farley Industries and became a public company in 1987. This initiated a strategic capital investment program for plant modernization and facilities and distribution expansion with a strong marketing direction that has resulted in an impressive, steady growth ever since. Between 1985 and 1992, the company added more

rope, including 65 employees at corporate headquarters in Chicago. Most of these locations represent state-of-the-art manufacturing facilities and capabilities that form the foundation for the company's total vertical integration that enables it to aggressively compete as an efficient low-cost producer in the basic apparel industry.

In 1992, Fruit of the Loom manufactured and sold more than 1 billion pieces of apparel in North America, Europe, and other markets around the world, as sales reached a record $1.855 billion. The company was also ranked 242nd on *Fortune* magazine's list of the 500 largest companies in the United States for the same year, up from 325th in 1987.

BRAND DIVERSIFICATION

A major turn in Fruit of the Loom's brand diversification efforts began in 1987 when the company intro-

family. The company has also introduced BVD Leisurewear® and Munsingwear® as separate upmarket casualwear labels, and has streamlined its hosiery business to focus on a full line of family socks marketed under the Fruit of the Loom® brand.

This remarkably successful expansion has also further enhanced the company's already solid presence in the growing imprint market, which includes blank T-shirts and fleecewear lines sold to screen and special process printers for customizing and resale. And today, Fruit of the Loom is one of the largest suppliers in the world of blank garments for this continually expanding specialty market, with its Fruit of the Loom® and Fruit of the Loom Best® labels.

Today, in addition to continuing steady gains with its basic lines of underwear for men and boys, and women and girls, the popular FunGals® and FunPals® brands of deco-

438

rated underwear for girls and boys have proven to be strong performers with a broad line of licensed children's characters that include Barney the Dinosaur and Batman. The recent introductions of Fruit of the Loom Baby Style® and Toddler Styles® have further strengthened the company's relatively new presence in the infant and toddler apparel market.

The colorful Fruit of the Loom logo and the exceptional level of both quality and value it represents are now more familiar than ever to consumers around the world as the company realizes its vision to be the international leader in basic apparel. Fruit of the Loom, with its growing product lines, expects to continue to set new standards for performance, as it builds on more than 140 years of success in the knit apparel industry.

Fruit of the Loom is a fully integrated manufacturer of basic family apparel, including underwear (bottom left) and casualwear (bottom right).

HOTEL NIKKO CHICAGO

AMERICAN LUXURY HOTELS HAVE TRADITIONALLY COMPARED THEM-SELVES TO THE FINE HOTELS OF EUROPE. BUT SINCE ITS OPENING IN THE AUTUMN OF 1987, THE HOTEL NIKKO CHICAGO HAS JUDGED ITSELF AGAINST THE BEST HOTELS OF JAPAN. BY COMBINING JAPANESE

ideas of service and efficiency with American friendliness, this international luxury hotel provides its guests a relaxed, comfortable stay for business travel, vacations, or weekend getaways.

The Hotel Nikko Chicago, owned by Japan Airlines, is one of more than 30 Nikko Hotels worldwide and one of seven in North America. Centrally located on the north bank of the Chicago River at Dearborn Street, the hotel is across from Marina City Towers and within walking distance of Chicago's famed State Street, Michigan Avenue, and Loop. Management and staff at the 421-room facility strive daily to uphold the ideals of its mission statement: "At Nikko Hotels our guests always find dedicated employees, attentive service, and quality facilities together in harmony."

According to Pete Dangerfield, vice president and general manager, the hotel's strong commitment to its employees is an important part of its recipe for success. Of the 450 original staff members, 190 are still with the hotel, a level of retention that is rare in the lodging industry. Monthly meetings allow employees to exchange information, get updates on hotel policies, and receive acknowledgement for excellence. "We believe that happy employees will provide better service for our guests," Dangerfield explains.

The Hotel Nikko Chicago (above) is centrally located on the north bank of the Chicago River at Dearborn Street.

From the elegant lobby area (top) to the Hana Lounge (bottom left) and the Benkay tatami rooms (bottom right), the hotel has the distinct feeling of Japan.

STEPPING INTO ANOTHER CULTURE

Entering the Hotel Nikko Chicago is a bit like stepping into another world, or at least another culture. "The Hotel Nikko Chicago has the distinct feeling of Japan," says Dangerfield. "It is an international luxury hotel with touches of Japan."

The decor of the lobby is comfortable and elegant. A 200-year-old,

hand-embroidered silk screen depicting the Nikko Shrine built by the Tokugawa Shogunate family in Nikko, Japan graces the entrance. More than $500,000 worth of contemporary and oriental art is on display throughout the hotel. A Japanese rock garden overlooking the Chicago River adds to the Japanese ambience.

One unique touch of the Hotel Nikko Chicago is its two tatami suites. Equipped with Japanese soaking tubs and bathrooms, these suites provide a uniquely Japanese experi-

ence. Guests sleep on futons on a tatami mat floor, and shoes are never worn in the suite. Each suite also features its own rock garden. A traditional western living room with television, sofa, love seat, and desk adds touches of American convenience to these distinctive suites.

SUPERIOR SERVICE AND AMENITIES

The primary goal of the Hotel Nikko's 400-plus employees is to provide more services and amenities to their guests than any other hotel.

"In addition to our concierge, five full-time guest relations managers attend to guest needs while they are here at the hotel," says Dangerfield. These staff members follow up on guest comments, review all arrivals, and make sure any special requests are filled.

After registering at the front desk, hotel guests are greeted by a bell-man who brings their luggage to their rooms and acquaints them with the hotel's features, including two restaurants, a gift shop, lounge, fitness center, the concierge and guest relations manager desks, and the Executive Business Center.

Located on the mezzanine level of the 20-story hotel, the Executive Business Center provides hotel guests with state-of-the-art communication tools, such as fax machines, IBM compatible and Macintosh personal computers, modems, and workstations. Paired with the hotel's secretarial and translation services, the center can accommodate the needs of virtually any business traveler. Selected equipment can also be rented for private use in guest rooms.

The hotel's fitness center, also located on the mezzanine level, is equipped with the latest in fitness equipment, including Stairmasters, Lifecycles, free weights, and sauna. To maximize guest convenience, exercise clothing is provided in the fitness center. The hotel also offers a professional massage service for the ultimate in relaxation.

According to Dangerfield, it is the little touches that make a big difference at the Hotel Nikko Chicago. In the 421 guest rooms and suites, guests will find robes, hair dryers, mini-bars, and an ample supply of toiletries. Sewing kits come with the needles already threaded. Wake-up calls include a choice of newspaper and hot beverage waiting outside the door each morning. The hotel's nightly turndown service leaves Godiva chocolates on every pillow.

ELEGANT JAPANESE AND AMERICAN DINING

Dining in the Hotel Nikko Chicago is a memorable experience as well. Traditional Japanese cuisine is served in Benkay, located on the lower level of the hotel. Named for a 12th century Japanese hero celebrated in No and Kabuki plays for his loyalty and faithfulness to his employer, Benkay offers guests the choice of four different dining experiences: a sushi bar, the Benkay-yaki room, the main dining room, and tatami rooms. The tatami rooms are private Japanese environments where guests sit on mats with their feet resting in recessed floor wells. Servers are dressed in Japanese kimonos. In the Benkay-yaki rooms, guests sit at U-shaped tables while their meal is prepared and grilled before their eyes.

The elegant Celebrity Cafe, which overlooks the Chicago River, serves a more traditional American menu with accents of Italian, Mediterranean, and Asian influences. The restaurant is open for breakfast,

lunch, and dinner.

Though only about 15 percent of the hotel's guests are Japanese business travelers, they have a strong influence on the exceptional level of service the hotel provides. According to Dangerfield, living up to Japanese standards is an important goal of everyone at the Hotel Nikko Chicago. "If we can provide the level of service they are comfortable with," he says, "all of our guests will benefit."

The Hotel Nikko offers extensive services for the business traveler, including an executive boardroom (above).

Luxury guest accommodations run the gamut, from the comfort and convenience of a standard room (top right) to the simple elegance of a Japanese suite (top left). Other unique options include the Presidential Suite, the Governor's Suite, and various luxury suites (left, top to bottom).

OAKWOOD CORPORATE APARTMENTS

THE NAME OAKWOOD CONJURES UP IMAGES OF A QUIET, WOODSY AREA IN THE COUNTRY, FAR FROM THE CONCRETE, GLASS, AND STEEL OF THE CITY. BUT THAT'S WHERE YOU'LL FIND OAKWOOD CORPORATE APARTMENTS— IN THE HEART OF CHICAGO'S BUSY RIVER NORTH NEIGHBORHOOD.

Oakwood has catered to the corporate traveler, offering flexible lease terms and accommodations for individuals seeking furnished apart-

Located in the popular River North area, Oakwood's 25-story Chicago complex features 304 move-in ready units with fully equipped kitchens and a fabulous array of unique features for luxury living.

ments on a temporary basis. The Chicago location is part of a nationwide network of apartment buildings managed by Los Angeles-based R&B Realty Group. Over the years, R&B has established and enhanced its national reputation as a leader not only in the corporate housing industry, but in the general field of property management.

A NEW CONCEPT IN LODGING

In the 1960s, R&B pioneered the concept of "singles" and "country club" apartment complexes. The company's founding partners, Howard Ruby and Robert Franks, also introduced the extended-stay apartment idea, which generally requires a stay of at least 30 days.

The 1970s saw a significant upswing in business travel and city-to-city job transfers. As corporations discovered that hotel costs were also on the rise, they began researching cost-effective alternatives to traditional lodging. Recognizing this entirely new market segment, R&B Realty responded by revamping existing apartment properties to target the corporate market.

The company soon brought its innovative ideas to Chicago in 1989, introducing the "corporate suites" concept at a luxury downtown location. Ever since, this concept has provided a unique and affordable alternative for individuals who need housing for a limited time. The corporate market now accounts for about half of R&B's business nationwide, with an impressive client list that includes more than 300 Fortune 500 companies.

In Chicago, Oakwood targets primarily corporate travelers who are participating in a training program, carrying out special assignments, or relocating to the area due to a job transfer. In addition, Oakwood works closely with representatives of the theater and film industry to assist them in finding affordable, convenient, and comfortable accommodations for their crews while working in Chicago.

CONVENIENCE AND AFFORDABILITY WITH TOUCHES OF HOME

Conveniently located in a 25-story high-rise complex, Oakwood's 304

units in Chicago feature unfurnished and furnished apartments, which are move-in ready with fully equipped kitchens and a fabulous array of unique features for luxury living.

A variety of floor plans are available, including studio, one-bedroom, two-bedroom, two-bedroom duplex, and penthouse apartments. On average, Oakwood units offer twice the space of standard hotel rooms at about half the cost. All rental agreements are based on a minimum 30-day stay, with flexible lease terms for up to 15 months.

The units include everything from televisions, VCRs, and stereos to telephone answering machines. Oakwood's recreational amenities— such as a fitness center, pool, sauna, and sun deck—are comparable to those usually found at exclusive resorts. Likewise, a 24-hour doorman, concierge service, linens, dishes, optional maid service, and laundry facilities are all available within the complex. Additional touches of home include immediate phone service, free cable TV, microwave ovens, plants, artwork, and other accessory items for each apartment. To further accommodate its corporate clientele, the Oakwood complex offers conference facilities, a business service center with fax machines, an on-site dry cleaning service, bicycle storage, covered parking, and controlled access entry with closed-circuit television monitoring.

Beyond the value and convenience that Oakwood's corporate clients enjoy, its location in the popular River North area allows residents to explore the active nightlife, famous restaurants, and other sights and activities available nearby.

"We try to offer a homelike atmosphere that is both convenient and comfortable," says Christina Mireles, marketing manager. "We

Oakwood's recreational amenities—such as a fitness center, pool, sauna, and sun deck—are comparable to those usually found at exclusive resorts.

are not a hotel. We differentiate ourselves from the more traditional lodging options because many people get tired of hotels, especially when their stay lasts for two or three months."

PROFESSIONALISM AND CUSTOMER SERVICE

As part of the R&B Realty Group, Oakwood benefits from a national corporate sales program and a staff of highly trained regional sales representatives. An individual or company interested in temporary lodging in Chicago can make a simple phone call to Oakwood's toll-free number, (800) 832-8329. On site, Oakwood's professional management staff and sales representatives take care of all of the preliminary details: hooking up electricity, setting up immediate phone service, arranging the weekly maid service, and placing all of the furniture and additional special features in the apartment for the new resident. With this distinctive service, new residents are afforded the luxury of a convenient and hassle-free transition

to their new home.

According to Mireles, it is Oakwood's primary goal to ensure that all of its residents are afforded the luxury of personalized service and quick response to their individual needs throughout their stay in Chicago. To that end, staff members strive for a superior level of customer service based on professionalism, courtesy, and genuine concern for every guest.

After decades of innovation in the property management and corporate lodging industries, Oakwood Corporate Apartments and its parent company continue to tailor their services to the needs of a growing clientele. Through in-depth market research, Oakwood will strive to add new services and additional locations for corporate suites throughout the metro Chicago area. Oakwood is setting the standards of luxury accommodations at the Chicago complex and surrounding area locations that will ensure comfort, convenience, and affordability for the corporate traveler of the future.

Oakwood Corporate Apartments offer convenience and affordability with touches of home.

CHUCK BERMAN, a native Chicagoan, received a bachelor's degree from Northern Illinois University in 1974. He has been a staff photographer for the *Chicago Tribune* since 1978, concentrating on news, sports, and art photography. Berman has received numerous awards from the Chicago Press Photographers Association and the Illinois Press Association.

JOHN BOOZ, formerly of Pittsburgh, graduated from the Art Institute of Chicago in 1984. He has worked on a free-lance basis for the *Chicago Sun-Times, Agence France Presse, People, Time, Downbeat,* and *Chicago* magazine, among others. Booz specializes in documentary and photojournalism, exhibiting his work locally as well as nationally. His most recent accomplishment is the publication of *Smart Start* by the Council of Basic Education, featuring 20 pages of Booz's full-page photos.

PATTY CARROLL, originally of Chicago, now lives in London and teaches photography at the Royal College of Art. She had been an Associate Professor of Photography at the Institute of Design, Illinois Institute of Technology since 1977. Her work has been exhibited nationally and published in several books, including *Spirited Visions, Women Photographers, Fabrications,* and *The New Vision: 40 Years of Photography at the ID*. Carroll is currently photographing Elvis impersonators.

ALAN KLEHR and W.S. CHURCHILL, based in Clarendon Hills, Illinois, have been a writing and photography team for over 10 years. Their work has appeared in *Forbes, Fortune, Newsweek, Modern Maturity,* and *Departures*. Klehr/Churchill's corporate clients include AT&T, IBM, Tenneco, Hyatt Hotels, and Norwegian Cruise Lines.

KELLY COSTELLO has worked as a free-lance photographer since 1990. A graduate of Memphis State University in 1985, she is pursuing a Master of Design at the Institute of Design, Illinois Institute of Technology. Her work has been exhibited nationally, including shows at Prairie Avenue Gallery in Chicago and Working Space Gallery in Memphis.

WILL CROCKETT graduated from the Brooks Institute of Photography in Santa Barbara and returned to Chicago in 1987 to shoot corporate and advertising images for Midway Airlines. His images of Tom Bosley, Betty White, Mike Wallace, and Paul Harvey for Midway's monthly inflight magazine led to assignments for *Time, Newsweek, People, Good Housekeeping,* and *USA Today*. Currently, Crockett heads a still photography, film, and video production company, The Image Source, in Aurora, with photographers Brett Patterson and Miles Boone.

TOM CRUZE grew up in Fort Wayne, Indiana and received his bachelor's degree from Indiana University in 1979. He works as a staff photographer for the *Chicago Sun-Times,* covering national political conventions, major sports competitions, and events of community interest. Cruze has received several awards from the Chicago Press Photographers Association, Illinois Press Photographers Association, and Indiana Press Photographers Association.

JON CUNNINGHAM has been a freelance photographer since 1975. His work has appeared in newspapers, magazines, yearbooks, books, brochures, audio-visual presentations, and annual reports. Formerly a chief photographer for *The Beacon-News,* Cunningham has earned a number of professional awards, including "The Best News Photo" in 1990 awarded by The Suburban Press Club.

WALTER DEPTULA, a Chicago native, has photographed on a free-lance basis since 1988. Due to his background in construction, major projects have included job-progress photography for such clients as INTEL and IBM. Deptula now co-publishes the *Chicago Scenes and Events* calendar with photographer Jeff Voelz.

CHARLES ESHELMAN, a self-taught photographer from South Bend, Indiana, resides in Chicago, where he heads Charles Eshelman Photography. His work includes editorial, corporate, portrait, and publicity photography. Eshelman's photography has appeared in *Chicago* magazine, *Publisher's Weekly, Wine & Dine,* and the *Chicago Tribune,* and has been exhibited at the Hubbard Street Gallery.

SAMUEL FEIN earned a bachelor of fine arts from the Art Institute of Chicago in 1975. He specializes in architecture, interior design, and still-life photography. His work has been included in many publications, including *Architectural Record* and *Chicago* magazine. Fein's prints have also been exhibited in a one-person show at the Chicago Cultural Center.

BOB FIRTH, originally of Minnetonka, Minnesota, attended the University of Minnesota and the Minneapolis College of Art and Design. Represented by Firth Photobank, he concentrates on nature, agriculture, urban, and heritage photography. Firth's images are included in a book to be released in 1993, *Landscape of Ghosts,* about the vanishing heritage of the Midwest.

MICHELE GIFFUNE graduated from Northern Illinois University in 1988 with a bachelor of fine arts in visual communication and earned a master of science and design from the Institute of Design, Illinois Institute of Technology in 1993. Originally from Buffalo, New York, Giffune moved to Chicago eight years ago to pursue her interest in the integration of normal photography, digital imaging, and multimedia.

ANDY GOODWIN opened Goodwin Photography in 1987 in his hometown of New Lenox, Illinois. Specializing in location photography, his clients include Ameritech, Motorola, and IBM. His work has been published in *Newsweek, Business Week, Chicago* magazine, *Entrepreneur, Success,* and *INC.* Goodwin received the Award of Excellence in 1989 for his self-promotion in *Communication Arts*.

GARY HANNABARGER graduated from the Ohio Institute of Photography in 1984, and has free-lanced since 1988. He specializes in editorial and portrait photography, and has been published in *Parade, Time, Newsweek, S.I. For Kids, TV Guide, Glamour, Working Woman,* and *Chicago* magazine.

KAREN I. HIRSCH, a Chicago-based free-lance photographer, has been featured in such publications as the *Chicago Tribune, Chicago Sun-Times, Graphis, Advertising Age,* and *Sail*. Her honors include a photography grant from Chicago's Department of Cultural Affairs and various awards from competitions sponsored by the *Chicago Daily News,* Eastman Kodak and Professional Photographers of America, and the 1990 Creative People Awards. Hirsch serves on the board of directors of the Chicago/Midwest chapter of the American Society of Media Photographers.

ADELE HODGE's assignments include editorial, corporate, portrait, and documentary photography for Citibank, Diners Club, Ford Motor Company, and NBC News. She has fulfilled editorial assignments for many local and national publications, including *Redbook, Essence, Black Enterprise, Chicago Tribune, Chicago Sun-Times,* and *N'Digo*. Hodge, who is on the board of the American Society of Media Photographers, Chicago/Midwest chapter, has had six one-woman exhibitions. Her work has also been part of the juried shows at the Beverly Art Center, Black Creativity at the Museum of Science and Industry, and New Image II by the Chicago Advertising Federation.

ROBERT C.V. LIEBERMAN, originally of Evanston, Illinois, received a bachelor's degree from the University of Illinois at Chicago in 1975. He has worked as a free-lance photographer since 1970. Lieberman's work includes editorial and industrial photography for such clients as *Northshore* magazine, YMCA, Chicago Botanical Garden, University of Chicago, Ryerson Steel, and Acme Steel. Lieberman lives in Chicago with his son, Noah.

PAUL L. MERIDETH has been a freelance photographer in Chicago for 10 years, concentrating on photojournalism, editorial, and corporate photography. He graduated with a master of fine arts from the Cranbrook Academy of Art in 1980, and has had his work published in *Forbes, Fortune,* and the *New York Times*. Merideth's documentary photographs of an AIDS hospice, exhibited at the Chicago Cultural Center, have received numerous awards from the Catholic Health Association and have been nominated for a Lisagor Award.

KEVIN O. MOONEY received his bachelor of science degree from Southern Illinois University in cinema and photography in 1980. Seven years ago, Mooney opened his Chicago-based studio, specializing in editorial, advertising, and documentary photography. His work has appeared in *Life, National Geographic, Forbes, Fortune, Runner's World, Chicago,* and many other national magazines.

JOSEPH OLIVER established his studio in Chicago in 1981. His areas of emphasis include underwater, automotive, and bicycling photography. His work has appeared in *Autoweek, Sports Car International, Playboy, Outside, Bicycling, Ocean Realm,* and *Photo Methods*. Oliver is currently director of photography for the Underwater Archaeological Society of Chicago and the principal photographer for the Lake Michigan Submerged Halocene Forest Study.

PANORAMIC IMAGES is a Michigan Avenue stock photo library specializing in large format panoramic views for advertising. Founded in 1987 by brothers Doug and Mark Segal, the firm represents the commercial artwork of 85 top panoramic photographers as well as the fine-art-for-advertising work of Mon-Tresor, a Japanese photo agency. Panoramic Images' clients include many major ad agencies and graphic design firms in the United States and Europe.

JASON PENNEY attended the University of Illinois at Chicago. He opened Jason Penney Studio, Inc. in 1992, specializing in fashion and portrait photography. Penney's work has been exhibited in various group shows in the Chicago area.

AL PODGORSKI has been a *Chicago Sun-Times* staff photographer for nine years. He was awarded "Photographer of the Year" three times in a row by the Chicago Press Photographers Association—the first time a single photographer had ever been so honored.

BOB RINGHAM has worked as a staff photographer for the *Chicago Sun-Times* for the past nine years. After graduating from Southern Illinois University with a bachelor of science in cinema and photography, Ringham worked for the *Daily Herald* in Arlington Heights, Illinois for six years. Ringham has covered a variety of events, including the 1985 Super Bowl and the Chicago Bull's championship seasons in 1991 and 1992.

RICH SAAL, originally of Springfield, Illinois, earned a bachelor of science in photography from Southern Illinois University in 1982. Since 1985, Saal has worked as a staff photographer for *The State Journal-Register* in Springfield.

DOUGLAS SEGAL grew up in Washington, D.C. in a professional photography family. He is a 12-year resident of Chicago, where in 1987, he and his brother Mark founded Panoramic Images, a photo stock agency specializing in large-format panoramic work. Although managing the transparency library of 85 photographers takes up most of his time, Segal occasionally sneaks out to shoot a few of his own.

MARK SEGAL has pursued the perfection of the panoramic image since 1972, focusing on commercial usage. He owns and operates three separate photography entities in Chicago, including Panoramic Images and its 50,000 stock and pan photographs. Segal's clients include Air France, American Express, Skidmore, Mobile, and Owings & Merrill.

ART SHAY, a Chicagoan since 1950, has worked as a free-lance photographer and writer for the *Washington Post* and a staff photographer for *Time-Life*. He has had over 30,000 photographs published — including 1,000 covers —in *Time*, *Life*, *Fortune*, *Sports Illustrated*, *New York Times*, *Forbes*, *Business Week*, and many others. Shay has worked on annual reports for 3M, National Can, and Baxter Labs, and his photographs have been included in more than 79 books. He has won 20 art director awards for advertising photographs. In 1959, he shot *Life*'s "Picture of the Year" of Khrushchev on an Iowa farm.

ALAN SHORTALL was born in Dublin, Ireland, and moved to New York in 1983. He parlayed his degree in photography into assisting jobs for established photographers before opening his own studio in 1986. Since his move to Chicago in 1988, his clients have included *Chicago* magazine, Statue of Liberty Foundation, Continental Bank, Scott Foresman, and numerous design firms and advertising agencies. Shortall's work has appeared in *Graphis*, *Communication Arts*, and a guide to Chicago commissioned by the American Institute of Graphic Artists.

NANCY R. STUENKEL has been a photojournalist for the *Chicago Sun-Times* since she graduated from Columbia College in 1978. Stuenkel's awards include the Peter Lisagor Award in 1981 and 1982 and a third place for illustration from the Illinois Press Photographers Association in 1986.

MIKE TAPPIN attended Northwestern University's Journalism School and the Institute of Design, Illinois Institute of Technology. He has been a free-lance photographer since 1971. His photography has been published in *Chicago* magazine, *Chicago Reader*, *North Shore* magazine, *Rolling Stone*, and *Arts and Antiques*, as well as brochures, annual reports, and educational and medical textbooks. Tappin's work was selected for publication in *Print* magazine's regional design annual in 1982 and 1992, and was also included in the *70th Art Directors Annual* by the Art Directors Club of New York.

RUSSELL THURSTON, a self-employed photographer and illustrator for six years, specializes in mixed-media photo-collage illustrations as well as assignment advertising and editorial photography. Thurston earned a master of fine arts in photography from The Art Institute of Chicago in 1985. He has had numerous assignments published in *Outside* and *Chicago* magazines, the *Chicago Tribune*, and various books.

JOHN WELZENBACH opened his Chicago-based studio, Welzenbach Productions, in 1975. His clients include Miller Brewing Company, Philip Morris USA, American Express, Kellogg Company, Kraft, Jamaican Tourist Board, and United Airlines. Welzenbach was one of the founders of the Chicago/Midwest chapter of the Advertising Photographers of America and served as the vice-president of its national chapter. Welzenbach is also the creator and president of the Chicago-based studio, Hot Shots Photographics.

JIM WRIGHT has been a free-lance photographer in his hometown Chicago since 1984. His photographs have appeared in advertisements, annual reports, brochures, audio-visual presentations, magazines, and newspapers. He was formerly photo editor for the *Louisville Times* and staff photographer for the *Courier-Journal* of Kentucky and the *Gainesville Sun* and *Orlando Sentinel-Star* of Florida. Wright has received numerous awards from the National Press Photographers Association and was named the Florida Journalistic Photographer of the Year in 1976.

RICHARD YOUNKER, a native Chicagoan, has been a self-employed photojournalist and poet for 19 years. Younker's photo essays have been published in the *Chicago Tribune's Sunday Magazine*, *Chicago Sun-Times Sunday Magazine*, and *Chicago Reader*. His work has also appeared in national magazines, such as *People* and *TV Guide*, and in three books, including *Our Chicago: Faces and Voices of the City*. Younker's most recent photography documents a family of commercial fishermen on the Mississippi River.